British Government
and Politics

EUROPE TODAY

Series Editor: Ronald Tiersky

British Government and Politics

Balancing Europeanization and Independence

Michael L. Mannin

ROWMAN & LITTLEFIELD PUBLISHERS, INC.
Lanham • Boulder • New York • Toronto • Plymouth, UK

Published by Rowman & Littlefield Publishers, Inc.
A wholly owned subsidiary of The Rowman & Littlefield Publishing Group, Inc.
4501 Forbes Boulevard, Suite 200, Lanham, Maryland 20706
http://www.rowmanlittlefield.com

Estover Road, Plymouth PL6 7PY, United Kingdom

British Library Cataloguing in Publication Information Available

Library of Congress Cataloging-in-Publication Data
Mannin, Michael L.
  British government and politics : balancing Europeanization and independence /
Michael L. Mannin.
    p. cm. — (Europe today)
  Includes bibliographical references and index.
    ISBN 978-0-7425-3684-5 (cloth : alk. paper) — ISBN 978-0-7425-3685-2 (pbk. :
alk. paper) — ISBN 978-0-7425-6777-1 (electronic)
    1. Great Britain—Politics and government. 2. European Union—Great
Britain. I. Title.
JN318.M26 2010
320.441—dc22   2009043144

Printed in the United States of America

To Harvey, Louie, Jude, Rowan, and Otis:
Britain and Europe's future

Contents

**Supplemental materials may be found on the book's website at
http://www.rowmanlittlefield.com/isbn/0742536858.**

Figures, Tables, and Textboxes

FIGURES

TABLES

TEXTBOXES

Preface

The political world has, in 2009, been turned inside out as "credit crunch" and recession have thrown decision makers into turmoil. A new US president promises new pathways—yet economic barriers foreshorten his choices. In Britain, a long-standing chancellor of the exchequer, turned prime minister, presents ideas for international economic solutions and receives plaudits for his boldness from a world audience. Yet at home the Labour government that he leads is the most unpopular since 1943. The mother of Parliaments is brought low by the systematic abuse of MPs' allowance claims, while honorable gentlemen and women scramble for the cover of "acting in good faith"—a highly likely tale for the public, which is about to vote in European Parliament and local elections. Indeed the political class as a whole is held, as one academic opined in a national newspaper, "in greater contempt today than at any other time since the eighteenth century."

The temptation for an academic writing about politics is to be led by current events. Currency matters, especially in textbooks that aim to explain the workings of a political system. It should not obscure, however, analysis and judgment of a more substantial kind: in this particular case, an approach to British politics that recognizes the complex nature of a sovereign nation-state that is also an integral part of a *sui generis* phenomenon—the European Union. In the past decade or so, many academics have attempted to reconcile notions of British exceptionalism and interdependence with such conceptual frameworks as multilevel governance, network analysis, and the core executive, all of which challenge the traditional Westminster model of British politics. More recently the notion of Europeanization in several guises has been applied to policy and institutional analysis and has led to a reassessment of political values and cultural assumptions. A healthy literature has emerged that both challenges and reinterprets British exceptionalism.

Yet, despite the best efforts of MPs to undermine the Westminster model recently, it lives on—as a battered "default" explanation of how things work in British politics for its citizens and political classes. Many basic academic texts, with notable exceptions, still reflect this state of affairs. The question of "Europe" is often confined to separate chapters of the "Britain in Europe" or "Europe in Britain" kind. Or it may be examined unevenly—where it is most apparent only—or not examined at all. The EU is often portrayed as an electoral problem, which it undoubtedly is for political parties. But it is also a *fact* of significance for British institutional and constitutional analysis, and it is worth mainstreaming this fact when examining all aspects of British governance. Not to do so gives an incomplete picture of where British politics is in the twenty-first century.

The text demands quite a bit from the reader. In "mainstreaming" the impact of the EU, it anticipates some appreciation of how the EU works, as well as a relatively open mind as to how the British system operates. Textboxes, tables, figures, and an appendix assist here, and extra reading is suggested at the end of each chapter. The reader is also referred to the Rowman & Littlefield website, where further dedicated material may be obtained. The study of any EU member state is difficult, it is contended, because of the peculiar status that the EU bequeaths to its component parts. This involves a complex interdependency based on a shared economy, common security, and shared values—most of which is treaty based. This text strives to make at least some sense of this complexity.

In the long process of compiling these chapters, I must thank several colleagues who so generously gave their time to comment on the text. They are Geoffrey Ponton, Peter Gill, Simon Lightfoot, Andy Hull, Bob Morley, John Vogler, Liz Sperling, and Charlotte Bretherton, who heroically read, corrected, and criticized the whole manuscript. I am particularly indebted to her for the support she offered. Claire House gave valuable research assistance, as did Joe Robjohns. I would also like to acknowledge the support of Martin Schain of New York University and staff and students at Amherst College, School of Political Science. I benefited from spells as visiting scholar and Loewenstein Fellow respectively, at each institution. My own university, Liverpool John Moores, School of Social Science, provided support for clerical services and Phil Cubbin, technical assistance. The European Commission, through its award of a Jean Monnet Chair ad personam provided financial support. I would also like to thank Professor Ron Tiersky, series editor, for the encouragement and occasional gentle deadline he suggested to me and Susan McEachern at Rowman & Littlefield for her patience and guidance. I am in awe of Eileen Brewer, who transcribed my work so well over several years. Finally my love and thanks go to Sue, who has for so long tolerated working holidays on my part.

Abbreviations

ALD	Alliance of Liberals and Democrats
BBC	British Broadcasting Corporation
BERR	Department for Business, Enterprise and Regulatory Reform
BEUC	Bureau European des Unions de Consummateurs
BMA	British Medical Association
BNP	British National Party
BSE	bovine spongiform encephalopathy (mad cow disease)
CAP	Common Agricultural Policy of the EU
CBI	Confederation of British Industry
CEC	Commission of the European Communities
CEECs	Central and East European countries
CFR	Chapter of Fundamental Rights
CFSP	Common Foreign and Security Policy of the EU
C of E	Church of England
COREPER	Committee of Permanent Representatives to the EU
DCA	Department for Constitutional Affairs
DCLG	Department for Communities and Local Government
DCSF	Department for Children, Schools and Families
DEFRA	Department for Environment, Food and Rural Affairs
DETR	Department for Environment, Transport and Regions
DFID	Department for International Development
DIUS	Department for Innovation, Universities and Skills
DG	Directorate-General of the European Commission
DMVS	double majority voting system
DOE	Department of Environment
DOH	Department of Health

DTI	Department for Trade and Industry
DUP	Democratic Unionist Party
DWP	Department for Work and Pensions
EA	Environment Agency
EAP	Environmental Action Programme of the EU
EC	European Community
ECA	European Communities Act
ECB	European Central Bank
ECHR	European Convention on Human Rights *or* European Court of Human Rights
ECJ	European Court of Justice
ECOFIN	Economic and Financial Affairs Council of the EU
ECSC	European Coal and Steel Community
EEB	European Environmental Bureau
EEC	European Economic Community
EIA	Environmental Impact Assessment
EMU	Economic and Monetary Union
EP	European Parliament
EPC	European Political Cooperation
EPG	Environmental Protection Group
EPP	European Peoples' Party
ERDF	European Regional Development Fund
ERM	Exchange Rate Mechanism of the EU
ESF	European Social Fund
ETUC	European Trade Union Confederation
EU	European Union
FCO	Foreign and Commonwealth Office
FIFA	Fédération Internationale de Football Association (International Federation of Football Associations)
FPTP	first-past-the-post electoral system
FSA	Financial Services Authority
G8	Group of Eight major economies
GDP	gross domestic product
Gha	global hectares
GMB	General and Boilermakers' Union
GOR	Government Offices for the Regions
GP	General Practitioner in British Health Service
HMSO	Her Majesty's Stationery Office
HRA	Human Rights Act
ICT	information communications technology
IEEP	Institute for European Environmental Policy
IGC	intergovernmental conference of the EU
IGO	Integrated Regional Government Offices in England

IMC	International Monitoring Committee
IMF	International Monetary Fund
IRA	Irish Republican Army
JHA	Justice and Home Affairs of the EU
JMC	Joint Ministerial Committee
LEA	Local Education Authority
MAFF	Ministry of Agriculture, Fisheries and Food
MEP	Member of European Parliament
MIG	Minimum Income Guarantee
MLG	multilevel governance
MOD	Ministry of Defence
MP	Member of (British) Parliament
MPC	Monetary Policy Committee
MS	Member State of the EU
MSP	Member of the Scottish Parliament
MTFS	medium-term financial strategy
NAP	National Action Plan
NATO	North Atlantic Treaty Organization
NCVO	National Council for Voluntary Organizations
NE	Network Europe of trade unions
NEC	National Executive Committee of Labour Party
NFU	National Farmers' Union
NGO	nongovernmental organization
NHS	National Health Service
NI	Northern Ireland
NICS	Northern Ireland Civil Service
NPM	new public management
ODPM	Office of the Deputy Prime Minister
OECD	Organization for Economic Cooperation and Development
Ofcom	Office of Communication
Ofgen	Office of Gas and Electricity Markets
Ofwat	Office of Water Services
OMC	open method of coordination in the EU
OSCE	Organization for Security and Cooperation in Europe
PAC	Parliamentary Select Committee on Public Administration
PC	Plaid Cymru
PCT	Primary Care Trust of NHS
PES	Party of European Socialists
PFI	Private Finance Initiative
PM	prime minister
PPP	public/private partnership

PR	proportional representation *or* public relations
PSBR	public sector borrowing requirement
PUS	permanent under-secretary
QMV	qualified majority voting in EU Council of Ministers
RAF	Royal Air Force
RRF	Rapid Reaction Force of NATO
RSPB	Royal Society for the Protection of Birds
SDC	Sustainable Development Commission
SDLP	Social Democratic and Labour Party
SEA	Single European Act
SEM	Single European Market
SEPA	Scottish Environmental Protection Agency
SERPS	State Earnings Related Pension Scheme
SHAC	Stop Huntingdon Animal Cruelty
SNP	Scottish National Party
TEC	Treaty establishing the European Communities
TEU	Treaty on European Union
TOA	Treaty of Amsterdam
TSD	Treasury Solicitor's Department
TU	trade union
TUC	Trades Union Congress
UK	United Kingdom of Great Britain and Northern Ireland
UKDEL	United Kingdom Delegation to the ECSC
UKIP	United Kingdom Independence Party
UKRep	United Kingdom Representative to the EU
UN	United Nations
UNEP	United Nations Environment Programme
UNICE	Union of Industrial and Employers' Confederations of Europe (now called BusinessEurope)
US	United States
USSR	Union of Soviet Socialist Republics
UUP	Ulster Unionist Party
VAT	value added tax

Map of Britain

Introduction

British Politics and Europe

It would be foolish for any political analysis of a national political system to underestimate the importance of the state. As a cultural, legal, and geographic boundary for the evaluation of a political system, the concept of a territorial state is of major advantage in terms of the clear edge that it offers to explanation as well the potential for comparative analysis. But it would be naive in the extreme if that same analyst could not see the limitations that a state-centered approach brings to the study of political systems, which are especially more than evident in a period of global recession.

So how far does the "state" still matter in modern politics? Britain is a rich example of both the limits and continuing importance of a territorial definition of a nation. Strategically located close to the coast of France and bounded by vital North Atlantic sea-lanes, Britain is both closely tied to and isolated from its European neighbors. Surrounded by water, this small, island country has well-defined boundaries but a multinational identity made more complex by its membership in the European Union, its "special relationship" with the United States, and its colonial heritage.

If statehood is defined by geography, then Britain seems to embody it clearly (see figure I.1). A set of islands including the northern part of the island of Ireland, it is strategically located between the North Atlantic Ocean, the North Sea, and northwest France. Its total area is slightly smaller than the state of Oregon, yet its coastline encompasses over 12,000 kilometers (CIA 2008).

There are, however, complications to a deceptively simple physical definition. Within the smaller of the two main islands, Ireland, British territory shares a border with a separate state, the Republic of Ireland, thus making it an awkward example for any landmass explanation of state

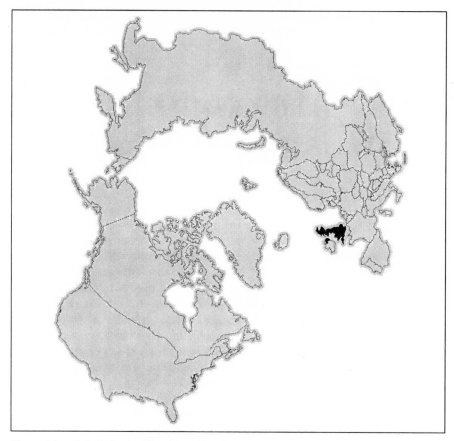

Figure I.I.   Britain in the Northern Hemisphere

boundaries. There are also three tiny but rich quasi-autonomous British crown dependencies, two of which sit close to the French coast, as well as many remote islands off the Scottish mainland. In addition, Britain comprises four distinct historical nations—English, Irish, Scottish, and Welsh—that combine into a somewhat more complex cultural, social, and geopolitical mix of British statehood.

In light of these basic facts, this text has two objectives. The first is to inform the reader about the character and organization of the British political system. This will be done within a conventional chapter structure, often with the use of information boxes and a dedicated website. The second objective is rather more ambitious. It is to explore the extent to which British government and policy has been "Europeanized." We will be defining our terms shortly; but by now the rationale for this volume should be apparent. With the assumption of a globalized world (of economies, communications, technologies, and politics) the *interdependence* between states complicates the analysis of an individual political system. For states, especially those that are members of the European Union, the concept of interdependence is highly relevant. So, explanations based on state exceptionalism alone fall considerably short of a satisfactory analysis of how a political system operates.

Contemporary political theorists have recognized this interdependence in different ways—within such concepts as the hollowed state, governance, multilevel governance, network analysis, and, of course, globalization. All these frameworks have been utilized by political scientists in their analyses of British politics (Gamble 1990; Giddens 1998; Rhodes 1988). But, while analysis based on unique features of a state may fall short, such notions remain strong in the perceptions of ordinary folk, politicians, and indeed academic observers. A belief in the uniqueness of a state is vital in establishing its integrity. In Britain, perceptions of British politics and government tend to fit around traditional themes of national sovereignty, long-established parliamentary democracy, a two-party system, a historic political continuity, and cultural homogeneity. These and other manifestations of British "exceptionalism" are also important to anyone observing Britain from outside—the complex can be made easy through notions of national characterization, personification, or just oversimplifying. We need this ease of access to make initial sense of complex reality. But, tested in the light of the complexities of *interdependence*, none of these exceptional characteristics represent unchallenged "truths" of the British political system. Nevertheless, they remain vital, for without their existence a case for interdependence cannot be tested!

SOMETHING DIFFERENT

There is, however, one aspect of British interdependence that cuts deep into its integrity as a sovereign state. Since 1973, and now together with twenty-six European states, Britain has been a member of the European Union (EU). Along with other member states (MS), interdependence is clearly designated by the *EU legal order* with economic, social, political, technological, and other *treaty-based agreements* that have cut deeply into aspects of government that were formerly the preserve of the state. We may make two leaps of faith here. The first is an assumption that the EU is an international organization that is *sui generis*—unique, exceptional: in its aims, composition, and working arrangements. It rests on a formalized interdependence, and its major components, its member states, accept and participate in this complexity. Thus, as component parts of the EU, *member states are also sui generis*—or at least worthy of distinction from nonmember states. The second leap is significant for the approach taken here: that, as Britain is one of twenty-seven sui generis member states, any analysis of Britain as a political system is obliged to *fully acknowledge* the extent to which EU interdependence shapes and is shaped by Britain. Hence, an analysis of British governance that fails to "mainstream" Europe is likely to miss vital explanatory features of its contemporary politics and, importantly, political change (Gamble 2003a; Bache and Jordan 2006; Bache 2008). Consequently, each chapter will mainstream and evaluate the impact of the EU on British politics and government in an effort to assess the extent of Britain's interdependence as an EU member state.

Already the warning bells should be ringing. If one accepts the idea of interdependence, how can the influence of different forms of dependence be distinguished? Is it EU, US, or global economic influences that are shaping, for instance, the nature of British economic decision making? What is meant by *Europeanization*? How can it be separated from events, circumstances, and trends that form part of "normal" political activity in Britain; and, even if we can pin Europeanization down, how can we measure its effects? These and other questions should be in the minds of the skeptical reader while considering the occasionally contentious conclusions reached in this book. At this point the reader who is unfamiliar with the characteristics of the European Union is invited to read the appendix that outlines the nature and institutions of the EU. Further information can be obtained from a dedicated Rowman & Littlefield website (http://www.rowmanlittlefield.com/isbn/0742536858). The next section grapples with the concept of Europeanization and its several dimensions.

EUROPEANIZATION

Driven by the "deepening" of the EU's policies after the Single European Act (1986), and in a post–Cold War environment that gave the EU a leading role in securing the emerging democracies of Central and Eastern Europe, the notion of Europeanization has both internal and external dimensions. We argue that it can be used in three ways: to encapsulate the consolidation and external projection of *European values*; in considering the *impact of EU integration*; and as a means of analyzing the *domestic policy processes* of the member states. Each of these is of course interrelated, but as we shall argue, distinctions in the focus of definition are necessary to allow the term a fighting chance to work effectively. It is worthwhile therefore spending time understanding the following terminology.

Europeanization as the Broadcasting of European Values

For one writer, Europeanization represents "the process towards increasing economic and political homogeneity and, consequently, the elimination of extremes in terms of economic policies or political systems" (Hettne 1995: 219). In this sense, the term is *developmental* and recognizes the spread of (West) European values of liberalism and capitalism. Thus authoritarian value systems in Southern Europe in the 1970s and Central and Eastern Europe in the 1990s were exchanged for representative government and the free market. These democracies sought external legitimation by accepting the rules of European "clubs" such as the Council of Europe, the Organization for Security and Cooperation in Europe, and, most significantly, the EU. Europeanization, in this context, underlined the opportunity for an autonomous, peaceful greater European family of states professing shared values. Thus, for Poland, the Czech Republic, Hungary, and others, a "return to Europe" after the end of communism marked a reawakening of past experiences (Mannin 1999).

A further external "value" dimension to Europeanization is its relationship with globalization, where Europeanization may be seen as either a part of a globalizing "process" or as a regional defense against it (Laffan, O Donnell, and Smith 1999; Wallace 2000). Here, the idea of Europeanization can be seen positively, as a transmitter of liberalism, the free market, and regional security, and thus as a door to global markets and economic survival. Or it may be seen as a negative phenomenon: a bastion *against* globalization. As we shall see, notions of a shared past with European values presents difficulties for many British people brought up on a historical diet of Europe as a problem or rival, rather than a solution. And perceived as an imposed set of values, Europeanization becomes another negative slogan in the vocabulary of the British Europhobe, as an infringement of national identity and state sovereignty.

Europeanization and EU Integration

In this sense Europeanization is associated with the continuing development of supranational governance within the European Union *"and thus the creation of a new institutional centre"* (Buller and Gamble 2004: 15). The search for a more effective EU policy system has been driven by the complexities of establishing a Single European Market, the moves toward Economic and Monetary Union (EMU) from 1992, the changes in the structures and processes of the EU to accommodate its expansion, and the need to promote member-state policies aimed at making the EU a globally competitive entity. EU integration has deepened rapidly during the 1990s. The implication is that the EU is now a *real* political system and can be studied as such. So "shared beliefs and norms are defined and consolidated in the EU policy process" and then are "incorporated in the logic of domestic (national and subnational) discourse, political structures, and public policies" (Bulmer and Radaelli 2004: 4).

Thus as part of the integration process, there has been necessarily an impact on the domestic political structures and processes of the member states. This might include *uploading* of particular member-state ideas and practices in the creation of EU-level policies, and *downloading* of EU policies once they are agreed. Therefore member states *adjust their domestic institutions and processes* to facilitate supra-governmental policy making. Thus, we observe in Britain institutional changes such as the creation of legislative committees and executive and bureaucratic units to facilitate involvement in supranational EU procedures, as well as changes in processes and personnel, such as the creation of special EU bureaus and employment of trained advisors. This and more must involve a redirection of government financial and political resources. In effect, the *processes* of policy convergence at EU level (integration) result in consequences for member-state governance (Europeanization), of which the effects are complex and varied.

Europeanization and Domestic Policy Making

Thirdly, the term describes "an incremental process reorienting the direction and shape of policies to the degree that EC political and economic dynamics becomes part of the organisational logic of national . . . policymaking" (Ladrech 1994: 70). The focus here is *domestic policy making* and its transformation through various interactions between the EU and its member states. These interactions may be *vertical* (up/down or down/up) or *horizontal*—between political actors across member states; they can also take place at the subnational level as a form of multilevel governance (MLG). Thus an interactive policy process emerges where member-state political actors have opportunities to *project* and shape EU policies in line with national or subnational desires; and *receive* EU Directives and Regulations, adapting them according to their domestic policy arrangements to fit EU objectives (Burch and Bulmer 2001).

Of course the reactions of a member state to EU objectives are likely to be affected by a range of domestic factors that may help or hinder effective implementation. One writer characterizes these differing responses as *"accommodation,"* where compatibility is rapidly achieved (for example, the absorption of EU legislation on equal opportunities into British law); *"transformation,"* where domestic processes need adapting to achieve policy change (for example, the creation of British regional administrative structures to assist administration of structural funding); *"inertia,"* where willingness to change is not apparent (for example, in some areas of EU environmental policy); and *"retrenchment,"* where negative national reaction leads to strengthened opposition to the policy (for example, in Britain, toward the Common Fisheries Policy) (Radaelli 2000).

Member states "share a general incentive to shape EU policies according to their domestic policy arrangements. They pursue diverging policy preferences and differ significantly with respect to their capacity to project and receive EU policies" (Borzel 2003: 4). In considering the capacity of the British system of governance to project and receive EU policies, much of the explanation of British politics will be developed in the forthcoming chapters.

British Politics and Europeanization: Applying the Concept

In light of these three foci of Europeanization, here is a general definition of the term: *Europeanization is a phenomenon promoting political change in the governance of EU member states, whose major source emanates from the EU as a supranational body of policy output, and is directed toward the absorption of EU core values and achieving policy objectives at the domestic level.* Thus the term has these ingredients: as a value system, a process toward EU integration, and a driver for policy change.

How far can this phenomenon be observed working within the British political system? It would seem that the term applies across a variety of political arenas or domains. To be applied without "conceptual stretching," we need to apply appropriate aspects of the term to the specific subject we are observing. Thus, studying the effect of the British media on public opinion would include the extent to which the British press, in particular, favors historic-traditional values over "European" values. An examination of the contemporary role of the British Parliament calls for an evaluation of parliamentary sovereignty against EU legal supremacy, but it also entails observations of the reorganization of parliamentary processes to meet the needs of member state/EU institutional interaction. An account of modern-day prime ministerial leadership, or of the role of ministers, would not be complete without recognition of the demands associated with participation in EU policy processes. To what extent, therefore, have the pressures of EU integration Europeanized the processes of political leadership and executive activity in Britain? Finally the impact of EU-directed policy is immediately apparent in British politics and needs recognizing and evaluating, as we undertake in the latter chapters of this book.

It must be pointed out that the use of one focus for the impact of Europeanization in specific arenas of British politics should not be an exclusive mode of analysis. For example, included in the heated debates about British membership of EMU is the broader issue of "Anglo-Saxon" versus "Continental" cultures and destinies; this runs alongside some calculated micro-debates on EMU's impact on the running of small businesses, should Britain join the final stage of EMU and adopt the euro. However, prioritization of one aspect of Europeanization offers initial clarity to the complex system of contemporary British governance within the EU.

ORGANIZATION OF THE BOOK

Chapter 1 outlines significant aspects of Britain's historical development and, in particular, its European connectedness. Here we follow the arguments of the historian Norman Davies, and others like him, who reinterprets popular Anglocentric, *Whig-imperialist* views of British history by questioning assumptions of unity and exceptionalism and illustrating the "island's" ties with its mainland, Continental Europe (Davies 1999). (See also textbox I.1.) This account of British political development forms a background to the second half of the chapter—an examination of conceptual explanations of British politics—each of which has inevitable historical antecedence. Chapter 2 is a contemporary snapshot of British society, examining external and domestic factors that are evident in exploring a rapidly changing social system.

Chapters 3 through 8 outline the institutional framework of British government and actors and processes that comprise the input side of the political system. After an initial review of the British constitution, chapters on representation, interest groups and the media, parties, and leadership test the explanatory power of the Westminster, prime ministerial/presidential, and multilevel governance models of British politics. In particular, the impact of European integration on British institutions and processes is highlighted, usually in the context of identifiable change and adaption to the EU, as it itself changes and adapts in a post–Cold War and global environment. Europeanization here is explored in the context of member-state responses to EU integration that, in Britain's case, has involved both institutional adaption and powerful public and political party reactions.

The remaining chapters, 9 through 12, examine the policy process and selected policy arenas, focusing on the extent to which British public pol-

Textbox 1.1. Identity and Whig-Imperial History

Since the cohesion of a political community relies on shared identities and an awareness of common origins and destinies, the interpretation of history is vital to this cohesion. The Whig-imperial view of British history is an optimistic perspective of Britain's
historical path, stressing "progress" for a unifying experience of economic development
and political maturity as Britain became "imperial, oceanic discoverers of the secrets of
free government and gradual progress" (Marquand 2009: 186). Historians like Macaulay
and Trevelyan adopted this view, celebrating the spread of British culture through imperial and economic hegemony as a positive world force. The stuff of school history for
much of the twentieth century was based on this approach and thus contributed to a
confident, popular view toward Britain and its place in the world. But as Marquand and
others point out, the economic, social, and political developments in the last quarter of
the twentieth century have confused this sense of common identity, as the loss of world
status, entry into the European Union, and a growing sense of Britain's multinational
and cosmopolitan society challenge this exceptionalist viewpoint. For Marquand there
is now a "vacuum of language" to describe Britishness that has led to an assertion of
English nationalism that sits uncomfortably with a twenty-first-century pluralist culture.

icy is influenced by its membership in the EU. The adaption of the policy
process to incorporate "downloaded" EU policies as well as the extent to
which British policy makers and implementers "upload" their policy preferences is illustrated. Where relevant, external influences—of the global
market, the United States, or international regimes—are also considered.
What emerges is a complex picture of external and internal pressures that
vary in their importance within different policy arenas. Thus, one can confidently illustrate the impact of EU legislation on most British environmental policy; however, an examination of British foreign policy and the
EU's role as an external actor is far more contradictory. A conclusion
draws together threads that inevitably intertwine and diverge.

The premise of this book is that British politics and government cannot be understood without a full acknowledgment of the impact that
membership in the EU and British engagement with it and other member
states has had on the British system. In no way does the author wish to
diminish the significance of what might be perceived as domestically derived phenomena—such as devolution; the Irish peace process; the welfare
state; Thatcherism and Blairism; or externalities such as global market instability and recession, terrorism, or the notion of the UK-US special relationship. It is contended, however, that the significance of these for Britain
can only be assessed in the unusual condition in which Britain and twenty-
six other member state have voluntary placed themselves: as a vital cog in a

sui generis EU system of governance. This fact should be the starting point for any journey through British politics today.

FURTHER READING

Among the many books that attempt to throw light on the politics and government of the EU, John McCormick's *Understanding the European Union* (2008) and Richard Sakwa and Anne Stevens's *Contemporary Europe* (2006) are excellent introductions. For a more advanced comprehensive analysis see Neill Nugent's *The Government and Politics of the European Union* (2006) and Helen and William Wallace and Mark Pollock's edited volume, *Policy-Making in the European Union* (2006). For a discussion of multilevel governance see Ian Bache and Matthew Flinders (2004) and for a debate about Europeanization in its different guises a reader, *Europeanization: New Research Agenda* is comprehensive (Paulo Graziano and Maartin Vink 2006). Its political implications are explored in Ken Featherstone and Claudo Radaelli's edited volume, *The Politics of Europeanization* (2003). Ian Bache brings together both concepts in *Europeanization and Multilevel Governance* (2008). Andrew Geddes (2004) and Bache and Andrew Jordan (2006) explore many of the fields developed in the course of this text. I am indebted to all above for their scholarship.

The Development of the British State
Stories and Models

It is beyond the scope of a text devoted to British contemporary politics to provide a detailed historical narrative that encapsulates the story of what Norman Davies calls "The Isles" (1999). Such a narrative is confined here, to Britain's experience of the twentieth century and especially the post–World War II era. The way the present is constructed, however, is influenced by the past, or rather the way the past story is told. Indeed the cultural framework within which a state seeks to sustain its legitimacy is dependent on the telling of a successful, believable history. The emergence of a British state has been a long and convoluted process and much of the popular telling of this story has been interpreted through the Whig-imperialist perspective described earlier. The assumptions contained within this perspective are powerful interpreters of Britain's past and thus also interpret the present for many of its citizens. What follows is a critical exploration of four themes that have played a significant part in explaining Britain's development from its pre-Roman, Celtic origins to its sui generis statehood within a European union.

A BRITISH OR ENGLISH STORY?

In constitutional terms, a united British Isles existed from only 1801 to 1922—from the Act of (Anglo-Irish) Union to the establishment of the Irish Free State. However, a united Britain (excluding Ireland) can be dated from 1707 to 1800 (the kingdom of Great Britain). One historian listed fourteen different "states" of the British Isles in 2,000 years of history (see table 1.1). The present writer has added two more—Britain and Ireland as EU member states from 1973. As the table shows, during the two

Table 1.1.   The States of the British Isles

Dates	State
To 1169	The High Kingship of Ireland
To 79	Ancient Celtic–British tribal principalities
To the 9th Century	The Land of the Picts (northern Britain)
43–410	Roman Britain
5th Century–1283	Welsh, Cornish, and Cumbrian principalities; Anglo Saxon Kingdoms
9th Century–1707*	Kingdom of the Scots
1066–1536	Kingdom of England (with Welsh, Irish, Channel Isles, and French provinces/colonies)
1536–1707*	Kingdom of England and Wales
1541–1801*	Kingdom of Ireland
1649–1660	The Commonwealth (First British Republic)
1707–1800	The United Kingdom of Great Britain
1801–1922**	The United Kingdom of Great Britain and Ireland
1922–	The Irish Free State, then Eire, then Republic of Ireland
1922–1973	The United Kingdom of Great Britain and Northern Ireland
1973–	UK: an EU member state.
1973–	Republic of Ireland: an EU member state

Source: After Davies (1999).
* Political settlement after the Civil War leads to a period of Commonwealth/Republic (1649–1660).
** Includes all the landmasses of the British Isles.

millennia, sovereign statehood for the two largest British Isles has existed for only 121 years; the larger isle, Britain, for 93 years; a partially united Britain for 531 years (with 410 years as a Roman province); a partially united British Isles (to include Northern Ireland) existed for 51 years. Since 1973 that state has pooled its sovereignty through treaty-bound obligations with other EU member states.

The British state is not only characterized by its fragmented past, but also by the other histories of its nations, that are both part of and a counter to any straightforward notions of a British history. Irish, Welsh, and Scottish histories provide different interpretations of events such as the Civil War period; Acts of Union; periods of religious persecution; or wars with France, Spain, and the Netherlands, whose effects were so consequential for Celtic nationhood. England as the dominant entity within the Isles has provided the power base through which an encompassing British state emerged, and accordingly, its history has until recently enveloped its Celtic neighbors. Therefore correction is necessary to recognize that the British story is composed of a "plurality of histories," not one, however appealingly simple that may seen to be (Pocock 2006).

It is because of the simplicity of such a British story that a Whig-imperialist interpretation took such a strong hold on the popular culture of Britons from the mid-nineteenth century. Though we note several contemporary factors that challenge this interpretation in chapter 2, a political dialogue about Britishness continues today. Indeed, one of Gordon Brown's first public campaigns was to reprise this debate. In doing so, an uncomfortable truth emerges: for many Celts, the British state was the result of English invasion of their nation, militarily, culturally, and economically; while for many English people, being British is the same as being English. Any contemporary attempt to reconstitute the notion of Britishness is complicated by its fragile historical basis. And this is compounded when one examines other assumptions that the Whig-imperialist paradigm has bequeathed.

A Relentless March of Liberal-Constitutional Progress?

One vision of the British past is its presentation as a gradual and upward path toward enlightened government, liberty, and stability through its ever-adapting constitutional monarchy. Thus the notion of a "freeborn Englishman" is linked to the Magna Carta (1215), when Anglo-Saxon freedoms challenged Norman despots; the Elizabethan defense of Protestant England from Spanish Catholic invasion (the Armada of 1588); and the superiority of Commons over Monarchy from the English Civil Wars and Republic in the mid-seventeenth century and its reinforcement in 1688 by the Glorious Revolution (see textbox 1.1). The Parliamentary Reform Acts of the nineteenth century and progressive social reforms accompanied by enlightened imperialism broadcast British values within the Isles and overseas (Marquand 2009). From this history emerges a confirmation of Britain/England as an imperious sovereign nation-state, with Parliament (Commons, Lords, *and* Crown) as the supreme legislator—and guarantor of hard-won liberties.

Other stories are available. Marquand identifies two other versions of the emergence of the British State: a democratic-collectivist view from Fabian socialists, and one from Conservative-nationalists. These notions are evident in the postwar Labour governments, 1945–1951, and in Conservative nationalist aspects of the Thatcher governments, 1979–1990. Both, he argues, end up accepting, in the case of a collectivist view, or eulogizing, in the case of a conservative approach, the notion of Crown-in-Parliament sovereignty. It is only an underwritten but long-standing third interpretation of British history—as a struggle between democratic republicanism and an imperial state—that fundamentally challenges this. So John Milton, Thomas Paine, J. S. Mill, and others present "outsider" perspectives to the Whig-imperialist notion of a British state (Marquand 2008; 2009).

Textbox 1.1. Magna Carta

On June 15, 1215, at Runnymede, King John was forced by an assembly of barons to sign a document, originally called "Articles of Barons," later referred to as the Magna Carta, or the "Grand Charter." The document formally recognized the traditional rights of barons—that is, to protect the rights and property of the few powerful families of the feudal system, not to provide universal protection of rights. The longest and most significant of the sixty-three clauses was Clause 61, or the "security clause." This established a committee of twenty-five barons who would oversee the enforcement of the document and who could meet at anytime to overrule the will of the king. The Magna Carta's primary purposes were to force King John to acknowledge ancient liberties, limit his ability to raise funds, and reassert the principle of "due process."

The significance of the Magna Carta extends beyond Britain to other countries such as the United States and Australia. It was cited in the resistance against the oppressive tactics of the Stuart kings and the creation of the 1689 Bill of Rights, the American colonial resistance to British imperialism, and the development of the US Constitution. The idea that the US Constitution is the "supreme law of the land" is borrowed from the supremacy of the Magna Carta. Moreover, the establishment of the Charter in 1297 as common law carries over into US affairs: the Magna Carta has been cited many times by the US Supreme Court. In British politics, this "incantation of the spirit of liberty" has been employed as a symbol of freedom against intervening forces, not least of which include the British state itself and inevitably, claim Eurosceptics, the "Brussels bureaucracy."

A Nonrevolutionary Tradition?

Two adjectives—*Glorious* and *Industrial*, are usually attached to the word *revolution* when used in a British context. The first, the Glorious Revolution (1688) is generally perceived as a nonviolent, almost joyous step toward a constitutional rather than monarchical political system; the second is a period of eighteenth- to nineteenth-century economic change that was the precursor to a British hegemony through to World War I. Though achieved at considerable social cost, this is also perceived as part of peaceful liberal progress.

The Glorious Revolution was more of a latter-day example of liberal interventionism, with 20,000 invading Dutch troops replacing, albeit temporarily, the English army in London (Jardine 2008). While confirming the salience of Parliament within a constitutional monarchy through a Bill of Rights, the executive voice of the monarchy continued to be heard into the nineteenth century (Davies 1999; see textbox 1.2). The revolution did, however, resolve the future succession to the throne, creating an Anglo-Dutch and, subsequently, a British-German Hanoverian dynasty that produced a permanent, anti-French rivalry that was to be

---

Textbox 1.2. The Bill of Rights

The coronation of William II and Mary was followed by the signing of an act declaring the rights and liberties of the subject and settling the succession of the Crown, better known today as the Bill of Rights. The immediate effect of the document was to legitimize the new monarchy and to delegitimize the old. James II was accused of many misdemeanors, including ignoring Parliament, illegality, interfering with elections, and favoring Catholics. The act set out to remedy these grievances by asserting the right of free elections and regular Parliaments and Parliamentary control over taxation, suspending statues, and a standing army. Catholics were banned from succeeding to the throne. The Bill of Rights granted political supremacy to Parliament and emerged as an instrument in the development of constitutional law. Its features are also evident in other authoritative statements of rights, including the US Constitution, the Universal Declaration of Human Rights, and the European Convention on Human Rights.

---

fought out in every world region during the eighteenth and early nineteenth centuries.

But revolutions in other countries also impacted on British political change. The American and French Revolutions provided both stimulus for and reaction against domestic political reforms and divided British public opinion dramatically. The challenge that American colonists threw out to the Crown/Parliament's sovereign authority is an example of that third interpretation of British political development, the struggle between democratic republicanism and the imperial state. In this sense, the War of Independence might be seen as a second English Civil War, with a successful outcome for republicanism and a people-based state sovereignty—but not on British soil! The French Revolution (1789), initially welcomed as an event likely to severely weaken Britain's Continental enemy, rapidly took on the image of a "political rabies" when the bloodshed and scale of destruction of the ancien régime became apparent. War with Revolutionary, and then with Napoleonic, France to 1815 focused the popular mind-set away from the radical aims of Thomas Paine toward the defense of Parliament and monarch, putting notions of American and French republican democracy and equality firmly on the back burner.

Demands for political reform in the nineteenth century had their violent edge, however: a crowd massacre in 1819 in St. Peters Field, Manchester, or the Merthyr riots in Wales in 1831 illustrate a more violent background to the first of three Parliamentary Reform Acts (1832, 1867, 1884). While a drip feed of political, social, and economic reforms contained Continental revolutions in 1848 "over there," they did not prevent Irish unrest. A political solution, Home Rule, was resisted by both Irish nationalists and northern unionists and brought Ireland near to civil war in 1914. It led to open revolt in the Dublin rising of 1916, an Anglo-Irish war (1919–1921), and partition and Southern Irish independence. Here was a domestic revolt and republican revolution against a sovereign "United" Kingdom.

There is one other caveat to the claim that Britain has avoided a revolutionary break with its past compared with US, French, or later Russian histories. Inasmuch as revolution in these cases was in part the result of external interventions in these states, historians of Scottish and Welsh politics can point to the impact of English interventions in their domestic affairs, culminating in their demise as separate state entities. Thus, "the Scots are well aware that in 1707 their forebears entered a new state . . . (y)et the English simply don't see it" (Davies 1999: 550). Wales was conquered (1284) and then arbitrarily incorporated (1536). The Welsh polity, which their hero Llewellyn and his ancestors had fostered, was uprooted. "Wales was now the first province within an English empire" (Davies 1999: 407). A case for a British nonviolent evolutionary history would seem to be dependent on which side of the English/Celtic border sits the judge.

Imperial Power and Broker to Europe

Among many successes in English history, Thomas Macaulay lists "how our country, from a state of ignominious vassalage, rapidly rose to the place of umpire amongst European powers; how her opulence and martial power grew together . . . how a gigantic commerce gave birth to a maritime power" (that sank every other power into insignificance), "how in the Americas, the British colonies rapidly became far mightier and wealthier than . . . the dominions of Charles the Fifth, how in Asia, British adventurers founded an empire not less splendid and more durable than that of Alexander" (Macaulay 1848). Except for the uncomfortable fact that most of the wealthy colonies in northern America had already been lost, his eulogy is the stuff of an imperial legend, and it underpinned nineteenth- and twentieth-century notions of British world hegemony.

Macaulay's perception of Britain as "umpire amongst European powers" echo's Mrs. Thatcher's notion of Britain's special contribution to Europe in "fighting to prevent Europe from falling under the dominance of a single power" (Thatcher 1988). Attempts at semi-detachment from Continental affairs are evident enough; total detachment has been impossible. And much of Britain's history is dissolved into a European mélange— whether political elites sought it or not. Most vividly, Continental invasions of Britain from the Romans through to the seventeenth-century Dutch, and English/British invasions of the Continent from the Plantagenet period to the 1944 Normandy landings, are the headlines of British military history.

Marriages between Scottish, English, and British and Continental royal houses reinforced diplomatic alliances from the thirteenth century onward. Rival claimants to the territories of Western Europe and wars of succession resulted. Norman-Angevin kings ruled England and parts of France for 200 years. The Tudors fought off French and Spanish claims to the English Throne—and claimed Continental territory themselves. William and Mary ruled Britain and the Netherlands; the Hanoverians ruled Britain and German states. Continental rivalries and alliances spread to the rest of the world, adding a European dimension to British imperial ventures.

After 1815, however, Macaulay's claim, that Britain was now the impartial broker of European politics, seemed plausible. Save for the Crimean War (1854–1856), the extension and management of a worldwide empire from Asia to Africa and Australia replaced Britain's direct intervention in Continental affairs. But at the back of this imperial prioritization lay a traditional diplomatic network of royal Victorian marriages that were helpful in assisting relatively peaceful settlement of disputes, as European powers attempted to carve up Africa and Asia. A sense of superiority that characterized British/Continental nineteenth-century relationships coupled with a detached perspective toward what was going on "over there" remains today an aspect of the Conservative-nationalist, Whig-imperialist, and liberal-collectivist perspectives mentioned earlier.

The loss of a first (American) empire was more than compensated for by the growth of a second. At its greatest reach after World War I had delivered parts of the Middle East as well as previously German colonies, the British Empire covered one-fifth of the world map in red—a map that was utilized by schools in the 1960s. With the monarchy at its head, with parliamentary democracy replicated in the white dominions (Canada, Australia, New Zealand, and South Africa) and with British legal administration superimposed in the African colonies and India, the imperial success of a Whig-liberal value system was broadcast on a global scale.

From this triumphalist scenario came a sense of cultural security and superiority through to the 1950s that was relatively undisturbed by the seamier sides of British colonialism. Periodic massacres, economic exploitation, arbitrary division of traditional ethnic lands, and the suppression of cultures did not fit such triumphalism, and were not much acknowledged until the collapse of the remaining Empire in the 1950s and 1960s (Marquand 2008; Davies 1999). Its demise brought new international challenges (see chapter 12), but it left significant historical memories. Imperial successes could be shared by all the nations of the Isles who had contributed to it; thus a sense of Britishness was fostered, indeed was underpinned by empire. But how to underpin Britishness in a postimperial world is problematic, and the current search for a new domestic national identification is in part the result (Gamble 2003a).

Up to the nineteenth century, it could be argued, British rulers had engaged for several centuries with two struggles. A domestic one, for unity with Wales, Scotland, and Ireland; and externally, for dominance within a European theater, engaging with Continental enemies and allies in order to achieve security and military and commercial dominance in the wider world. Colonial wars in North America, India, and the West Indies were extensions of those European rivalries. After 1815, secure in naval supremacy and despite the debacle in the American colonies, direct involvement in Continental affairs was replaced by the extension and management of a world empire extending to Africa, Asia, and Australasia. Europe was "over there," a set of potential allies and enemies to be managed by political brokerage and royal marriages.

BRITAIN IN THE TWENTIETH CENTURY: WORLD WARS, COLD WAR

The early twentieth century evidenced some cracks in a comfortable Whig-imperialist scenario. The concern to catch up with economic and military rivals, especially Germany, together with demands for social reform from the Liberal Party and labor organizations, created a dynamic period of reform before the onset of World War I. The 1906–1909 Liberal government produced social legislation commensurate with the needs of expanding demand and an increasingly complex industrial economy. Resistance to these interventions by the Conservatives was to result in the Lords voting down a spending budget that included a "supertax" on the very rich. This challenge to Commons supremacy was resolved by the Parliament Act of 1911, which reduced the House of Lords' power to delay House of Commons legislation to one month for financial bills and two years for all others.

The Great War

The agreements reached at the 1878 Congress of Berlin, and the glue of Victoria's dynastical linkage to the Continental monarchies, broke apart under the strain of twentieth-century economic and imperial rivalries. Britain's alliances (entêntes) with France (1904) and Russia (1906) led inevitably to confrontation with Germany when Austro-Hungary and Russia clashed over the assassination of Archduke Ferdinand in Serbia. Between 1914 and 1918 over 750, 000 British troops died; 2,500,000 men were casualties. In the Battle of the Somme 60,000 men fell on the first day (July 1, 1916); 300,000 soldiers, by then conscripts as well as volunteers, were killed or wounded at Passchendaele (August–September 1917).

The horror of this "Great" war was to have profound effects on the thinking of British elites and populace.

For the war to be won it was evident that mobilization of the peoples of Britain and the empire was necessary. It was not just Celtic and English blood but Indian, Canadian, South African, Australian, Asian, and African as well. But not withstanding the combined might of empire forces and portentously for the rest of twentieth-century international politics, it was the arrival of US "doughboys" in the trenches (1917) that proved a key factor in the outcome of this "Great War." In the war at home, women were to play an integral role in the economy and in providing military support. The government, especially after the formation of a national coalition under Lloyd George in May 1915, took more powers than any absolute monarch of the seventeenth century. Wartime central organization, in both size and scope, was to alter the administration of British domestic policy thereafter.

The Interwar Years

Politically, the Liberal Party was the major loser from these events, and despite the success of Lloyd George as a war leader, it was to suffer resounding defeat in the election of 1918. While Lloyd George survived at the head of a coalition of loyal Liberals and Conservatives, it was the Labour Party that was to emerge as the effective second force in British Politics. Women over thirty had won the right to vote during the hostilities. The electorate increased in size from 8 million (1914) to 21 million (1918). This new pool of working-class voters was effectively fished by a party ideologically bolstered by the growth of sister socialist movements in France, Italy, and Germany, and controversially, by the 1917 Russian Revolution.

Nor could issues of empire be put aside. While the British imperial writ stretched even further after the Treaty of Versailles (1919), which established British "protectorates" in what is now Jordon, Israel, and Iraq, old imperial relationships between the white Dominions and India could not be sustained. Pressures toward independence and the creation of the Commonwealth were soon to emerge. An attempt to resolve the Irish question was made in the shape of partition. In 1922 the Irish Free State and Ulster were created; a decision whose consequences are still evident today.

While there were some attempts at social reform, especially in the provision of housing ("Homes fit for heroes" was an election slogan of 1918), the dominant Conservative group within the postwar coalition government was intent on a return to prewar "normalcy." This included the return of the coal and steel industries from a period of wartime nationalization to private ownership and reestablishment of the international value of the pound (gold standard) at prewar levels (in 1925). This forced considerable deflation on an already depressed economy. A decline in world trade, industrial unrest culminating in the General Strike of 1926, and persistent high unemployment in the traditional and generally northern and Celtic regions of the UK assisted the fortunes of the Labour Party, which formed minority governments in 1924 and 1929–1931. After a National Government (1931–1935), economic fortunes changed somewhat in the mid-1930s, just in time to face another world war.

British Politics and World War II

Remembrance Day, September 11 each year, commemorates the deaths of military personnel and civilians in all wars that Britons have experienced. The futility of World War I is a cliché, but it remains a persistent characterization of attitudes toward the military losses that caused untold personal tragedy to almost all the British population. This may be vividly contrasted with the popular characterization of World War II. While thoughts of World War I on Remembrance Sunday produce a shocked recognition of the individual soldier's sacrifice, World War II produces a sense of national satisfaction, of a job well done and, for some, a massive sense of national pride. The tragedies—defeat in France 1940, the fall of Singapore in 1942, the air "blitz" on London and other towns, defeat at Arnheim in 1944, and the fear of missile attack on Southern Britain—are countered by the "miracle" of Dunkirk and the (air) Battle of Britain (1940); the desert Battle of El Alamein (1942); and the Normandy (France) invasion (1944) to final victory in 1945.

A united military purpose produced a high point of national unity: Welsh, Scottish, English, and Irish (from both North and South) joined in the war effort, as once again did the Empire/Commonwealth. Women once again donned factory overalls, uniforms, and farmers' boots. The rationing of both necessities and luxury goods was applied, formally anyway, across all classes. Total war was met by total government, with the 1935 Parliament extended until the war was over. Though there were still by-elections (special elections) and some strikes, national unity was maintained and, especially after the decisive moments of US and Soviet entry into the hostilities as allies to Britain, postwar visions of a better future were to aid in sustaining the public morale.

The Beveridge Report (1942) presented soldiers and civilians with a postwar plan for a comprehensive social security system. Reports on regional policy, urban planning, and, in 1944, a White Paper committing the government to full-employment policies, underlined the inevitability of a postwar Keynesian (interventionist) economic policy. The Butler Education Act of 1944 not only promised modern public secondary education for all, but the opportunity of social mobility through educational attainment.

When the European war ended in May 1945, the Labour Party, sensing that their political tide was high, withdrew from the coalition. In the election that followed, the wartime leader, Winston Churchill, was defeated. The Labour Party's Clement Attlee won in a landslide victory. Churchill and his Conservative ministers were less trusted in winning the peace than they had been in winning the war.

THE POST-1945 LEGACY: FINDING A NEW ROLE

The end of World War II meant the collapse of the prewar world order and the rise of new phenomena—particularly the international involvement in European and world affairs of the United States and the USSR. As well as promoting the ideological and military rivalries of the Western and Eastern blocs, the end of World War II also hastened the end of the empire, an adjustment that Britain's politicians and public acknowledged with difficulty. The Cold War ran through to the last decade of the century, and its impact on British domestic politics and foreign policy was a determining factor throughout the period.

This new dynamic, together with an associated decline in Britain's position as a world economic player, needed to be reconciled with the triumphalism of a successful war outcome: for Britain had "stood alone" for two years before the welcome military support of the United States and Soviet Union became available; and the shared view of elites and population was that Britain remained a world player. This idea constituted a problematic cultural legacy during later adjustments to a regional European rather than a global view of Britain's international position, and it continues to color attitudes and behaviors within the British political system.

Post–World War II triumphalism helped to shape domestic politics in a rather more direct manner. Peace ushered in social democracy and a Keynesian political economy that was to last through to the mid-1970s; this was apparent in both Labour and Conservative "consensus" politics. The welfare state established during the 1945–1951 Labour governments was consolidated under subsequent Conservative and Labour administrations. The nationalization of important industries such as gas and electricity, coal, steel, and rail transportation completed a genuine revolution in domestic policies when compared to the prewar period. Even after the return of Conservative administrations (1951–1964), Britain remained firmly in the mainstream of a postwar West European mixed-economy philosophy that emerged in each of the states destined to join the European Union. That philosophy, translated into votes, meant that until 1970, Labour and

Conservative parties regularly polled close to 90 percent of the votes cast in British general elections.

The postwar Labour government, however, was far less radical when considering domestic institutional reform. Several European countries—notably France, Italy, and (West) Germany—made serious institutional changes to their structures of government in response to prewar and wartime experiences. Others, like Poland, Czechoslovakia, Yugoslavia, and East Germany, created political systems in response to the strictures of their dominating neighbor, the USSR. Victorious and not having been invaded, no significant changes to British political institutions were thought to be necessary, apart from reducing the delaying powers of the House of Lords as a second chamber. The British political system administered a new welfare program and mixed economy through a centrally directed, London-based, single-party government. A nineteenth-century parliamentary system had grafted upon it a massive twentieth-century welfare state, and, though able to operate through the discipline of national political parties, it was to prove wanting in the delivery of a pluralist democracy that could effectively check the executive and administration.

Equally, the economic problems of the 1950s and 1960s industrial decline, technological obsolescence, uncompetitively priced exports, and a vulnerable currency (the pound sterling) were not assisted by an era of "stop-go-policies": successive Labour and Conservative governments attempted to manipulate economic conditions to their advantage prior to an election—inevitably to the detriment of the economy. Attempts to replace Keynesian "demand management" with more balanced-budget approaches were thwarted by strong trade union representation, often culminating in bitter strikes, such as the miners' strikes of 1972 and 1974 against the Conservative Heath administration and the "Winter of Discontent" of 1978–1979 during the Labour Callaghan government. These domestic circumstances were exacerbated by the rise in oil prices and the collapse of the postwar Bretton Woods system, which had, until 1973, provided a degree of certainty for the trading activities that were so significant for the UK's economy and international standing.

One response to this catalog of problems was reluctant recognition that Britain's economic future might be better protected by joining the European Economic Community. Initially rejecting membership of the European Coal and Steel Community (1952) and the EEC (1955–1957), the shock of the Suez Crisis in 1956 and economic decline during the late 1950s led to a change of diplomatic tack on the part of both Conservative and Labour governments (George 1990; Young 1998). A mixture of British government miscalculation and French reluctance to admit a halfhearted partner thwarted initial applications in 1961 and 1967. It was not until 1972 that a more confident and positive application, led by Europe enthusiast Prime Minister Edward Heath, proved successful. A subsequent Labour administration endorsed this major step in a new direction by referendum in 1975.

Membership in the EU did not solve Britain's domestic ills. A spent Labour administration was replaced in 1979 by the first Thatcher government, which created new parameters for economic policy—the Thatcher "revolution"—and fundamentally challenged most of the Keynesian assumptions established in the period following World War II.

From Thatcherism to Blairism: The Search for New Coordinates

There is some debate in British political and academic circles as to whether the extended period of Conservative government under Margaret Thatcher (1979–1990) and then John Major (1990–1997) was genuinely revolutionary when compared with the consensus politics of the previous era (Kavanagh 1997). Facing serious economic problems, Mrs. Thatcher's political fortunes were changed with the popularity of victory in the short Falklands/Malvinas war (1982) with Argentina. A massive electoral victory in 1983 provided the necessary political impetus and legitimacy to commence a controversial journey that lasted long after her demise in 1990. A retreat from state ownership of economic assets via denationalization of gas, water, and electricity industries was made electorally popular by their sale at knockdown share prices on the open market. This, together with the right-to-buy policy established for social housing tenants, engendered a new neoliberal slogan, "property owning democracy," based on individuals with a personal stake in the market.

Less palatable for the regions and communities unable to make the adjustments necessary to join these market-led opportunities was the abandonment of full employment as a macroeconomic goal and the use of supply-side (monetarist) policies devoted to containing inflation. The result was levels of unemployment in some economic sectors and regions not experienced since the 1930s; and the end of the corporatist collaboration with trade unions that was a major feature of postwar consensus government. A miners' strike (1984–1985) led to the bitterest industrial confrontation since the general strike of 1926 and polarized the nation. The miners, and subsequently the Labour Party in the 1987 general election, were roundly defeated on a continuing wave of popular support for "Thatcherism." A deeply wounded Trade Union movement lost membership and much legal protection during her period of office.

Parallel to the Thatcherite search for an end to the "dependency culture" of the welfare state was a similarly strident external presence in the shape of a strongly restated nationalism supported by a global vision of Britain's external role. Mrs. Thatcher's close relationship and shared ideological outlook with US president Ronald Reagan underscored an un-compromising foreign policy that included enhancement of the "special" British-US relationship, strong support for NATO, and strident anticom-munism. Similar support was offered by Mrs. Thatcher's successor, John Major, for the first Iraq War (1990–1991). Militarily, British defense expen-diture reached a Cold War high point of 5.3 percent of GDP in 1985, re-flecting the political will of the British government to fulfill international obligations and thus preserve Britain's role as an international player.

The EU: Deepening and Widening

Thatcherite conservatism, with its neoliberal economic policy and new na-tionalism, fitted uncomfortably with the one-nation Toryism of the 1950s and 1960s. It also fitted uncomfortably with the rapid change evident in the EU during the 1980s. Conservative support for EU membership during the 1970s was reinforced initially by the Thatcher government's enthusi-asm for completion of the unified European market provided for in the 1986 Single European Act (SEA). Freer access to a Continental market, especially for Britain's successful financial services sector, complemented a globalist free market vision for Britain's economic future.

However, during the last few years of her premiership, Mrs. Thatcher took an increasingly anti-EU line on many issues. Thus, the other side of market integration—social solidarity in the shape of a Social Charter and the federalist vision of Jacques Delors, then EU Commission president, and French president Mitterrand—was opposed by a skeptical Prime Minister Thatcher. This stance, together with indecision over British participation in the European exchange rate mechanism (ERM), sowed seeds of unpopu-larity for the leader a decade into her post. Domestic unpopularity, together with party division over EU policies, led to her resignation in 1990.

At the same time, the ending of the Cold War had altered external cer-tainties for Britain and the rest of Europe. The collapse of Soviet and East European Communism beginning in 1989 produced new challenges that presented the EU, as a regional economic power, with a stabilizing role in a new era. As the EU responded to this challenge through consideration of a more federal future and an extended membership, the Conservative Party, now led by the more pragmatic John Major, split into Europhobic, Eurorealist, and Europhile wings. The Labour Party opposition was con-tent to encourage these divisions and adopt a more balanced pro-EU line as John Major struggled to sustain party unity.

Following an unexpected electoral victory in 1992, with a Commons majority of only twenty-five, John Major was continually pressurized by the neoliberal, Eurosceptic right of his party to stand against the federal-ist direction of the EU. Despite achieving "opt-outs" from the single currency and the Social Charter, and weakening moves toward an EU Common Foreign and Security Policy (CFSP), his claim of winning treaty concessions "game, set, and match" could not disguise the federalist direction of the 1992 Treaty on European Union (TEU). Beset by serious internal divisions over Europe, Major's administration went from crisis to crisis. Ejection from ERM after two years in 1992, serious disagreement over the EU ban on British beef in 1996 (following the BSE mad cow crisis), and disputes over further EU institutional reform undermined Major's authority within his party and the country at large. But the period of his premiership is significant in that several factors combined to reinforce a perception of British exceptionalism characterized by "European deviance," which has proved difficult for subsequent governments to alter.

New Millennium, New Labour, Old Problems

If a Eurosceptical perspective within the Conservative Party is one continuing legacy of Thatcherism, so also are consequences of her economic policies that needed to be addressed by a Labour Party searching for an election-winning formula after seventeen years of opposition. There were some signposts of redirection to be examined as opposition and counter-strategies began to emerge. The impact of neoliberal policies was felt heaviest in the Celtic regions and Northern England. Here was a breeding ground for nationalist reaction and demands for self- and local government as a response to the seeming disregard of London. The seeds for constitutional reform were sown in the latter years of Mrs. Thatcher's administration as academic and opposition discussion examined the possibilities of correctives to Conservative rule. Much of this often cross-party debate could be seen in the publications of Chapter 88, a radical manifesto for a total overhaul of the constitution, to which an aspiring Labour government had to respond. A Constitutional Convention argued for a Scottish legislature. As David Marquand states, "the road to the most far-reaching reconstruction of the British state for nearly three hundred years was open" (Marquand 2008: 338). With some trepidation the Labour Party faced these demands for radical constitutional change.

While it was initially easy for a new Labour leader, Tony Blair, to adopt a constructive policy toward expectant EU partners, responding to the neoliberal restructuring of the British economy presented more difficulties, not least within his own party. Between gaining the party leadership in 1994 and winning a landslide election in June 1997, Blair and his team modernized both the Labour Party machine and its policies. The party, already adjusting to a post–Cold War agenda of market capitalism, the environment and public sector reorganization was, under Blair, forced further toward a "third way," neither socialist nor neoliberal. At its core were policies on social inclusion, welfare to work, private sector stimulation through low taxes, and social investment for jobs—with a particular emphasis on "education, education, education." Clause 4 of the Labour Party Constitution (1918), which required control over the "commanding heights of the economy," was dumped, and the position of the unions and constituency parties within the parties was weakened. In external affairs, Blair looked toward a close association with a Clinton-led Democratic United States and, importantly, a new and leading role in an EU that was to be guided away from the protective aspects of a European social model toward Blair's open-market third way. The concept of Britain as a transatlantic bridge between the United States and Europe was an attractive if ambitious platform for external policy. Blair's resignation in June 2007, undefeated in three elections, has led to controversial assessments of the impact of his administration on British politics, and they are discussed in subsequent chapters.

A Convoluted History Lesson

Much of Britain's political development in the second millennium was intertwined with ideas, values, and events in mainland Europe. Britain's imperial role was shaped as much by rivalry, wars, and deals with Continental neighbors as by independent defense of British interests. Shared and contradictory values, philosophies and cultural experiences abounded. Christianity and secularism, liberalism and traditional conservatism, individualism and collectivism as well as nationalism and regionalism, elitism and egalitarianism are as much the contradictory characteristics of French and German political development as British experience. Britain's earlier development of constitutional monarchy and liberal representative institutions was an export to Continental states emerging from imperial domination in the nineteenth century. In turn, democracy, egalitarianism, and collectivism may be seen as radical Continental imports to nineteenth-century Britain. The mix of these philosophical and ideological experiences may be different in Continental state development, but they constitute shared elements of a European political culture.

Nevertheless, there are also some notable ideological and experiential exceptions that give claim to notions of Britain distinctiveness. The absence of violent revolutionary change in the past 350 years; the gradual nature of constitutional development through convention and piecemeal legislation; and the continuity, consolidation, and popular support for Parliamentary sovereignty and constitutional monarchy, are significant factors to include in claims to British political exceptionalism within a European context. As a consequence, the politically extreme ideologies of the twentieth century, fascism and communism, found in British pragmatism and moderation a poor breeding ground compared with Continental Europe.

Yet, events since 1945 have confronted those exceptionalist characteristics. Britain is multicultural now to an extent almost unimaginable to pre–World War II society. The nations of Scotland, Wales, and Northern Ireland have a stronger institutionalized status through devolution. Britain is economically "globalized" more than any other European economy, as well as being embedded within the regional economy of the EU. Yet that very embeddedness is problematic, for its peoples and its politicians, not least because the "exceptionalist" images of British political culture seem so powerful. How, then, to model and thus to simplify these complexities so as to establish an essence of the contemporary British political system?

CONTEMPORARY MODELS OF BRITISH POLITICS

An analytic model in political science should organize facts so as to bring clarity to what otherwise might be a disorganized collection of information. But since model builders choose the facts and the ordering of their relationships, they spring from an underlying value-laden frame. Therefore, when it comes to building a country-based model, there must be recognition of potential bias associated with issues such as ethnocentricity, competing values, and historic interpretation. Here we present three contemporary models of British politics that emphasize different factors, each based on differently derived assumptions. Each presents a set of related political data that is organized systematically. As such, each has an input/output process and a range of gatekeepers that order political demand. Each is a simplification of reality but, more significantly, is also a reflection of a complex of ideas stemming from different assumptions about the nature of British politics in the twenty-first century. They provide, therefore, competing starting points for the analysis of how British politics works today. However, a further more contemporary perspective must also be acknowledged—*Europeanization*. It is the recurrent message of this book that, unless the impact of the EU on explanations of contemporary British politics is tested, we will exclude a potentially determining factor of how the system works.

The Westminster Model

A description of the Westminster model is contained in textbox 1.3. It has been much emulated, especially by Commonwealth countries, and, more recently, by some states emerging from Communism in Central and Eastern

Europe. As such, it has obtained a status as a simple and effective framework for translating citizen demands into government action. It has been adapted to meet the particular political circumstances of countries as diverse as Italy, the Bahamas, Ireland, and India. In "pure" form, its characteristics are: parliamentary sovereignty, a mixed executive-legislature, strong cabinet government, adversarial politics, a unitary state/unified civil service, and a rule of law shaped by legislative will and legal interpretation. The model, lends itself to centralized policy output within a clearly established state: Parliamentary will is therefore the expression of national sovereignty, through time-limited majoritarian party rule.

If there is a historically derived paradigm within which the model operates, it is the Whig-Liberal view of British political development reflected in both John Locke's seventeenth-century individualism and Edmund Burke's eighteenth-century conservatism. That is, the citizen within a specific geographical constituency votes for both a representative of her/his interests and a political "intellectual samurai," as George Bernard Shaw labeled members of Parliament (MP). In the former capacity, the individual's

---

Textbox 1.3. The Westminster Model

Britain is a constitutional monarchy with the queen as the figurehead of state. Politically, it is a parliamentary democracy whose national politicians are elected to the House of Commons by a first-past-the-post, single-member-constituency electoral system. The members of the second chamber, the House of Lords, are primarily appointed by party leaders in the House of Commons. It is currently under reform. While the Lords plays a formal, revising role in the process of legislation, the Commons is in practice the most politically powerful chamber. Its constitutional authority to legislate on any matter (parliamentary sovereignty) is enhanced by its role as the major source of the British executive—the prime minister, cabinet, and departmental ministers. The government is created from the ranks of the party able to command a majority in the Commons. Formally, the government survives as long as it commands the support of the Commons—in practice the majority party, or until a Parliament ends (maximum five years). The final choice of an election date lies with the prime minister. Parliamentary parties provide the opportunity for majoritarian government; a party in the majority will not share power with recognized opposition parties, whose task it is to oppose and wait their electoral opportunity. There is, thus, no separation of legislative-executive functions; but while senior judges have seats in the Lords, there is in practice a clear separation of the judicial from the political process. The PM and cabinet have a collective responsibility to the Commons, and individual ministers have a direct accountability for their department's activities to Parliament. At its best, the Westminster model delivers responsible cabinet government with the prime minister as first among equals (primus inter pares).

private interests can be advocated publicly; in the latter case—and mediated by the political tendencies of MPs as measured by party affiliation—the legislator does battle on behalf of constituents' broader values and the national interest, exercising her/his best judgment. "In every English gentleman," suggested G. B. Shaw, "we have got our samurai." Thus Burke, the Whig conservative; John Stuart Mill, the liberal; and Shaw, the socialist, share this perspective. Politicians, according to the Westminster model, whether guided by superior social standing or ideological inclination, apply their judgment on behalf of their constituents to achieve the wise public outcome.

Furthermore, a majoritarian, adversarial parliamentary process provides the representative with clear but limited and transparent decision-making choices. The cabinet executive, emanating from the majority parliamentary grouping, has the opportunity to process policy effectively, sheltered from factional interest within the limits of a five-year time frame. Thus, a limited, responsible, representative government emerges.

Before evaluating the Westminster model, it is important to emphasize the iconic status that it has enjoyed, especially with politicians themselves. Parliamentary sovereignty is an attractive and powerful concept in its simplicity and liberal democratic application. Adversarial, majoritarian procedures are equally simple and democratically appealing to voters looking for straightforward answers to complex problems. The model's history engenders a strong public loyalty to the system—if not necessarily as recently demonstrated to the politicians operating it! The unitary nature of the state is manifest in the focus of domestic political attention on leaders in Parliament, and therefore any challenge to Parliament's sovereign position, domestically or externally, can be interpreted as a fundamental attack on British national independence and unity. Its public status is reinforced by politicians' periodic resort to the model as a shield of national independence. This is underscored by an external perception of the British political process as innately stable.

The issue of parliamentary sovereignty and the EU is examined in subsequent chapters. Here we will simply argue that there are particular limits that EU treaties have recently imposed on the independence of all member states' legislative bodies and legal systems; which includes Britain. The concept of unlimited legal competence and the right to make or unmake any law whatsoever—examined, famously, by the nineteenth-century jurist A. V. Dicey (1959)—seems more a reflection of a political commentator writing in the mid-1880s, at the time of imperial hegemony, than a realistic assessment of political power within the British contemporary state.

Notwithstanding the breakup of a United Kingdom in 1922 when Southern Ireland gained independence, the idea of British state unity is now challenged by the devolved political institutions recently established in Scotland, Wales, and Northern Ireland. This devolution, together with the occasional deployment of referenda and their potentially binding political effects and the Human Rights Act (1998), which obliges compatibility of Parliamentary legislation with the European Declaration of Human Rights, challenges what Dicey claims as the most dominant feature of the Westminster model—the sovereignty of Parliament!

The case against the Westminster model rests not only on the validity of this key concept but also on its descriptive power. Can we assert that the relationship between the House of Commons and the Cabinet—the mixed executive—adequately describes the balance of political power in Britain? A simple electoral-chain-of-command process (voter to MP to minister to bureaucrat to citizen) for the Westminster model is challenged by external, especially EU, intervention in British domestic politics. It is also challenged by the claims of those who view British politics as a battle between diametrically opposed party armies whose main aim is to achieve electoral superiority over each other. Since the determining force for that battle is political and executive leadership, a quasi-presidential perspective of the British political system has emerged.

Quasi-Presidentialism (Prime Ministerial Government)

As textbox 1.4 shows, this model springs from several of the characteristics of the Westminster model. However, while the latter is clearly focused on the salience of Parliament, the quasi-presidential model reflects the evolution of the British executive and the factors that recently have allowed this to take place.

In this model, the relationship between the voter and the politician is mediated by electronic written media and Web-based industries that have undermined conventional constitutional and party political networks. This is to the advantage of public leaders whose access to and potential manipulation of communications media is extensive. They are assisted by the media's need to personify and simplify political messages. Since the media, especially television, have become the major source of electoral information, traditional political institutions have become less important, with a result that political communication comes mostly through the leader. This situation is common in many Western political systems, where leaders and media seek each other out in order to present attractive political messages to customers, audiences, and voters. The consequences are several, including the politics of sound bites, with voters' decisions made increasingly on style rather than substance.

A further common trait that has enhanced the role of the executive leader in Western democracies is the globalization of politics and eco-

---

Textbox 1.4. Prime Ministerial Government

Here the prime minister as leader of the majoritarian party in the House of Commons enjoys a popular legitimacy via a de facto direct relationship with the voters. Thus the voters' choice is shaped primarily by the consideration of who she/he wishes to lead the country for five years. The two main political parties' choice of a party leader is made with this overridingly electoral factor in mind. As such, the individual MP, the parliamentary party, and members of the cabinet and ministerial team are willing to be politically subordinated to leadership decisions. The prime minister makes the most important policy decisions with or without the advice of his/her ministerial colleagues. The prime minister enjoys support from the PM's office and staff, which advises outside of party or ministerial perspectives. He/she leads and coordinates policy with the overriding aim of sustaining popular support. Quasi-presidential power comes from various mainly conventional sources, such as patronage; party leadership; the cumulative authority of the post itself; and the ability to appoint and fire senior colleagues, to choose the date of elections, and to command a public audience. The growth of state intervention since World War II, access to a pervasive media, and a relentless involvement in international and EU affairs have all enhanced the "presidential status" of prime ministerial leadership.

---

nomic decision making. The prime minister thus has taken the role of international leader in such organizations as the UN, G8/20, and the EU. Also, the PM's role is enhanced in terms of leading national responses to global challenges that have, in turn, stimulated economic and political change domestically. The neoliberal policies that were thought necessary to change Britain in the 1980s were both a response to global economic trends and a reflection of Mrs. Thatcher's close association with the then US president's "Reaganomics." The Clinton-Blair relationship similarly fed third-way perspectives that reflected, in part, shared (globalist) views of economic policy and its political consequences. International events, from the Falklands intervention to conflicts in Bosnia-Kosovo, Afghanistan, and Iraq, and now the global economic crisis, have given scope for a prime minister to be seen as *un uomo d'azione* (man of action) that has led, with the prominent exception of Iraq, to considerable enhancement of prime ministerial reputations.

While a quasi-presidential epithet could be attached to such historical British prime ministers as Walpole, Lloyd George, and Churchill, the concept may be set in a more contemporary paradigm associated with modern elite theory. Here Joseph Schumpeter (1962) offers a model of democracy analogous to an economic-choice model of voting behavior. This model, in turn, informed the rational-choice theorists of the 1950s–1970s (Downs 1957; Riker 1962; Coleman 1973). Taken a stage further, the neoliberalism and consumerism of the 1980s and 1990s have constrained ideological choice for political parties—thus enhancing the importance of leadership in winning elections. Hence, the constant battle for the middle ground through the personification of political well-being and "feel good" for the voter/consumer in the shape of quasi-presidential (prime ministerial) presentation.

As chapter 8 illustrates, there are considerable doubts concerning the value of this perspective. Empirical observation suggests that not only is a quasi-presidential epithet ineffective when applied to the radically different prime ministerial styles of PMs such as Margaret Thatcher and John Major, but the power dynamics are so complex that it lacks consistency, even when applied to one incumbent over her/his period of office. The model remains a variant of the Westminster model, for the PM/president remains indirectly rather than directly elected. Powerful countervailing institutions and processes such as the maintenance of backbench and Cabinet loyalty, the Parliamentary timetable, and the limits of the electoral cycle will cut even the most presidential of premiers to size. Thus, the complexity of the executive/voter relationship is not served by the simplicity of the quasi-presidential model. There are other perspectives on the British executive that build in more complex and incorporative factors to describe power and process at the center of British politics. The concepts of "core executive," which encapsulates the complexity of decision making, and "multilevel governance" (MLG), which recognizes the impact of Europeanization, illustrate the continuing search for inclusive explanations of the contemporary British political system.

Multilevel Governance

A *governance* approach to the study of a political system switches our attention away from institutions and processes toward how societies organize. Governance thus includes not just the contribution of traditional political institutions and actors but voluntary societies, business organizations, quasi-autonomous public agencies (more unfortunately entitled "quangos"—quasi autonomous nongovernmental organizations), and religious structures—the "little platoons" of civil society, as Edmund Burke would term them. A governance approach recognizes that these platoons have now obtained regimental status in social organization; and also that the public/private, state/civil society boundary is inadequate in exploring how policy is created and implemented.

Blurred boundaries are the result of the complexity of contemporary political output, the recognition of important linkages between the public and private sectors, and the inability of the state to keep up with demands made upon its domestic policies. There emerges the need for what the European Commission has termed "partnership" and "subsidiarity" in the policy process. This manifests itself in both formal and informal ways: in the creation of "nonpolitical" regulatory, advisory, and implementing agencies; the emergence of new "policy communities" in areas such as health and the environment; public-private initiatives and partnerships; the application of business techniques to public-sector management; and the periodic initiatives of government to deconcentrate civil bureaucracy either geographically or functionally.

Much of the debate regarding a governance approach is not new to British politics. Edward Heath's Conservative government (1970–1974) introduced public-sector reforms that entailed deconcentration and "hiving off" (privatization). This was evidence of the "failure of the state" to effectively deliver the postwar promise of comprehensive social welfare (Cornford 1975). State failure, leading to what was subsequently called its "hollowing," was the result of external interventions in the British political system and internal political demands for regional/local autonomy and better delivery of public services. Thus the vagaries of world economic trends and crises, EU membership, and unresolved domestic issues over political identity and voter expectation of welfare delivery combined to produce political change—from "above" and "below."

Cornford's observations have proved particularly apposite over the subsequent thirty years. Conservatives in the 1980s and 1990s talked of "rolling back the state," a property-owning democracy, and a consumer society where government's role is reduced to regulation rather than provision. New Labour did not significantly challenge these policies, but stressed the need for "joined-up government" to make sense of the proliferation of agencies in the public service.

Labour inherited not only the Thatcherite "market" approach to the role of the state but also a significant external dimension to Britain's domestic political scene in the shape of a "deepened" EU. The Single European Act (1986) and Treaty of European Union (1992) produced a supranational layer of governance of some substance. In a range of domestic and external policy areas, European Union institutions and processes now interact with Britain's domestic processes to produce the notion of MLG—and in some situations, considerable governmental change (see textbox 1.5).

The assumptions behind an MLG approach contrast with those of the Westminster and quasi-presidential models in several ways. The state is presumed to be layered rather than centralized, and the clear lines of political responsibility—to Parliament/minister or to quasi-president are not evident. Sovereignty is neither national nor parliamentary, but shared. The executive, whether cabinet-based or prime ministerial, is segmented, as is the bureaucracy responsible for policy implementation. The primarily political nature of the parliamentary and quasi-presidential models becomes

Textbox I.5. Multilevel Governance

Multilevel governance shifts the notion of politics to include the various modes of social, political, and economic organization through which social life is structured. It recognizes the significance of markets, hierarchies, and formal and informal networks in this structuring. It also recognizes the salience of links between internally devolved public institutions, central government, and externally significant supranational organizations in the creation of many areas of public policy. In the case of Britain, the increased competences of the European Union, the moves toward devolution (Scotland, Wales, and Northern Ireland) and deconcentration and delegation of responsibilities to a variety of regional, local, quasi-public, and private bodies have resulted in what may be termed a "differentiated polity." In many policy areas, horizontal and vertical links are a vital aspect of a complex policy process, and an analytic model of British politics may be constructed to include the connectivities between: the European Commission and Council; the Council of Ministers; the ECJ; Westminster and Whitehall departments; the devolved assemblies and local governments; regional government offices and agencies; hospital trusts and universities; and other social partners including interest groups, private interests including trade unions, and commercial/employer groups/organizations.

more legally based as EU treaties and specifically designated quasi-federal (devolved) layers of government take responsibility for policy areas. A complex of ideas such as social partnership, functional expertise, subsidiarity (deconcentrated responsibility), shared citizenship, and quasi-constitutional legal hierarchy bind these layers together.

Controversially, MLG assumes the interdependence of Britain as a state within a global and particularly European context. Notwithstanding the controversial aspects of the assumptions behind it, MLG suffers also from problems associated with its application. In particular, while it seems an appropriate analytical frame to examine *some* aspects of the British polity— such as regional or environmental policy—other aspects remain firmly in the grip of the central state machinery. Its use as an analytic model may thus be limited. Nevertheless it does allow consideration of a key factor in the explanation of contemporary British politics—the relatively new contested but vital dimension of Europeanization discussed in our introduction.

CONCLUSION

A conceptual model should simplify complexity and focus attention on what is believed to be the essence of a social phenomenon. When compared, the different foci of the three models and their assumptions about what is significant in explaining British politics look plain enough. The historic Westminster model—with Parliament clearly at its center and liberal, representative, unitary government formed by a cabinet responsible to Parliament—encapsulates the myths and realities of British political development: in shorthand, it is the Whig-liberal tradition. Proponents argue that it has both an intrinsic value—it encapsulates British exceptionalism—and a fundamental explanatory power, through the trump card of parliamentary sovereignty and its defense of individual liberty. Ultimately, the essence of the British polity is contained within the House of Commons, where all political life commences and eventually ends.

The focus of a quasi-presidential explanation, by contrast, is upon a "command model" of British government (Hennessy 2001). It is rooted in a realist view of contemporary politics, whereby the demands of the electorate and the role of government have resulted in the preeminence of national leadership at the expense of Parliament, party, and cabinet. The phenomenon is not unfamiliar throughout Continental Europe, either in its contemporary form or from imperial/monarchical experiences and traditions. Globalization and European integration have increased the international demands on the prime minister, enhancing her/his role as an external actor. The ubiquity and immediacy of modern media technology have fundamentally altered political communication to permit direct citizen-politician relationships—to the advantage of a quasi-presidential premier. The "personification" of government, together with the simplification of political issues, is the outcome of a new mode of political communication and a consumption-oriented electorate. Thomas Hobbes, writing amid the disorder of the sixteenth-century English Civil War would recognize the imperatives of this contemporary Leviathan.

Multilevel governance contrasts with both Westminster and prime ministerial models. MLG transcends state boundaries. It centers on the concept of civil society and the interaction of its "social partners"—unfamiliar territory for insular British perspectives. Government institutions are important as location points or gatekeepers for social partner interaction, but they remain only one part of a broader whole. In the case of Britain, the recently added layers of devolved government that now form a significant part of the policy process have structured the relationship between civil society and government. Devolution and EU integration produce a semi-federal rather than unitary structure to British politics, enhancing both democratic (representative) and pluralist (social partnership) opportunities for demand input. Problematic in this equation is the tendency for professional networks to take greater control of a complex of political gates—in effect the superiority of the bureaucratic and entrepreneurial "expert" over the ordinary citizen. A lack of clear-cut accountability also encourages public cynicism.

It is evident that most states are experiencing global and supranational pressures; many are also experiencing domestic pressures for internal reform, devolution, and autonomy. The global economic crisis of 2008–2009 is a vivid reminder of financial interdependency. The twenty-seven EU members were already experiencing supranational pressures of Europeanization that both integrate and complicate their statehood. These factors support a multilayered view of political systems, especially in the sui generis (unique) environment of the EU. This is not so unfamiliar to European historical experience, which also includes Britain. Hierarchical overlapping authorities, of empire, nation, and religion, were the stuff of European (including British) experience to the eighteenth century. MLG and multiple identification, for example, with the Catholic Church, Scottish nation, and British monarch, were and still are examples of overlapping authority/identity.

Though the Westminster model, with its historic status and appealing mythical summary of statehood, has a familiar ring, twenty-first-century Britain is more than any one nation-state and is driven by global, regional, and domestic forces that need incorporation within any analysis of its parts. As such, Westminster, quasi-presidential, and MLG models of British politics represent a simplification of competing contemporary "realities" and historical perspectives of British politics. And enhancing or colliding with the assumptions of each of these models is the dimension of Europeanization—the new kid in the conceptual block and the recurring theme of this book.

FURTHER READING

Two books by Norman Davies, *The Isles: A History* (1999) and *Europe: A History* (1996) give both breadth and depth for an understanding of Britain's emergence as a European state. The case for a more insular perspective is made by J. G. A. Pocock's *The Discovery of Islands* (2006). For a twentieth-century examination of competing notions of British democracy see *Britain since 1918: The Strange Career of British Democracy* by David Marquand (2008) and also Alex Gamble's *Between Europe and America* (2003a). Britain's relationship with its continent is traced in Keith Robbins's *Britain and Europe, 1789–2005* (2005). For a summary of postwar consensus politics and Thatcherism see *The Re-Ordering of British Politics* by Dennis Kavanagh (1997). A comprehensive reader, *Blair's Britain, 1997–2007* edited by Anthony Seldon (2007), covers the whole period of the Blair premiership. For a conventional view of the Westminster model, see David Judge, *Political Institutions in the United Kingdom* (2005) and for a quasi-presidential perspective, *The British Presidency* by Michael Foley (2000). The notion of multilevel governance can be explored in Rod Rhodes, *Understanding Governance: Policy Networks, Governance, Reflexivity, and Accountability* (1997) and also his *Beyond Westminster and Whitehall* (1988).

②

Economic and Social Change

This chapter examines the factors that have contributed to social change in Britain and identifies the political consequences of that change, especially in the last quarter century. Several phenomena have interacted to produce contemporary conditions that create, in the Western industrialized world, and especially in Britain, a greater propensity for social and political change than has existed since the long and uneven experiences of industrial revolution in the nineteenth century. These phenomena are: the globalization of economic forces; the communication revolution associated with information technology; and, in the case of Britain and the rest of Europe, the integration of political economy in the shape of the European Union. As a starting point, we will comment on each of these factors in relation to Britain's social environment, before presenting a snapshot of recent changes.

GLOBALIZATION

Britain, by virtue of its island status, its need to trade, and past imperial aspirations, has needed to engage with the world to survive. Whether as part of the Roman Empire; engaging in Continental European diplomacy and war; or emerging as a competitive world trader and, eventually, as nineteenth-century imperial hegemon, the "external" has been part of Britain's political and economic reality throughout history. As such, contemporary globalization may be seen as another external phenomenon that the British state and economy must respond to and hopefully benefit from. The term *globalization* "is used with enormous elasticity and, often, with too little precision" (Krieger 1999: xiii). But in setting the scene for an explanation of change in British society, we recognize a contemporary reality: the increasing erosion of economic, technological, political, and societal space between states and peoples.

How to tame the beast was the quest of both Thatcherite and Blairite policies—and, since the impact of global forces is diverse, so is the range of potential state responses. The structure of the British economy is particularly open to global forces. And in recent years, as "a specialized producer of relatively low wage, low tech, low added value products," it has benefited from free-flowing foreign direct investment, especially from Japan and the United States (Krieger, 1999). The result has been labor-market (and thus social) changes of considerable dimension during the past quarter century. Conversely, Britain's vulnerability to global economic downturn is more than evident in the impact of a finance-driven world recession beginning in 2008.

EUROPEANIZATION

The term *Europeanization*, like *globalization*, has been used to describe a variety of phenomena that have influenced the recent development of British politics. We have identified three interdependent usages of the term to refer to: (1) the spread of European values, (2) the processes of integration in the EU, and (3) the impact of EU membership on the discrete policies and processes of member states. Whether utilized in any of these guises, or whether seen as a defense against or a complement to globalization, membership in the European Union has created an external dynamism for change in British society. The Single European Act (1986), Economic and Monetary Union, enlargement to EU27, and labor-market migration, together with the controversial issue of a new European constitutional settlement, have disturbed assumptions regarding state sovereignty, national identity, and the future of a "United Kingdom."

THE TECHNO REVOLUTION

Technological innovation has been a permanent feature of social change for many centuries. To take a historic example, the railway age brought with it an economic demographic and social revolution that percolated throughout Western Europe and North America, initially, and to most parts of the developing world by the end of the nineteenth century. In the twentieth century, the automobile facilitated changes to the mode of production and provided fast and available transportation for ordinary folk. In the twenty-first century, just one aspect of the Internet and telecommunications revolution is the use of "the Net" by one-quarter of the world's population and, staggeringly, one-half who use cell phones (ITU 2009).

Sources of innovation were previously limited to advanced industrial countries such as the UK, France, Japan, Germany and the United States—and were exported over a long period via nationally located entrepreneurship. National dominance and gradual change have been replaced by diverse transnational interventions that have spread almost viruslike from innovative source to global sites of consumption and production. Strategies for innovation, production, and marketing need a global perspective, and changes to production processes to encourage innovation and economies of scale have created a demand for cheap, flexible, labor as well as for technical skills. For Britain, recognition of such demands formed the mission, initially, of the Thatcherite "economic" revolution and subsequently the Blairite and Brown mantra of labor flexibility and investment in education for skills—a Britain fit for a global purpose. The social costs involved, as well as the political change necessary, have been considerable. Encouraging "green" technology entwined with the search for economic strategies to help lift Britain out of recession is the current driver for radical change.

THE POSTWAR WELFARE SOCIETY

Britain is a rich country according to OECD economic league tables, whether measured in terms of domestic product or income (see table 2.1). Historically, this relative well-being has existed for some three hundred years. What has changed is the economic base of that well-being and the consequent social characteristics that emanate from changing economic conditions.

Table 2.1. G7 Countries GDP per Capita: $US (2007)

Country Name	GDP per Capita
United States	45,845
United Kingdom	35,134
Japan	33,577
Canada	38,435
Italy	30,448
France	33,188
Germany	34,181
Russian Federation	14,692

Source: IMF (2008).

The defining feature of postwar Labour government was the establishment of a welfare state. Welfarism had several effects on the structure and culture of British society. Postwar expectations of a better quality of life and a universal welfare system that promised a healthy, well-educated, and financially protected future introduced a sense of equity to British society. This feeling was based on a new role for an interventionist state and a basic consensus on that role among the political parties. There was, however, no great social revolution—a number of persistent socioeconomic factors saw to that.

Postwar Keynesian economic and welfare policies placed a Band-Aid across an economy that for many observers had been in decline since the 1870s (Hobsbawm 1999; Barnett 1972). The public provision of welfare after 1945 produced massive organizational structures, not the least being the National Health Service, which was, by 2004, the largest employer in the world outside the Chinese army. Central decision making in both the public and private sectors became the norm. The private sector moved from one characterized by small companies prior to World War I to a growing domination of large, merged companies. For instance, by the 1960s the British car industry had been transformed into a handful of large, transnational volume players, compared with thirty-plus British-owned companies that had existed before World War II. There are no British-owned volume car manufacturers today. Nationalization had the same effect on the transportation, energy, and mining sectors. By the early 1980s more than 40 percent of manufacturing was undertaken by the largest 100 private companies, and employment in the public sector amounted to 30 percent of the workforce.

This concentration met its response in the growth of union membership and the consolidation of trade unions, which in turn produced a high profile for the central union organization, the Trades Union Congress (TUC). Business organizations such as the Confederation of British Industry (CBI) also organized to combat the power of trade unions and to lobby governments. In effect, the conditions for conflict between class-based organized interests were more evident in the 1980s than at any time in contemporary British history. For one commentator, Britain was "a society more centralized, more dominated by giant organizations and more permeated by class organizations . . . than almost any other economically advanced country" (Moran 1985: 12).

Questions about the ungovernability of the British state had already led to International Monetary Fund (IMF) intervention in 1976 to correct a massive decline in the value of the pound. The intervention was conditional on a cost-cutting response by the then Labour government and public spending was reduced by 6 percent (to 44 percent) in 1978. Thus the Keynesian postwar settlement effectively ended with the 1976 IMF intervention. It was buried politically in 1979 with the defeat of Labour and the return of the Conservatives under Mrs. Thatcher—a "conviction" not "consensus" prime minister who promised to tackle Britain's image as the "sick man of Europe" through market-led solutions. This was adapted to a New Labour social market vision of Britain in the twenty-first century. It altered but did not entirely replace the 1940s societal expectations of a welfare state, and has in turn been severely challenged by the impact of global recession since 2008.

INCOME, WEALTH, AND WELL-BEING

The impact of the welfare state is examined in subsequent chapters. (See also the book's website.) Here we look at changes in income pattern and wealth distribution that may give some initial guide to whether social market Britain is a more equal society now than fifty years ago. One immediate caveat regarding what may or may not be considered a low or high income needs to be stated. Approaches to income distribution are relative, both temporally and spatially. Possession of enough income to meet the costs of running a car, cell phone, flat-screen TV, or satellite/cable service may now be considered a necessity. This was not the case fifty years ago. Thus, "low income" is a contemporaneous and relative term.

To some extent a progressive income tax and social security system, together with state provision in education, health, and family-income support had led to more equal income distribution in the period 1945–1980. However, since then, income distribution has become more differentiated. Taking low incomes first: people in Britain whose income was below 60 percent of the median stayed at around 14 percent of the population between 1961 and 1980. From 1987 to 2000 around 17 percent of the population lived on 60 percent of the median income. A similar pattern can be observed when considering top income earners. The top 1 percent of earners, who in 1945 had shared 10 percent of the total earned income of the country, shared around 5 percent during the 1960s and 1970s. From 1980 on, their share of personal incomes rose steadily to above 10 percent by the end of the millennium. To 2007, however, poverty alleviation policies directed toward poor families and senior citizens has slightly reduced income inequality, and measures taken in 2008–2009 to stimulate a flagging economy have also led to further poverty alleviation.

For the average Briton until 2008, income has risen around 2.5 percent per year since the mid-1980s. Prior to 1979, during the period of consensus welfarism, levels of income taxation had tended to equalize income. Since 1979 income equality has climbed, peeking around the turn of the century and then slightly declining. Thus, while the average Briton today is better off in absolute terms, those who care to look at incomes above their own may feel relatively left behind.

This may be even more apparent if one compares incomes in different parts of the country. Regional differences have been a characteristic of the economic history of Britain in the twentieth century. Table 2.2 shows average weekly household incomes between 2001 and 2003, and the highest and lowest within the English regions. Unemployment follows a less consistent pattern.

While there has been some amelioration of income disparities through the redistribution and taxation policies of postwar governments, wealth inequality—the ownership of assets that may provide income—is far more unevenly spread than income, with little change to that spread in the past twenty years. As table 2.3 shows, only 8 percent of wealth (1976) and 7 percent (2005) is owned by 50 percent of the poorest half of the British population. Without house purchase, a popular way of acquiring some foothold in the wealth stakes, wealth distribution was even more skewed toward the richer half of the population. The impact of a fall in house prices on wealth distribution since 2007 is however unpredictable for most, and for some disastrous, as unemployment leapt to 2.2 million (as of May 2009).

Table 2.2.   Richer and Poorer Britain: Regional Indicators (2005)

Region	Mean Income £	% Earning over £50,000	% Unemployed
London	29,947	9.5	7.6
Southeast England	26,328	8.5	4.4
East of England	24,401	6.8	48
Wales	19,007	3.00	4.7
Northeast England	19,127	2.8	6.7
Northern Ireland	19,705	3.2	4.4

Source: ONS (2007).

Table 2.3.   Distribution of Wealth

	1976	2002	2005
Top 1%	21	23	21
Top 5%	38	43	40
Top 10%	50	50	53
Top 25%	71	74	72
Top 50%	92	94	93
Rest 50%	8	6	7

Source: ONS (2009b).

Measured in income and wealth, Britain at the beginning of the twenty-first century remained a society with considerable economic inequality. Within the EU15, Britain ranked fourth highest in terms of unequal income distribution, with only Spain, Greece, and Portugal more unequal. Denmark and Sweden were least unequal (Townsend 2004: 30). This seemed confirmed in research conducted in 2008 that placed Britain third in a list of developed countries with regard to income inequalities, behind Portugal and the United States (Wilkinson and Pickett 2009). As recession bit, a public backlash especially against high earners in the financial sector was followed by a political response in the 2009 budget, when the chancellor of the exchequer delivered a 50 percent tax rate on high incomes.

DEMOGRAPHIC CHANGE

Britain had a population of just under 61 million in 2007, compared with 38 million in 1901. As table 2.4 shows, England has by far the largest share (84 percent), with the populations of Wales, Scotland, and Northern Ireland declining in relative terms over the past century. Scotland's population is projected to remain static to 2031. England's population increased by 62 percent between 1901 and 2007, while Scotland experienced an increase of only 14 percent.

Since population change depends on the net effect of births, deaths, and migration it is worth commenting on these phenomena so as to gauge the impact of demography on British society. While birthrates have fluctuated, with booms in the early part of the twentieth century, after World War II, and during the 1960s, birth rates have declined since the 1970s, as they have done for West European and North American societies generally. However this decline has been more than offset by a parallel decline in mortality rates, especially in infants and childhood. In more recent years, the death rate among older people has also fallen, as standards of

Table 2.4.   Population of Britain (thousands)

	1901	1971	2001	2007	2031 Projection
England	30,515	46,412	49,450	51,092	56,800
Wales	2,013	2,740	2,910	2,980	3,300
Scotland	4,472	5,236	5,064	5,144	5,100
N. Ireland	-	1,540	1,689	1,719	1,800
UK	-	55,928	59,113	60,975	67,000

Source: ONS (2009a).

living and medical science have improved. Life expectancy for women, as in similar societies, is higher than for men, though the birthrate of boy babies is higher than girls. Thus there are more women than men in the British population, and markedly more older women than older men.

Again this is the situation throughout the EU. Britain has an aging population, with women beginning to outnumber men after the age of fifty. In 1901 one person in twenty was over sixty-five; by the end of the century this figure was one in six. A projection by the Office of National Statistics (ONS) for 2016 suggests that, for the first time, the number of people of retirement age (currently sixty-five) will exceed those just entering the workforce at sixteen.

Internal Migration: An Urbanizing Britain

British folk do not move around as much as the US population. During the 1990s around 4 percent of Britons moved to other parts of Britain. In the United States the figure was around 17 percent (Jacoby and Finkin 2004).

Changes in economic and industrial patterns during the twentieth century, however, produced some movement in population from the coal, steel, textile, and shipbuilding industries of northern Britain and Wales to the light industries of the Midlands and service sectors of southern Britain. There has also been an outflow of people from urban centers to suburban and provincial localities. This urban decentralization was evident during the 1980s, not just in such unemployment black spots as Liverpool, Manchester, and Glasgow, but also within inner London. So while the southeast and southwest of England had experienced net gains in population by the turn of the century, London experienced a net loss of 48,000 due to internal migration. This has been offset, however, by international immigration—as would be expected, given London's world-city status.

Movement of population has resulted in wide variations in population density. The highest concentration of people inhabits Greater London—the lowest the Highlands of Scotland. There are approximately 380 people living in a square kilometer of England compared with 66 in Scotland. Close to 90 percent of Britain's population lives in urban areas. Over half the population inhabits an area only 6 percent of the total landmass. Britain is thus overcrowded, but in small parts only. Thus any assessment of the impact of international immigration over the past fifty years must be set in the context of this imbalance of population density.

International Migration: The World Comes to Britain

Until recently Britain has enjoyed a relatively liberal reputation for immigration, and its people made use of its imperial legacy as a source of migrant opportunity. A pattern of migration to the dominions and colonies dating from the nineteenth century continued through until the mid-twentieth century. Around 1 million Britons migrated, particularly to the white dominions. In the second half of the twentieth century this was reversed as the populations of former colonies entered Britain to permanently transform the demographic profile of Britain's major cities. By 2001 people from ethnic minority groups comprised 8 percent of Britain's population compared with 1 percent in 1951. Significantly for population growth in the new millennium, ethnic minority groups have both a younger age profile and higher fertility rate than the indigenous population. The ONS (2009a) reported a net inflow of migrants between 1996 and 2006 was around 3.9 million. In contrast, the net outflow (1996–2006) was around 1.97 million. Thus, international migration has become important in determining British population change, and between 1999 and 2002 it contributed 80 percent of the country's population increase.

In 2002 there was an inflow of 69,000 from the Commonwealth and 120,000 from countries other than the EU. Notably, since the expansion of the EU to Central and Eastern countries in 2004, Britain benefited from an inflow of mostly skilled workers, particularly from Poland, Lithuania, and the Czech Republic, who took full advantage of the opportunities for free movement of workers within the EU established by the Single European Act (SEA). Around 48,000 arrived in 2004. Up to 2007, estimates of East European labor migration to Britain varied between 600,000 and 900,000, mostly from Poland. The majority returned to their home countries within two years, and with the decline in employment opportunities and the falling value of the pound since 2008, this source of labor migration has declined. This inward movement of population to Britain, the greatest since the Norman invasions, has produced periodic press and political debate, but for the most part has been received by a relatively acquiescent British public. The advantage of cheap labor provided by young, white, Christian, and well-educated newcomers is perhaps a major aspect of this reception. The flow of British workers in the other direction, to Continental Europe, is small. In 2005, over 30,000 Britons packed up for sunnier climates in Spain, and 17,000 moved to France to work and, more often, to retire.

SOCIAL CHANGE AND GENDER

A complicated mix of economic and demographic change, together with technological development, produces conditions for social change. Like all post–World War II Western democracies, this change has been particularly marked in gender relations and the role of women. Opportunity for female employment increased as Britain's economy changed from industrial to a service-sector base. A declining birth rate, provision of welfare services, and a universal education system, together with changing perceptions of gender roles, combined to produce considerable increases in female labor participation rates, especially for married/cohabiting women. Approximately three-quarters of this group were economically active by the end of the century. Overall, women's participation in the labor force increased from 56 percent (1970) to 72 percent (2000). However, inequality in pay, at around 18 percent less for women in 2008, promotion, and opportunity remain, with women still performing a disproportionate amount of child rearing and domestic activities despite equal pay and equal opportunities legislation, much of this of EU origin (ONS 2008a).

Changes to the structure of the British economy, in part associated with the growth of the public sector but also the growth of a service sector sensitive to global markets, has produced job opportunities that have sustained the activity of women in the British economy over the past fifty years. However, the nature of this expansion has not allowed a parallel change in gender equality with men, particularly in professional and managerial positions. Moreover, although improved since 1997, the percentage of women in British politics—as decision makers, representatives, and senior administrators—is well below the 51 percent that females comprise of the British electorate (textbox 2.1).

Factors associated with gender and social change are further complicated by such crosscutting phenomena as ethnicity, class, education, and religion. The battle for gender equality, commenced in the 1960s in Britain, remains unfinished. Although many issues are "mainstreamed" and dealt with institutionally, legally, and sometimes culturally, a postfeminist debate has become a part of twenty-first-century British politics, to the dismay of many feminists of the 1960s and 1970s.

ETHNICITY: NEW HORIZONS OR URBAN GHETTOS

If it is true that the position of British women has been transformed during the second half of the twentieth century, the ethnic mix of (especially urban) Britain has produced similar dramatic transformations. The increase in British population to over 60 million is in no small measure associated with net migration from people of ethnic minority origin. In a fifteen-year period the percentage of immigrants in the total British population rose to 7.9 percent (2001) from 5.7 percent (1991), with four out of ten living in the London region (25 percent of London's population). A far wider range of origins is evident in migratory trends over the past fifteen years. Where Ireland, India, Pakistan, and the Caribbean were the major

---

Textbox 2.1. Women in Public Life (2008)

Women hold over 35 percent of all public appointments:

- Local magistrates, 50 percent
- School governors, 54 percent
- Chairs of NHS Boards, 35 percent

Women in politics are seriously underrepresented:

- Cabinet members, 26 percent
- MPs, 20 percent (9% in 1996)
- English local councillors, 29 percent
- British MEPs, 26 percent

However in regional government, women are more prominent:

- Welsh Assembly, 47 percent
- Scottish Parliament, 33 percent

Source: Women and Equality Unit (2008).

---

origins of immigration thirty years ago, new immigration emanates from South East Asia, Africa, and—particularly since 2004—Eastern Europe. There has been a steep decline in Irish and Caribbean net migration, as many choose to retire to their land of origin. By contrast, Continental EU states have provided a stream of mainly educated, young, skilled labor to British society, adding a further dimension to the cultural mix (IPPR 2005).

With differing skills and aptitudes, the life experiences of migrants vary considerably; and issues of assimilation, cultural diversity, and multiculturalism are periodic political hot potatoes. While some ethnic minority groups are proportionately more likely to be of younger working age, their economic success is not guaranteed. At the end of the last century 15 percent of Bangladeshi males aged between twenty-five and forty-four, and 70 percent of young females, were economically inactive. This contrasts with 6 percent Indian males and 48 percent Indian females in the same category. Figures for the white majority grouping were 6 percent and 23 percent respectively. Afro-Caribbean boys between the ages of eleven and fifteen are, in some areas, fifteen times more likely to be excluded from school and twelve times more likely to be imprisoned by their eighteenth birthday.

Concentrations of minority ethnic groupings, usually in urban areas, have led, it is argued, to the emergence of racial ghettos. Not all of these areas are associated with deprivation: a small and vibrant South Korean community has centered itself in a predominantly white London suburban area of New Malden. Indian communities have prospered in suburban Birmingham and London. Long-established Chinese communities in Manchester and Liverpool have carved out a socioeconomic niche within their respective urban communities. However, other minorities have found little consolation in ethnic zones of poverty, and the discontent of the minorities and surrounding white majority areas has resulted in racialism; public unrest; and, on occasion, violence in areas such as Bradford, Blackburn, and Birmingham.

A drift toward racial segregation similar to the urban US experience is inevitable claim several observers, notably the Chairman of the Equality and Human Rights Commission, Trevor Philips. Language and religious and other cultural differences are reinforced by this segregation, encouraging the type of anomie evident in the backgrounds of the "London bombers" (2005), several of whom are British Asians. Others argue differently. Indices of segregation, save in Belfast, where there has been a rising Catholic/Protestant ghettoization, have fallen between 1991 and 2001. Concentrations of ethnic minority groups are, however, characterized by personal isolation and, where job opportunities are minimal, by poverty. Thus "Cut up Britain horizontally rather than by neighbourhood and you will find majority/minority areas . . . [for] . . . above the fifth floor of all housing in England and Wales a minority of children are white." Segregation, it can be argued, is a product of "inequality, poverty, wealth and opportunity not of race and area" (Dorling 2005: 15).

THE CLASS FACTOR: DEFINING OR DECLINING?

If Dorling is right in this explanation of ethnic differentiation, then a significant factor governing life chances in Britain is the familiar notion of an economically based class system. Class remains, like the monarchy, a significant and persistent totem of the British social system. In fact it could be argued that the monarchy and class system are symbiotic, and thus an important aspect of British political exceptionalism. The monarchy is historically representative and the pinnacle of the class system. Both enjoy an importance as part of the external perception of British life yet have recently been de-emphasized as determinants of British political culture. Yet both remain as impediments to radical social change.

The class structure in Britain is now formally described in terms of occupational identity (see textbox 2.2). The Industrial Revolution led to an organization of labor based on types of economic activity that brought

Textbox 2.2. Registrar General's
Socioeconomic Classifications

Commencing in 1851, the British population was officially graded in occupational classifications summarized by 1911 to represent "social grades." These were later referred to as "social classes." Thus were inaugurated the Registrar General's Social Classes (RGSC), renamed in 1990 as Social Class Based on Occupation. From 2001 the ONC classified socioeconomic groups using "analytic classes." The concept of a British class system remains formally sanctioned, albeit redefined. Students, incidentally, are deemed not classifiable.

1990

A	Upper middle class	Higher managerial/administrative/professional
B	Middle class	Intermediate managerial/administrative/professional
C1	Lower middle class	Supervisory or clerical and junior managerial/administrative/professional
C2	Skilled working class	Skilled manual workers
D	Working class	Semi and unskilled manual workers
E	Those at lowest levels of subsistence	State pensions or widows (no other earnings), casual or lowest-grade workers

2001

The National Statistics Socioeconomic Classification Analytic Classes 2001

1		Higher managerial and professional occupations
	1.1	Large employers and higher managerial occupations
	1.2	Higher professional occupations
2		Lower managerial and professional occupations
3		Intermediate occupations
4		Small employers and own account workers
5		Lower supervisory and technical occupations
6		Semi-routine occupations
7		Routine occupations
8		Never worked and long-term unemployed

Source: ONS (2003).

wage rewards commensurate with their market value. That market value governed wage levels and employment security inevitably determined life chances for those involved. In general terms, skilled and unskilled manual labor and domestic service were the lot of the British working class; the notion of a middle class that comprised managers, service providers, educators, and bureaucrats emerged as part of capitalist organization. In these phenomena there is little to distinguish the development of the British class structure from that of its Continental neighbors or the United States.

But in Britain, with no experience of political revolution or military invasion, a nineteenth-century capitalist class structure was grafted onto an already existing socioeconomic structure of which the monarchy was the symbolic pinnacle. As such, the essence of class in British society is an amalgam of economic and traditional determinants; and its persistence lies in the continued, albeit much less overt, contribution of its aristocratic (upper-class) stratum. While there may be evidence of historical elites in other social systems based on region (Parisian metropolitanism), religion (Italian political Catholicism), or antecedence (the North American white Anglo-Saxon Protestant), the prior and continued existence of a hereditary social grouping with considerable economic wealth and an accepted social standing, helps perpetuate a perception of class-based social relations in twenty-first-century Britain.

Before examining the validity of British class exceptionalism, it is important to recognize the changes in social divisions that mark twentieth-century Britain from the nineteenth century. As we suggested earlier, especially in the past thirty years, changes to the historic base of the British economy have resulted in rapid decline of working-class occupations, together with a commensurate rise in white-collar middle-class jobs (see table 2.5). While the table masks the considerable range of skills and incomes in each category, there is no doubt that occupational class has changed markedly, and spectacularly rapidly, since the 1970s. Skilled manual workers, the backbone of the British labor movement, comprised only 14 percent of the labor force at the end of the century, compared with 30 percent at its beginning; the growth in white-collar jobs, especially clerical and lower professional occupations (mostly) in the public sector, had increased over the century from 4 percent to 29 percent. Automation and

Table 2.5.   Occupational Class in Britain (1911–2003)

	1911	1951	1971	1991	2003
Middle Class	25.4	35.8	45.3	53.3	60
Working Class	74.6	64.2	54.7	37.7	40

Source: Adapted from Halsey (2000); and ONS Socio-Economic Classification (2003).

computerization since the 1970s has produced a demand for a labor force commensurate with new technological demands, the key to which is education and skills training.

Education, it is argued, produces the life opportunities necessary to overcome traditional barriers to achievement and thus provides a social mobility that cuts across the rigidities of a class-based social structure. The free market and technological change, supported by a flexible and skilled labor force, also facilitate social mobility. Add to these factors the impact of women in the labor market and the conditions for class mobility increase as life opportunity and income increases. Lifestyle changes support the class mobility thesis. As table 2.5 illustrates, in thirty years, a larger proportion of the British population began to enjoy a style of living previously the preserve of a white-collar minority. From the point of view of consumption, there has emerged an evident opportunity for entrance to a middle-class lifestyle variously termed as popular capitalism, a stakeholder society, or consumer democracy—and thus a potentially classless or meritocratic society.

The consequences for voting preferences, party politics, and government policies are dealt with later. Here, we argue that the tenacity of class designation in British society remains rather more deeply embedded than in the aspiration to own a three-bedroom semi-detached house, car, and wall-mounted flat-screen digital television. The *trappings* of a middle-class lifestyle may be available as a larger proportion of British families fall into the average income group in jobs designated as middle class. But within that designation the income of a senior barrister (a Queen's Council) may be ten times that of a call-center operator. An *ascribed* social status to a traditional middle-class is still strong and is manifest in such distinguishing features as accent, dress, housing location, membership of social organizations, and educational pathways. These are but some of the often subtle differentials that continue to mark an ingrained superior and inferior social status in Britain. The historic fee-based "public" schools remain predominantly the preserve of children of the traditional upper and middle classes. Paths to Oxford and Cambridge are more heavily trodden from those public schools, and access to political and economic elites remains easier for those fortunate few who tread this public school/Oxbridge pathway.

Undoubtedly, measurements of social mobility in the second half of the twentieth century indicate a more permeable class structure than had existed in the previous fifty years. State educational provision and health and welfare services, plus the growth of white-collar industries in the public and private sectors, provided employment opportunities for aspirant working- and lower-middle-class individuals to progress up the social ladder. One survey of mobility found that 26 percent of men born in the period 1900–1909 reported an upward mobility when compared with their father's occupations; this compared with 42 percent of those born between 1940 and 1949, beneficiaries of the British welfare state, who had enjoyed upward mobility. Women born in similar periods, however, reported less optimistic progress (22 percent and 36 percent respectively) (Heath and Payne 2000).

Other factors stand against evidence of a declassing society. We have already alluded to regional economic differences crudely designated as a North/South divide. London and the southeast provide a more consistently friendly economic environment for social progression than most other regions of the UK. This was especially true of the Thatcher-Major period of government (1979–1997), when high levels of regional unemployment produced the phenomenon of underclass: ghettos of low-status, penniless people with limited skills and life chances—a disenfranchised anomic nonclass (Murray 1990).

Since 1997, the New Labour government has taken advantage of an improving economic performance and introduced policies directed to eradicate this phenomenon. But some twelve years on, wealth remains unequally distributed even with the expansion of property ownership, and there is some evidence that there is widening of income differentials because of New Labour's moves toward indirect (regressive) taxation and away from income-based (progressive) revenue raising. Arguments for the persistence of a traditional class structure based on social and occupational criteria remain and have been recognized by the Brown government in the introduction of an Equalities Bill (April 2009) that seeks among other objectives to impose a duty on public bodies to help reduce class inequality in the provision of their services.

It can be argued, however, that a more differentiated model of social structure emerged in the late twentieth century. Delineation of class now depends on a range of factors such as ethnicity, geography, consumption, and education. Propensity to move between classes is enhanced or weakened by these factors. The growing tendency in British society to assign oneself to a class, that is, to self-assess one's social status, may well be explained by the complexity of social fragmentation. Consequently, as we shall see in subsequent chapters, political behavior is much less amenable to class analysis. Nevertheless, traditional working-, middle- and upper-class values, whether assigned or ascribed, remain a "default" factor when the very British activity of "classing" oneself, or others, is being undertaken.

RELIGION AND SOCIAL CHANGE

At the beginning of the twenty-first century, Britain remains, as it was at the beginning of the twentieth century, an ostensibly Christian society.

In 2001, 71 percent of the population identified themselves as Christian, with Islam next at fewer than 3 percent. Non-Christian groups in total amounted to only 6 percent of the population. Sixteen percent stated they had no religion. This apparent preponderance of Christianity, however, belies a cultural indifference to religious influence that has been marked, predominantly in the last thirty years, by a dramatic decline in regular church attendance. Thus, in 1970, around 9 million people in Britain perceived themselves as active members of Christian churches. This number had reduced by over a third by the end of the century. The decline was especially evident within the larger Trinitarian churches with the largest of the faiths, the Church of England, worst hit (*Social Trends* 2004). By then the population had become almost evenly split over whether to believe in God, or some form of higher power—or not. If there is evidence of a religious revival, it is within the non-Trinitarian Churches (Mormons, Jehovah's Witnesses), and particularly the growing numbers of Muslims, Sikhs, and Hindus in British society. Even in the more established Christian churches, Afro-Caribbean groups show a greater propensity to religious identification than the majority population. It is, thus, in ethnic minority rather than white British society that religiosity is sustained. This, however, amounts only to a small overall percentage of the population.

Is Britain therefore best described as a mainly godless society? An examination of the peculiarity of the largest church in Britain gives ambivalent answers to this question. Eighty-five percent of British Christians nominate themselves as Church of England (C of E). However, only 15 percent attend church once a month, with the majority attending only for ceremonies associated with "hatchings, matchings, and dispatchings." The C of E is an established church, that is enjoys constitutional recognition as a state church. The monarch is at its head and, as a clear statement of its separation from the Church of Rome, no Catholic can become a king or queen of Britain. So a clear-cut constitutional position is paralleled by studied indifference to religious practice on behalf of its lay members. The genius of the church, suggest its apologists, is incorporating the disinterest of most English people through its benign tolerance of unenthusiastic membership and, at the same time, enjoying an aura of institutional permanence as part of the fabric of the state. If there is public support for the C of E, it seems it is patriotically rather than religiously based! This is periodically reinforced through its association with royal occasions, joyous and tragic. Its presence therefore "suits mutually convenient purposes for church and state" (Paxman 1999: 100).

The established church, indeed most British Christian churches, has played, save in Northern Ireland, a limited role in British politics in the past 200 years. Neither Christian socialism nor Christian democracy is overt in the image or organization of the major political parties. Religion is a matter for the individual with God, "the ultimate good chap"—a sort of moral default structure with a vague defensiveness against central dictates of the Continental Roman Church (Paxman 1999). One little example of C of E tolerance in 2009 was the willingness of the Liverpool Cathedral authorities to host a cultural exhibition that included the music of John Lennon's "Imagine" ("Imagine there's no heaven" . . .)!

To be overtly religious is a no-go area for leading politicians. Unlike US leaders, any strong reference to divine guidance would be considered slightly mad. When asked about the reported religious perspectives of Prime Minister Blair, his press officer replied, "The Labour Party does not do religion." Only after leaving office did Tony Blair publicly address his deep religious convictions. Gordon Brown was happy to remind the US Congress in 2009 of his upbringing as a Presbyterian but in connection with the social responsibility of wealth creation rather than personal morality. Moral stances, where they exist, tend to come more from newspapers and nonconformist or Catholic groups rather than from the established church.

But the C of E, with its persona of all-encompassing toleration and its reluctance to interfere with people living their own lives, has, therefore, contributed to a sense of nationhood and to individualism. The contrast with more strongly focused faiths is not missed by benignly indifferent English folk. As such, Catholicism (practiced in many countries of the EU) and, more recently, Islam are viewed warily as part of the peculiarity of "otherness."

THE PROBLEM OF IDENTITY: TOWARD A MODULAR SOCIETY?

First, it is worth emphasizing that the notion of Britain and being British is a political construct. That most political of playwrights, William Shakespeare, was being evidently "politick" in referring to Britain, rather than England, in plays written after the death of that most English of queens, Elizabeth I, and in deference to the new "unity" of Scotland, England, and Wales under James I (James VI of Scotland). A hundred years later, after the Act of Union, some acts of Parliament referred to Scotland as North Britain, England as South Britain, and the "the hugely ambitious took to calling Ireland 'West Britain.'" (Paxman 1999: 20) The term *Britain* then became synonymous with empire, the *pax Britannica*, as Scottish, Welsh, Irish, and English soldiers, administrators, entrepreneurs, and settlers played their part in the establishment of an imperial diaspora. Citizenship is of the rather pompously termed United Kingdom of Great Britain and Northern Ireland (UK). It is as a subject of the UK that access to the job market of the EU may be obtained. There is, however, no official national day to celebrate the United Kingdom. Cause to fly the Union flag is limited. As a global brand icon the "Union Jack" may be seen on more T-shirts in New York City than in suburban gardens of Birmingham or London. Union flag waving is usually preserved for royal events, such as trooping the color, for the queen's birthday, the Olympic Games, the Orange Parades in Northern Ireland (as a defiant reminder of Protestant loyalty), and the last night of the proms. The latter ends in annual musical homage to Britain's imperial past and closes with a rousing chorus of "Rule Britannia," in which citizens are reminded that Britons "never, never, never shall be slaves."

So Britishness emanates from historical circumstances and its association with empire rather than a set of shared political ideals. But Scottish, Irish, Welsh, and English cultures are readily available for clearer senses of national identity—each with quite different cultural traits and historical myths. As empire fades and is replaced by a growing consciousness of regional nationalism, so has emerged the British identity crisis.

There are several aspects to this crisis. England has always provided the majority population of Britain, and the unity of the British Isles owes much to its dominance over Celtic neighbors. As we have seen, Britishness for the English has often been seen as coterminous with English history and identity. This worked well while the triumphalism of empire and, importantly, World War II provided an umbrella beneath which the four nations of the Kingdom could share a successful external presence: "Our Finest Hour." If one says "since the war" to most British adults over forty, even today they will know exactly where to locate their thoughts.

Once this triumphalism was challenged—by the demise of empire, economic decline, globalization, and the love/hate relationship of Britain and its Continental neighbors—England's British external face, based on myths of past glories, was less tenable. This goes some way to explain the emergence of a defense of Englishness against the "other"—whether that be the European Union, immigrants, or people of color—manifested in a reluctance to learn other languages and some pretty hysterical and sometimes xenophobic outbursts, most notoriously associated with football (soccer) partisanship. A manifestation was the English (national) celebration of victory over the Australians (a friendly colonial "other") in a cricket match test series (the Ashes) in 2005, the joyous celebration of which was only matched by England's solitary success in World Cup Final soccer against the old adversary, West Germany, in 1966. Cause to celebrate English nationalism is limited, and cause to celebrate Britishness is equally limited. A successful Olympics Team UK in 2008 enjoyed a short-lived island-wide celebration. The 2012 London Olympics may provide a similar opportunity.

Celtic Society

A second point is that the celebration of Britishness as Englishness is made all the more problematic by a growing sense of regional identity in Wales and Scotland. While almost certainly a product of many factors, not the least the policies of support for parallel cultures (multiculturalism) by successive British governments, one writer perceives the principal cause as a reaction to globalization, which has led to "an increase in nationalism, devolution and self determination and a resurgence of concern about ethnicity and cultural identity in almost all parts of the world, including the so-called United Kingdom" (Fox 2004: 14). This, together with the promotion of regions, partnership, and multilevel governance by the EU, has allowed a new confidence for Celtic identities. So, while being English may be more clearly delineated by the resurgence of Celtic nationalisms, it is confused by the loss of the British-English version of identity. There is, however, no great demand for the emergence of an English Assembly and there is similarly little demand for English regional assemblies, despite the Blair government's attempts to air the issue in referenda. Only one referendum was held, in the northeast of England (2004), and this resulted in rejection of the idea. So the Westminster Parliament, despite its preponderance of English MPs, still represents Britain.

A Modular Society?

Immigration, not just from the British imperial diaspora but more recently also from Europe, has produced a further complexity to the idea of a British "imagined community," shared "fates," and deep "historical memory" (Anderson 1991). Terms like *British-Somali* or *British-Korean* may give both identity and citizenship status, but they do not lead easily to British nationalism—a concept still predominantly defined by Englishness. Second-generation migrants may not identify themselves as English with the same ease with which their US cousins see themselves as American. Educated in England, the leap to being culturally English is considerable and remains a difficult act of choice. A growing number of "counternarratives"—of black history, Islamic values, even of European identity—produce differing versions of past or future belonging, especially in Britain's cities. The result is an identity conundrum as British identity, already challenged by its Celtic fringe, is set "amidst competing territorial, ethnic and supranational attachments and a complex of shared institutional authorities" (Krieger 1999: 164). The homogeneous society evident to politicians and academics in the 1950s Krieger now describes as "modular," that is, with interlocking but separate parts. Thus assumptions pertaining to class, ethnicity, and shared history are challenged through migration and social and economic change and its political consequences. These consequences are evident already—in the individualization of 1980s Thatcherism, in the Blairist New Labour policies of devolution, and in the use of focus groups by the major parties to clear ways to gain support from sectional interests and groups. Gordon Brown's concern with the weakness of a British identity led to a brief and inconclusive public debate on the issue in the early period of his administration.

Uncertainty concerning the impact of globalization and Europeanization have exacerbated a historic sense of defensiveness against "the other" that is inherent in British (particularly English) culture. An uncertain sense of destiny breeds negative and defensive attitudes, among which anti-Europeanism is very evident. The search for a new identity, a new citizenship, and thus the creation of a new Britishness is an uncomfortable outcome of the radical social changes that became evident in the later years of the twentieth century.

CONCLUSION

Several contemporary paradoxes demand political attention. Big interventionist government capable of delivering effective welfare is called for; so is the right to enjoy the benefits of a freer market, increased consumer choice, and an appropriate disposable income. High expectations of "joined-up government" are met by subnational and local demands for autonomy. An uneasy recognition of the multicultural nature of contemporary British society is matched by the search for a common identity capable of holding this social complex together. Globalization presents the benefit of cheap, diverse, and technologically advanced goods and resources. It also brings with it the movement of peoples and the receipt of ideas that can destabilize and, in extreme, cases terrorize. Finally, the European Union presents at once a regional defense against external destabilization and yet another attack on Britishness. While the free movement of EU citizens provided for by the SEA has encouraged inflows of good-quality labor to Britain, it has also produced yet another "other" to be suspicious about. Media publicity about illegal immigrants and East European "mafias" fuels doubts about "Europe" and its values, especially as British values are ill defined. Social change toward "modular society" thus challenges both national (British) and regional (EU) visions of social order.

In the past thirty years external factors (globalization, technological innovation, and Europeanization) have provided the backdrop to some remarkable changes in British society. Even in a recession Britain has become a richer, more urbanized, more demographically complex and culturally diverse society. Internal factors such as the economic domi-nance of the southeast of England, Celtic devolution, the growing signif-icance of women's roles in the economy, and the increasing expectations of an aging population combine against this external backdrop to produce a multicultural, dynamic, but uncertain society. As against this picture of dy-namism, the persistence of income and wealth inequalities, the uncertain-ties of economic recession, the complexities of an idiosyncratic class system, and strong regional and national subcultures provide a more static view of Britain's social makeup. The glue that has held British society together—the imagined community, shared fates and memories of the past—seems rather less adhesive in the twenty-first century.

FURTHER READING

For an account of Britain's rise and fall as an industrial power read Eric Hobsbawm's *Industry and Empire* (1999). Michael Moran's *Politics and Society in Britain* (1985) reflects clearly the working of the class system at its twentieth-century zenith. *Social Trends*, a series of contemporary papers about British society, is available via the Office of National Statis-tics website. A discussion of inequality is contained in Ian Townsend's *In-come Wealth and Inequality* (2004) and also in a comparison of Britain with other developed nations in *The Spirit Level* by Richard Wilkinson and Kate Pickett (2009). Aspects of British class and religion and the prob-lem of Englishness and Britishness are discussed in two readable and amusing accounts: Jeremy Paxman's *The English: A Portrait of a People* (1999) and Kate Fox, *Watching the English* (2004). For a splendid histori-cal critique of the monarchy see David Starkey, *Monarchy: From the Mid-dle Ages to Modernity* (2006). A serious analytical discussion of Britain's diversity and its consequences is in Joel Krieger's *British Politics in the Global Age* (1999).

3

British Politics and Constitutional Change

We start with a much-trumpeted but somewhat misleading "fact": that unlike almost all states in the world, Britain's Constitution is unwritten. Unlike the US or French Constitutions, whose texts may be viewed in original format or read verbatim in the appendices of legal or political science texts, the British Constitution has a more ethereal presence. To read its component parts from original sources would place a rather large dent in an extended summer vacation, for they are scattered in time and space across a thousand years of political development and are housed in various repositories. From the Magna Carta (1215) to the lord chancellor's statement to the House of Lords in 2003 that he was attempting to abolish himself, the constitution may be found in Royal Charters and prerogatives; English Common Law; Parliamentary Statute Law; conventions (sometimes evidenced in parliamentary records); and international, especially EU, treaty obligations (see textbox 3.1). This would involve visits not just to London, but also to Edinburgh, Cardiff, Belfast—and to The Hague, Brussels, and Strasbourg as well. It would be more time efficient to buy a comprehensive academic text that represents the nearest attempt at a codified statement of all these disparate elements (Johnson 2004; Bogdanor 2005a).

An enduring typology of constitutions into written/unwritten categories informed academic commentary for much of the twentieth century, perhaps reflecting the conceit of writers who wished to laud the exceptional status of the British experience (Dunleavy 2006: 332, Johnson 2004: 14). In effect, only Israel and New Zealand might be seen as other significant examples of the unwritten constitution, and much of the New Zealand Constitution is formally contained within a Constitution Act. Perhaps of more use in placing the British Constitution into a

Textbox 3.1. Sources of the Constitution

English Common Law	Judge-made law and precedents that become part of custom and practice of the legal process: Significant in issues of civil liberties and legal "due process."
Parliamentary Statute Law	Created by Parliament—the Supreme Lawmaking institutions after due process of legislation.
Crown Prerogatives	Executive powers derived from the monarch and exercised by ministers. Important in foreign affairs and issues of security.
Conventions	Binding rules of government practice, e.g., collective and ministerial responsibility; the PM as a member of the House of Commons.
EU Law and other International Sources	EU Law has precedence over UK law after the European Communities Act (1972). Also ECHR is now mainly followed in British law (1998). ECHR decisions accepted by British courts.
Works of Authority	Legal or political learned works accepted as guides to constitutional practice, e.g., T. Erskine May on parliamentary practice (1844 as revised).

comparative box are its customary basis and the resultant flexibility—allowing a government to enjoy easy adaptation of existing constitutional practice to cope with changing political circumstances. The extent to which a twenty-first-century public still views tradition, convention, custom, and practical good sense as a framework for liberty, democracy, and government accountability is explored below.

THE "BACK-OF-THE-ENVELOPE" CONSTITUTION

The Westminster model as a constitutional icon undoubtedly attained a status emulated especially, but not only, in Commonwealth countries. It is as a model of British governance expressive of powerful historical and cultural phenomena, whose particular characteristics provide a bundle of shared myths around which a national political identity has emerged. As such, thoughtful descriptions of its institutions and their processes are not just accepted as "what happens" in British politics, they provide the constitutional legitimization to "what happens." Nevertheless, if doubts remain about the nature of the British constitution in the absence of a codified version, there are no doubts that the British system of government embraces *constitutionalism* in its operation. This implies government that abides by the rule of law, upheld by an elected assembly that must be periodically legitimized by the people, that is, the continual maintenance of a liberal democratic political order. The advantage of a customary constitution is that "it expresses to a substantial degree the political practices, habits and traditions of the country concerned" (Johnson 2004: 18). As such, the flexibility offered by its "unwritten" form allows practice to adapt to the demands of the people—all of which may look like a virtuous constitutional circle.

There are, however, some flaws in this traditional logic. What happens if the historic social traditions of constitutional practice are less and less recognized as a protection for liberty and democratic responsiveness? For a "social tradition crumbles as soon as enough people cease to treat it as a guide to their behaviour" (Johnson 2004: 18). We have previously noted major changes in the social composition of Britain, as well as a deterioration in the willingness of societal groups to defer to political elites—a premise on which important aspects of British constitutionalism are based. And what if the protection of individual rights by Parliament, as the sentinel of the people, is undermined by executive action, or the dubious behaviour of MPs removes citizen respect for the office? The "war on terror" and 2009 expenses scandals provided situations that undermined the legitimacy of both political elites and institutions. What if the *united* aspect of United Kingdom is challenged, not just on the familiar territory of the Irish question, but in Scotland and Wales? Inevitably, the legitimacy of London-based unitary government is then undermined.

Faced with these challenges, the Blair and Brown administrations have introduced several constitutional innovations that might well be seen as pragmatic responses in line with the much-praised traditional and empiricist approach to constitutional adaptation befitting a "'sort of back of the envelope type race" (Hennessy 1995: 9). We explore below first the principles and then the characteristics of Britain's constitutional envelope.

THE PRINCIPLES OF THE CONSTITUTION: THE BACKDROP TO CHANGE

Common features of constitutional government are the phenomena of consent and limitation—which in general terms emerge in the obligation of people to abide by the rules legitimately created by a state, and legal limits to a government's power in creating those rules. The balance between citizen obligation and limited government varies between states, and debates about rights—of government, groups, and individuals—have been the stuff of European political thought for centuries. The principles of a British political tradition, and thus the essence of the constitution, are contained in two doctrines—*the rule of law* and *parliamentary sovereignty* (see textbox 3.2).

Textbox 3.2. Immutable Constitutional Principles

Parliamentary Sovereignty

This term describes the authority of the linked parliamentary institutions of the British state—Crown, Lords, and Commons—to make or unmake any law. Its peoples must obey and the judicial system must accept and implement parliamentary law passed by due legislative process. Parliamentary authority has no limits. Formally, parliamentary statutes are superior to any other kind of law. *As such, no law made by Parliament can bind a future parliament.* Parliament is formally the arbiter of not only domestic law but also constitutional law. An act of Parliament could legally abolish the monarchy, providing the monarch signed the bill, or rescind British membership of the EU. No other body either internally or externally constituted can overturn parliamentary legislation. In effect, Parliament is "omnipotent."

The Rule of Law

According to the nineteenth-century constitutional lawyer, A. V. Dicey, the rule of law is of equivalent significance to parliamentary sovereignty in defining the nature of the Constitution. It has a universal place in liberal democratic thought, being the process by which all relationships within a state are governed: that is, by duly constituted legal means. It should ensure equality and impartiality of treatment when laws are applied, rapid redress of grievances, and freedom from arbitrary arrest. Governments and citizens are bound to act within the law and, as such, the rule of law is a constraint on both government and people. Implicit in the British system is an independence of the judiciary and a practical, if not clearly formal, separation of powers such as is evident in, for instance, the US Constitution. Such ethical principles as natural justice, reasoned and reasonable judgment, fairness and proportionality, form the ethos of the judicial and policing process in applying the law.

In the British system there exists a tension between parliamentary sovereignty and the rule of law emanating from the lack of a codified statement that could separate guidance from governing function, the mixed (executive-legislative-judicial) elements of the Parliament system, and the potential clash with parliamentary "omnipotence."

The Rule of Law

The rule of law is a concept evident and practiced in all countries that claim to be liberal democracies. The European Declaration of Human Rights and the role of the European Court of Human Rights (ECHR) are now adopted as an aspect of domestic law in all EU states. Evidence of its practice formed an important part of the conditions to be met by aspirant members of the EU, and criteria for evaluating how far prospective entrants matched EU standards were established during the period leading to the 2004–2007 enlargement. An ever-growing body of international law emanating from treaty obligations between states, the UN system, and international adjudication by the International Court of Justice adds a further external dimension.

The rule of law is thus an internationalized maxim for, but also a process within, domestic government. One hallmark of the British legal system has been a reliance on customary practice and convention. This has established the independence of the judiciary, rather than any clear codified statement that establishes judicial separation from the executive, or the codification of the law or a hierarchy of laws that would give supremacy to judicial (constitutional) interpretation and thus a supreme jurisprudence. This can be contrasted with the US Supreme Court or the French and German Constitutional Courts, which have clear judicial functions, identify "superior" laws, and establish particular constitutional procedures before change can be made to what are considered fundamental rights.

Sovereignty

The backstop for the maintenance of the rule of law in Britain is a second principle, of parliamentary sovereignty. Famously, the historical omnipotence given the "mother of Parliaments" allows it to make or unmake any law, be it statute or common. Neither can one Parliament bind another to any law that it makes. In effect, to quote the eighteenth-century judge William Blackstone, Parliament "can do anything that is not naturally impossible." The simple, indeed almost brutal, nature of this doctrine needs some explanation and qualification.

The English Parliament consisted of three institutionalized components—monarchy, Lords, and Commons. The Bill of Rights (1688) and subsequent changes subordinated monarchical power to Lords and Commons and has resulted in a sort of "republican monarchy" (Starkey 2006). Enfranchisement during the nineteenth and twentieth centuries confirmed the dominance of Commons over Lords, and regular elections, at least every five years, provide a popular check on the notion of parliamentary sovereignty. The term *constitutional monarchy*, in a United Kingdom of Great Britain and Northern Ireland, formally describes the end process of the Crown-in-Parliament's development from an English divine-right monarchy to a twentieth-century British, representative, democratic political system.

The problem for constitutional reformists is that, despite the historic genius of periodically adapting and rebalancing power relationships between executive, legislature, and judiciary, the foundations of the constitution simply have not changed. The Commons, purportedly the bastion of an established popular sovereignty, are controlled, through a disciplined majority party system, by those elected ministers (and especially the prime minister) whose constitutional, as distinct from political, source of power rests on royal prerogative—in effect what some see as an *elective dictatorship*. Parliamentary sovereignty is, in essence, executive sovereignty. Hence, Britain might be categorized as "the last of the *anciens regimes* of Europe, possessing the only constitution to have been drawn up before the modern era" (Gamble 2003b: 22). Controversial reform issues tumble out of such an analysis and include: the establishment of a solid popular sovereignty based on citizenship; the formalization of the independence of the judiciary and thus the affirmation of the rule of law; the rebalancing of executive and legislative power; the appropriateness of a historic English constitutional settlement to the political aspirations of Scottish, Welsh, Irish, and even English, nations; and recognition of the constitutional implications of British membership of the EU.

Before examining these implications, it is worth considering the major features of the British political system as it entered the twenty-first century. Here we examine the consequences of Britain's formal status: as a constitutional monarchy, a unitary state, a fused system of government, and as an established member of the EU.

THE LAST ANCIEN RÉGIME

The continued existence of monarchy is not unfamiliar in Western Europe; of EU states the Netherlands, Belgium, Luxembourg, Denmark, Sweden, and Spain have hereditary heads of state, as do non-EU states Liechtenstein, Monaco, and Norway. Pretenders to the thrones of Romania, Bulgaria, and Hapsburg Austria are active in their country's politics. The Spanish monarchy was restored after authoritarian rule ended in 1975, and in Bulgaria the ex-king, Simeon, was the elected prime minister in 2001–2005. Even in established republics such as France, Italy, and Poland, an informal titular aristocracy enjoys some social standing as a reminder of monarchical traditions. Constitutionally, politically, and socially, monarchy touches twenty-first-century Europe as a shared historical experience for all countries, save federal Switzerland and the Vatican. But there are, it can be argued, a number of features that, when combined, delineate the British from other European monarchies as a distinct feature of the constitution and political process. We can examine this significance under three heads: the Crown-in-Parliament; the monarch as head of state; and the royal family as social phenomenon.

As already mentioned, by convention and common and statute law the British Crown is a constitutional element of a "sovereign" Parliament. There are roles that the Crown must perform as part of that process—what Walter Bagehot called its "dignified role," and it would be simplistic to describe these activities as purely formal, historically symbolic, and ceremonial in nature. Thus the queen must read whatever is put in front of her when outlining the government's annual legislative program, grant the PM's request for a dissolution of Parliament and a consequent election, and accept the resignation of a prime minister or the offer to form a government that the leader of the largest party (or person able to sustain a majority in the Commons) makes to her when "called to the Palace." Apart from a few personal awards, honors are made at the behest of the PM and her/his advisors. Her assent to a parliamentary bill is mere formality.

The Queen's prime minister and other political leaders oversee her representative role as head of state, as head of the Church of England and the Commonwealth, and as head of state of some Commonwealth countries. The monarchy in Britain survives, it is argued, because of its nonpolitical role—despite its constitutional presence in so many aspects of the British political process. But if the modern monarchy strives for political obscurity, its social presence remains overt, curious, and often controversial.

There are a number of elements to the social presence of the Crown and its public face, the royal family. Constitutionally and traditionally, at least from Victorian times, the monarchy has provided a moral template for Christian, family, and civic values. Being "supreme governor" of the established church (the C of E) gives little other choice; the 1953 coronation of Elizabeth II affirmed the monarch's duty to sustain and abide by the moral standards of British society (Johnson 2004: 70). In itself a tall order, the subsequent activities of her children during the 1990s, culminating in the spectacular death of Princess Diana in 1997, provided disturbing publicity for an institution dependent on a quiet and dignified presence for its survival in contemporary British politics.

The royal family as media fodder has politicized the institution during the past twenty-five years, but has not massively undermined its public popularity. While individual members of the royal family are depicted as heroes and villains by the hungry mass media, opinion polls show a consistent public support for the institution, averaging around 72 percent since 1990. The long-term future of the monarchy is less confidently supported, with only around 40 percent of subjects believing that it would still exist in fifty years (Mori Opinion 2005; Norton 2004).

This public ambivalence is difficult to explain without acknowledging the contradictions of societal continuity and change in contemporary Britain. The Crown in its dignified, moral dimension represents, on the one hand, the pinnacle of a traditional class-based society, deferential and quiescent to elite-based solutions to problems. However, a family with immense inherited wealth and massive personal advantage, accompanied by an often-fallible public image, sits on top of a heterogeneous, mobile, and economically expectant society where, for many, consumption is "king." Passing this contradiction on to other generations to solve is a neat way of avoiding the queen's current subjects having to choose between conflicting public visions of the past, present, and future.

There may be other factors, however, that have allowed a constitutional anachronism to survive into the new millennium. There is no evidence that any government in the past or present century has seriously considered a constitutional reform that includes radical change to the position of the monarchy. Leaving aside the electoral dangers in such a step, there are solid pragmatic reasons for keeping the monarchy in place. As its stands, the Crown is capable of confirming the legitimacy of other constitutional reforms that might otherwise disturb the stability of the political system. Thus, devolution for Scotland and the limited reform to the House of Lords were confirmed and legitimized by royal approval. The monarchy also provides an extra layer of international presence for the PM—through her role of head of state with all its intimidating grandeur. Of more significance, however, is the protection of prime ministerial powers that the concept of royal prerogative offers, for "unlike any other democratic constitution in the world . . . it is not the people but the Crown-in-Parliament that is legally sovereign (Gamble 2003b: 32). For the PM, who exercises authority in the name of a historically authoritarian monarch, this has meant an extensive list of powers that have enjoyed little parliamentary control. In 2008 however, the Brown government stated its intention to refer use of the prerogative for several executive actions to Parliament for ratification (see below).

DIVERSITY IN UNITY?

A constitutional monarchy together with national parliamentary sovereignty would seem to imply the inevitability of a uniform system of government and a unitary state. This is also not an unusual European experience, given the monarchical origins of most states within the region. Only Switzerland, Belgium, and Germany are clear-cut examples of nonunitary European states. But closer examination of the governmental processes in France, Spain, and Italy, and now Britain, reveals a somewhat different picture, as EU states have responded to demands for political and organizational decentralization through regionalization. Membership in the EU has also challenged the unitary state and led to a new perspective on center-periphery relations that might better be termed as multilevel. Britain's unitary characteristic is similarly challenged by contemporary factors, but it may also be questioned historically and culturally.

The Local State

We might first examine the contention that the British constitution underpins "a structure of government that was in some degree unified rather than unitary" (Johnson 2004: 41). Beginning in 1945, local-government service provision, particularly for education, social services, and housing, existed side-by-side with a heavily centralized welfare state. There was no regional or local prefect, as in France or Italy, to provide a coordinative central direction to local services. There were only two forms of representative government—at Westminster and at the local level. It was a mainly two-tier system that, until the reforms of 1972, was based around geographical counties, some of Norman origin. The growing significance of national parties in local politics in the 1970s and then a range of financial controls during the Thatcherite 1980s eroded local autonomy, such that today only "lip service continues to be paid to the idea of local institutional pluralism" (Johnson 2004: 43). There is no constitutional protection available to British local governments from the encroachment of central-government decision making, nor has a local financial base ever been sufficient for even the richest unit to enjoy the protection of local resource independence (see chapter 5).

Historic Diversity Recognized

As against this lack of local autonomy, there are both historic and contemporary examples of governmental diversity, illustrative of the lack of definition of the British state that emanates "from its highly unsystematic design and structure" (Johnson 2004: 50). The oldest examples of that diversity are the tiny Channel Islands, accurately described in French as *Les Isles Anglo-Normandes*, and the Isle of Man, midway between Britain and Ireland, which have existed for centuries as quasi-autonomous states with loyalty to the Crown but independence from Parliament, save for their defense and representation in foreign and EU matters. They have the hallmarks of a US state or German Länder, but without representation in the British Parliament. Guernsey, Jersey, and Man have taken full advantage of this independence to become rich offshore financial centers, attracting the suspicious attention of watchdogs from the OECD, the EU, the British Treasury, the New York District Attorney, and most recently the G20 London Conference of 2009 (Mannin 2006a). Their fiercely guarded historic quasi-independence has been recognized by Britain; in 1972 a codicil to the European Communities Act committed the Islands to membership of the EU Customs Union only.

More recently they were included as participants in the British/Irish Council (or Council of the Isles), a consultative body set up within the Good Friday Agreement (1998) to "promote the harmonious and mutually beneficial development of the totality of relationships amongst the people of these islands."

In effect, together with the North-South Ministerial Council (see chapter 5), there now exist within the system of British constitutional governance two councils composed of international and subcentral governments with formal and equal rights of input to an, albeit limited, set of functions. The devolved institutions associated with Northern Ireland are discussed later; at this point we wish to refer only to the historic and problematic status of the province as part of the British state. With internal political divisions over its future as part of Britain, and despite formal withdrawal of the claim by Ireland for its "return" (in 1998), the validity of the concept of a United Kingdom remains questionable (Rose 1982; Nairn 2000).

The Celtic Nations

It is the Labour government's creation of Scottish, Welsh, and revived Northern Irish devolved governments that represents the most recent challenge to the notion of British unitary government. Labour's introduction of Celtic devolved government (1998–2006) and the creation of a metropolitan-wide London Assembly in 2000 have engendered two interconnected debates. The first is around the issue of how far devolution is going. Is it the first step in the breakup of Britain into independent states of a federal rather than unitary constitutional structure? (Nairn 2003; Bogdanor 1999; Trench 2004) The second, in the light of Celtic devolution, is how to govern an *England* that has no equivalent national assembly, only one somewhat limited regional government notably in London and thus is represented by the *British* Westminster Parliament? Both these issues crop up in attempts to answer the "West Lothian Question" raised by the Scottish MP, Tam Dalyell, that is: "Why should English MPs have no right to vote on matters devolved to the non-English parts of the UK, while MPs from those territories remain fully entitled to vote on all English matters?"

(Johnson 2004: 196). The question, raised by Mr. Dalyell in the 1970s, has been made current by Labour's Devolution Acts and the consequent rumblings in parts of England for more effective representation of English interests than the Westminster Parliament seems to offer.

A Quasi-federation?

If the unwritten or customary base of the British Constitution encourages analysis in terms of "what happens," then it might be argued that Britain is now *a de facto federacy*. Commentators have presented support for this thesis in categorizations of a "new federalism" that are in part a response to the contradictions that have emerged from global/EU/state/local relations and pressures. Thus the British state is characterised as a decentralized union with federal features (Watts 1999: 8) or a quasi-federation (Elazar 1987) or at best a unified set of nations rather than a unitary nation-state (Johnson 2004). A counterblast to these arguments is the equally powerful assertion first made by an ex-Lord Chancellor Hailsham in 1976, that Britain has become a politically centralized elective dictatorship. Nevertheless, if a unitary state still exists, it does so within a set of devolved arrangements that, in terms of the evolution of British government, are now constitutionally established. Its continuation may depend on the tensions between the effect of regional demands for autonomy and the pressure of centralized political decision making as well as, we shall argue, the impact of an external tension: EU membership.

First, however, we explore a third major feature of the British constitution—the mixed or fused nature of its legislative/executive arrangements.

MIXING POWERS—OR MIXED-UP GOVERNMENT?

Revolutions in France, the United States, and Russia or wars of unity for Germany and Italy or the radicalism of reformist periods in Sweden or Norway have provided impetus in these states for institutional change that evidenced a historic break with the past. Whether this resulted in a republican constitution or a massively reduced position for the Crown in the shape of a reformed constitutional monarchy, a clear distinction between executive, legislative, and judicial functions emerged in the form of a written constitution. The result was, for Continental liberal democracies, a legally embedded system of rights and duties with clear constitutional processes for dispute adjudication (see the book's website).

In contrast, Parliament has long been the formal meeting place of the component parts of the British political elite. Its full title—the Palace of

Westminster—denotes the traditional court purpose that it once had, as a place where monarch and subjects met to discuss the ordering of state affairs. Since those affairs were primarily "ordered" by the monarch, her advisors— Lords and Commoners, judges, bishops and crown bureaucrats—provided a complex mix for an institution that represented the elite and class structure of initially English and then British society.

The Executive-Legislative Mix

Britain's contemporary Westminster system may still be characterized as a parliamentary court, but with a single-party government that dominates the legislature with a powerful executive straddling Parliament and a centralized Whitehall (i.e., the government bureaucracy, which is collectively referred to as Whitehall after the street on which its offices are located). Doctrines of cabinet-collective responsibility for policy, ministerial accountability, and civil service loyalty represent the constitutional conventions of fused legislative/executive/administrative processes and also give credence to the closed and elite administrative landscape of British governance (see chapters 8 and 9 and Dunleavy 2006: 317). Exponents of this traditional constitutional landscape argue a strong empirical case for its validity. The Constitution has transformed to meet the needs of universal suffrage and complex policy demands made of a still elite-led but now representative, responsive, and accountable system of limited party government. An ever-present and vigilant media may be relied upon to question politicians about these processes and associated policies.

The fusion of executive and legislative relationships was, for Walter Bagehot, writing in the mid-nineteenth century, "the efficient secret of the English [sic] constitution" (as quoted in Hennessy 1995: 96). While the cabinet, as the nerve center of the system, may have lost its position as "the most powerful body of the state" (Hennessy 1995: 96), there still exists a hidden wiring that sustains the hardware of constitutional function and process. A "software"—of awareness of precedent, flexibility, pragmatism, and careful management of change—"makes the irrational work better," creating the conditions whereby the body politic is made constitutionally relevant and acceptable to the British people. Striving to sustain this system in revised form is for many academics "a prize worth fighting for . . . as ancient polity meets new millennium" (Hennessy 1995: 207; Norton 2003).

The Problem of Accountability

These *fused* legislative/executive arrangements in British politics rest for their efficiency on a unique balance of formal and informal constitutional practice that is currently under considerable scrutiny. First is the problem of executive power and its accountability. As we argue later, executive power, and more specifically prime ministerial power, has, for many commentators, increased to an extent that neither the constitutional pull of the Commons nor the political push of a governing party is effective in controlling the tendency toward "elective dictatorship." Sitting at the intersection of three sources of power, Parliament, party, and government, the PM escapes from the restrictions of parliamentary control for as long as she/he occupies the space in that intersection (Hennessy 1995: 16–17). Critics of the Thatcher and Blair administrations were quick to argue for the reinstatement of cabinet government; more constitutionally established parliamentary accountability for the PM through the removal of Crown prerogatives; legislative reforms; or, more radically, the creation of a quasi-presidential separation of powers.

The problem of executive accountability is also related to how effective the current fused system is in representing national/sectional and individual interests. The electoral process for general elections, a first-past-the post, majorities system based on geographic constituencies, provides for individual voter representation as well as that of group interests within the MP's territory. The link between protection of individual rights, articulation of local interests, and determination of collective national interests is contained within Commons procedures that exalt the role of MPs and show "intellectual samurai" fighting (and compromising) on behalf of their constituents. While this role remains, the majoritarian system, when combined with the discipline of the parliamentary party, has produced stable, single-party government throughout most of the twentieth century.

As a general rule however, elections end up underrepresenting losing parties and overrepresenting the winners through a "lopsided electoral system" (Fielding 2005). A more detailed analysis of the nature of Britain's party system follows in chapter 6. Here we simply point out the reluctance of governing parties, including a Labour government committed to constitutional modernization, to change the national electoral system and thus give up the advantage it bequeaths in an executive-dominated political system.

The Judiciary: At Arm's Length from Government?

We have mentioned the somewhat uneasy constitutional paradox between notions of parliamentary sovereignty and the application of the rule of law. Not only are judges constrained by the potential superiority of statute law, and thus Parliament, over Common Law, their independence from the executive and legislature has, until recently, been seen as constitutionally confused by the fusion of senior judicial roles within the British legislature and executive. Once again we can see the link between monarchical tradition and judicial delivery of the monarch's writ through Crown Courts and the gradual emergence, through convention and legal process, of an independent judiciary (see textbox 3.3).

However this process has been clouded in the minds of the public and many critics of the Constitution by the functions that, until recently, have been exercised by the most senior of judicial appointments, the lord chancellor. He, for there has so far never been a female incumbent, was the political head of the judiciary entitled to sit as an appeal judge in the House of Lords and, as a senior member of the cabinet, also had a major role in

---

Textbox 3.3. Sources of Judicial Independence

- The Bill of Rights, 1689, and Act of Settlement confirmed the autonomy of the judiciary in implementing the law and assured the security of tenure of judges. Judges' salaries were separated from annual parliamentary control by payment through a separate Consolidated Fund.
- Recruitment of judges is conventionally from an independently self-regulated group of senior advocates (barristers) whose practice and training is highly regulated by a profession that is organized in relatively small private units.
- Judicial appointments are characterized by a background of long and successive legal service. High pay within the legal profession assures material independence and contributes to a degree of social prestige within a class-structured society. Judges can only be dismissed when Commons, Lords, and the Crown agree.
- Though overtaken by statute and now EU law, the Common Law developed a judicial interpretive tradition that focuses on individual rights and conduct and the ownership of property and the right to use it. There is a traditional respect for judge-made law that has historically regulated the life of individuals in British society.
- The growth of public policy, and thus statute law, has been subject to judicial interpretation and review based on the principle of equal application of the rule of law. Even the Crown can be proceeded against in its own (Crown) courts (Crown Proceedings Act [1947]). Public bodies may thus be judged to be "ultra-vires" (working outside their powers) or judged to be interpreting the law not intended by Parliament.
- The occasional reluctance of ministers to accept judicial opinion is balanced by a culture of restraint by the judiciary in reviewing the implementation of policy.
- Matters that may be considered by the ECJ, and particularly since the Human Right Act (1998), or the ECHR, have meant that British judges must apply the law in relation to their interpretation of "European" rather than existing or new British legislation or what a government may want.
- The Constitutional Reform Act (2005) and the creation of a Supreme Court, Judicial Appointments Commission, and new functions for the Lord Chancellor and Lord Chief Justice have enhanced to some extent the separation of powers.

the executive. A similar three-headed status exists in the role of attorney general. Thus the danger of viewing the British judiciary as an "arm of government," albeit within a convention of strong judicial independence, according to one lord chancellor, "throws some light on the persuasive dominance in contemporary political life of an executive outlook" (Johnson 2004: 140) (see the book's website).

Another lord chancellor, Lord Faulkner, went some way in rectifying this constitutional three-in-one phenomenon when, in 2003, several radical steps were taken to enhance judicial independence. His proposals included the abolition of the title lord chancellor and new roles for his successor; a new independent Judicial Appointments Board for England and Wales; an ombudsman and Office for Judicial Complaints; and, most surprisingly, a form of Supreme Court for the United Kingdom. While most of these proposals were achieved in the form of a Constitutional Reform Act (2005) the title, lord chancellor, was retained and included in the new office of minister for justice. The chancellor/minister no longer sits as a judge, and the lord chief justice is now head of the judiciary. The twelve appellate law lords now sit separately from the House of Lords, though they will not change their appeal responsibilities.

The Supreme Court is "certainly not a supreme court in the American mould" (Johnson 2004: 256). The new court cannot strike down legislation for its unconstitutionality; its function remains that of the Appellate Committee of the House of Lords, as the final court of appeal in criminal and civil law cases. The Judicial Appointments Board takes from the lord chancellor the task of recommending the appointment of judges. The changes represent a modernization rather than a radical reform of Britain's fused constitutional arrangements. But perhaps a clearer raison d'être for these reforms may be seen when one sets them in the context of Britain's constitutional relationship with the EU and the influence of the European Convention on Human Rights (ECHR) (Johnson 2004: 255–58).

EU MEMBERSHIP: DIRECT AND INDIRECT CONSTITUTIONAL EFFECTS

> Constitutionalism, more than anything else, is what differentiates the Community from other transnational systems. (Weiler 1999: 221)

By the time Britain joined the European Community in 1973, the role of the ECJ and the enforcement and interpretation of Community Law had already constitutionalized EU–member state relations. In a landmark case, *Van Gend en Loos* (1963), the ECJ clarified the direct effect of EC Laws on individuals in member states and their right to have EC law confirmed in their favor by national courts. In a further case, *Costa v ENEL* (1963), the ECJ asserted the superiority of EC Law over domestic law. In 1970 the ECJ went further "to hold that community law even took precedence over the constitutions of member states" (Page 2003: 38) In effect, on joining, Britain was not just another member of a trading arrangement, but had become part of a supranational constitutional process, a fact that most British political elites and the public have failed to come to terms with (see textbox 3.4). Dealing with the constitutional "facts" of EU membership has become, for politicians and also for many academic commentators, an exercise in obfuscation, either in terms of denial of its significance or, for anti-Europeans, warnings that the end of civilization (at least the British version) is nigh. During the period prior to entry in 1972, the Conservative government under Mr. Heath stressed the economic advantages, as did the Labour government in the period of renegotiation and the referendum in 1974–1975 (Butler and Kitzinger 1976). When the constitutional implications of membership became more publicly evident, during the latter part of the Thatcher administration and in negotiations leading to the Treaty of Union under the Major premiership, denial was replaced by a strongly articulated defense of the status quo. Thus any further loss of "sovereignty" was nonnegotiable.

In the end, however, successive British governments have signed EU treaties—in Maastricht (1992), Amsterdam (1997), Nice (2000), and Lisbon

---

Textbox 3.4. An EU-British Constitutional Time Line

1972	The European Communities Act
1975	Referendum confirms British membership
1986	Single European Act expands EC policies and introduces qualified majority voting in its Council of Ministers
1991	*Factortame* case confirms EC law precedence over parliamentary statute.
1992	Parliament ratifies TEU and institutional changes: opt-outs make it palatable
1997	Parliament ratifies TOA; agrees to incorporation of Social Chapter
1998	Human Rights Act: incorporates ECHR into British law
1999	First British PR election to EP: requirement of TOA
2000	Parliament ratifies Treaty of Nice
2005	Government agrees to ratifying referendum for EU constitution; EU Constitution stalls after French/Dutch referendum rejection
2007	Government agrees on an EU Reform Treaty (of Lisbon) with opt-outs and then argues no referendum is necessary
2008	Parliament ratifies Treaty of Lisbon

(2007)—that have resulted in a progressive erosion of political sovereignty. In 2005 the Labour government, with all other member-state (MS) governments, agreed to the proposal for a European Constitution that, subject to a referendum, would have reduced still further the supremacy of the British Westminster system. The danger of losing that referendum was averted by the prior rejection of the Constitution in French and Dutch referenda in 2005. However, the issue was reviewed during the 2007 German presidential election and during the Irish referendum in 2008, when a "no" vote stalled its ratification. The issue will eventually return to haunt future governments. As much of the Constitution is contained in the Lisbon Reform Treaty, the issue of a referendum on what many consider to be yet another episode of eroded sovereignty is still live (see textbox 3.5).

Pooling Sovereignty?

There are two issues of sovereignty that, inevitably, are interrelated. The first is a debate about the extent to which the legal sovereignty of Parliament still exists after Parliament agreed to the terms of accession contained in the European Communities Act (ECA) in 1972. Since then, Community legislation has domestic legal effect; that is Community legislation automatically becomes part of British law and, where there is any conflict between existing or future legislation, Community legislation will always take precedence. In effect "Acts of Parliament are no longer trumps" (Page 2003: 40). Inevitably supporters of Parliament's ultimate sovereign rights point to the fact that Parliament can repeal the 1972 Act: bye-bye EU. But this solution to preservation of a historic pillar of the British Constitution has a somewhat desperate character; for inasmuch as the Monarch's assent to an act is formally still a matter of her choice, but politically is a de facto obligation, Parliament's repeal of the ECA and disentanglement from the EU would seem politically untenable. For one eminent constitutionalist and Eurosceptic, Britain lost both its political and legal sovereignty with entry to the EC in 1973, and subsequently became "a unit within a federal system and so deprived of the essentials of self government which are presupposed by the constitution" (Beloff 1998: 170).

The matter has been complicated by the development of a stronger role for the judiciary in the interpretation of the ECA and EC law. This has been reinforced by the Human Rights Act (HRA) (1998) that, while not giving the judiciary powers to strike down legislation through incompatibility with the Council of Europe's ECHR, has increased the opportunity for judges "to interpret parliamentary legislation in terms of a higher law" (Bogdanor 2001: 22). An extension of the HRA to include citizen rights and duties has been somewhat cautiously proposed by the Brown government (Ministry of Justice 2007). The implication here is that judges are beginning to "formulate

Textbox 3.5. The 2007 Reform Treaty (Treaty of Lisbon)

- A Reform Treaty—not a European Constitution
- No mention of flags, anthems, mottos, or other symbols of common destiny
- Old terminology retained (regulations, directives, decisions, etc.)
- Double majority voting system (DMVS) for Council of Ministers (decisions need 55 percent of member states representing 65 percent of EUs population)
- Increase in decisions taken by DMVS: Forty to fifty new areas (Britain allowed to opt out of criminal matters/police cooperation)
- National veto retained in foreign and defense policies, taxation, social security, and cultural policy
- Elected president of the European Council: term of two and a half years.
- Foreign affairs to be coordinated by a High Representative (not called a foreign minister). Post combined with Commissioner for External Affairs
- Beginning 2014, Commission to be reduced in size (selected for five-year term on a member-state rotation basis)
- EU has a "legal person status" within the competences agreed by member states
- Charter of Fundamental Rights agreed (CFR). Charter is however only a protocol.
- Minor changes to national parliaments right of reasoned opinion on EU legislative proposals
- EU solidarity in case of energy supply problems
- Processes established to increase or decrease EU competences as well as voluntary withdrawal from the EU.

Britain's "Opt-Outs"

- Protocol to prevent CFR from allowing EU courts to strike down British laws on social and economic rights
- Protocol to safeguard British criminal law system and police processes (opt-in procedure available)
- Protocol to affirm Britain and Ireland's limited participation in the Schengen Treaty
- Veto power over social security policy changes
- Affirmation of member-state superiority in foreign affairs and national security unless an agreed common policy is established.

a corpus of constitutional principles in the area of human rights. That is something quite new" (Ministry of Justice 2007: 23). This may hinge, however, on the establishment of a clearer separation of powers than has existed before—an issue that is considered below when we examine Labour's constitutional modernization program.

The other aspect of sovereignty involving EU membership and the direction of British constitutional change is associated with state (external) sovereign rights. There are several interconnected points here. Membership in the EU and the subsequent development of the EU's competences (sphere of powers) into the domestic policies of its member states has "emptied the distinction between foreign and domestic affairs of much of its former significance" (Page 2003: 40). As subsequent chapters illustrate, this is evident not just in the specific constraints on external trade policy that EU membership brings, but in agricultural, competition, and environmental policies to list but a few.

Constraints on national independent decision making, it is argued, have been compensated by pooled decision making at the EU level, and thus *shared sovereignty*. However, the accountability of a British government is realized through its fused relationship with the Commons. This delivers a popular mandate and thus legitimacy for government that rests, in turn, on Parliament's sovereignty. Inevitably, any change to this familiar equation has been difficult to sell to the electorate. Encroachments on a government's capacity for independent decision making can be interpreted as undermining the very basis of British representative democracy itself (Johnson 2004: 32). Here we may contrast the German Basic Law that, in the first line of its preamble, resolves its people to "serve world peace as an equal partner in a united Europe"—a strong constitutional endorsement of European integration that would seem impossible in Britain.

However, the consequence of EU membership is that the British government needs to "deal" in Brussels on behalf of its electorate. This inevitably diminishes its accountability to Parliament, reinforcing the view that, in so many areas of public policy, the executive, by agreeing with other member governments to proposals that automatically make EC law, has assumed "the constitutional function and power of Parliament" (Page 2003: 44).

Paradoxically, therefore, we might argue that while the notion of EU pooled sovereignty has diminished the executive's capacity for independent external action, its capacity to work independently from parliamentary scrutiny and accountability has increased. Thus an additional role of the Parliament of any member state is to effectively scrutinize the actions of its government within the EU—an issue for both EU and British constitutional reform. The adaptation of the British Parliament and executive in the context of EU policymaking is examined in chapters 4 and 8.

From British Subject to EU Citizen?

A final area involving an EU dimension to British constitutional change relates to representation and citizenship. The TEU gave EU citizenship rights to all member-state citizens. In practice, these are limited to the right to vote in local and EU parliamentary elections, subject to residential requirements within any EU member state, and the right to assistance from any EU member state embassy or consulate in a non-EU member state. Symbolically, all EU citizens hold passports of a similar size and format. Citizenship is complementary, rather than equivalent to or replacing national citizenship. For Britain, EU citizenship extends domestic rights that had previously been offered to Irish and some Commonwealth citizens. Of much more significance is that EU citizenship offers the right to work as well as to move freely and to reside in any EU member state. In practice, the TEU constitutionalizes the economic rights established in the SEA with regard to free movement of people throughout the EU. Knowledge of these citizen privileges in Britain remains low, though it may have been enhanced from 2004 to 2008 with the influx of workers from the new East European member states as Slovak laborers, Polish plumbers, and Hungarian dentists come to reside (often temporarily) in Britain. For some Britons however, the burgundy-colored EU-style passport is an anathema, to be hidden within a larger traditional black mock UK cover as they pass through airports.

Subsidiary Effect?

Two other constitutional effects are, in part, associated with EU membership. Since the TEU there has been a somewhat unsystematic attempt to implement the concept of *subsidiarity*, allocating EU policies to their most *appropriate level* of governance, be that in Brussels or at regional/local level. This seems to support the associated concept of multilevel governance (MLG). For British governments, subsidiarity has often been seen as an opportunity to renationalize policy areas or as a reason to sustain national control over potentially supranational policy areas. Currently the Conservative Party talks of the need to repatriate the Common Fisheries Policy; both Labour and Conservative parties resist moves to incorporate aspects of Justice and Home Affairs policies in the Community (supranational) orbit of EU pillar policy making. Whether by coincidence, as in the case of devolution to Scotland, Wales, and Northern Ireland, or design, in the case of English regional governance, the mechanisms for subsidiarity have emerged in British governance. While not the only force for change, what is evident is an embryonic MLG structure "evolving within and against the Westminster model" (Flinders 2006: 135).

Changes in the practice of British governance have often paralleled the requirements of supranational governance in the EU. Thus, "the timing, scope, and impact of change in English regional governance" to 1997 "was significantly driven by the Structural Funds and thus by the European Union," and the effect was to bring Britain closer to the Continental European idea of a "Europe of the Regions" (Burch and Gomez 2006: 90). Indeed, in a government White Paper, *Your Region, Your Choice* (DTLR 2002), several references were made to the significance of regional governance in providing a participative element in the implementation of EU regional policies. The paper also pointed out that, within the EU, only the English regions lacked some form of directly elected government (Mather 2004).

Britain in a Europe of Regions

A second effect is the network of direct contact with EU institutions and other European regions. Both the Scottish Executive and Welsh Assembly have joined with such powerful Continental regions as Bavaria, Catalonia, Flanders, and North-Rhine Westphalia in seeking a more powerful voice for regions that enjoy legislative capabilities, the so-called "Regleg" group. This has created a network of "constitutional regions" that have argued for recognition of their special status in any EU constitutional reform. This position was supported by the British government, at least in part, when arguing during the European Constitutional Convention for a more powerful EU Committee of Regions (Bort 2005); and, with government approval, Scottish ministers have represented British interests in the EU Council of Ministers in what are deemed appropriate areas, such as fisheries policy.

So, while there are no constitutional rights of participation similar to those won by the German Länder during the TEU ratification process, there are emerging, in typically pragmatic fashion, conventions that give the devolved governments an "external" presence. The strength of these conventions depends on the existence of a politically friendly dialogue between Westminster and the devolved assemblies—a factor that could unravel when center and periphery are politically opposed. However, any future EU constitutional settlement that gave more powers to EU regions would amount to an external endorsement of devolution in Britain, tying it "to the governance of the EU, in an integrated multi-level governance system" (Bort 2005: 312). There is, however, another scenario: having ventured down the route of devolution, any future British government may be faced with demands, especially from Scotland, for independence within the EU.

Representation in the EU

The European Parliament (EP) is unique in that it is the only assembly of any international organization to be directly elected. As such, it is a part of the constitutional representation of British public opinion and has a legitimating role for the activities of politicians in an EU context. Since the European Single Act (1986) the EP's involvement in legislative processes has expanded and its powers to reject legislation have also increased, especially after the Amsterdam Treaty (1997), through the extension of the process of co-decision with the Council of Ministers (see chapter 5).

Since 1999 Britain has come in line with other member states and abandoned its traditional single-member majoritarian electoral system for the EP in favor of proportional representation—a regional list system in mainland Britain alongside an already existing constituency proportional representation (PR) system in Northern Ireland. The EP electoral regions are utilized as part of the electoral process in Scottish and Welsh elections. While domestic calculations have weighed heavily in the use of hybrid electoral systems for Scottish and Welsh legislative elections, forms of proportional representation are also used in Northern Ireland and London regional government. It is noteworthy that it is only the House of Commons and English and Welsh local government that continue to be served by the single-member majority system. However, despite the extension of its competences, the EP lacks a public profile, and turnout for EP elections, throughout the EU, has been low (44% in 2009). British EP electoral turnout (39% in 2004 and 35% in 2009) is toward the lower end of the scale, comparable with that experienced in local elections.

In examining this "European" effect, public discourse is at least encouraged to consider, for instance, why PR is suitable for EP elections yet not for general elections, whether the Human Rights Act based on the ECHR has enhanced individual rights, or why a written constitutional treaty is appropriate for the EU but not for Britain. It is in the light of this external backdrop that we examine below Labour's constitutional "revolution."

THE CONSTITUTION AND LABOUR: MODERNIZED, REVOLUTIONIZED, OR TRAUMATIZED?

Twelve years of Labour government (1997–2009) have seen more constitutional change than had been undertaken in the previous century. From the operational independence offered to the Bank of England days after their first election in 1997, to the drafting of a further Lords reform bill in 2007, successive Labour governments have dealt a series of constitutional shocks to the British body politic.

Why So Many Reforms?

Several factors have been suggested for this plethora of reforms. The first is associated with preelection promises by New Labour to deliver modern government for the new millennium. Modernized government was to support the domestic, European, and global aspirations of British society. Second, after thirteen years of Conservative government and Labour opposition, both the voting public and Labour Party were open to radical and challenging "solutions" to a set of problems emanating from central government policy failure, and the public perception of closed and corrupt elites that needed cleansing and opening up (Flinders 2006).

A cross-party approach, that fitted New Labour's pluralist direction, was encouraged through campaigning organizations such as the Scottish Constitutional Committee, Charter 88, and Democratic Audit. Constitutional reform had previously been the particular interest of the Liberals and, for a short time after the election, Liberal Democratic leaders sat on a cabinet subcommittee on constitutional affairs in a temporary spirit of consensus. More pragmatically, constitutional reform was relatively easy to fit into Labour's early legislative timetable: the 1997 election pledge to maintain public expenditure levels at those set by the Conservatives to 1999 did not allow for any major social or economic initiatives.

The period 1997–2001 represents Labour's application of a liberal-pluralist agenda to constitutional reform. Scottish and Welsh devolution, London government, a Human Rights Act and a Freedom of Information Act, and the abolition of hereditary peers all indicated a radically different dimension to a party that, during previous periods of office, had shown little interest in reducing the power of the executive to deliver centrally directed, redistributive policies. Though there were some attempts to reform Parliament, including a further commitment to Lords reform, the pressures to deliver public services and also a new level of security after 9/11 led to a turning from the liberal-pluralist to the (centralist) Whitehall view of constitutional reform.

Despite this waning of enthusiasm, the government found reason, in the latter half of their second Blair administration, to reestablish its reform agenda. Under considerable pressure from its policies on Iraq and public service reform, the government took a further constitutional leap in 2003 when a Constitutional Reform Bill and a House of Lords Bill were announced. The albeit short-lived creation of a Department for Constitutional Affairs was an indication of Labour's recommitment to its modernization program, and in 2007 a further attempt to get agreement over Lords reform was presented to the Commons. To add to the government's failures, separate plans for regional government were set back by a referendum no vote by northeast electors in 2004.

On succeeding to the premiership, Gordon Brown and Jack Straw, the new justice minister, attempted to address unfinished issues in the Green Paper *The Governance of Britain*, which asked two fundamental questions: "How should we hold power accountable, and how should we uphold and enhance the rights and responsibilities of the citizen?" (Ministry of Justice 2007: 5). There followed a piecemeal set of actions, proposals, and discussion points, some of which changed constitutional practice or the procedures of governance, or attempted to invigorate political participation. Several of the proposals, especially those that increase parliamentary oversight of the executive, were intended to be applied as new constitutional conventions with immediate effect. Others involve new legislation or actions by Parliament to take advantage of what seems a fair reforming wind. One immediate step was a legislative program statement, prior to the queen's speech, that allowed Commons and public alike the opportunity to assess the government's intentions several months in advance. The change agenda was revisited in 2009, and all parliamentary parties scrabbled to rectify the crisis of public confidence that occurred after the telegraph allowances scandal (see the book's website).

TOWARD A EUROPEAN MULTILEVEL CONSTITUTION?

Bagehot wrote his seminal essay, "The English Constitution," in 1867 in the context of an emerging British world hegemony and the increasing dominance of liberal ideas. As one historian put it, "Judged by continental standards of liberalism . . . Britain could fairly claim to be the home of 'the Mother of Parliaments,' of the rule of law, of the Bill of Rights and of free trade. Britain was the most modernized and industrialized country in Europe, and supposedly the most open to liberal ideas" (Davies 1999: 807). It was to London that Continental revolutionaries such as Mazzini and Marx fled, either explicitly extolling or implicitly enjoying the benign if imperfect liberalism of the time. English state omnipotence, an imperial reach, and a certain smugness associated with the island's avoidance of revolutionary change—as a consequence of the superior maxims of gradualism and adaptation—produced a marketable export: the Westminster model. Great Britain presented a confident, autonomous statehood and appeared to provide a pathway for Continental political development—for Italians, Germans, Spaniards, Greeks, and Austrians struggling to emerge from autocracy.

Fast-forward 133 years to 2000: Larry Seidentop's reexamination of the characteristics of the British constitution asserted that, in relation to its contribution to democracy in Europe, Britain "has lost its voice" (Seidentop 2000: 65). He supports his conclusion by pointing to the lack of a written constitution that can clearly deliver a "rights minded society" (Seidentop 2000: 69). British democracy, he argues, was historically assured by "decency and common sense"—akin to the constitutional "software" referred to earlier. The Thatcherite market-led social revolution of the 1980s provided only an economic liberalism "stripped of its political and moral dimensions," and the loss of autonomy of local government, together with the decline of ideological debate, also "stripped British liberalism from its idealism" (Seidentop 2000: 77).

At around the same time the European Union and its member states embarked on processes of widening and deepening—as a consequence of

the Single European Act and, after 1989, to extend membership to fledg-
ling democracies of Central and Eastern Europe. As "the least constitutionally literate people in Europe" who are capable of equating "federalism
with centralization" (Seidentop 2000) and espousing "a visceral anti-
Europeanism" (Mandelson 2007), the British contribution to debate on the
future constitutional shape of the EU has been severely curtailed, suggests
Seidentop (2000), and the nineteenth-century exportability of the Westminster model is now impossible.

Apologists for the current state of the constitution can deflect Seidentop's critical assessment in a number of ways. One claim of traditionalists, who support the conservation of the Westminster model, is its
ability to adapt and survive—a hallmark of a stable and responsive political system. On face value, the system survived the considerable onslaught
of EU membership in 1972 and the impact of New Labour's reform agenda
at the turn of the millennium. The constitutional monarchy and parliamentary sovereignty are still the most immediately evident characteristics of an exceptionalist state. The Scottish Parliament is devolved, not
sovereign; the new Supreme Court cannot strike down parliamentary legislation; the HRA is open to executive interpretation; and general elections to the Commons remain a PR-free zone. Any notion of radically
changing the status of the monarchy is off any party agenda. Finally, increasing EU powers have been successfully absorbed within the Westminster-Whitehall embrace.

The problem for modernizers is that they perceive the recent changes
as unfinished business. All the main parties, as well as Scottish, Irish,
and Welsh Nationalists, have a perspective on the future that implies that
continuing modernization is very likely. Further modernization of the
constitution may be inevitable given the scandal concerning MPs' use of
their expenses and allowances in 2009. These may involve the extension
of devolved government and a stronger role for local government. Despite
its limitations, once operating, the Supreme Court may prove an active
institution in checking executive power. What emerges are three modernizing assumptions—the notion that Britain has developed into a multilevel system of governance; that the codification of human rights has
been achieved throughout the British Isles; and that mechanisms are
needed to balance the strength of the British executive over a relatively
weak Parliament. These themes present challenges to traditional "Anglo-Saxon" constitutional values and practice (Dunleavy 2006: 340).
Textbox 3.6 contrasts the characteristics of these traditional values with
those that can be identified as "Continental." The modernization of the
British constitution, it can be argued, has brought the political system
closer to shared generic European values than was postulated at the turn
of the century.

Textbox 3.6. Variations in Constitutional Values

Postwar Continental Variant		Generic European Values		Anglo-Saxon Variant
pooled	⟵	sovereignty	⟶	parliamentary
collective	⟵	rights	⟶	individual
codified	⟵	rule of law	⟶	customary
consensual	⟵	elective Law making	⟶	adversarial
proportional	⟵	peoples representation	⟶	majoritarian
superior court	⟵	final arbitration	⟶	Commons
corporate formal	⟵	social representation	⟶	competitive informal
legal equal	⟵	citizenship	⟶	subject-traditional

Generic European values expressed through such ideals as freedom of the individual, limited government, the rule of law, and a predominately Judeo-Christian moral code are not just the backdrop to European constitutions but have spread, if unevenly practiced, across continents. Listed above are a set of constitutional practices that represents a post–World War II variant of European values that have emerged in Continental Europe. These are contrasted with Anglo-Saxon constitutional practice—itself a variant of generic European values. The differences between these may not be great, but they lead to considerable, often emotional, debate about fundamental principles of government, in particular, the extent to which Anglo-Saxon values are to be overtaken by Continental values: in effect the Europeanization of the British state and thus its distinctive traditions. The values and characteristics listed often represent a false dichotomy, but their political potency in the Britain-EU public debate is powerful.

A more radical approach to change in the British Constitution emphasizes and welcomes the decline in the central notion of state sovereignty in the context of external pressures. There are several explanations for this. The first is a postmodern one: that cultural and social diversity, much more evident in Britain today, has made the values of the Westminster system less relevant than it was fifty years ago. A differentiated polity is better analyzed in terms of networks and multilevel governance (Bevir and Rhodes 2003). A second explanation reflects a globalist view, where global interactions "have pushed control of many critical issues far beyond the level where single-country politics makes sense" (Dunleavy 2006: 337). The third is one that has permeated this chapter; the impact of EU membership and its implications for member state sovereignty and governance.

CONCLUSION

In the view of Lord Beloff, the British Constitution is no longer operative because Britain is already a unit within a federal system "and is deprived therefore of the essence of constitutionalist self government" (Beloff 1998: 170). This somewhat dramatic conclusion is rebutted by others, but Beloff supports his assertion by pointing out enforced changes to British constitutional practice entailed by membership in the EU. The superior role of the ECJ in certain areas, and the support for its authority within British courts, undermines the legislative capacity of Parliament. The need to second-guess the ECJ's stance on legislative issues, together with the application of qualified majority voting (QMV) in the Council of Ministers, has curtailed the domestic power and independence of government. If the British constitution *is* what it *does*, as we suggested earlier, then Britain is already part of a quasi-federal entity and is closely involved in a political process characterized by shared or pooled sovereignty in many aspects of public policy. Formal and informal interactions between the Westminster-Whitehall and EU institutions, such as attendance at presidency and Council meetings, representation in the EP, and participation in ECJ procedures, are evidence not just of Europeanization of policy processes but also of constitutional practice.

Reform of the British Constitution, therefore, cannot be separated from the notion of European integration—and its full acknowledgment as an integral aspect of "what happens" in British politics today. If this analysis is correct, then further reforms of devolved regional and local government, consideration of the role of MPs, and the accountability of ministers within the EU policy process are matters for consideration as part of British constitutional debate. The EU derivation to this debate however, has been carefully avoided or demonized by mainstream politicians, or sanitized by the perpetuation of traditional myths of national and parliamentary sovereignty. For example the government's 2007 Green Paper barely mentions the EU in its list of sources for the British Constitution and omits any reference to EU treaties and laws (Ministry of Justice 2007: 16). The Europeanization of the British Constitution, both in terms of values and emerging conventional practice, is perhaps only the latest element to be included in a typical British "back-of-the-envelope" approach to constitutional reform.

FURTHER READING

For a conventional perspective on the British Constitution prior to the Labour reforms see Peter Madgewick and Diana Woodhouse, *The Law and Politics of the Constitution of the United Kingdom* (1995). More critical and contemporary analysis is available in Anthony King's *Does the United Kingdom Have a Constitution* (2001) or *Our Republican Constitution* by Adam Tompkins (2005). Vernon Bodganor's reader *The British Constitution in the 20th Century* (2005a) and Nevil Johnson, *Reshaping the British Constitution* (2004) give critical evaluations of the Labour reforms as do chapters in the Developments in British Politics series edited by Patrick Dunleavy and others (2003, 2006). For a strong Eurosceptical perspective of British sovereignty see Lord Beloff's "Amery on the Constitution: Britain and the European Union" (1998). Andrew Gamble presents the alternative debate in chapter 2 of *Between Europe and America* (2003a). The "United" in United Kingdom is explored critically in work by Tom Nairn: *The Breakup of Britain* (2003) and *After Britain* (2000). Issues of the direct effect of EU law and parliamentary supremacy are discussed in *Britain in the European Union: Law, Policy and Parliament*, edited by Philip Giddings and Gavin Drewry (2004) and Bogdanor (above). The consequences of British constitutional exceptionalism and the need for rights-based reform are forcefully presented in Larry Seidentop's *Democracy in Europe* (2000).

4

Parliamentary Representation and the Legislative Process
Models of Representation

There were, until the introduction of EP elections in 1979, only two forms of direct representation available to the British citizen—at the parliamentary and the local levels. The character of that representation was broadly similar. Essentially, both national and local representation in British politics is formally characterized by the *trustee model* (see textbox 4.1). The basis of representation in the House of Commons and at the local level is a territorial constituency, where one person, in the case of the Commons, or one to three persons, in the case of English and Welsh local government, represents the collective interests of all citizens living within that constituency. An Electoral Commission attempts to adjust the size of constituencies relative to population movements against the need to sustain communities of interests and localities (Judge 2005: 34).

This historical and legal commitment to territorial representation has consequences for the citizen's relationship with the Commons and its organization. It implies that an individual seeking redress, assistance, or even just advice may see the local councillor or MP as a first port of call in any government-related problem that may occur. This willingness and trust is based on an understanding of the representative's problem-solving skills and status (Judge 2005: 34). In turn, parliamentary procedures that underline the formal constituency basis of an MP's authority reinforce the representative's status in the eyes of the constituent. All of this is underpinned by a first-past-the-post (FPTP) electoral system whereby the winner, implicitly the best person for the job, is elected. As we shall argue below, this FPTP system tends to reinforce the elitist nature of representation inherent in a political system where land, property ownership, and commercial success were traditionally locally derived within a class-based social order.

Textbox 4.1. Models of Representation

The Trustee Model

Representation is entrusted to a person who is deemed capable by virtue of superior abilities of looking after the interests of those who have conferred their faith in the better judgment of the person they elect to public office. Edmund Burke and later J. S. Mill advocated this essentially elite view of representation.

The Mandate as Representation

It is the party composed of elected representatives that offers a collective choice on public issues through the prioritization of issues in a clearly stated political program. The individual representative is subordinated to the party. The task of the representative is to carry through the mandate from which he or she gained elected public office, that is, to support or oppose the government of the day. The role of the voter according to Joseph Schumpeter is to periodically accept or oppose the politicians who seek political office via their parties' electoral strengths.

Representation through Delegation

Here the interests of an individual or community are expressed directly by someone chosen to communicate their more or less express wishes. There is little room for the personal views of the representative in this context. Delegated representation is often accompanied by mechanisms that give the elector the ability to influence control over the delegate such as "recall" or the use of referenda. Tom Paine and Jean-Jacques Rousseau present, in different ways, this participatory form of representation.

The Mirror Theory

Representation is facilitated by reflecting the social structure of society in a fairly proportionate manner. Thus, depending on the elements of a social structure, ethnic groups, men/women, age groups, gender, subnational groupings, or economic interests would gain proportionate access to representative forums. The assumption is that the interests of respective social groupings can only be effectively represented by mechanisms that end up in a "fair" balance between the several components of a society.

This "principle of distinction" (Manin 1997) has continued into the twenty-first century, surviving the impact of twentieth-century party-based electoral organization and egalitarian notions within socialist thought. Though contemporary MPs, as we shall see, are more professional—in the sense of being career politicians—their profile remains predominantly white, male, middle-class, and university educated. Commons salaries and supporting (and recently controversial) allowance payments place MPs in the top quartile of earners. In effect, though changed in its social composition, the representative system remains elite based and is, through its constituency basis, as territorially bounded as it was in the nineteenth century; as such, it could be argued that representation through the notion of a trustee model is out of tune with what we have previously referred to as the "modular society" of contemporary Britain (Krieger 1999).

There is, however, little doubt that the advent of political parties had considerable impact on the trustee model. If trustee representation favors the individual's relationship with the representative, then party organization and the emergence of a party system aggregates the political demand of like-minded individuals and places an ideological badge on the representative—and thus a constraint on his/her ability to make independent judgments on behalf of constituents. For the most part, British political parties "nationalize" the political agenda, thus loosening the geographic context of parliamentary democracy through a *mandate* system of representation.

British political parties are powerfully disciplined organizations, and this is reflected in the organization of legislative business in the Commons. The pursuit of a government mandate, and clear opposition to it, is the very essence of British party government. As such, this model of representation through the mandate has been layered over the historic/social notion of trustee representation. As a relative newcomer in British political development, its presence is more evident in the practice of legislative politics than might be suggested by the formal rules of the House (Judge 2005: 39). The juxtaposition of these two models, together with the FPTP winner-take-all mode of election, provides an adversarial framework for the British representative process. Both models sustain the elite-based nature of representation, but the distinctly national and partisan perspectives of party government undermine trustee representation.

The MP, whose legal basis is a constituency but whose electoral legitimacy comes from a party badge, has a difficult job: Does individual/constituency or party/national interest come first? While most MPs stand on the moral high ground of their "trustee role," the reality of British government is that it is party dominant. One somewhat infamous description of the MP's role in the Commons was by the Labour Prime Minister Harold Wilson who, when facing a 1960s backbench rebellion, suggested that just like pet dogs, the rebels were there on public licence and, just like misbehaving dogs, their licences could be revoked!

In such circumstances there is not much room for reflection on the *delegatory* or *mirror* theories of representation in the formal process of British politics. Delegation is best evident in trade union politics and, until the 1990s reforms, in the Labour party. The recent use of the referendum as a delegatory mechanism has been usually as a means to solve thorny constitutional or local issues and may be used to deal with the problem of euro membership, the Constitutional Treaty, or domestic electoral reform (see

Table 4.1.   Significant Referenda

		For	Against	Turnout
1975	Membership in the European Community	64	36	65%
1979	Welsh Devolution	20	80	59%
1979	Scottish Devolution	51*	49	64%
1997	Scottish Devolution	74	26	60%
1997	Welsh Devolution	50.3	49.7	50%
1998	NI Good Friday Agreement	71	29	80%
	London Government	72	28	34%
2004	North East Regional Government	22	78	48%
		For	**Against**	**High/Low**
2001/02	Referenda for the establishment of directly elected mayor (32 held)	11	21	64% / 10%

* Did not reach government-stipulated electorate threshold.

table 4.1 and the book's website). Attempts to introduce mirror representation have also been piecemeal. Both the Labour and Conservative parties have struggled with selection mechanisms to produce a better gender balance for electoral candidates. Ethnic minorities, except in areas where they are dominant, struggle to gain prominence in constituency representative selection procedures. The FPTP system of election, which remains in parliamentary and Welsh and English local elections, presents a barrier to broader-based representation. As such, ideas of representation that favor an exclusive, elitist notion have remained in the ascendancy, seeming to justify "what to many diverse groups in society . . . seem to be palpably undemocratic processes" (Judge 2005: 36 and below).

STILL REPRESENTING BRITAIN? THE COMMONS AND THE LORDS

We discussed in chapter 3 the myth and reality of parliamentary sovereignty and the broader picture of a multilayered constitutionalism that, in historical terms, has emerged quite recently. While the trustee model reflects the abiding character of individual and constituency representation in Britain, party politics has modified the notion of trusteeship through its crosscutting discipline and doctrine of the mandate. Parliamentary sovereignty and trusteeship, as partners in the philosophy of British representation are, in turn, challenged by the dominance of the British executive over Parliament and party and by the institutions and processes of multilevel governance, in that devolved assemblies and EU institutions challenge the preeminence of Parliament as the centerpiece of British representative democracy.

In a review of the impact of ten years of Blair government, one commentator asserted that the prime minister left the House of Commons "in a far worse state than he found it. The place is a glimmer of its former self, a Parliament of political shades, where business is curtailed by government managers, where the prime minister rarely votes . . . the chamber has rarely seemed so listless, so disconnected from the government of the British people, so lacking in self confidence and authority" (Porter 2007). But another discussion of Parliament suggests that "the Blair government—particularly in the period 2001 to 2005—resulted in a partial rebirth of Parliament," even though little was intentional on the part of the Labour government! (Cowley 2006: 55) So what to make of these seemingly contradictory evaluations? We discuss below the role of the Commons, its recent difficulties and attempts to "modernize" its activities; the position of the House of Lords; and, finally, the role of Parliament within the multi-level system of governance that affects so much of the twenty-first-century British political system.

Parliament: Still an Icon?

First, it is worth mentioning the footprint of history that has anchored Parliament's role within the system. While we can point to its ability in adapting to social change, it is its permanence, its starring role in historical events, and simply its longevity that have given Parliament a cultural and, indeed, iconic status that has both domestic and external recognition. Its imposing London manifestation, a neo-Gothic building by the Thames (that dates from only the 1850s), has been etched further into the psyche of its citizenry by the daily broadcast of its presence on radio and TV and through the imposing sound of "Big Ben," or rather the collective bells of Parliament's clock tower, the nation's time check. While not wishing to overstate the case, the familiar image of Parliament enjoys an affection that contrasts with the more negative perspectives that the British public may have toward the people that occupy the buildings. This was reinforced in 2009 by the public disclosure of detailed allowance/expenses claims made by MPs, which reduced citizen trust in their honorable representatives massively (see textbox 4.2 and the book's website).

The Commons: The Representative Role

The Commons' existence as a forum for democratic representation creates, as in all assemblies, the conditions that allow its multiple functions: as legitimator of public policy, as legislator, as a forum for the expression

---

Textbox 4.2. (Dis)Honorable Members?

Backbench MPs are paid £64,766 ($97,150). Ministers receive more (between £94,000 and £194,000—the PM's salary). Successive governments have failed to address what some MPs have considered a relatively low basic wage, preferring to offer "allowances" of up to £23,000 ($34,500), so that their backbenches living outside of inner London can fund their office and a second home necessary to carry out their national and constituency duties. MPs have proven reluctant to disclose details of their allowances, eventually agreeing to release generalized information in the summer of 2009 and in advance of a formal review of MPs' allowances by the Committee on Standards in Public Life.

In May, the broadsheet *Daily Telegraph* obtained a detailed listing of how MPs had spent their allowances and provided it to an astounded public. The *Telegraph* list included MP claims for housing loans already paid back; property deals to make capital gains with no tax paid; claims to clear a moat (£2,000); the purchase of a duck island (?) and £8,000 television set (rejected); £115 to change twenty-five light bulbs; backbench married MPs who claimed for two second homes; and a minister who bought and sold her second home three times in one year, failing to declare the profit made to the Inland Revenue. MPs from all parties as well as ministers and senior Conservative front-benchers were involved. Nearly all claimed not to have broken any rules and to have acted "in good faith."

An angry public demanded retribution. The Speaker of the Commons, a defender of the existing system, reluctantly resigned. A junior minister "stepped down," as did an advisor of David Cameron. Many MPs announced that they would not be on the ballot at the next election and some were referred to the police for investigating. Both Labour and Conservative parties lost opinion poll points and members in what was considered a calamity for the political classes the likes of which had not been experienced since before the 1832 Parliamentary Reform Act. The Trustee model of Parliamentary representation and the institution of Parliament itself took a massive battering.

Source: Independent, 15 May 2009; Observer, 10 May 2009; Daily Telegraph, 12 May 2009.

---

of public and other opinion, as a major recruiting ground for executive public office, and as scrutinizer of those public office holders—in effect it is the key to representative and responsible government. So who are MPs?

The first and most obvious characteristic is that they are members of (mostly) long-established political parties. Save for a handful, MPs are in the Commons because they wear a party badge. Though a small number defy party discipline on occasion, and many more will proclaim their primary obligation is as a constituency-elected representative, their existence as MPs depends on their party allegiance. More than this, though the percentage has declined over the past fifty years, the great majority of MPs are either Labour or Conservative. In the last three general elections Conservative and Labour MPs won more than 75 percent of available seats.

However, the 2005 election produced the highest total of non-Labour/Conservative MPs (24%) and the greatest number of Liberal Democrat MPs, (sixty-three, or 9%), which suggests a need to reconsider the notion of two-party politics that dominated the parliamentary scene from 1945 to the 1980s. When the total share of the 2005 vote for the two major parties (67.5%) is compared with the average Labour/Conservative vote between 1945 and 1970 (91.6%), there is evidence of a considerable erosion of support for the two parties (Bartle and Laycocks 2006; Webb 2000).

But this is not reflected in the party political makeup of the Commons that is preserved by the unrepresentative outcome of the FPTP electoral system. In 2005, Labour's much-reduced electoral lead over the Conservatives (2.9%) sustained a substantial majority of sixty-six seats. The Conservative vote increased by only 0.6 percent, yet they gained thirty-three Commons seats. But the Liberal Democrats gained 3.9 percent, and won only eleven extra seats. This, it must be remembered, was achieved on a turnout of only 61 percent of the total electorate. Thus, "out of every five members of the electorate, one voted for Labour, one voted Conservative, one voted for one of the other parties—but two did not vote at all" (Bartle and Laycocks 2006: 78).

An examination of the socioeconomic background of MPs provides a critical if not unexpected commentary on the character of the British representative system. As can be seen from table 4.2, MPs are predominantly male, middle-aged, white, and middle class—a situation not unfamiliar throughout Western liberal democracies. When one adds educational background to the profile, a picture of elite domination emerges. One-third of MPs in the 2005 Parliament went to fee-paying schools (8% nationally). Three-quarters were college graduates, of whom over one-third attended Oxford or Cambridge. Around 40 percent are from the professions, with the teaching and legal professions dominating (around 18% and 10% respectively). Interestingly, the percentage of "party professional MPs" has doubled (to 14%) between 1992 and 2005. Manual workers have declined to 6 percent. The most significant change is in the number of women representatives. There were only 3 percent in 1979—the year that Mrs. Thatcher was elected. By 2005, this had increased to 20 percent, more than doubling from 1992. The increase was predominantly the result of the Labour landslide of 1997, together with the adoption of all-women shortlists, when 24 percent of Labour MPs were female (Blair's Babes). In 2005, Labour female MPs amounted to 28 percent of Labour's total (355). Females, however, make up 51 percent of the British population. No such radical change is evident in the ethnic complexion of the House. It was not till 1987 that the first four postwar nonwhite MPs were elected. By 2005 this had increased to fifteen (2.3%). The 2001 census showed an 8 percent nonwhite population in Britain. The 2007 regional elections provided Scotland and Wales with their first ethnic minority representatives, both elected on nationalist tickets.

Table 4.2.   The Socioeconomic Background of MPs

Election Year	Average Age	M/F Balance%	Occupation %	Ethnicity Totals	Education
1992	50	91:9	Professions: 41 Businesses: 24 *Admin: 24 Manual: 10	White: 645 Nonwhite: 6	Public School 46% University 69% (Oxbridge 30%)
1997	48.8	82:18	Professions: 43 Businesses: 18 Admin: 30 Manual: 9	White: 650 Nonwhite: 9	Public School 41% University 72% (Oxbridge 36%)
2001	49.8	82:18	Professions: 43 Businesses: 17 Admin: 38 Manual: 8	White: 657 Nonwhite: 12	Public School 39% University 73% (Oxbridge 30%)
2005	50.6	80:20	Professions: 39 Businesses: 19 Admin: 35 Manual: 6	White: 631 Nonwhite: 15	Public School 33% University 74% (Oxbridge 30%)

*The term *Admin* includes white-collar workers, political organizers, publishers, and journalists.
Sources: House of Commons (2005); Sutton Trust (2005).

One characteristic is the length of parliamentary service that MPs enjoy. In 2007, 81 percent of MPs had been in the Commons since 2001. Only eighteen had no parliamentary experience when elected in 2005. Even in the landslide of 1997 over 60 percent of MPs had served in the previous Parliament. Since the number of career politicians has increased during the past few years, it is probable that the average length of Commons service, around twenty years, is unlikely to decline (Norton 2007).

Although major parties have engaged with issues of gender and minority representation recently, the composition of the twenty-first-century Commons does not reflect the social and demographic changes in British society over the past thirty years. It does, however, reflect socioeconomic change, in the greater representation of Britain's broader middle class—at the expense of upper-middle- and working-class representation (Rush 2001). Professionals—whether from traditional professions or as professional politicians—dominate. This, together with the considerable improvement in MPs' salaries and supporting expenses, has resulted in a "marked growth in the number of career politicians . . . who devote themselves to Parliament or rather to their parliamentary careers" (Norton 2005: 24). A contemporary parliamentary party may thus be characterized as elite-professional, or a cadre party—tightly controlled and seeking to maximize its vote by presenting the best image of the national interest that it can demonstrate (Childs 2006 and chapter 6). For the MP, therefore, the need to cultivate a constituency is her/his contribution to the cadre-based party machine. Paradoxically, MPs are increasingly focusing on their constituents' needs, "which would have been unimaginable 50 years ago" (Cowley 2006: 55). In a limited sense, and maybe for the wrong reasons, British MPs have maintained at least one characteristic of the intellectual samurai. But what about their other roles?

Still Legitimating?

The political essence of the Commons is the party system. Once elected, parties invade the Commons and shape its processes and output. The House divides into a dominant governing party and the opposition, with the next-largest party enjoying the title of Official Opposition. Except for relatively short-lived periods when a governing party has not enjoyed a clear majority, or in times of dire crisis when national coalitions have been formed, a winner-take-all system of government has emerged through the majoritarian system. It is thus an *adversarial* system, civilized by the formal rules and traditions of parliamentary behavior.

Between 1945 and 2005 government parties have had absolute majorities for fifty-six of the sixty-year period. Even during the periods when there has been a small majority, for instance between 1964 and 1966, the Labour government of the day was able to pursue its policies reasonably effectively. Providing the discipline of the party can be sustained, the governments can control the Commons through its democratically achieved mandate.

With this built-in political legitimacy, and with so much of government policy having been through the party manifesto mill, which involves detailed party discussion, it is the ministers who monopolize the legislative process, who introduce bills, manage their progress, and expect their content to emerge pretty much as originated. Though MPs—as private members—have the opportunity to introduce a small number of bills each year, it is public legislation that dominates the business of the Commons. The legislative process, summarized in textbox 4.3, gives formal opportunities for both MPs and Lords to throw out, amend, or accept a bill. However, given the party discipline that normally prevails, both government and opposition can be expected to play their normal roles—that is, the governing party consistently winning and opposition parties consistently losing. The majoritarian, adversarial process is continued in standing committees, making bills difficult to amend unless a minister sees advantage in the proposals being made. For the most part, opposition MPs will try to hinder the bill's passage for as long as possible, and government

---

Textbox 4.3. The Legislative Process

All bills on their way to become laws must pass through both the Commons and the Lords. The stages of this process are broadly similar for each House and consist of:

First Reading	The title of the bill is read out; then, at least two weeks later:
Second Reading	There is a debate on the principles of the bill.
Committee Stage	Details of the bill are considered and amendments are proposed. This takes place in one of several general standing committees, or if deemed important enough, on the floor of the House.
Report Stage	The bill is reported to the whole House; some other amendments can be made.
Third Reading	Bill is approved by the House.

Most bills commence in the Commons, though some go to the Lords first. If the Lords amend the bill and the Commons (i.e., the government) do not approve these changes the bill is returned to the Lords. Generally, the Lords, as an unelected House, will be reluctant to delay a bill for a full parliamentary session before it, like all bills, goes forward to Royal Assent. This has not been refused since 1707.

MPs, encouraged by their party enforcers (Whips), will sit on their hands to save time. The committee stage is effective in progressing government wishes, but it ranks relatively low in its primary task of legislative scrutiny (Brazier 2004).

A few statistics from the Blair era illustrate the largely formal role of the Commons in passing legislation. Between 1997 and 2005 the Labour government experienced only two defeats to its legislation. These were both on November 9, 2005, when two votes were lost on the number of days that a person suspected of terrorism could be detained without a formal charge. In April 2009 Gordon Brown experienced a first Commons defeat by three votes over government proposals to grant only limited rights of entry to Britain to ex-Ghurkha soldiers who had served in the British Army. These were the first defeats for a government since 1995, when the Conservative government lost a vote on an EU fisheries motion.

There have been, however, many occasions when the government has responded to Commons pressure and amended or, indeed, substantially changed its legislative intentions. In fact, about 90 percent of amendments that are successful in standing committees are accepted. This is often to head off disquiet among backbench party members rather than face political embarrassment and loss of precious legislative time. Examples are the bill to establish Foundation Hospitals in 2003 and the Higher Education Bill (2004), where, in both cases, the government bowed to backbench pressure. The latter passed its second reading by five votes only after the promise of substantial revision at committee stage (Norton 2005). However, in quantitative terms, it is the House of Lords that seeks to amend government legislation more than the Commons, as we shall see.

A built-in Commons majority, a clear-cut adversarial "them or us" perspective on politics and party loyalty, and an overwhelming need for solidarity when facing the electorate give every advantage to a government in getting its own way in the Commons. Since around a third of MPs in a governing party hold some form of governing office, from cabinet minister to parliamentary private secretary, the tentacles of collective loyalty, if not collective responsibility, stretch deep across the government benches. But while the opportunity to stop the progress of government policy proves elusive, there are opportunities to force amendments to government action. And since the Major and Blair governments, there has been a revival in backbench activities that have produced many policy retreats, if not defeats (see the book's website). It is with this in mind that one of the first steps of the Gordon Brown premiership was to acknowledge the Commons, and the importance of its legitimizing role, by offering some new areas of responsibility, including the opportunity to ratify treaties and approve parliamentary recall and dissolution. Brown, however, also faced backbench revolt within months of his accession over issues of taxes and the arrest of terrorist suspects, and later, there was rebellion over proposals to reform the expenses of MPs and privatization of the Post Office.

Scrutinizing Government

Within an adversarial, dominant-party parliamentary system, such as Britain's, the task of scrutinizing what the government does is not easy. The political and institutional resources available to a government are vast. Ministers manage Commons business through the whips' office, working within Commons procedures and with the agreements of opposition whips—whose time as government whips will come soon, they hope. "Usual (business) channels," therefore, involve collusion between government and would-be government party managers and have been described by the veteran parliamentarian and ex-Labour Minister Tony Benn as "the most polluted waterway in Europe" (Rogers and Walters 2006: 100). Scrutiny of government business takes place, therefore, within priorities and a time frame set by the Commons party elites, who indicate the significance of their decisions in a weekly circulated document known as—"the Whip." Any item underlined three times is vital and needs the backbenchers' presence in a vote and total loyalty when speaking. A politically neutral speaker and deputy speakers preside over the House business and impose formal procedural rules.

In terms of general criticism of government policies, debates on issues or on the principles of legislation are, for the most part, ritualistic partisan affairs. Governments can rely on their Commons party machine to win through in the end. What has been evident for several years is a more relaxed attitude by the Labour and Conservative whip to backbench rebellion. However, this might well have been the result of executive disdain for the role of Parliament rather than any benevolence on behalf of the Blair government. There were some signs that the Brown government wishes to reverse this perception, especially in the light of the low public esteem in which the Commons is held currently (see textbox 4.4).

There remain, however, other opportunities for scrutiny. Questions to Ministers, both oral and written, provide an opportunity for the opposition and backbench MPs to attempt to open a secretive bureaucracy and to embarrass ministers in public. Oral questions to ministers take place for an hour, Monday to Thursday, with the minister generally able to answer critics, given the thorough briefing provided by their civil servants. The more difficult questions may be lost as time runs out, resulting in the answers emerging as written statements. "Question Time," suggest two eminent commentators, has become "an opportunity to tell the story the way ministers see it" (Rogers and Walters 2006: 328). Prime minister's Question Time, every Wednesday for half an hour, is essentially a mini party political broadcast on behalf of the leaders of the two major parties—a debate between gladiators and an opportunity for both to show their mettle to backbench MPs and, if newsworthy, to national and even international TV audiences the same evening.

Scrutiny by Committee

A more effective, if much less exciting, form of Commons scrutiny takes place within the various select committees that operate during a parliamentary session. During 2007 there were thirty select committees, of which nineteen were designated departmental committees, paralleling the responsibility of Whitehall ministries. There were also seven joint select committees within the House of Lords, in such areas as human rights and climate change. The House of Lords had a total of twenty-six select committees. Membership of select committees mirrors the Commons party balance, but the chairs of select committees may be opposition backbench MPs. The committees are small, eleven or so members who have skills or show a particular interest in the committee subject area.

Each committee, with the notable exception of the Public Accounts Committee, has only a small permanent staff but can make use of tempo-

---

Textbox 4.4. Modernizing the Commons

Since 1997 a Select Committee of Modernization has produced a series of reports that have lead to piecemeal changes in Commons procedure. Leader of the House Robin Cook (2001–2003) pushed through some substantial changes, but the impetus for change was lost after his resignation in 2003 over the Iraq war. A further period of reform was promised by the Brown government. The impetus for change increased considerably with the 2009 expenses scandal. Particular reforms already implemented include:

- The programming of some legislation, that is, fixed time limits for legislative scrutiny agreed consensually;
- Some bills subject to "prelegislative scrutiny," that is, select committee scrutiny after second reading.
- Bills no longer need to be "lost" but may be carried on from one session to the next.
- Select Committee chairs are paid to do the job;
- Additional debating opportunities in nearby Westminster Hall, especially to debate Select Committee reports;
- Changes to timing of parliamentary day; Friday now mainly a "constituency day"; parliamentary timetable established early for the year to assist backbench diary making;
- PM's Question Time starts at 12:00 Wednesday; oral questions now need only three days' notice:
- Time-limited backbench speeches regularly applied.
- Pre–queen's speech consultative process on legislative program.

  Further reforms may include:

- Annual parliamentary debates on major departments' plans;
- Increased parliamentary scrutiny of public appointments;
- More transparency within the intelligence and security services;
- Simplification of financial committee information;
- Introduction of process for citizens' e-petitions;
- Major reform of MPs' allowance/expenses procedures.

---

rary researchers and experts to investigate particular matters (see the book's website). The Public Administration Committee also enjoys support in one aspect of its role as the committee to which the parliamentary commissioner for administration (the ombudsman) reports. With the assistance of 230 staff, the ombudsman examines and reports on maladministration in central government departments. The chairs of select committees meet in a Liaison Committee that, since 2002, has received a biannual visit from the prime minister to discuss both domestic and foreign affairs. The presence of Tony

Blair at these meetings was, in part, a counter to the many who criticized his interest and attendance in the Commons as minimal throughout the ten years of his premiership.

Despite the horseshoe arrangement of the chairs in committee rooms, partisanship filters through when reports are presented. This may be in the shape of a majority/minority report, but more often is implicit in the production of an agreed position that tends toward a rather bland analysis. This, of course, varies with the quality of the membership and the subject under consideration. There can be no effective comparison between a British Commons committee and a congressional committee, whose role is to contribute to the separation of institutional powers by which the presidency is checked in the use of executive authority. But this is not to say that select committees do not, on occasions, collect government scalps. As an example, the relatively young Select Committee on Constitutional Affairs (set up in 2003) criticized and then watched the resignation of a Family Courts Advisory Board, wrung a formal apology from the lord chancellor over the treatment of a committee witness, and produced a report on the Constitutional Reform Bill that contributed to the government changing its decision to abolish the post of lord chancellor (Rogers and Walters 2006: 375–76). Indeed, their very existence gives them deterrent potential "throughout the corridors of power" (Norton 2005: 136). The Modernization Committee produced useful, if less than radical, proposals for Commons reform. The proposals that were accepted helped strengthen backbench opportunity to "connect" with the public and constituents and have also improved the efficiency of the legislative process. But there was little in them that provided opportunities for more effective scrutiny of government business (Cowley 2006).

As suggested earlier, Gordon Brown, when taking over from Tony Blair in June 2007, offered a series of reforms that gave opportunities for a broader Commons scrutiny of government policy creation. This, together with offering executive accountability to Parliament for several areas previously excluded as royal prerogatives, seemed to indicate a greater sensitivity to Parliament than had been evident during the Blair years (CM7170 2007). However, the fallout from the 2009 MPs' expenses scandal and a wholesale reconsideration of legislative-executive arrangements—a work, it seems, in progress—has confounded the process (see the book's website).

The House of Lords

We opened the discussion of Parliament by noting the weight of history in shaping its contemporary status. There remains no similar institution in Europe that, until very recently, offered an opportunity for its aristocracy to enjoy a privileged position within an otherwise modern political process. Similar European institutions for noble representation were swept away by revolution, foreign invasion, or radical reform. Britain's claim to neither invasion nor sudden social shock goes part of the way to explain this political anomaly. The historian Norman Davies adds to this explanation of the preservation of the British aristocracy, and with it "The Lords." He suggests that the "tenacity of the British aristocracy . . . at the top of a class-based political system had something to do on the one hand with its unparalleled penetration of all institutions, including commercial firms and businesses, and on the other hand with its masterly command of social emulation . . . [they] . . . stayed on top because so many other groups loved to co-opt or to ape them" (Davies 1999: 623). There remained into the twenty-first century no shortage of candidates wishing to take up the privilege of joining the House, albeit only now within their tenure as life peers (see chapter 6).

As textbox 4.5 shows, reform of the Lords has been slow and piecemeal. By 1911 the ability of the Lords to stop a democratically elected government getting on with its business was constitutionally precluded by the Parliament Act. Delaying powers were restricted further in 1949 to only one parliamentary session, and the hereditary membership of the House was pierced by the Life Peerage Act (1958). Though emasculated, the Lords survived by making itself a useful part of government business—trading on the qualities of "independence, expertise, and experience." It claimed to do what the Commons could not: spend more time improving legislation; scrutinizing governments' delegated powers; and, in a less partisan manner, holding a government to account. It also provided a useful extra source of ministerial recruitment: Gordon Brown made used of the Lords as a fast track for the return to government of the ex-minister and European commissioner Peter Mandelson in 2008. The Lords have continued to provide moral and constitutional guidance through its life peers, bishops, and judges (House of Lords 2007). In effect it can provide a gentle, civilized, historically validated check on the potential of five years of party dictatorship in the Commons.

Successive Labour governments—in the 1940s, 1960s, and 1970s, only tinkered with this anachronism, either from fear of the consequences of challenging a historic pillar of constitutional monarchy, or because they had better things to do with their time. From 1997, however, New Labour seemed prepared to commence a radical attack on the class-based nature of Britain's second chamber. The 1999 reform, however, resulted in unintended consequences for the government. It increased the patronage of the prime minister who, between 1999 and 2000, appointed over 250 life peers to replace the hereditaries. In doing so, the previous inbuilt Conservative majority was replaced by a rough balance whereby Labour, Conservative, and nonaligned peers each hold just over 200 seats, with Liberal Democrats around eighty. However, whereas hereditary peers had previously attempted

Textbox 4.5. The Slow Death of a Hereditary Assembly

1867	Reform Bill—elected Commons, male suffrage
1893	Lords reject Irish Home Rule: call for its abolition
1909	Lords reject "Peoples" budget
1911	Parliament Act. Limits Lords powers over money bills and only two-year delay on Commons legislation.
1949	Only one-year delay of Commons legislation allowed.
1958	Life Peerage Act—life peers could be appointed
1963	Peerage Act (renunciation of peerage permitted)
1999	House of Lords Act limits hereditary peers to ninety-two
2005	Constitutional Reform Act—removes Law Lords to a Constitutional Court (by 2010)
2007	Commons vote for 80–100 percent elected upper house
	Lords vote against a wholly elected upper house
	Green Paper promises substantially or wholly elected second chamber and review of its powers (CM7170)

Political Complexion of the House of Lords

	1999	2007
Conservative	473	208
Labour	168	212
Liberal Democrat	67	78
Cross Bench (neutral)	310	201
Law Lords	12	26
Bishops	26	26

Average daily attendance has risen since 1999 to around 350, compared with 300 in 1980s, and rose to over 400 by 2006. Only 131 are female. Unless government ministers or Law Lords, they do not draw salaries but may claim £287 in daily allowances. Average age is sixty-eight. Between 1975 and 1979 the then Labour government was defeated in the Lords on average sixty times per annum. Between 1979 and 1997, Conservative governments were defeated on average thirteen times annually. Between 1997 and 2006 the Labour government was on average defeated forty-five times per annum.

to avoid confrontation with the elected government, the mainly appointed assembly has taken a more positive perspective on its activities. Thus between 1997 and 2001, their Lordships defeated government legislation on 128 occasions; between 2001 and 2006 the government lost in the Lords 302 times. As one commentator put it, "If the government hoped it had created a poodle of an Upper Chamber, then it was very much mistaken" (Cowley 2006: 52). The Lords held up legislation in such areas as terrorism prevention, hospital reform, and its own reform.

It is ironic that the reforms breathed new life into the second chamber with such effect that it has proved a substantial force in holding the government to account. A further irony is that, in the last year of his administration, Prime Minister Blair and several colleagues within his office were interviewed by the police in connection with an investigation into an alleged breach of a 1925 Act forbidding the purchase of peerages by making "contributions" to party funds (cash for honors). The act had been a response to a notorious episode of honors buying after World War I during the Lloyd George administration. It is against this background that the Commons finally voted for a reform of the Lords that would entail the democratic election of at least 80 percent of the upper house (February 2007), having failed to agree on a similar reform three years earlier. Their Lordships promptly rejected the reform despite a generous transition period that would allow existing life peers and the ninety-two remaining hereditary peers to retire, resign, or die out.

We have already discussed the significant constitutional change to the Lords involving the removal of their judicial role and its replacement by a Constitutional Court (2009). This left a reformed but still unelected House with the functions of scrutiny; revision; and, where considered necessary, delay of an elected government's program. The increasingly active role played by the Lords has, however, led to a growing weight of party opinion that a fully elected upper house with Commons party disciplinary practice might be easier to control. Thus, even the Conservative Party has proposed a fully elected upper house, and also that it be renamed the "Senate." In July 2007 the Brown government proposed a wholly or mainly elected chamber as well as examination of the appropriateness of second-chamber functions (CM7170 2007).

Much of the historic debate surrounding Lords reform has concentrated on its lack of democratic legitimacy, and thus its composition, with little discussion of what a potentially popularly elected upper chamber might do in a reconstructed political system. Would such an institution accept the politically inferior position to the Commons to which its predecessor was resigned? If elected on a regional list system, as some have suggested, would its constituencies present an added or competitive voice to a nationally elected Commons? Would its current claim to constitutional functionality—as an expert and independent voice within the policy process be lost in a newfound political legitimacy? How would the concept of hereditary monarchy be affected by the removal of a title-based assembly; and, within the broader picture of contemporary British politics, what relationship is there between Lords and Commons reform and the realities of devolved governments and Britain's position within the EU? It is to consideration of these interrelationships between what otherwise might be seen as competing areas of representation that we now turn.

THE EU: DROWNING OR POOLING SOVEREIGNTY?

"Parliament remains a marginal actor in the policy process" (Cowley 2006: 54–55). Despite attempts to "roll back" the state, the imperatives of economic and social intervention, the development of the party machine, and an electorate whose vision of government is shaped by a media personification of political leadership all contributed to the marginalization of the legislature, not just in Britain but throughout Europe. There may be dispute about which legislature is weakest, but to generalize, most governments with a favorable political breeze do not have to work very hard to gain support of an assembly that has a favorable government majority. This is not to say that, where MPs perceive that their leadership is losing the support of the electorate, their loyalties are not challenged. However, their role as deliberators, scrutinizers, and legitimizers has been made more complex by their position in European multilevel governance. Since 1973, when Britain joined the EU, and since 1999 when devolution was set in place, where do parliamentarians sit within this complex interinstitutional political process?

Coordinating Legislative Decentralization

We pointed out in the previous chapter the representational problem that the West Lothian question presents: that Scottish (and Welsh and Northern Irish) MPs can vote on issues that pertain to English interests—but devolved powers have taken many policy arenas away from MPs and into regional parliaments, resulting in an asymmetric pattern of representational responsibilities. Parliament's ability to scrutinize Celtic affairs has been reduced still further by the downgrading of cabinet ministers and departments responsible for the national regions. However, this decentralization of legislative responsibilities is complicated by the responsibilities that the British government still has in applying EU directives and regulations across Britain in a way acceptable to Brussels. National coordination on behalf of the devolved authorities therefore seems inevitable (Judge 2005: 219). Hence many bills requiring devolved processing (almost half between 1999 and 2003) start in the British Parliament so as to ensure compliance with EU obligations (Judge 2005: 185–86).

Though disappointing to Celtic-nationalist or devolutionist opinion, this should not be surprising: 50 percent of important legislation now emanates from the EU and, since the British government is responsible for its enactment, this centralized role of processing EU legislation is impossible to avoid. Parliament remains, therefore, the key domestic legitimator within this multilevel process. But is it up to the task of representing, deliberating, and scrutinizing in this complex process? Here we can observe the "double-democratic deficit" that EU political systems share. This refers, first, to the evident problem of democratic accountability that exists between EU institutions: the lack of accountability of the European Commission to the European Parliament, or the opaque decision-making process in the Council of Ministers. The second element of this deficit is the inability of many national parliaments to effectively scrutinize the activities of their respective ministers as they deal with EU business.

The British/EU Legislative Nexus

The parliamentary committee processes designed to keep check of the British/EU nexus are outlined in the book's website. Both Commons and Lords are beset by well over 1,000 EU documents a year. These include consultation papers, proposals for legislation, common or joint positions, decisions, directives, and regulations—in effect, documents ranging from international agreements on climate change to the definition of what is a chocolate bar. Commission consultation papers might involve comments on potential global strategies to combat terrorism or regulations on the hours truck drivers may work in a twenty-four-hour period and the breaks they must take. In each case, Parliament is invited to acknowledge, comment, recommend, broadcast, or just accept EU policy and legislation. In doing so, whether it comments critically on a proposal or just acknowledges receipt of an EU regulation, it legitimates the action of the British government within the EU, thus providing an important public scrutiny role in EU matters.

The two EU select committees in the Commons and Lords complement each other. The European Scrutiny Committee in the Commons reports on around a third of the roughly 1,000 documents it receives and, where necessary, will recommend a debate on the issues that will take place in one of three European Standing Committees or, less likely, on the floor of the House. For each EU document there will be an explanatory memorandum from the Whitehall department concerned that will be accepted in most cases as a critical review of the impact of the document on British policy and/or law. The Lords European Union Committee is an altogether different scrutinizer in that its reports are much more detailed, often across broader areas of policy, and they amount to only around twenty-five a year. It is composed of several policy-specific subcommittees that involve more than seventy members in their work. Government ministers and civil servants, especially from the Foreign and Commonwealth Office (FCO), as well as ambassadors from the EU state holding the presidency, may be interviewed (Rogers and Walters 2006: 399).

While scrutiny takes place in the Lords and Commons, a minister cannot take part in a Council of Ministers agreement to a proposal. She/he must wait until the committee has reported and/or the matter has been decided in debate. Potentially, therefore, this "scrutiny reserve" can delay Council decision making and, at its most effective, can alter the outcome of a proposal by shifting the position of a minister in Council deliberations. However, ministers can, and generally do, opt to merely "take note" of parliamentary opinion unless there is considerable political reason why they should accept advice.

The scrutiny of EU business by the British Parliament has encouraged civil servants to take seriously the need to keep Parliament informed about government/EU activities. Specialist select committees allow expert scrutiny and "offer much more of a challenge to the executive than the much larger ad hoc standing committees" (Bale 2005: 98). However, a number of problems remain, some of which are associated with British parliamentary practice and others that are part of the second aspect of the democratic deficit—that of the EU institutional process itself.

As with other select committees, the support necessary to fulfill a comprehensive scrutiny of policy is inadequate. Both Commons and Lords must prioritize the areas they investigate. In the case of the European Scrutiny Committee, there exists a lack of interest in its work, manifested by the low attendance at its meetings. Moreover, when debates on EU issues are held, as one House of Commons official put it, "they become generalized and end up sounding much the same" (House of Commons 2005: 19). Much like the British public, many MPs allow "raw opinion" to validate what happens in the EU rather than informed judgment. This was perhaps one argument against reinstating a specific European question time in the Commons, a practice that had existed until 1985 (House of Commons 2005).

But the issue of effective scrutiny of EU matters by Parliament has wide implications for the representation of citizens' affairs and is not effectively carried out either by the Commons or the EP with its own scrutiny agenda. Member-state governments have shown only limited sympathy with proposals to extend to their assemblies rights of scrutiny and delay beyond those established in the Treaty of Amsterdam. Therefore, since Parliament and the EP present parallel processes of scrutiny for the British/EU citizen, the question of bilateral cooperation between these legislatures arises. This is extremely limited. The National Parliament Office, established in 1999, reports to the European Scrutiny Committee and acts as its "eyes and ears" in Brussels. An EU-wide Conference of European Affairs Committees provides an opportunity to meet colleagues in similar roles and, on occasion, there are bilateral meetings with European scrutiny MPs from other national parliaments (Hansard Society 2006).

A recommendation from the Commons Modernization Committee to create a Joint Parliamentary European Committee as a link between Brussels institutions has to date not been implemented. A similar committee of thirty-three Bundestag members and eleven MEPs operates in Germany. In evidence to the Modernization Committee, the Confederation of British Industry recommended greater formal connectivity between Parliament and the EU, but some parliamentarians resist too close a connection because they "fear that formal contact with their counterparts in Brussels (and Strasbourg) would endanger the clear separation of their respective institutions" (Hansard Society 2006: 6). There are other MPs who see the role of Parliament with the EU as technical, given the supranational and intergovernmental processes that lead to "imposed" rule making. Others take no interest, and this evident reluctance to engage with the process "amounts to a failure of political will" (Hansard Society 2006: 13). But this, in turn, is only a reflection of more fundamental issues associated with party attitudes and policy toward the EU.

CONCLUSION

Notwithstanding parliamentarians' spectacular "own goal" regarding their allowance payments, it was the specific intention of the Brown government to "strengthen Parliament and renew its accountability," for it is "a major symbol of what it means to be British" (CM7170 2007: 40). This will also no doubt be the aim of an incoming 2010 administration (see textbox 4.6). However, a cleaner trustworthy and effective Parliament begs the question of the role of national parliaments in the EU political process. That, in turn, involves issues of principle (a federal Europe?); a democratic deficit (how or whether to resolve it); and, inevitably, the political hot potato of EU Treaty (or constitutional) reform. Whether from a Eurosceptic or Europhile perspective, it might be concluded that "only if *national* Parliaments are *seen* to have genuine influence over the decision-making process in Europe will their members, and the wider electorate, take a greater interest in such matters" (Hansard Society 2006: 14). This is explored in the next chapter.

FURTHER READING

For a comprehensive and accessible look at Parliament, *How Parliament Works* by Robert Rogers and Rhodri Walters (2006) is excellent. A broader examination of the role of Parliament is taken by Philip Norton

---

Textbox 4.6. A Climate for a Parliamentary Revolution?

The spring/summer 2009 allowances scandal led to a series of political commitments to parliamentary reform from each of the three main parties. David Cameron demanded a "new politics" to achieve "a massive sweeping radical re-distribution of power. From the state to citizens; from government to Parliament; from Whitehall to communities; from EU to Britain; from judges to the people from bureaucracy to democracy." To achieve this he proposed: fixed-term parliaments; "free" votes for MPs in legislative committees; MPs to control the legislative timetable and the selection of committee chairs; further limits on the PM's prerogative powers; publishing the expenses of all high-paid public servants; giving local government a general competence to make local decisions and to raise local funds. He recommitted a Conservative government to a referendum on the EU Lisbon Treaty.

The prime minister committed the government to a constitutional renewal bill and all party debate on major parliamentary reform. A cabinet colleague, Alan Johnson, raised the issue of a change in the electoral system to some form of proportional representation—an issue endorsed by the Liberal Democratic leader, Nick Clegg. The latter also demanded the end of the House of Lords and a thorough reform of party funding. As one political commentator put it "The MPs expenses saga has raised much bigger questions than whether an elected representative has the right to claim for a massage chair or a duck house."

Source: Independent, Wednesday, 27 May 2009.

---

in *Parliament in British Politics* (2005). Philip Cowley examines Parliament and Labour administrations in Dunleavy et al. (2006) and also in Anthony Seldon's (ed.) *Blair's Britain* (2007). Access to research papers as well as general information may be obtained directly from House of Commons and House of Lords websites as well as the Hansard Society, who published Alex Brazier's edited volume, *Parliament, Politics and Law Making* (2004). The Hansard Society has provided a critique of the role of Parliament in examining EU legislation (2006), as do Philip Giddings and Gavin Drewry, *Britain in the European Union* (2004), and Digby Jones in a critical Foreign Policy Centre Paper (2005).

5

Beyond Parliament
Multilevel Representation

The year 2000 ushered in a new layer of institutional representation for British citizens, in the shape of Scottish and Welsh devolution together with the hope of a renewed Northern Ireland Assembly. This means that for voters in these areas, and the London region, there are distinct levels of representation and arenas of legislative capacity within which they are entitled to engage. What is unusual in such a situation is that Britons also have vital interests, alongside their fellow EU citizens, that need representing at supranational as well as national and regional local levels; we shall return to the significance of this in the concluding part of this chapter. We commence with a look at the oldest and closest form of British representation—local government.

LOCAL GOVERNMENT: FROM A CONSTITUTIONAL BALANCE TO ADMINISTRATIVE NECESSITY

Despite its long history, local government throughout Britain does not enjoy the constitutional status afforded to its counterparts in the federated systems of the United States and Germany or its codified recognition in France or Italy. Though formed by royal charters and acts of Parliament and sometimes originating from Anglo-Saxon and Norman times, local government has evolved as politically and constitutionally inferior in status to central government. A simple example: the towns of Chatham near London, with its Royal Charter of 1525, and Chatham on Cape Cod, in the United States, incorporated in 1712 within the Royal Charter establishing the colony of Massachusetts, originate from similar monarchical favor. Chatham, Massachusetts, remains today a small but autonomous local government; local government in Massachusetts enjoys the protection of a state constitution and an obvious status within US democracy. No such status exists for British local government. Chatham, Kent, has been swallowed up in the conurbation of Medway, whose boundaries have changed on three occasions since 1974. The latest structural reform in 2009 replaced forty-four districts and county local governments with nine "super" authorities. The ancient county of Cheshire disappeared overnight to be divided into East and West Cheshire unitary authorities.

The Character of Local Government

Until the end of the nineteenth century, local government administration provided an extra-parliamentary platform for men of property, leisure, and wealth to sustain social as well as political control. "It was the interface between social structure and political institutions in Britain" (Seidentop 2000: 71). Intertwined parliamentary and local elites provided protection for local autonomy and this helped resist a growing encroachment of central executive power. But this constitutional balance "was an informal aspect of the constitution, relying on deference and a social hierarchy to limit the growth of state power" (Seidentop 2000: 71). Indeed a commentator at the time saw a danger in emerging local democratic practices as "keeping up a permanent fever of contention" in quiet country parishes that had "long lived in perfect amity" (Lecky 1908: 239).

Today there are 433 principal local authorities and approximately 9,000 community-level councils. British citizens elect approximately 22,000 councillors to their local authorities, of whom the majority are members of a political party. After the English elections of May 2007, 5,315 were Conservative; 1,877 Labour; and 2,171 Liberal councillors. All other parties and groups elected 1,122 councillors. In effect, and especially since structural reform in 1974, local government in Britain has become party politicized, though there has been a rise in the number of representatives who classify themselves as "independents." However, outside of those local elections that have been combined with general elections, turnout has been notoriously low, on average around 40 percent. Northern Ireland's sectarianism has contributed to a higher vote (55%) compared with England's 33 percent (1995–2006). While turnout in lower-order elections throughout the EU is much lower than in national elections, Britain has consistently been at the bottom of any ranking prior to the 2004 EU expansion. Thus France (65%), Germany (58%), Denmark (69%), and Spain (67%) all provide higher average local-election turnouts. It must be pointed out that there is little evidence that much interest has *ever* been taken in local politics by the average British voter during the twentieth century, for even when councils ran everything from education and trains to gas and water supply, "British voters still remained shy of local voting" (Wilson and Game 2006: 235).

For those anticipating a "mirror" representation of local communities, the profile of local councillors in Britain makes uncomfortable reading. In 2008, in England, 68 percent of councillors were male and the average age was 59; 40 percent were retired. But while fewer than 4 percent came from ethnic minority backgrounds, overall, much higher minority representation is recorded in some urban councils. Councillors on average represented around 3,000 electors, which is higher than any ratio among the fifteen countries using the euro; Italy and France with similar populations have ratios of 1:597 and 1:118 respectively (Wilson and Game 2006; Local Government Association 2009).

This raises issues regarding the democratic legitimacy of local government that have been compounded by the powerful influence that central government has demonstrated in the past sixty years. Since 1945 especially, local government has been co-opted into the vital central tasks of welfare provision and the creation and maintenance of public infrastructure. Accordingly, its importance to central government and citizen alike has increased massively; however, any nineteenth-century semblance of local autonomy has declined as the functional demands made upon it have altered its raison d'être within a complex system of multilevel governance. Since 1972, successive governments have changed the structure and functions of local government in an attempt to achieve service efficiency for a dynamic economy and demography. Consequently, local discretion has been funnelled into a set of ever-narrowing administrative controls and financial limits.

Provincial metropolitan government has come (1972) and gone (1986). Greater London government has come (1963) gone (1986) and come again (2000) (see the book's website). Wales, Scotland, and Northern Ireland, with devolved national governments, have single-tier local councils with some community-level councillor meetings. England has a mixture of first- and second-tier and unitary authorities, plus parish/community-level councils. The structure is further complicated by the numbers of joint authorities, action zones, public/private partnerships, police authorities, and housing associations that now make up a complex system of local governance.

A Creature of Statute

Functions as well as structures have also come and gone, for, unlike their French, US, or Swiss counterparts, there is no power of general competence to take on any activities that they wish other than those expressly forbidden. In Britain the reverse pertains—local councils can only do what Parliament gives them power to do. If they go beyond their powers they will act *ultra vires* (outside of their powers) and are legally culpable. They are, in effect, "creatures of statute." As such, these creatures shouldered the burden of educating and housing their citizens during the postwar period, only to have this role gradually eroded by successive Conservative and Labour governments. Since the 1980s their role in the provision of police, transport, and emergency services has been similarly challenged through a succession of structural reforms and functional initiatives involving the use of joint authorities, agencies, public/private initiatives, and the voluntary sector. We may thus legitimately distinguish between local *government* and local *governance* in Britain, which now consists of a collection of overlapping civil, official, and private organizations all providing services for local communities.

One final problem for local government autonomy throughout Britain is its lack of financial independence. Local property tax, currently called the Council Tax, varied between 13 percent and 22 percent of English local government funding between 1976 and 2006. Though there is a business property tax, it is set and redistributed by central government. Central government grants, which are highly regulated, form the major source of local finance: specific and general government grants contribute to around 60 percent of local government expenditure. In no other EU country is the financial discretion of local government so restricted. Britain, it can be argued, lacks the financial means necessary to support "a robust local democracy" (Wilson and Game 2006: 222).

Europeanizing and Modernizing Local Governance

As in all EU member states, British local government has a considerable role to play in implementing EU policies, with many local areas receiving significant funding for EU-approved projects. In some cases, such as the implementation of environmental regulations, the impact of the EU has been coercive; in others, such as some local authorities' pursuit of EU Structural Funding by direct Brussels lobbying, the EU has proved an ally in their battles for funding and independence (Marshall 2006: 103). This "local Europeanization" adds a further dimension to the changes taking place in British local government and has contributed to tensions between center and periphery. In 1997 the Labour government signed a European Charter for local self-government, indicating its commitment to local autonomy and effective local service provision. The EU may well prove a valuable external source in maintaining British local autonomy that is ill supported by conventional British constitutional practice. The EU also provides a significant coordinative pressure on service delivery—a point that we return to later.

Labour's reforming zeal has been directed toward the internal workings of local government and its decision-making processes. By the Local

Government Act (2000) the long-established executive committee structure has been replaced by one of three executive options: a directly elected mayoral system most famously adopted for the Greater London area; a mayor and council manager; or an indirectly elected council leader and cabinet system (a local "prime ministerial" executive). This, together with the mantra of achieving "best value" for service provision, which includes the publication of performance tables, has increased pressure on politicians and local officials to respond to government demands and initiatives and to consult with "social partners" to achieve "better performance" (DTLR 2001). Gordon Brown's government underscored this theme as part of a constitutional reform package in 2007 that aimed to empower local citizens by encouraging local initiatives through petitions and community management of local services (CM7170 2007). It could be, however, that the government's contributions to changing local democracy may fail from the unintended consequences of its policy of devolution, to which we now turn.

DEVOLUTION: LETTING THE TIGERS LOOSE?

The term *Celtic Tiger* has been applied to Ireland's remarkable economic renaissance during the 1990s. For Celtic regions still within the British state, Ireland's example has become part of a debate reinforced by the arrival of several small states as full members of the EU: that is, given the relatively protected status of small states within the EU, are there now opportunities for Scotland, Wales, and Northern Ireland to exist as independent entities within a European rather than British Union?

As table 5.1 illustrates, there are several small states within EU27 of comparable size and economic strength to Britain's Celtic nations. In explaining devolution, however, domestic factors remain paramount, with several of these factors specific to each of the countries concerned.

Scotland: Back to the Future?

Until 1707 Scotland had its own Parliament and after the Act of Union still retained its own legal system, its own established church, and separate educational traditions. Scots' representation at the national level was within a House of Commons that slightly overpresented the Scottish voter; the emergence of a Scottish Office in Edinburgh allowed for the administrative deconcentration of Scottish home affairs from Whitehall. A Grand Committee composed of Scottish MPs oversaw legislation as it affected Scotland, and a secretary of state for Scotland sat in the cabinet. Prior to 1997, therefore, Scotland's affairs were already operating through

Table 5.1.   EU Small States and British Nations: A Comparison (2007)

	Population (Millions)	Area (000km²)	GDP-ppp ($ billions)	GDP Per capita -ppp	EU Status
Cyprus	.79	.92	36.5	46,900	Member State
Estonia	1.30	45.2	29.4	21,100	Member State
Denmark	5.50	43.1	208.4	37,400	Member State
Ireland	4.16	70.2	186.2	43,000	Member State
Latvia	2.24	64.6	89.8	17,400	Member State
Lithuania	3.56	65.2	59.6	17,700	Member State
Luxembourg	.36	.36	38.6	80,500	Member State
Malta	.40	.31	21.9	53,400	Member State
England	51.20	130.40	2047.0	40,790	No Status*
N. Ireland	1.70	14.15	56.0	31,671	Region (NUTS 1)
Scotland	5.10	78.77	193.0	37,511	4 Regions (NUTS 1)
Wales	2.90	20.78	87.0	29,183	2 Regions (NUTS 1)
Britain (UK)	61.90	224.9	2383.0	39,086	Member State 9 Regions (NUTS 1)
EU27	497.20	4,454.3	14712.2	28,213	

Sources: CIA (2008); ONS (2008a).
* England has no official EU status but is divided into nine statistical (NUTS 1) regions (Nomenclature of Territorial Units for Statistics).

a quasi-independent administrative, legal, and political process. This, together with a partly differentiated media industry, allowed a "Scottish political system" to be identified (Kellas 1989).

Scotland's share in the success of the British Empire, and solidarity with England in defense of the Islands during two twentieth-century world wars, masked murmurings about further independence from the union, but after some twenty-five years of post–World War II economic decline, Scottish national identity became a matter for public debate following the discovery and exploitation of North Sea oil and gas reserves. "Scottish oil" and its benefits became a rallying call for the Scottish National Party (SNP), which enjoyed sufficient electoral success in the 1970s to demand devolved powers. A beleaguered Labour government passed bills to establish both Scottish and Welsh assemblies, but in referenda (1979) the Welsh and Scottish electorate failed to support the devolution agenda convincingly. Though Scottish devolution was won in the referendum (52%–48%) on a turnout of 64 percent, failure to reach a required 40 percent of the *total* electorate precluded the plan's implementation.

The advent of Thatcherism and seventeen years of Conservative government had two effects: neoliberal policies accentuated Scotland's economic woes, leading to the virtual extinction of the Scottish Conservative

Party and the revival of, primarily Labour, but also Liberal Democrat and Scottish Nationalist representation. Opposition to "London" reinvigorated the debate regarding Scottish self-government, this time with an attentive Scottish Labour majority and a more receptive national Labour opposition, anxious to sustain its political resurgence in the Celtic peripheries. A similar political scenario could be observed in Wales.

The establishment of a Scottish Constitutional Convention in 1989, with both Labour and Liberal Democrat attendance, was to have considerable influence on the devolution debate within the resurgent New Labour elite of the 1990s. What the Convention recommended was a halfway house between a centralized state and true independence. Devolution of power to a revived Scottish Parliament elected through a form of proportional representation—the Additional Member System (AMS)—was considered to be sufficiently radical to gain support from Scottish voters who saw London government as anathema and sufficiently acceptable to more unionist opinion. Both the Conservatives and SNP initially opposed this hybrid solution, but subsequently accepted and actively involved their party machines in what amounted to a Scottish national parliamentary system.

In its White Paper and resulting Scotland Act (1998) the Labour government utilized many of the recommendations of the Constitutional Convention, utilizing political perspectives that reflected the broad range of opinion included by the Convention in a "language of Hope" (quoted in Judge 2005: 182). The new Scottish system was based on the guiding principles of power sharing, evident public accountability, easy access, broad participation, and equal opportunity. These principles are evident in several processes of the new Scottish Parliament. (A table that compares the political features of the Scottish and other devolved governments may be found on the book's website).

Election to Scotland's 129-member Parliament is through the AMS, where 73 MSPs are elected through the traditional FPTP (Westminster) process and 56 MSPs via PR party-list system from eight Scottish regional constituencies. In agreeing to this system, the Labour government recognized that power sharing between at least two Scottish political parties would be inevitable; this would, in turn, lead to a reduction in adversarial party politics, and thus a distinct break with the legacy of an English tradition of winner-take-all politics. The reestablished Scottish Parliament elects an executive that can bring legislation before its SMPs in devolved matters. Reserved matters, however, remain the responsibility of the Westminster/Whitehall nexus, and these are extensive. Westminster also exerts its constitutional superiority through Section 28 of the Scotland Act, which states an ultimate power of the British Parliament "to make laws for Scotland." As against this constitutional stick, the Scottish executive/Parliament has an impressive list of domestic policy arenas within which to produce primary legislation, has limited tax-raising powers of plus or minus three pence in the pound on income tax, and a de facto legitimacy based on a regional/national constituency that is more equitably represented through PR and power sharing. A referendum in 2000 had approved devolution by 74 percent on a turnout of 64 percent.

Though not the first example of a devolved government in Britain (see below), a Scottish Parliament has had considerable impact on representation and legislative processes in Britain, directly for the Scottish voter and indirectly on the British "union." The use of an AMS electoral system has created a distinctive scenario in post-devolution Scotland. The first two elections in 1999 and 2003 resulted in Labour as the largest party entering into a coalition with the Liberal Democrats, together with a revival of Conservative fortunes. The SNP enjoyed second-party status taking one in five votes. Coalition politics in this period reinforced the objectives of the Scottish Convention to achieve a new and distinctive style of politics. Scottish parliamentary procedures and the necessity to compromise within the Scottish executive coalition in part confirm this difference (Judge 2005). There was some evident friction in Labour Party policy also between Edinburgh and London, particularly in regard to student higher education tuition fees (abolished), teachers pay (higher), and personal care for the elderly (free).

Of significance for the 2007 elections, and at the behest of the Liberal Democrat partners, the Scottish executive extended proportional representation to Scottish local government when a single Transferable Vote System was used for the first time. The results of the 2007 elections proved a significant test for a system designed to preserve rather than destroy the Union. The SNP, though in a minority, replaced Labour as the largest party and formed a minority government. Many previously Labour local councils also lost out to an SNP and Liberal Democrat resurgence. In effect, Scotland has emerged as a clearly different political entity and one that is unlikely to return willingly to the secondary status that it occupied during the twentieth century.

Despite this evidence of a working devolution of power, the practicalities of policy coordination, especially in ensuring that reform schemes—for instance in social security or health care—and EU obligations are uniformly applied, has led to a continuation of Westminster/Whitehall involvement not envisaged by the Scottish founding fathers (Judge 2005: 185 and chapter 4).

WELSH DEVOLUTION—OR BIG LOCAL GOVERNMENT?

The Welsh Assembly, unlike the Scottish Parliament, has neither power to pass its own (primary) legislation, nor any taxation powers. It has executive authority but only within the limits of primary legislation set by the Westminster Parliament; that is "transferred functions" from "a patchwork of over 400 laws from present and past statutes" (Jeffrey 2007: 142). This lack of legal independence is one factor in the evident enthusiasm of the mainly Labour-dominated Assembly to distinguish itself from Westminster. Another factor, at least until the elections of 2007, was a dominant Welsh Labour Party whose socialist traditions, personified in the leadership of Rhodri Morgan, attempted to place "clear red waters" between the Assembly's policies and Westminster's New Labour "revisionism." These factors, together with the pressure on the Assembly to achieve legitimacy, have produced some policies that can be seen as distinctly Welsh in their application and origin. Thus, health prescription charges have been abolished, and the Welsh NHS has been reorganized to match local authority boundaries. A children's commissioner and a Homeless Commission have been established, rankings of schools were abolished, and free milk for school children under seven (a minor welfare-state icon of the pre-Thatcher days) was reestablished. The 2007 Assembly elections produced a weakened Labour representation, in coalition with Plaid Cymru (The Party of Wales), whose left-nationalist credentials make it a strange bedfellow for a supposedly social-market British political partner.

Currently, Wales represents a somewhat curious form of devolution. Even after the Wales Act (2006), when members of the Welsh cabinet gained a more distinctive status and further executive powers, the Assembly enjoys only a weakly defined devolved status. Plaid Cymru, as a nationalist party, has been concerned to call for cultural distinctiveness rather than the full-blown independence demanded by the SNP.

Political elites, and indeed the Welsh Assembly itself, have articulated demands for a constitutional status similar to Scotland, but there remains little evidence of public desire in Wales for parity with either Scotland or Northern Ireland. A commission set up by the Westminster government in 2004 recommended a Scottish model for Wales, in part to simplify the confusing result of a devolved system based only on secondary powers (Richards Commission 2004). Its conclusions were sidelined by the central government, encouraged by Welsh Labour MPs, who saw a danger to central government policies from the new Welsh Assembly. Further independence may rest on the direction of Scottish devolution in that, if it progresses, it provides a catch-up target for those who seek parity for Wales.

NORTHERN IRELAND—DEVOLUTION ON TRIAL

The extent to which devolved powers have been granted to the Celtic regions has been shaped by their antecedent relationships with Westminster—

a historic path of dependency is evident in each case. This is more than evident in Northern Ireland, where the past continued to fuel belligerence and turmoil to the very end of the twentieth century (see the book's website). Attempts to overcome historical divisions form a backdrop to the Good Friday Agreement (1998) and the subsequent attempts to build institutions and processes that lock together otherwise deadly protagonists. A potpourri of institutional devices has emerged, several of which are antithetical to the trustee model of representation and Westminster system. They are currently (2009) being applied in what may be a last chance to reach a political solution acceptable to this beleaguered society.

Toward a Constitutional Solution?

The concept of a "United Kingdom" may be immediately questioned when considering the situation of Northern Ireland. Since 1922, when thirty of Ireland's counties proclaimed an Irish Free State, the position of the remaining six Protestant majority counties and their continuing allegiance to the British Crown have proved bitterly contentious. Claims by Irish Republicans for a united Ireland have been pursued and resisted in the North by both political and violent methods. As many British, Irish, and other European citizens were killed in the period of "the Troubles," 1969–1996, as were killed in New York on September 11, 2001.

Under John Major and then Tony Blair, with the considerable support of Irish, US, and other politicians, a peace initiative was undertaken, culminating in the "Good Friday Agreement" of April 1998. The agreement was ratified by 70 percent of voters in Northern Ireland, but the effective working of it was not helped by periodic community violence or the principled stands taken by the Democratic Unionist Party (DUP) and Sinn Fein, the two largest parties in the Assembly. Despite two elections, 1998 and 2003, the political divisions that had haunted Anglo-Irish relations remained into the twenty-first century. The power-sharing executive functioned between 1999 and 2000, was suspended, and then reinstated, only to be suspended again from 2002 to 2006. The 2005 general election confirmed the dominance of the DUP and Sinn Fein, and shortly afterward the IRA announced a formal end to its military campaign.

In 2007 Sinn Fein stated its willingness to cooperate in the policing arrangements for the province. The Assembly was reconvened and new elections were called (March). An executive was constructed a few months later. The executive since then has struggled to overcome both internal policy divisions and external shocks, the latest being the murder of two British soldiers and a policeman by dissident terrorists (March 2009). Devolved responsibilities are similar to those of the Scottish executive, except for security issues, the courts, and legal and prison service. These may be devolved if the Assembly agrees to request the transfer.

The US government, especially during the Clinton administration, played an important role in facilitating the peace process. Also, unquestioning financial support for the Republican cause from Irish-Americans has dried up, especially after the violent lesson of 9/11 changed attitudes among some parts of the US public. A further international dimension concerns the extent to which European integration has began to erode cross-border divisions economically, socially, and politically. Both Ireland and Northern Ireland have benefited from (EU) structural and agricultural funding support, some of which was directed toward cross-border peace and cooperation. A de facto currency interchangeability between the pound (Northern Ireland) and Euro (Ireland) has emerged since 2001. This has helped a recession-hit Northern Ireland economy as the 2008 decline in the pound sterling has produced a welcome upsurge of Irish consumers in Northern Ireland's shopping malls. Supranational perspectives on Irish futures have helped to mitigate some of the historic parochialism of domestic politics that has led to so much unhappiness and division during most of the second half of the twentieth century.

The Good Friday Agreement (1998): A Constitutional First

Signed by eight of Northern Ireland's political parties, the Good Friday, more formally Belfast, Agreement, is a *consociational* arrangement (CM3883). That is, it seeks to provide formal processes through which divided communities can reach accommodation on the basis of political bargaining, and so reach mutual understanding. This is facilitated by the principles and supporting mechanisms of community power sharing; the application of proportionality in public-sector employment and resources; mutual cultural recognition; and, where appropriate, the use of the veto for minorities. As a prior condition to establishing consociational mechanisms, a set of interlocking international and intergovernmental agreements was outlined in order to produce an external framework that would help engender a sense of internal security for otherwise diametrically opposed (Irish) nationalist and (British) unionist views. These agreements were, in principle, *confederal* and involved concessions of sovereignty on the part of two EU states, Britain and Ireland. As such, the agreement was ratified by referenda in both Northern Ireland and the Irish Republic (May 1998).

The agreement therefore contains three interlocking forms of devolution: *Consociation* is evident in the establishment of a devolved NI Assembly/government and was facilitated by the use of PR in Assembly and local elections, and the composition of the Northern Ireland executive (cabinet) is proportional to party strengths. Qualified majority voting is to be applied on all key decisions including the election of first and deputy first minister (one each from nationalist and unionist communities), the budget and allocation of ministerial posts, and assembly scrutiny committees. First and deputy ministers have equal powers but do not appoint the other ten ministers, who make up the Executive Committee. They are appointed by their political parties in proportion to Assembly-member strength. This complex system worked imperfectly until 2002, when direct rule was reimposed. The 2007 elections led to a further attempt at shared government with the DUP leader, Ian Paisley, and Sinn Fein leader, Martin McGuinness, for many years deadly enemies, as first and deputy leaders respectively.

An *intergovernmental* mechanism for dialogue and cooperation also operates in the shape of a North-South Ministerial Council (NSMC). This follows, in part, the example of the EU Council of Ministers and allows Northern Irish and Irish ministers to reach mutually acceptable agreements on issues of cross-border interest, much of which is of EU origin. This has involved Irish and British constitutional adjustment. Finally, a *confederal* institution, the British-Irish Council, which includes representatives from Irish, British, Scottish, Welsh, Channel Isle, and Isle of Man executives, provides an east-west dialogue and a balance (so placating unionist opinion) to the north-south dialogue within the NSMC. The Council met even during the period of direct rule (Judge 2005).

This intergovernmental link is one of several that have emerged in British politics recently. The next section deals at length with a longer established intergovernmental link—between Britain and the EU—focusing on how British citizens are represented in the most complex element of its multilevel structure.

THE EU AND THE REPRESENTATION OF BRITAIN'S CITIZENS

It is worth again rehearsing why the British citizen needs representation within the EU. Foreign and Commonwealth Office figures give reason enough. The EU is Britain's biggest trading market at 51 percent. In 2004 British companies exported £111 billion worth of goods to other EU member states. It is estimated that over 3 million jobs in Britain are linked to the EU market, of which 2 million are in the manufacturing sector. Access to the EU Single Market has proved an important factor in encouraging inward investment from the United States, China, and Japan. The EU negotiates international trade deals on behalf of its members (including Britain), and EU-wide employee mobility and many employee rights are guaranteed through Single Market legislation, as are many consumer rights. For the British taxpayer, membership in the EU costs annually £175 per head of the British population, though this reduces, it is argued, to £50 per head once EU funding for projects and agricultural subsidies are taken into account (FCO 2007).

Swathes of domestic policy in such areas as the environment, public health and safety, equal opportunities, employment and competition law, agriculture and fisheries, and product design and safety are regulated by EU legislation. The security of member states, whether defined in terms of the environment, border protection, terrorism, or international crime, is more and more shaped by EU decisions. Common foreign policy positions, though fraught with difficulties, have also emerged to deal with common EU interests; and limited defense cooperation exists.

The EU has a direct impact on the well-being of Britain's citizens in most of their daily existence and, since the EU is reliant on its member states to implement agreed policies, British institutions *at all levels* are directly engaged with putting into effect those policies. Representatives and bureaucrats at local, devolved, and national levels of British politics all have responsibilities in implementing policies that originate not in the Westminster Parliament but from EU institutions. Approximately 50 percent of domestic legislation emanates from Brussels. Therefore is the British citizen represented effectively at this supranational level?

The British-EU Nexus

EU institutions are described in the appendix. Since January 1973 the British government seats a representative at the Council of Ministers and at meetings of the European Council, recommends for appointment members of the European Commission and European Court of Justice, and sends delegates to the Committee of the Regions and Economic and Social Committee. Despite being outside the eurozone, the governor of the Bank of England sits on the General Council of the European Central Bank. British citizens directly elect members to the European Parliament (EP). Beneath this formal representation is a complex bureaucratic structure coordinated by Britain's Permanent Representation (UKRep), a super-ambassadorial presence in Brussels. The Committee of Permanent Representatives (COREPER) and over 250 functional working parties that compose a semi-formal bureaucratic representation with considerable influence over policy outcomes support the meetings of the Council of Ministers. Britain has her share of bureaucrats and experts on these committees, as do all other member states.

As table 5.2 illustrates, British representation in EU institutions takes various forms. Directly elected British MEPs enjoy a formal democratic legitimacy; ministers are British government representatives enjoying the

Table 5.2.   Formal British Representation in EU Institutions

Institution	Relationship with MS	Representational Form	Numbers
Council of Ministers	Intergovernmental	Appointive	appropriate minister
Committee of Permanent Representatives	Intergovernmental	Appointive	2
European Council	Intergovernmental	Appointive	I (PM)
Commission	Supranational	Appointive	I
European Parliament	Supranational	Direct Election	72
Committee of Regions	Intergovernmental	Appointive	24
Economic and Social Committee	Intergovernmental	Appointive	24
European Central Bank (General Council only)	Interinstitutional	Appointive	I
European Court of Justice	Supranational	Appointive	I
Court of Auditors	Supranational	Appointive	I

Note: In addition there is formal British expert representation in the many working parties (around 250) of the Council of Ministers; there is also opportunity for considerable formal influence over the EU's program on a periodic basis when a member state holds the presidency of the Council (rotational every six months). Britain's last presidency was in 2005 (June–December).

status of "the Crown," with an accountability to Parliament when attending Council meetings, and the same is true of the prime minister at European Council sessions. Similarly, Brussels-based British civil servants, assisted by the coordinating role of UKRep and the FCO, are directly accountable to their Whitehall base and, through the relevant ministerial accountability, to Parliament. As we shall see, the representational link is less clear for the position of the one member of the European Commission, currently the trade commissioner, Catherine Ashton, who is recommended for appointment by the British government. The supranational perspective on decision making by the Commission overrides particularistic national stances, though the "tone" of policies emanating from a directorate-general may reflect the commissioner's political and cultural background.

British judges and auditors must adopt a more clear-cut supranational perspective, despite being appointed after recommendation by the British government to the ECJ or the Court of Accounts. While there are representational opportunities for British local and regional governments and social partners (trade unions, business groupings, and civil associations) in the Committee of Regions and the Economic and Social Committee respectively, these institutions are advisory and relatively weak in their contribution to EU decision making. This is also true of British representation on the General Council of the European Central Bank, whose capacity to influence the direction of Eurozone monetary policy is extremely limited. British influence in these areas is, of course, significantly affected by its nonparticipation in the Eurozone.

In general, the extent of formal representation of British interests within the EU is shaped by three factors. First is the capacity of British representatives or appointees to act in a partisan manner. This is a function of the extent to which the EU institutions are intergovernmental or supranational in character. Second is the position that those institutions hold in the decision process: since the Council of Ministers and its supporting "back offices" of COREPER and working parties play such a significant role in the legislative process, the formal opportunities for member states' influence on outcomes is considerable; the roles of the Committee of the Regions and the Economic and Social Committee are minimal in contrast. Finally, the EU legislative process has several formal pathways, and thus varying opportunities for access and influence. Whether the issue is subject to veto or qualified majority voting (QMV), whether the policy is being dealt with through co-decision procedures, whether the legislative outcome is a directive (framework law) or regulation (with direct effect) are factors that influence the extent and depth of opportunity for a member state to represent its own interest. On achieving membership any EU state enters a modern policy Byzantium.

Britain in the Council of Ministers

The Council of Ministers lies at the center of EU decision making. It is, ostensibly, an intergovernmental body where member states, represented by the appropriate minister, argue for their country's interests, eventually reaching a common EU position. If, therefore, its processes are *intergovernmental*, its outcomes are *supranational*, in many cases binding on all member states. It is a legislature through which all proposals from the Commission of the European Communities (CEC) must be approved. But it also has executive functions that "provide leadership and steer the pace and direction of European integration, especially in areas of diplomacy and foreign affairs" (Lewis 2007: 155). It shares its legislative functions with the CEC and, more and more, with the EP, and shares its executive responsibilities with the European Council and presidency. Much of the legislation that reaches the statute books in Britain passes through the

Council, so the role of Britain's representatives is an integral and crucial aspect of the British political process.

British ministers attend Council meetings appropriate to their policy area and are authorized to act on behalf of the government in accepting the eventual outcome of legislative proposals. The number of meetings within each policy area varies, but ministers from DEFRA, which includes agriculture, fisheries, the environment, and food production/safety, tend to be the ones most frequently making the London–Brussels trip. Less frequent flyers are ministers for education or the Department of Health, whose tasks are less influenced by EU policy competences. On occasion, ministers from the Scottish executive and Welsh Assembly attend meetings on agriculture or regional policy matters as representatives of the British government.

Every Whitehall Department contains a European unit that supports ministerial and other EU-associated activities. Notably the British Treasury has not shown as much enthusiasm as the Foreign Office in matters European. This is partly reflected in a less than diligent attendance by the former chancellor, Gordon Brown, at Council (ECOFIN) meetings. He attended only two of eleven ECOFIN meetings in 2006 (43%); his counterpart from Germany attended 80 percent (Ludford 2007). Attendance of senior British ministers at Council meetings between 2003 and 2006 varied between 80 percent for the General Affairs and External Relations Council, to 26 percent at Transport Council meetings. This seeming lack of interest by some cabinet-level ministers, however, may well reflect confidence in their more junior colleagues and the strength of bureaucratic preparation and support offered by UKRep. Indeed, one commentary claims that the British executive enjoys "possibly the best political and administrative machinery for handling EU business"—as a result of a centralized political system and a tried-and-true, efficient administrative machine "located within the proven Whitehall model" (Nugent and Mather 2006: 130).

Decisions: Lost in Translation?

The significance of a well-prepared position on a policy item is evident when one considers the experience that ministers face in Council meetings compared with their usual Whitehall/Westminster environment. In the cabinet or cabinet committee, a minister sits alongside up to thirty-five colleagues and civil servants; in the Commons there may or may not be considerable numbers of MPs in attendance, but ministers will always face an opposition front bench, taking, generally, an antagonistic view of the policy proposals under discussion. There is a press and public gallery and in-house TV and radio listening to and interpreting every last word.

In an EU Council room, on the other hand, the gallery contains interpreters from twenty-seven member states relaying simultaneous translations of the proceedings in eleven official EU languages. Ministers and officials for the other twenty-six member states listen and adjust official positions as required. Officials and occasionally ministers confer over lunch in corridors, as the meeting is slow to resolve issues and spreads into the evening and maybe the night. There is no external witness to "what can seem rather chaotic proceedings" (Geddes 2004: 108).

The search for acceptable solutions in public policy in a democratic society involves inevitable compromises, and British politicians are no strangers to this. In the mainly adversarial atmosphere of Westminster politics, however, compromise is a pre-public activity. Once out in open parliamentary space, the government of the day has a policy line that is seldom crossed—a U-turn, like lunch, is for wimps, and a parliamentary majority is seldom breached. No such advantage exists in the Council of Ministers, where the issues and actors, save in defined areas of rigid national interest, are forced to seek best national value within inevitable compromises. While the chance to veto certain proposals still exists in areas such as taxation or constitutional change, the "default" procedure for EU legislation is co-decision, which in the Council of Ministers involves the application of QMV.

Since the Treaty of Nice (2000), the use of QMV has been extended considerably. Currently Britain enjoys, with France, Germany, and Italy, a "weighted" vote (29) compared with, for instance, Belgium, Czech Republic, Greece, Hungary, or Portugal (12 votes each). Compromise through alliance with other member states is always potentially necessary in order to reach the weighted majority total of 245 of the total votes cast (345). Beginning in the 1980s the need to promote the Single Market was, for British governments, an issue that had overridden their more sceptical view of QMV when it was extended to other areas, such as health and safety or environmental regulation.

Opportunities to "upload" British interests in Council proceedings are also affected by the sometimes quite distinctive decision-making cultures that exist in each Council and also by the level of expertise, and indeed interest, of national officials (Westlake 1999). The ability to influence the decisions within an Agriculture Council with strong French representation always to the fore, or ECOFIN with Britain outside of the Eurozone, may be contrasted with more evident British influence in trade or competition issues. This influence may well be based on expertise evident in working party and/or COREPER meetings. What emerges is a complex picture of decision making, whereby parts of the British executive and bureaucracy have gained considerable independence from domestic scrutiny in the shape of parliamentary or media observation. While this facilitates supranational (EU) solutions to British and other MS (member-state) issues, this pooled decision-making process undermines the independence of the national executive while simultaneously losing accountability to the British Parliament and public.

The European Council and Presidency

The European Council, rather than the Council of Ministers, is the meeting place of heads of government. This forum takes place two or three times within the tenure of the member state that holds the presidency. Since 1974 some of the most significant strategic decisions in EU history have been made here. It has emerged as an agenda setter, a broker of deals, and an international actor on behalf of the Union. A member state holding the presidency is expected to sustain the momentum of existing policies as well as gain an opportunity to shape the future agenda of the EU, though this is bounded by the contributions of the previous and following presidencies, to ensure continuity and coordination.

As befitting the presidential and prime ministerial status of its members, the European Council receives far more public attention than the Council. The issues discussed are often important and controversial, and opportunities for "grandstanding" and "leadership" are available. Thus, one of the first occasions for Prime Minster Blair to present his diplomatic credentials to the world was at the Amsterdam Council immediately following his first general election success in June 1997. At this meeting he marked an attitudinal change to the EU by not only agreeing to sign the Charter of Social and Workers Rights previously rejected by the Major government, but also careering around the streets of Amsterdam on a bicycle, leading an assortment of prime ministerial and presidential colleagues in his symbolic wake. Blair's last appearance on the international stage was at the summit (June 2007) when the issue of a revived constitutional treaty (now Lisbon Treaty) was agreed.

Other prime ministerial spectacles of note include the somewhat less *communautaire* "handbagging" episode when Mrs. Thatcher, at the 1984 Fontainebleau Summit, demanded and eventually got "our money back" in the shape of an EU budget rebate. Similarly, in an unusual demonstration of forthright leadership, John Major announced his success in winning opt-outs from the euro and the Social Contract after the (1992) Council Summit at Maastricht, as "game, set, and match" to Britain. Subsequently, in 1996, he was to exclude Britain from all Council meetings in an attempt to reverse decisions to ban the export of potentially infected British beef during the BSE "mad cow disease" episode.

There have been two recent occasions, 1998 and 2005, when Britain has held the presidency. In 1998 the major task was to continue the process that would lead to Stage III of the Economic and Monetary Union (EMU) and thus the establishment of the euro. This was successfully advanced, despite Britain's self-exclusion from the final stage. Issues associated with enlargement of the Union to Central and Eastern Europe, and Turkey, were also pursued, as was the "Blairist" agenda of labor-market flexibility and structural economic reform. In 2005, a more isolated Blair government, especially after EU divisions over the Iraq war, was forced into agreeing to a reconsideration of Mrs. Thatcher's hard-won budget rebate that now seemed less justifiable in relation to Britain's relative economic position in an enlarged Europe. In front of a quizzical electorate and forceful opposition, the prime minister, also the president of the European Council, agreed to a reduction in the size of the British budget rebate in return for a nebulous consideration of the future of agriculture policy. As some newspapers ruefully observed, "game, set, and match" to then French president Chirac.

For any British prime minister the short, intense meetings of the European Council offer both opportunity and potential failure. To win arguments without creating enemies and tensions builds political credit within the EU and in the broader international community. A reformed labor market, or movement away from external agricultural protectionism, would win plaudits from some EU and many US interests, for instance. It also would carry a fair share of, albeit begrudging, domestic applause. It is, however, easier to gain domestic approval by winning "game, set, and match" in the proclaimed national interest, or indeed by not playing the game at all; but this risks isolation and opprobrium within the EU, as John Major found to his cost in the 1990s. Attempting to be at the heart of Europe, as both prime ministers Major and Blair intimated was their aim, may be received well in Brussels, but enjoys considerably less audible support in a suspicious domestic environment.

The European Commission and British (Mis)representation?

One problem, as we argue below, is that for Europhobes the Commission has come to represent the institutional "dark heart" of Europe. Yet its role in recent years has been beset by political and procedural changes that belie its reputation as the secret, guiding hand of European federalism.

It is a supranational body, though many of its activities are directed to mediating member states' interests and negotiating solutions between the Council of Ministers and the EP. Formally, it has the exclusive right to initiate Community legislation. It has an international role in representing EC interests in trade negotiations; once policies have been agreed, it has an executive role in their implementation, but it relies on the member states to apply directives and regulations. It has, however, a responsibility to check the effectiveness and legality of a member state's implementation of EU policies and can, where necessary, instigate legal proceedings via the ECJ. Finally, it has legal responsibility for initiating and distributing the EU budget.

For British Europhobes, the Commission remains their worst euro nightmare—federalist, monolithic, faceless, technocratic, and undemocratic—an army of foreign bureaucrats bent on regulation and intervention in the sovereign affairs of the British state—as well as being corrupt! The Commission is an easy target for such newspapers as the *Sun, Mail,* and *Express* in their scorn of "Brussels bureaucracy." Unlike the European Council and the Council of Ministers, where at least some political accountability to Westminster may be observed, the Commission is portrayed as beyond the control of the British citizen (see chapter 7).

In some respects the Commission has conformed to this stereotype—for instance, in 1999, the Santer Commission was forced to resign over allegations of corruption and inefficiencies that were music to a Europhobic ear. However, much of this criticism rests on a (deliberate?) misconception of the role and power of the Commission by the British press to the public. The current twenty-seven-member body is appointed "by common accord" of the member states and requires EP ratification on an individual basis. Britain can recommend for appointment one commissioner, currently the commissioner for trade. Peter Mandelson, who has a controversial and very public presence in British politics, held this appointment until 2008. Previous government-recommended Commission appointments include Neil Kinnock, leader of the Labour Party until 1992 and deputy commission president; Christopher Patten, a Conservative minister and last governor of Hong Kong; Leon Britton, a Conservative chancellor, who with a predecessor, Lord Cockfield, commissioner for the internal market, made a considerable contribution to the implementation of the Single Market; and Roy Jenkins, a deputy leader of the Labour Party who was president of the Commission from 1977 to 1981.

The usual political background of Commission appointments scarcely encourages facelessness on behalf of the incumbents, who have, on many occasions, expressed strong opinions for both EU-wide and domestic consumption. These ex-politicos, appointed to initiate policies in often conflicting areas (for instance consumer protection versus market deregulation), cannot, therefore, be placed in a single box. Thus it is more accurate to think of the Commission as a "multiorganisation" rather than a monolith (Geddes 2004: 101).

Each commissioner has a personal "cabinet," which, until recently, was likely to be dominated by nationals from her/his country. This would lead to networking opportunities in specific policy areas that allowed a member state, via permanent representatives, a window into forthcoming Commission proposals. Lord Cockfield's British-dominated DG cabinet of the mid-1980s assisted initially favorable outcomes for the Thatcher government in the legislation creating the Single Market (Allen 1992: 42). By contrast, DG Agriculture has been criticized as a French fiefdom. Since the Prodi Commission (1999–2005), attempts have been made to internationalize cabinet staffing, thus weakening the national fiefdom argument (Egeberg 2007).

The Commission in 2006 totalled 27,354 full and temporary administrative staff; the EU's population is 496 million. This compares with the 50,000 staff employed by the Birmingham City Council, which provides services for 1 million people. In terms of public access, Commission culture is far more open than the corridors of Whitehall, as academic researchers and interest group representatives will attest. Other reforms, led by then British deputy president of the Commission Neil Kinnock, indicate a growing responsiveness by the Commission to its external critics. This, together with the reputation that UKRep has achieved for delivering coherent British positions and solutions, belies the critical, often belligerent stance taken by parts of the British press in its analysis of the Commission's role in British politics.

Viewed as a single institution, the Commission fits uneasily into the British policy process. It is an international political bureaucracy initiating policies that make up half of Britain's domestic legislative output. Its ability to "download" policy and then evaluate the effectiveness of British implementation of EU policy is matched by what seems a limited opportunity to upload British government interests. The process seems dangerously unbalanced, especially when compared with the apparent simplicity of British parliamentary accountability.

However, the Commission is but one institution. It is interlinked with the Council system, with its considerable British government presence, and the EP, with direct representation of British voter interests. How far, therefore, is the EP a corrective to this democratic deficit?

The EP as a Representative Institution

Britain elects 72 members of the European Parliament (MEPs), a number similar to that of France and Italy. The total number from January 2009 was 736 for the election of 2009. Since 1999, MEPs have been elected by a system of proportional representation chosen by their member states. In Britain's case, this is a regional list system, a strongly party-based system contrasting with the candidate/constituency system in parliamentary elections. When Britain changed to the PR "the level of disproportionality plummeted . . . the effective number of parliamentary parties more than doubled . . . and there was a noticeable increase in the proportion of women MEPs from 19 percent to 25 percent (Farrell and Scully 2005: 977).

Since direct elections were instigated in 1979, the EP has grown in importance within the EU policy process. Its legislative role, for a long time mainly consultative, was enhanced by the SEA (1987), through a new *co-operation procedure* with the Council, for many new policy areas. The TEU (1992) introduced another EP/Council shared process, *co-decision*, which was subsequently expanded under the treaties of Amsterdam, Nice, and Lisbon. Around 50 percent of all EU legislation is advanced through the co-decision procedure (see the book's website).

The EP scrutinizes and must approve the EU budget, can approve or reject a new Commission and its president-designate, and comments on and potentially influences the appointment of individual commissioners. The Council must seek the EP's approval for the accession of new member states or association agreements with other states. Thus, the EU has developed a two-chamber legislative procedure "in which the Council represents the states and the European Parliament represents the citizens" (Hix et al. 2003: 355). Its most effective work is in the committee system, for which, unlike its US congressional counterpart, it gets little publicity (358). It has become, in this new century, a much stronger institution than it was at the beginning of the 1980s and, as such, has a formal authority worthy of the attention and interest of its electors.

The British, and many other EU voters, do not seem to have recognized this situation. Turnout in Britain for the four elections held between 1979 and 1999 under the familiar single-member constituency system averaged 35 percent. In the two elections held under PR it reached a nadir of 24 percent (1999) rising to 39 percent (2004). In 2009, turnout across the EU varied from 91 percent (Belgium) to 20 percent (Slovakia), averaging 43 percent overall. Britain's turnout was down to 34 percent. Only five member states polled above 60 percent, indicating a sense of "second-order importance" for this unique public forum. Though the average is higher than in US congressional elections, it is still lower than turnout in MS national elections, despite a recent trend to declining numbers in these "first-order" polls.

British or European Representation?

Before discussing why this is, it is worth exploring the character of the EP and of the MEPs who represent the British citizens. First, MEPs, once elected from their national/regional constituencies, sit not in national but in transnational party groups. In other words, representatives elected with Labour, Conservative, or Liberal Democrat national labels will sit and interact with like-minded colleagues from other MS national parties, in such groups as the Party of European Socialists (PES); the European Peoples' Party (EPP), a center-right grouping; or the Alliance of Liberals and Democrats (ALD). These groups are not only fairly coherent in their legislative activities but they also show a degree of intragroup party cooperation not evident in the British parliamentary system.

The reasons for this are partly ideological, partly procedural, and partly political (Hix et al. 2003), but the groups do present a very different political culture for British MEPs compared with their domestic experiences. They have the difficult task of balancing a range of interests to be represented—a Liverpool-based Labour MEP has individual, local, and northwest regional interests; party interests; national interests; and, given the Europhile perspectives of many British MEPs, EU-wide interests to represent! It is, therefore, not surprising that MEPs, in such cross-pressured circumstances, "think deeply about their role and (have) reached differing, individual interpretations of it" (Scully and Farrell 2003: 279).

EP elections produce, on face value, a broader representation of British voters' interests than the general elections. This was to some considerable extent the result of the PR system utilized to vote in MEPs (see table 5.3). Thus the Green Party gained two seats in the EP but was unable to win any seats in the (2005) Westminster Parliament. The United Kingdom Independence Party (UKIP), that seeks complete withdrawal from the EU, gained thirteen seats to equal Labour in terms of EP representation. This, together with votes for the British National Party (BNP), indicates that

Table 5.3.   2004/2009 EP and 2005 General Elections: Votes Cast and Seats Won

**Nationwide parties	2004		2005		2009	
	%	seats	%	seats	%	seats
Labour	22.5	19	36.3	355	15.7	13
Conservative	26.7	27	33.2	198	27.7	25
Liberal Democrats	14.9	12	22.6	62	13.7	11
Green Party	6.2	2	1.1	0	8.6	2
UKIP	16.1	12	2.3	0	16.5	13
BNP	4.9	0	0.7	0	6.2	2
National Turnout	38		61		34	
Regional Parties (% of regional vote)						
Plaid Cymru	17.4	1	12.6	3	18.5	1
S.N.P	25.2	2	17.5	6	29.1	2
Sinn Fein*	28.3	1	*24.3	5	25.8	1
DUP*	32	1	*33.7	9	18.1	1
Ulster Unionist*	16.6	1	*17.8	1	17.0	1
SDLP*	15.9	0	*17.5	3	16.1	0
Seats Total	78		646		72	

* Elected by STV system (Northern Ireland only)
** In England, Scotland, and Wales only

over 25 percent of citizens cast their ballot for an anti-EU-system party. This, however, must be seen in the light of a turnout of only 34 percent. For the first time, the BNP gained two seats in 2009 as protest votes hit the Labour vote hard. One-quarter of Britain's MEPs are women; this compares with one-fifth of MPs in the 2005 Parliament.

Why does the EP, despite its democratic format, its legislative partnership with the Council of Ministers and Commission, and the EU's growing influence over the lives of British citizens, still fail to ignite the interests of more than four out of ten voters? Several factors account for this. First, the EU seems of much less significance in the lives of EU citizens than national governments. This is a result of the second and third factors: a low, virtually nonexistent, coverage of the EP in the British media; and third, the mental distance that citizens put between themselves and Brussels compared with London, Edinburgh, or Cardiff. The EP competences in trade or environmental policy are simply far less relevant to the average citizen than the health, social security, or education policies of the national or regional government. Fourth, there are in EP elections no "results" in terms of maintaining or dismissing a government. This fact, coupled with a final factor, the consensus-style decision making within the EU, removes the partisan excitement that is evident in national electoral competition. This disinterest encourages "a widespread lack of understanding of how the EU institution operates," which is "accompanied by a significant proportion of the press who are overtly hostile to the EU" (Corbett et al. 2003: 359).

The EU and a Democratic Deficit

The problems listed above are summarized in the term *democratic deficit,* which can be applied to two interrelated problems: the lack of democratic control that seems apparent between the EU institutions and the relatively weak authority of the EP vis-à-vis other EU bodies; and the lack of democratic control that British citizens have over the decisions of the EU. The democratic deficit is, in turn, bound up in the national sovereignty debate raised in the previous chapter that amounts to a "de-parliamentarianization" of national political systems. This has disenfranchised the EU citizen by allowing the executives of member states more "unaccountable" power as they participate in EU decision making (Chryssochoou 2007: 362).

Without a Parliament with the ability to effectively call an executive and bureaucracy to account for its actions, EU legitimacy is open to public challenge. For EU citizens there are at least two parliaments whose task it should be to call decision makers to account—the EP and their national assemblies. Reduction of any democratic deficit, therefore, should involve recognition of this dual mandate and the relationship between interrelated political processes. This was to some extent recognized in the proposals for the Constitutional (now Lisbon) Treaty that sought to introduce a range of democratic devices, including an enhanced role for national parliaments (see the book's website).

These proposals were received both in Britain and elsewhere in a manner that indicates the dilemmas of supranational democracy. For those that accept the importance of democratizing EU institutions, the proposals did not address such issues as the continued unaccountable role of the European Commission, whose unique powers to initiate legislation remained. Neither were the powers of national parliaments to call to account ministers legislating on behalf of their countries satisfactorily enhanced. Overall the democratic deficit was still evident. The more Eurosceptical critics, of whom there were plenty in Britain, perceived even these relatively limited reforms as "federalist" and therefore increasing the already existing threat against domestic political institutions that the EU demonstrated. For the Conservative opposition, UKIP, and other Eurosceptic players, the Lisbon Treaty produced the obverse of democratic reform. The proposed creation of a president of the Council and a single representative for foreign affairs confirmed their federalist take on the issue.

During 2005, when debate on the Constitutional Treaty was at its height, British public opinion was generally negative, but mostly confused. One poll recorded that, while only 10 percent were strongly in favor of the treaty and 25 percent were strongly against, 21 percent were generally in favor but could in debate be persuaded against, and 27 percent were generally against but could possibly be persuaded to be in favor. Sixteen percent did not know! (Mori Opinion 2005) A Eurobarometer poll of the same year recorded a general distrust of EU institutions by the British public (58%). However, distrust in the British Parliament was also low (51% of those polled). But of those polled, 55 percent felt that Britain had benefited from EU membership and supported the idea of common policies in defense (71%) and immigration policy (74%) (European Commission 2005). Subsequent Eurobarometer polls confirm this generally confused perception. The difficulty, therefore, of conducting a sensible public debate on the EU as a democratic institution is evident enough.

CONCLUSION: BRITAIN'S DEMOCRATIC DEFICIT

In 1970 the British citizen was able to elect, through an FPTP system, representatives to the House of Commons and to local government. Thirty years later, those citizens living in the Celtic national regions and London had, in addition, a regional representative; all citizens could elect a member of a European Parliament; and a variety of electoral systems to do this had been introduced (see chapter 6). Half of new British law emanated from an external source—the EU—and domestic legislation, previously the domain of a Westminster Parliament, was being processed within a shared devolved environment that has effectively reduced the Commons and Lords to "English" assemblies. Scottish, Welsh, and Northern Irish MPs, however, continue to play their part at Westminster as part of a still-powerful majoritarian, adversarial, and central government–dominated parliamentary process.

But, while the concept of parliamentary sovereignty is challenged, whether through the notion of pooled sovereignty with other EU member states or shared sovereignty with the devolved assemblies, the cultural myth and constitutional reality of a legally sovereign Parliament persists in the minds of most British citizens; many MPs; and, in their public role, among British ministers of state. There exists, therefore, a most fundamental contradiction in such popular notions as trustee representation and Commons supremacy: they simply do not match the reality of twenty-first-century British multilevel governance; but these notions continue as the "default mode" of the national representative and legislative system.

This disjuncture has important consequences when observing the several attempts made in the past few years to modernize Parliament and to integrate devolved with central governance. The first and overriding point to make is that several modernization initiatives—whether House of Lords reform, devolution, or improving Commons efficiency and openness—have been implemented without the open acknowledgment of a Europeanization of British governance. If we use the term Europeanization in its least controversial sense, in terms of its impact on domestic policy, the ability of British representatives to shape policy from the EU legislative factory is relatively limited. As we have seen, not only is parliamentary scrutiny of EU matters lacking, but also the level of Commons involvement and interest is less than it ought to be. Neither is there effective cooperation between the British MEPs who are more involved in policy scrutiny than their domestic counterparts.

If we take Europeanization to mean integration, that is, the incorporation of norms, beliefs, and processes into the discourse and political structures of member states, then Parliament and other domestic representative structures have adapted rather than transformed themselves in the light of this EU integration process. The Scottish Assembly has gone further than others in appreciating the need to adapt its relatively new practice to the external realities of the EU; yet it finds, with the other devolved assemblies, that it must rely on the British central government for direction in its engagement with the EU. As for British parliamentary engagement, its role is mainly "downstream," though the right of scrutiny provides a "burglar alarm" mechanism that is frequently ignored by both parliamentarians and government ministers.

There remains a systemic divide between EU and MS political processes, which is part of the democratic deficit. The British representative system is a victim of that divide, but does not help itself by what seems at times a bemused perspective on the issue of EU integration itself. If European integration also involves the acceptance of a set of particular shared values, then Parliament, and the Commons in particular, sits uneasily within those values. Political leaders spend much of their time avoiding discussing the consequences of integration and, therefore, the British Parliament misses the opportunity to play an educative role on this issue for its citizens.

Representation for British citizens, and scrutiny of their governments, is no longer just about parliamentary samurai and local worthies and notables. Local democracy has been eroded, first by the imperative of central government's need for a local agency, and second by the plethora of deconcentrated local services demanding a community input for their delivery. Parliament, confounded by "big government" and the elective dictatorship of a disciplined party majority, now competes with devolved national assemblies for a meaningful role in the lives of citizens; and arching across local, devolved, and national representative systems are the intergovernmental and supranational processes of the EU that bring with them a representational system of directly elected MEPs and indirect representatives (British ministers in the Council of Ministers).

For the ordinary citizen, coming to grips with multilevel representation and establishing a clear picture of who to hold to account for what, the temptation to place one's head in the sand is great. Some of this complexity is clearly in the public domain. Devolution has brought with it a consciousness of political difference in Scotland and Wales. Economic and political revival in Northern Ireland also brings the chance of new local choices and an association with Ireland previously outside the political agenda. Meanwhile, the notion of an English Parliament has taken root in the discourse of some English political communities. The impact of devolution on the role of Parliament, one can safely argue, is likely in the long term to be profound.

It may seem, therefore, somewhat strange that a similarly profound impact on the traditional base of the British representation system, through EU membership, has been subsumed within existing processes and is, whenever it is allowed a public face, crudely and often negatively received. It is debated, legislated upon, and legitimized by a hybrid, parallel legislative "system." Within the British Parliament, a small number of MPs and a rather larger group of Lords members attempt to scrutinize the activities of their ministers in Europe and the resulting proposals for, and output of, EU laws. Externally, a small and dedicated group of ministers, civil servants, and technical experts participate in a foggy policy process with other MS colleagues, to create laws acceptable to all member states. Directly elected British MEPs enjoy some legislative powers but little public recognition in Britain. The cooperation between these parallel worlds is limited and, to some considerable extent, rejected by a Parliament concerned to maintain its historic sovereignty. At the same time political parties lack the will to lead public opinion toward a coherent multirepresentational system. Ultimately, EU institutional change is a domestic reform issue—and one that British political parties must discuss openly with British citizens.

FURTHER READING

For a comprehensive and readable examination of most aspects of British local government see David Wilson and Chris Games's *Local Government in the United Kingdom* (2006). Adam Marshall illustrates the impact of the EU on local government in Bache and Jordan (2006). A discussion of the decline in public interest in local government is contained in Simon Parker et al. *State of Trust* (2008). For an introduction to Britain's devolved government see Mike O'Neill's edited volume *Devolution and British Politics* (2004), or more succinctly in Michael Moran's *Politics and Governance in the UK* (2005). The emergence of a Scottish political system is explored in Tom Nairn's *After Britain* (2000) and in Jo Murkens et al. *Scottish Independence: A Practical Guide* (2002). For Welsh devolution, see *Delineating Wales* by Richard Rawlings (2003). The painful progress to the resolution of Northern Ireland's place in UK and Irish politics is explored in Jon Tonge's *Northern Ireland: Conflict and Change* (2002) and his *The New Northern Ireland Politics* (2005). Simon Bulmer et al. (2002) examine the relationship between Britain's devolved government and the EU policy process. "The English question" is examined in Robert Hazell's edited volume of the same name (2006). Britain's representation in Brussels in its various manifestations is described in Anthony Forster and Alistair Blair *The Making of Britain's European Foreign Policy* (2002). The role of UKRep is explained by David Allen and Tim Oliver (2004). Andrew Geddes describes the problems for British ministers in their Council of Ministers deliberations in *The European Union and British Politics* (2004). David Farrell and Richard Scully in *Representing Europe's Citizens?* (2007) and Richard Corbett et al. (2007) give insight to the role of an MEP.

6

Parties and Why
Citizens Vote for Them

It is easy, but misleading, to present Britain as an example of a moderate, two-party system. The Westminster model and a parliamentary culture of civilized, adversarial politics, together with the first-past-the-post (FPTP) system, certainly point us toward that conclusion. Political groupings, as they emerged in twentieth-century British politics, fitted into this environment. The Continental alternative was either authoritarianism or multiple polarized parties, reflecting the antithesis of Britain's virtuous gradual development (Sartori 1976). The inability of antisystem parties to take root even during the economic and political instabilities of Britain in the 1930s, was testimony to a party and electoral system that contained excessive demands and preserved institutional continuity. Indeed the adaptive capacity of the Conservative and Labour parties and their willingness to work within a flexible parliamentary system contributed to the preservation, some argue freezing, of the class-based nineteenth-century social cleavages to which both parties owed their origins (Lipset and Rokkan 1967).

The conditions leading to Britain's categorization as a moderate two-party system were, first, the focus on Westminster politics for party interaction; second, the acceptance by political parties, after World War II, of Keynesian economic solutions to domestic problems; and, third, the lack of either regional, religious (save for Northern Ireland), or ethnic cleavages that might allow other political forces to occupy sufficient political space to challenge the dominance of the two parties of government. In addition, the FPTP system does no favors for third, fourth, or fifth parties, as the return of parliamentary seats to Liberal Party votes through to the 1997 election testifies.

But the moderate two-party model existed from 1945 through to 1979 only. Indeed it had eroded by 1977, when the Labour government was forced to conclude a parliamentary accord, the so-called "Lib-Lab Pact," as its Commons majority dwindled. Moderate bipartism was further challenged—first, by the neoliberal perspectives of the Thatcher-Major governments beginning in 1979, when centrist electoral competition was replaced by a more polarized left-right divide; and, second, by the resultant splits in the Labour Party, leading in 1982 to a reformist liberal–social democrat coalition, when Liberals and social democrats of the Labour party formed the Liberal and Social Democratic Alliance, winning 25 percent of the vote and twenty-three Commons seats in the 1983 election. This alliance was renamed the Liberal Democrats in 1988. Though their success was short lived, the lack of an effective, electable opposition throughout the 1980s led some commentators to claim that Britain had turned into a *dominant party system*, where one party, the Conservatives, was permanently in office—similar to the dominance of the Japanese Liberal Democrats, or the Indian Congress Party of the 1950s and 1960s. A further challenge to the application of a two-party model was the existence, alongside national electoral competition, of the underresearched environment of British local politics that historically included coalition patterns of many types (Bulpitt 1967; Copus 2004).

Events during the 1990s also challenge the presentation of British politics "as emblematic of the two-party pattern" (Hague and Harrop 2007: 248). The erosion of the two-party system may be explained in terms of the emergence of postmaterialist issues that include consumer, gender, and environmental politics and, it is argued here, European issues—all of which disrupted the two-party divide (Hague and Harrop 2007: 57). These and other issues contributed to the breakdown of class alignments that had been the backbone of the Labour/Conservative duopoly.

It is instructive to contrast the configuration of British party politics in 1945 with that of the situation sixty years later for the election of 2005. In the first post–World War II election, 89 percent of the vote was shared by the Conservative and Labour parties (table 6.1). By 2005 this had dropped to 68 percent. Three-quarters of the total 1945 electorate turned out to vote for 640 MPs, of whom only 37 did not obey the Labour or Conservative whip. In effect, two-party dominance was clearly evident in the national legislative systems, leading to one-party dominance in the executive systems. In 2005 a majority of 66 gave clear executive control to the Labour party. But out of 646 MPs, 92 were from other parties, voted in by one-third of 2005 voters. Only 6 out of 10 electors contributed to this result. Since any PR voting system would have distributed Commons seats more equitably, it is difficult not to conclude that although "the era of two party politics may not be quite dead . . . at the Westminster level, it is kept alive by the continued existence of the single-member plurality (FPTP) system" (Childs 2006: 56).

Table 6.1. Seats and Votes in General Elections since 1945

Elections	Conservative Seat No	Conservative Vote %	Labour Seat No	Labour Vote %	Liberals* Seat No	Liberals* Vote %	Others Seat No	Others Vote %	Total No of MPs	Electoral Turnout
1945	210	39.6	393	48	12	9	25	3.4	640	75.5
1950	298	43.4	315	46.1	9	9.1	3	1.4	625	83.6
1951	321	48	295	48.8	6	2.6	3	0.6	625	84
1955	345	49.7	277	46.4	6	2.7	2	1.2	630	76
1959	365	49.4	258	43.8	6	5.9	1	0.9	630	78.7
1964	304	43.4	317	44.1	9	11.2	0	1.3	630	77.1
1966	253	41.9	364	48.01	12	8.6	1	1.5	630	75.8
1970	330	46.4	288	43.1	6	7.5	6	3	635	70
1974 (Feb)	297	37.96	301	37.2	14	19.3	23	5.6	635	81
1974 (Oct)	277	35.8	319	39.2	13	18.3	26	6.7	635	72.8
1979	339	43.9	269	36.9	11	13.8	16	5.4	635	78
1983	397	42.4	209	27.6	23**	25.4	21	4.6	650	72.7
1987	376	42.3	229	30.8	22***	22.5	23	4.4	650	75.3
1992	336	41.9	271	34.4	20	17.8	24	5.9	651	77.7
1997	165	30.7	418	43.2	46	16.8	30	9.3	659	71.4
2001	166	32.7	412	42	52	18.8	29	6.5	659	59.4
2005	197	32.3	356	35.3	62	22.1	30	10.3	646	62.2

* Liberals are now Liberal Democrats.
**Northern Irish MPs are counted as "others" from 1974 on.
***In 1983 and 1987 "Liberal" includes SDP/Liberal Alliance.
Source: Electoral Commission (2009); Butler and Butler (2006).

Besides the more varied history of party politics in local government, other electoral arenas had emerged by 2005 that reflected very different party configurations. Thus, by 2009 Britain's several electoral arenas have produced political outcomes that included:

- A Labour/Welsh Nationalist coalition Assembly government in Wales faced by an opposition of Liberal Democrats and Conservatives.
- A Scottish Nationalist minority Scottish executive opposed by a fragmented opposition of Liberal Democrats, Greens, Conservatives, and a still substantial Labour Party.
- A consociational Northern Irish executive with executive posts distributed across four parties including Sinn Fein and the Democratic Unionist Party (DUP).
- EP representation that consists of eleven different parties: Conservative, Labour, Liberal Democrat, Scottish National Party (SNP), Plaid Cymru (PC), Greens, British National Party (BNP), the anti-EU United Kingdom Independence Party (UKIP), and three Northern Ireland parties. These operate within transnational, rather than national party groupings.

Prior to the 2007 regional elections, Wales and Scotland experienced Labour/Liberal Democrat coalitions, and Greater London was led until 2004 by an independent mayor, seeking support from an Assembly of five different parties.

Britain now has a multiplicity of electoral arenas within which parties can interact and the number of significant parties competing in each of the systems and winning seats of value for coalition formations has increased (textbox 6.1). More than this, however, the ideological and territorial representation of parties, and thus the potential for polarization, has increased. There is, therefore, a potential for *fragmented pluralism* in these several arenas, in a manner that would have been thought inconceivable sixty years ago. Table 6.2 shows party representation in the national and regional assemblies that now operate in Britain. Thus, the potential for coalition executive government, especially in the Celtic regions, is high when one observes the political balance of their legislatures. Some authors suggest that there is potential for coalition contagion to spread to Westminster as early as the next general election. The major parties are calculating that they may be better served by supporting some form of proportional representation for national elections rather than facing the uncertainties of a FPTP system within a fragmenting party system (Dunleavy 2006: 333).

Textbox 6.1. Voting Systems in Britain Today

House of Commons	Single-Member First Past the Post (FPTP)
English/Welsh Local Government	Single- and Multimember (FPTP)
Northern Ireland Assembly and Scottish Local Elections	Single Transferable Vote
Scottish Parliament Welsh National Assembly London Assembly	Additional Member System
European Parliament	Proportional Representation List System
London and other elected mayors	Supplementary Vote System

There are several factors that may lead major party elites to consider such a radical voting system change for elections to Westminster. As we mentioned above, postmaterialist issues have cut into the traditional notions of a left-right ideological divide and resulted in party realignment to incorporate these issues. Also, there are opportunities for smaller or new parties to compete by offering regional rather than national solutions. Partisan de-alignment, assisted by the erosion of trust, social divisions, class de-alignment, and the crosscutting nature of postmaterialist issues, has impacted on party membership and voter turnout. Mass organization and catchall electoral tactics no longer produce levels of turnout previously taken for granted by party leaders. Changes to voting systems have been seen as a panacea for this decline. Thus, the national Labour Party calculated that, with a PR system, while it would be unable to sustain an absolute majority in a devolved Scottish Parliament, it would remain the largest and therefore dominant party. This proved a miscalculation, for in 2007 the SNP was elected by one seat as the largest grouping. For the Conservatives, despite their initial reticence, devolved elections have meant a welcome return to Scottish and Welsh politics after many years with limited or no parliamentary representation. As Dunleavy warns, "analysts need to face the fact that a multi-party system already exists in every region of the UK, not excepting the metropolitan heartland regions of England" (Dunleavy 2006: 331).

Table 6.2. Political Parties in British Assemblies (2009)

	Con	Lab	Lib	SNP	PC	SF	DUP	SDLP	UUP	UKIP	BNP	Greens
House of Commons	197	356	62	6	3	5	9	3	2	–	–	–
Scottish Parliament	17	46	16	47	–	–	–	–	–	–	–	2
Welsh Assembly	12	26	6	–	15	–	–	–	–	–	–	–
Northern Ireland Assembly	–	–	–	–	–	28	36	16	18	–	–	–
European Parliament	25	13	11	2	1	1	1	0	1	13	2	2

THE LABOUR PARTY

The 2005 general election was the third electoral success for Labour under the leadership of Tony Blair. His leadership of the party lasted from 1994 to 2007, ten years of which were as prime minister. Only Mrs. Thatcher's leadership of the Conservative party has lasted longer in the twentieth century (1975 to 1990 with eleven years as premier). During this period the Labour Party was transformed from its divided unelectable self—it had not won a national election since 1974—to the very model of a modern party animal (see the book's website).

Since 1980, the "lurch to the left," as a response to the success of Mrs. Thatcher's neoliberal Conservative Party victory, has had two results. The first was the division of the party in 1981, when part of its social democratic wing left to form a new alliance with the Liberal Party; and, second, the humiliating electoral defeat of 1983, when Labour's socialist manifesto ("the longest suicide note in political history") sought to take Britain out of the EU and commence the renationalization of British industry. Under the new leadership of Neil Kinnock there commenced a party modernization, and though defeated in 1987 and 1992, Kinnock handed over a party firmly in the social democratic tradition of contemporary Europe attuned to the importance of its public image as an electoral asset. Under the short period of John Smith's leadership, one-man-one-vote for leadership election was introduced in 1993, which significantly reduced the influence of the trade unions: a National Policy Forum reduced the powers of the party's National Executive Committee (NEC).

Under the Blair-Brown leadership beginning in 1994, the centrality of Labour's socialist origins was symbolically abandoned when Clause Four of the 1918 Constitution, which directed the party to control the "commanding heights of the British economy," was ditched in favor of a relatively elastic commitment to "a community in which power, wealth and opportunity are in the hands of the many and not the few" in the new (1995) Labour Constitution. *New Labour* was still a "democratic socialist party," but one that had accepted the inevitability and advantages of the market. New alliances could thus be forged with business leaders who were invited to advise, serve in, and donate to a competent market-friendly party of social justice (see textbox 6.2).

The policy leaps that were undertaken also needed the most careful presentation to voters and business and financial audiences. The first steps to the professionalization of image making were undertaken during the 1992 election. Borrowing ideas, particularly from the US Clinton Democrats, a centralized media operation was established within the new London party headquarters. "Being on message" and "spinning" have become part of the political vocabulary of British politics; the effect has, however,

---

Textbox 6.2. Blair's New Labour Ideology (1994–2005)

- A commitment to social justice—and the market
- Economic growth and individual opportunity
- A stakeholders society in public and private goods
- The state steers, but does not row
- Communities provide, not the state
- Social inclusion, but political decentralization
- Globalization as opportunity; the EU our neighbor and a flexible labor market our friend
- A proactive foreign policy to enhance democracy and social justice

---

not always furthered Labour's political objectives and has become part of the problem rather than solution of image representation: the medium emerged as the message for the Blair government (see chapter 7).

One substantial change is evident in Labour's parliamentary makeup. While the selection of candidates for Commons seats is still influenced by existence of an NEC list (all candidates selected must be approved by the NEC), constituencies since 1997 have been permitted, and indeed encouraged, to adopt all-women shortlists, 50 percent of which were designated as "winnable seats" for the 1997 and 2005 elections. The result was an increase in Labour women MPs from 37 out of a Commons total of 60 in 1992 to 101 out of 120 in 1997. In 2005, 98 Labour women MPs were elected of whom 30 were from all-women shortlists. This, together with other internal equality guarantees, has moved women's concerns and perspectives "from the margins towards the centre of the political agenda" such that "issues such as paternity leave, flexible working, a national child care strategy . . . are concerns over which the parties (now) compete" (Childs 2006: 75).

Labour in Government (1997–2009)

Coinciding with the resignation of Tony Blair and the virtual coronation of Gordon Brown as his successor, the Labour Party circulated a pamphlet listing 300 changes to public policy made during their ten-year administration. These claims make interesting reading for any member who may have joined during the 1970s. Some still fit a 1970s socialist agenda: the party in government claimed to have taken 2.1 million people out of poverty, created the first ever National Minimum Wage, banned foxhunting and fur farming, abolished hereditary peers from the Lords, signed the European Working Time Directive; invested £260 million in transport each week since 1997; lifted 2 million pensioners out of hardship; increased central investment in schools from £700 million in 1997 to £7 billion in 2007; and achieved the lowest level of unemployment since 1974. Other changes would not be out of place in an evaluation of a 1980s Thatcherite government: Labour had increased home ownership by 1.5 million; encouraged an increase by 16 percent of small businesses; cut corporation tax to 30 percent, long-term capital gains tax from 40 percent to 10 percent, and would raise the inheritance tax threshold to £325,000 in 2009; increased investment in policing by 33 percent since 1997, employing the highest number of police officers ever; and established a "heroes return home" scheme for World War II veterans. Liberal Democrats would not be upset with Labour's establishment of a Human Rights Act, Celtic devolution, the creation of a Disability Rights Commission, a Minister for Women, a Sex Discrimination Act for election candidates, and a Freedom of Information Act. Nor were parliamentary reforms, especially the establishment of a "Supreme Court" and more powerful scrutiny committees, unwelcome to Liberal Democrats (Labour Party 2006).

Thus constitutional and organizational reform from 1985 to 1995 and radical policies once in government provided the Labour leadership with the party platform necessary to address a changed demography, a realigned political center, and a radically different external scenario of global and European interconnectivity. Though not always effective, professionalization of the party, public relations, top-down organizational change, and the powerful leadership of the Blair/Brown tandem was characteristic of a modern cadre party (see the book's website). Now in its twelfth year, the Labour government faces challenges to the "social market" assumptions of the Blair period as policies to assist Britain out of recession necessitate massive (old Labour) state intervention. Labour's main opponents, the Conservatives, have inevitably reacted to this challenge.

THE CONSERVATIVE PARTY

By 2005 the Conservative Party found itself in much the same electoral condition as the Labour Party in 1992. Both parties had lost three consecutive national polls. Both had attempted some degree of modernization to overcome historic failures, but not enough to convince a sceptical public, and within a year after a third defeat, each was to take on ideological changes that borrowed the more successful formula of their adversary. However, after losing power in 1997, the Conservative Party was "shell-shocked" (Norton 2001: 70). Not only was the parliamentary party halved, with several senior Tories losing their seats, but also the scale of the defeat, not experienced since 1906, meant that the road back to power was unlikely to be a short one. Some twelve years later, with two more election defeats and four attempts to appoint a winning leader in between, the party caught up in the opinion polls and by 2008 surpassed a battered Labour government. Its leader since 2006, David Cameron, described himself, perhaps unwisely, as "heir to Blair." There was a scent of electability in the air.

After all the Conservative Party *was* the twentieth-century party of government. A Conservative Party leader was prime minister for seventy-seven years of the century, whether supported by a Conservative, national, or coalition government, and until 1945, the party survived on an image of continuity and stability, a patriotic and imperial party capable of defending Great Britain from the ravages of Continental militarism and socialism.

In the postwar period the party showed its electoral adaptability. Building on established local social networks—for instance, the Church of England was known until the 1980s as "the Tory Party at prayer"—Conservative constituency parties produced funding and foot soldiers such that, by the 1950s, its direct membership was larger than the Labour Party at close to 3 million. Its women and youth sections and its local Councillors were powerful pressure groupings in its central office and at the annual conference. Leadership and parliamentary party were ruthlessly united in their abiding aim to win elections and form governments.

In adapting to the welfare state and Keynesian economics in the third quarter of the twentieth century, the Conservative Party accepted the shift to interventionist, high-tax policies. It was justified as both necessary to place the party at the new center of voters' aspirations and morally correct as part of the obligation to serve and preserve one nation—Benjamin Disraeli's nineteenth-century concern. Harold Macmillan, of noble background and prime minister from 1957 to 1963, perhaps best represents this pragmatic idealism. In the 1930s, his tract, "The Middle Way," argued for a controlled free market with social aims, especially in relation to unemployment. By 1959 the Conservative election slogan "you never had it so good" seemed the high water mark of one-nation Toryism, and it was Macmillan who also recognized the limits to Britain's external economic security when, in 1961, he made the first overtures for British membership in the EEC.

By the mid 1970s as the postwar Keynesian consensus broke, the response of the Conservative Party was again ruthlessly pragmatic. The one-nation conservation of the 1950s and 1960s was replaced by a neoliberal market-led approach to domestic policy. Led by a redoubtable middle-class science graduate and lawyer, Margaret Thatcher, "solutions" to the inflationary ills of the British economy were presented to an angry and frightened electorate as radical government intervention to reduce state expenditure; let market forces rebalance the economy; and accept, at least for a temporary period, the resultant social misery. Radical economic reform was, however, accompanied by a respect for traditional Conservative social values of family, patriotism, duty, property, and an individual right to strive for wealth and personal security. *Neoliberalism* combined with *neoconservatism* to produce a new center-ground of politics, for which Thatcher's Conservatives were rewarded with three election victories. A fourth, under the leadership of John Major continued her policies through rail privatization and the introduction of market-driven solutions for welfare policies.

Several factors, however, eroded the electoral success of Thatcherite policies during the 1990s. First, the political cost of the market experiment—unemployment at unprecedented levels, a north-south economic divide, the decline in quality of public services—produced internal strains within a party divided between "wets," whose predilections were to the one-nation Toryism of the middle century, and "drys," Thatcherite loyalists who dominated the party, especially after the 1992 election. Second, the long uninterrupted period of Conservative rule produced an "Acton effect," whereby the semblance of "absolute power," as Lord Acton opined, "corrupts absolutely": a series of financial and sexual scandals undermined John Major's "back to basics" campaign of social responsibility and traditional morality (see the book's website). Finally, and equally spectacularly, the Conservative Party, having supported the drive to extend the market to the EU through the Single European Act, turned from its pro-Europeanism to Euroscepticism and suffered, like the Labour Party during the 1980s, massive internal division (Heppell 2002).

Conservatives and the "Europe" Problem

Just as the Labour Party began to reconsider its anti-Europeanism, Mrs. Thatcher's Conservatives were being led in the opposite direction. The Bruges Speech (Thatcher 1988), when their leader summed up EU policies as "socialism through the back door," was a commentary on the impact of nonmarket provisions of the SEA. Her growing Euroscepticism, and the associated backbench divisions, were strengthened by Britain's entry into the European Exchange Rate Mechanism (ERM), a reluctant decision on her part at the behest of her then chancellor, John Major, and foreign secretary, Douglas Hurd. Shortly afterward, her continued stridency toward the EU, together with the unpopularity of the new local tax policy (the "poll tax") led to a leadership challenge and her resignation (1990).

Her successor, John Major, inherited a party more evidently divided on the EU than during most of the 1980s. As the pace of integration increased, parliamentary and extra-parliamentary Eurosceptic factions, such as the Bruges Group, No Turning Back, and the European Foundation, fuelled the debate and were met by pro-EU groupings, such as Positive European and the Action Centre for Europe (Baker 2003: 6). Prime

Minister Major, despite his 1992 electoral success, was not assisted in his attempts to sustain backbench unity by a succession of EU "problems." The Treaty on European Union (TEU) presented a serious challenge to Major's leadership when, after a series of defeats on the bill implementing aspects of the treaty, the Tory Party whip was withdrawn from eight intransigent Eurosceptic MPs in 1994 (i.e., although they retained their seats, they were suspended from the party). Matters were not helped by the ejection of Britain from the ERM (September 1992); this was a massive blow to the Conservatives' reputation for sound economic management. In a bid to shore up his authority, John Major resigned his leadership (June 1995), subsequently winning a victory over the neoliberal Eurosceptic, John Redwood, by 218 votes to 89. But this was scarcely a ringing backbench endorsement. Finally, and in part to placate his divided backbench, Major took an uncompromising stand in the "national interest" when faced with the EU-imposed ban on British beef products following the discovery of BSE infection (mad cow disease) in 1996. This had the effect of further polarizing an already divided Conservative Party—which turned into arguments about whether EU membership was in British interests "when faced with dirty tricks" by other member states (Geddes 2004: 220) For Dennis Kavanagh (1997: 212) "more than any other issue in the 1992 Parliament, Europe dragged down the Conservative Party and sapped the authority of John Major."

The elections of 1987 and 1992 had reduced the Europhile wing of the Conservative Party to minority representation, and the issue itself was no longer perceived as part of a foreign economic policy but as a fundamental issue of national sovereignty. The party from 1997 to 2006 became "a relatively united, anti-European, right wing ultra nationalist/market libertarian party" (Baker 2003: 12). The implications of this for electoral politics in Britain are discussed later.

Conservatives in Opposition (1997–2009)

As became clear during the first Blair administration (1997–2001), the Conservatives' major problem was to relocate to the new electoral middle ground on which New Labour had so successfully camped. The Conservatives were to struggle in response to a political scenario that contained so many of their own core values, as well as the added promise of caring public intervention. A party reorganization was also necessary since membership had dwindled to fewer than 200,000, with an average age that guaranteed most were in receipt of old age pensions. Electorally, the party was provincial, rural, middle-class and English.

William Hague, elected shortly after the 1997 election, moved to emulate some of New Labour's organizational reforms. He sought both to democratize the party and provide the levers of central control necessary to engage with a national constituency. This partial democratization of the party has extended the choice of members in electing political representatives who reflect their values; the problem was that those values were not necessarily shared by the electorate at large. Defeated in 2001, William Hague resigned to be replaced by Ian Duncan-Smith, who, though winning by a three-to-two margin, proved to be both unpopular with the electorate and eventually his backbench. The self-proclaimed "silent man" lasted only two years before his opinion poll rating confirmed his unelectability as prime minister.

Elected unopposed, Michael Howard, as with Hague and Duncan-Smith, failed to locate Conservative policies sufficiently close to the middle ground of twenty-first-century British politics. Howard led his party to its third defeat in 2005 but substantially reduced Labour's majority in the process. Despite his unpopularity after the Iraq invasion, Blair and the Labour Party "successfully occupied much of the Tories' traditional policy space for over a decade" (Cowley and Green 2005: 67).

The election of David Cameron was, to some considerable extent, a major attempt on behalf of both party members and MPs to ditch this image and to truly modernize the party. The leadership choice, once MPs had completed their part in the process, was clear enough: a tough center-right candidate, David Davies, whose orthodox stance on moral issues and the economy, contrasted with the "compassionate conservatism" proclaimed by a youthful and photogenic David Cameron, an old Etonian who embraced much of the New Labour agenda. Despite David Davies fitting the more traditional views of Tory constituency associations, members at last voted for the man most likely to win the next general election. Cameron then commenced both a policy and image makeover of the party that markedly improved the opinion ratings of the Conservatives.

One of his first acts was to attempt to increase the selection of ethnic minority and women candidates in winnable seats as an evident modernizing reform. This has had mixed success, as constituencies have been reluctant to implement a centrally provided "A-list" system involving equal numbers of males and female candidates, together with minority representatives. Policy reform has gradually captured public attention with a stress on environmental issues, global poverty, social inclusion (including recognition of different sexual lifestyles), social justice, and community responsibility. Improved public services, especially in health and education, rather than tax cuts became Conservative priorities. However in the run-up to a 2010 general election the Cameron leadership faces the problem of dealing with economic policies that challenge many of these modernizing planks aimed at achieving electoral success. Cameron, like his post-1997 predecessors, remains openly Eurosceptical and suffered the loss of one backbench Tory MP to Labour for this stance on the very day of Gordon Brown's accession to the premiership. In Cameron, however, the Conservatives have recaptured sight of their core objective—to govern again.

The Liberal Democrats

The repositioning of the Conservative Party makes the center of British politics look crowded for a Liberal Democrat Party seeking a clear position in the middle. With varying and limited degrees of electoral success since 1945, the Liberals in Britain have attempted to present a case for their worth. Liberal parties throughout Europe have been faced with the tactical choice of either a neoliberal or social liberal pathway in the face of a social democratic and Conservative or Christian Democratic squeeze. Britain's Liberals have to date defined themselves in the social liberal and thus center-left mold. Their problem has been twofold: how to sustain a distinct manifesto platform in the face of "policy squeeze"; but also, a problem unique to the British FPTP system, how to maximize a sometimes respectable share of the national vote in terms of parliamentary seats. For the German or Italian liberal parties a more proportionate electoral system guaranteed a roughly equivalent number of parliamentary seats that strengthened their claims to a pivotal role in coalition formation. This has happened only once in British post–World War II national politics (1977–1978) during the Lib-Lab Pact, sustaining the Callaghan government for one year, through a Parliamentary "accord."

Between 1945 and 1979, the Liberals' share of general election votes ranged from 2.5 percent (1951) to 19.3 percent (February 1974), when they returned fourteen MPs. From the formation of the alliance between twenty-nine ex-Labour MPs and the Liberals in 1981 emerged the Liberal Democrats, which provided the first opportunity to break the two-party mold of British politics. In the 1983 election they gained 25.4 percent of the vote and returned twenty-three MPs. But a broken Labour party still retained 209 seats, with only 2.2 percent more of the vote share. This first opportunity for party realignment faded as Conservative successes up to 1992, and Labour recovery, continued to squeeze Liberal Democrat electoral opportunities. The 1997 election seemed to offer new opportunities for a third party, as the possibility of a hung Parliament was in Labour's strategic calculations. Thus, cooperation emerged over such issues as Scottish devolution and electoral reform—a holy grail for the Liberal Democrats as well as tacit acceptance of tactical voting. However, the massive electoral majority won by New Labour destroyed any hope of a coalition government. For a period to 1999, Tony Blair included Liberal Democrat representation on a Joint Cabinet Committee on Constitutional Reform.

This unravelled as the preelection consideration of PR reform for Parliamentary elections was pushed off the Labour agenda.

A mixture of factors, including targeted anti-Tory voting, had resulted in forty-six Liberal Democrat MPs being elected on 17 percent of the vote in 1997. By the 2005 election this had increased to 22 percent and sixty-two MPs, the strongest Liberal presence in the Commons since 1923. But, for many Liberal Democrats, the 2005 results were another failure to break the mold, given the unpopularity of both the Labour government and the Conservative opposition. The party had moved to the left on many issues and made some gains against Labour but did less well against the Conservatives. A "twin targeting" electoral strategy brought uneven benefits (Fieldhouse and Cutts 2005).

Since 2000, however, the Liberal Democrats have served in coalition governments in Scotland, Wales, and many local governments, some as the majority party. In relative terms their representation at the national level is the highest in eighty years. Yet their ideological and electoral significance remains challenged by the crowded political center and the continuing disadvantage that the FPTP system presents to any third party in British politics.

NATIONALIST PARTIES: CELTIC, BRITISH, AND ENGLISH

The opportunities for multilevel electoral contests after 1999, and their associated PR systems, have given fresh opportunities for several parties whose raison d'être is the enhancement and protection of their nation. Britain now has ethnic nationalist parties, in the shape of Plaid Cymru and the SNP, and the defensive nationalism of United Kingdom integrity through the DUP and UKIP. It also retains the residue of ultraright nationalism expressed by the British National Party (BNP). What is missing from this listing is any clearly identifiable party of English nationalism, reflecting the problematic and confusing nature of British/English identity. The author once was confounded by a voter in an English (Liverpool) local government election, who spoke with a strong Yorkshire (northern) accent, wore a (southern) Surrey County Cricket club sweater, and announced that he was going to vote Scots Nationalist. The "Beware Alsatians" sign on the garden gate should have been sufficient warning!

The presence of nationalist parties at several levels of representation and in various executive processes has diluted the notion of a British-only political agenda to which major parties must refer. Party competition has a fourth nationalist dimension that all-British parties (Labour, Conservative, and Liberal) must now address, with consequences for the central, London-based authority of each organization. As we have illustrated,

Celtic nationalist parties are inevitably most successful in their national assemblies. A Scottish minority SNP government, a PC/Labour coalition, and a Sinn Fein/DUP/other party coalition are currently operative; as are many coalition, minority, and power-sharing local governments in each of the devolved nations. In the 2005 general election, Welsh and Scottish nationalist parties fared less well than in 2001, with three and six MPs respectively. No mainland parties operate with any electoral effect in Northern Ireland, though the Conservatives have a Belfast office and the Social Democratic and Labour Party has some association with the Labour party. At EP level the 2004 and 2009 elections returned Welsh, Northern Irish, and Scottish nationalist MEPs, giving representation for nationalist aspirations at every level of British politics.

Elections for the EP Commons and devolved assemblies give a picture of differing voter responses to nationalisms. In the case of the SNP and PC, now that devolved assemblies are firmly established, it may be that a nationalist vote at parliamentary elections is more likely to be a protest or demonstration of ideological commitment. Votes that are cast for devolved assemblies, however, may be considered differently in that they have the possibility of impacting on the shape of devolved government. Both the SNP and PC, in the third devolved election in 2007, obtained shares of the total vote (47% and 15% respectively) and seats sufficient to form minority SNP and Labour/PC coalition executives.

For nationalist voters, therefore, it might be argued that these elections are taking on first-order significance and thus the electoral appeal of nationalist parties must be to a broader range of "rational" voters. Further, since the objective of both parties is to achieve independence, voters have a greater awareness of the consequence of their actions. For the Labour Party, especially in Wales and Scotland, the necessity of tactical collaboration can fit uncomfortably with central government policies. Thus the party competition now evident will continue to develop a distinctive Celtic dimension, with issues that are politically unique and potentially problematic to central government.

In Northern Ireland, Irish nationalism and unionism (which may be perceived as a particular form of British nationalism) run ideologically in opposite directions. The 2005 general and 2007 Assembly elections resulted in the two most extreme protagonists, the republican Sinn Fein and the loyalist DUP, consolidating their positions. The consociational power-sharing agreement, bolted together by constitutional mechanisms and reinforced by British and Irish government joint intervention, has created conditions for "the maintenance of a benign sectarian apartheid" (Tonge 2005a: 147). With an electorate becoming more antipathetic to extremism, but still evidently divided on nationalist issues, the possibility of power sharing and the opportunity to enjoy the recent relative economic prosperity of the province in safety "represents some form of progress, albeit curious, compared to previous decades of political violence" (Tonge 2005a: 147).

Two other parties worthy of consideration in the context of British nationalism are the BNP and UKIP. The BNP is the current manifestation of extreme-right fascist opinion previously represented by the National Front, itself an amalgam (from 1967) of Empire Loyalists, a previous BNP, the Great Britain Movement, and Oswald Mosley's 1930s Union of Fascists. Like its predecessors, its main plank has been the race card; the 1970s slogan "there ain't no black in the Union Jack," its involvement in serious riots in Oldham and Bradford in 2001, the appearance of the French *Front Nationale* leader Le Pen on a 2004 EP election platform, and its more recent criticisms of the influx of East European workers have provided the party and its leaders with a notoriety that mainstream parties find hard to ignore. In the 2005 general election the BNP fought 130 seats, where they averaged 3.5 percent of the vote. In the 2004 EP elections their national vote reached 4.9 percent, coming close to electing an MEP in four regions of the North and Midlands. By 2009 the EP elections delivered two BNP seats from the North West and Yorkshire regions on 6.2 percent of the vote. Their significance, however, has been more for the response by the major parties to their persistent background noise on race and immigration that, until the 2001 election, had been low on the electoral agenda. Islamic terrorism and extremism since 2001 has presented the BNP with the opportunity to claim to reflect "mainstream opinion," with propaganda directed especially at areas of Muslim population.

UKIP has also played the immigration card—but in the context of their primary objective of bringing Britain out of the European Union. In particular the party seeks to stop all economic migration from Europe as part of a rapid staged withdrawal from all EU obligations. Founded in 1993, UKIP gained 16 percent of the vote and 12 seats in the EP elections in 2004, claiming over 10,000 members, located primarily in southern and southwestern England. They have attempted to operate as a right-wing alternative to the Conservatives and have become the home of dissident Europhobic, mainly English, Tories. In 2008 one Conservative MP resigned to join UKIP and Roger Knapman, ex-Conservative MP, became a UKIP MEP and was until 2006 the party's leader. Concern for any major impact on the 2005 performance of the Conservatives, however, was ill judged. UKIP gained only 2.3 percent of the vote and lost 461 constituency deposits (through failing to gain more than 5 percent of each constituency vote). However, in the 2009 EP elections they maintained their 2004 share of the vote at 16.5 percent and gained one extra seat.

Both UKIP and the BNP, "whose ideational variables center on the issues of state, nation and sovereign authority . . . connect European integration with immigration as threats" (Geddes 2006: 132). UKIP's EP success in 2004 and 2009 was the result of several factors, not least the lack of priority given to EU matters by the electorate in general elections (see below). However both parties seek that element of the electorate susceptible to Europhobic, xenophobic, and racial ideas that mainstream parties do not articulate comfortably. As such, their ability to touch the electoral sensitivities of the larger parties and to garner a protest vote is their greatest tactical weapon, giving them, it might be argued, more influence than their inconsistent electoral performance indicates.

POSTMATERIALIST PARTIES

Environmental parties are a permanent feature of the European party landscape. Britain's Green Party emerged in 1985, reaching a high point in the 1989 EP elections when it secured 15 percent of the vote under an FPTP system—but no seats. The mainstream parties have absorbed many of the Greens' policy planks, with the consequence that its electoral impact in parliamentary elections has been limited. In 2005 the Green Party fielded 229 candidates, receiving 1.1 percent of the overall vote. It has proved more successful in PR competitions, gaining two EP seats in 2009, though it lost ground in the 2007 Scottish Parliament election, when its representation dropped from seven to two. In a few local areas, in towns like Brighton and Oxford, the Greens have performed well and have formed part of local-government coalitions in a handful of councils. The party now has a broad agenda for education, transportation, and economic policy and exists as both a party of protest and as a pressure group.

An environmentalist plank is also part of RESPECT (Respect, Equality, Socialism, Peace, Environment, Community, and Trade Unionism), a party based on a "coalition of left wingers disillusioned with the policies of New Labour" (Kavanagh and Butler 2006: 49). Trading on anti–Iraq war and socialist policies, the party pulled support from the Socialist Workers Party, Muslim groups, and leftist Trade Unionists. Its figurehead, the Scottish ex-Labour MP George Galloway, also had links to the Scottish Socialist Party, which has enjoyed some presence in the Scottish Parliament and local government. Galloway successfully fought the Bethnal Green seat in London during the 2005 election. RESPECT also performed well in several other inner-city constituencies where there was a high representation of Muslim voters. The party is representative of the attempt by disillusioned socialists in several European states to find a postmaterialist niche in what might be identified as an ever-more-exclusive political spectrum.

PARTY MEMBERSHIP, APATHY, AND FUNDING

There has been a considerable decline in membership of the main parties in British politics since the 1950s. Labour claimed 850,000 members in 1953 and an allocated membership (and subscription) from several million union members. The Conservatives claimed an individual membership of around 2.75 million. In 2007 this figure had fallen to 320,000. The Labour Party had not only suffered the loss of around 700,000 members, but also a decline in trade union (TU) support as New Labour disentangled itself from its historic TU associations. Several unions disaffiliated themselves from the party, and TU membership had itself declined during the 1980s. Decline in party and TU membership was also accompanied by a decline in national electoral participation. In 1979, 78 percent of the electorate participated in Mrs. Thatcher's first victory. By 2005 only 61 percent turned out for Tony Blair's third election. By the 2009 EP and local elections, fought in the shadow of recession and the allowances scandal, the turnout had dropped to 34 percent.

Decline in frontline political activity is a European-wide phenomenon and is most evident in the last twenty-five years of the twentieth century (Hague and Harrop 2007: 238; Pattie et al. 2004). There are a number of reasons for this situation. Socioeconomic change, as well as a less hospitable political and legal environment in Britain, has had its effect on trade unionism. Consumerism, different work-life patterns, the growth of issue-based politics and organizations, and the decline in class-based political culture have all contributed to partisan dealignment and a reduction in the propensity to join political parties. There is also a change in the mode of political communication that has allowed parties, perhaps at their peril, to discount their membership base. Electronic media, from TV to mobile phone and Internet, allow both mass and individual contact with parties and, importantly, their leaders. This was made widely evident in the Obama presidential campaign in 2008. The ability to target key groups or constituencies is enhanced by sophisticated marketing techniques. The presentation of political messages and personalities and the organization of party resources to allow this to happen is a key feature of the professional or cadre party of the twenty-first century (Webb 2000).

There are, however, some difficulties with what amounts to "a brave new world" analysis of party political communication. A declining membership base means a strain on local campaigning and impacts negatively on party finances. As one commentator suggests "with more elections to fight than ever before, an electorate with fewer partisans, and a lower turnout, political parties (still) need members willing to campaign irrespectively of whether this means actually delivering leaflets or sitting in offices telephoning potential voters" (Childs 2006: 69–70). Both Labour and Conservative parties have attempted to address the problem of their aging membership base, as well as making it easier for would-be members to join and make rapid progress in the party internally and as candidates for elections. There is a dilemma here. Party members are only a small percentage of electors, less than half a million out of 46 million in 2005. The balance, therefore, between giving the membership a voice—the right to control candidate selection, elect party leaders, and shape or negate policies—as against giving the national party and its leadership the opportunity to engage with the electorate is, to say the least, problematic.

Who Pays for Parties?

Declining party membership also means declining finance, as subscription levels and funding activities decrease. Unlike many European democracies, Britain has not moved to a comprehensive system of public funding for party activities. The traditional, voluntaristic nature of party activity, together with what is currently a negative perception of the activities of political parties and politicians in general, has made the provision of public funding (taxpayers' money) politically difficult (Ipsos MORI 2006). Yet, there is a need for a radical overhaul of party funding. In the twelve-month period before the 2005 election, the main parties spent around £90 million (£65 million in 2001). However, only around one-third of Labour's finance was provided by membership sources; for the Conservatives just over two-thirds. The shortfall in both cases is made up by donations and loans from individuals, trade unions, and "other" sources. Whether from business or trade unions, such funding is perceived by many people as potentially corrupting and associated with favoritism and sleaze.

Following the Neill Committee proposals, the Political Parties, Elections and Referendum Act (2000) provided for much more regulated and open information on party finance, with a requirement for donations of over £5,000 nationally and £2,000 locally to be recorded with the Electoral Commission. There was also a limit on the amount parties could spend on both national and local campaigns. However, the act did not solve the acute cash problem that all main parties have experienced in fighting expensive media-based elections, now at the devolved as well as the national level. Moreover, recourse to loans that, until 2006, did not have to be declared, resulted in another item for the sleaze box of party politics, for between 2006 and 2007 several senior political figures were investigated by the police in the "cash for honors" case. Subsequently, Tony Blair, himself interviewed during the investigation, commissioned a report on the future of party financing. The Philips Report (2007), while recommending that public financing was necessary, also recognized that this went hand in hand with a considerable effort on behalf of political parties to improve their public image (Philips 2007). The furor over MPs' expenses in 2009 also led to further calls for party finance reform, as it was revealed that several MPs had utilized their expenses allowance as a means to fund their constituency party activities (see the book's website).

VOTING AND PARTY PREFERENCE

In a contemporary analysis of voting in Britain, David Denver contrasts voting patterns in the 1950 and 2005 general elections to illustrate what appear to be profound changes in voter choice during the period (Denver 2007: 30). We have already pointed out the dominance of the two-party model that produced a 90 percent share of the vote for the Conservatives and Labour in 1950. By 2005, this had fallen to under 70 percent of the to-tal vote (see table 6.3). Of note also was the decline in citizens willing to come out to vote, by 25 percent, during the same period: this despite ex-panded opportunities to cast a ballot by mail (see the book's website for an examination of voting behavior over the past sixty years).

In a contemporary analysis of political choice in Britain, Clarke et al. (2004) explain what has been termed the *valence model*: How does the voter come to an evaluation of her/his relationship with a political party? One element, evaluation of one or another political team's competence, is for many simplified (personified) in the credentials of party leaders; sec-ond, the issues considered most important by the voter will direct her/his vote toward the party that "seems" most able to handle the issue, which gives some room for parties to establish reputations through the quality of their campaign. Thus Labour, out of power since 1979, managed to pres-ent itself as tough on crime and its causes in 1997, thus stealing a previous

Table 6.3.   Voter Identification and Voting Volatility: Change since the 1960s

	Mean 1964–1966	1997	2001	2005
Identity with a party	90	93	89	81
Very strong identifiers	42	16	13	10
Identify with Conservative or Labour	81	76	73	63
Very strong identification: Labour or Conservative	40	15	11	9
Switched party vote from previous election	10	25	22	24
Decided during campaign	12	27	26	33

Source: Denver (2007) (sourced from British Election Studies).

issue trump card from the Conservatives. Finally, voters return to the vital ingredient of economic competence, that is, whether the future of an individual's economic world is best served by one or another party (Clarke et al. 2004). For Gordon Brown, the 2009 world recession presented an opportunity to claim, albeit not without dispute, competence in "seeing Britain through" massive economic problems. However, other issues, not the least being the parliamentary allowances fiasco and resulting public cynicism, were equally decisive, especially to smaller parties seeking to maximize electoral support in local and EP elections (2009).

WHICH ELECTORAL ISSUES ARE MOST IMPORTANT?

Opinion polls confirm that issues that are close to personal experience, "bread and butter issues," are the ones in which British folk show most interest. Table 6.4 shows the NHS, law and order, and education, together with economic interests, as the most significant for the voter between 2001 and 2005. In 1997 unemployment was also in the top three. Though their salience might differ over time it is evident that issues that are external to domestic priorities, or ideological issues (nationalization/privatization, human rights/community, security), do not easily enter the electorate's consciousness. Thus, issues that seem to exercise the interests of parties and the media are not always at the forefront of the consciousness of the electorate. In particular, immigration and asylum and EU matters have consistently failed to appear in the top five issues that interest the majority of the voting public. As we have seen above, the Conservative Party remained massively divided over the EU throughout the 1990s. The Blair government between 2001 and 2005, and in particular the PM himself, was attacked for their support of the Iraq war. But neither the Conservatives' defeat in 1997 nor Labour's limited victory in 2005 was singularly

Table 6.4.   The Most Important General Election Issues: Voters' Priorities (2001, 2005)

2001	Priorities	2005
Health Service	1	Health Service
Law and Order	2	Education
Education	3	Law and Order
Economy	4	Taxation/Public Expenditure
Taxation	5	The Economy Generally
Pensions/Taxation	6	Asylum/Immigration
Asylum/Immigration	7	Fight against Terrorism/Iraq
Europe	8	Europe

Source: ICM (2001, 2005).

explained by these factors (Denver 2007; Geddes 2005). EU issues in 1997 added to the general sense of incompetence that the electorate felt about the Conservative government; and Iraq in 2005 added to the general disillusion and distrust of the Labour prime minister. Iraq, as an issue, was ultimately outweighed by the "valence" assessment by a (small) majority of voters that Labour's economic competence over time was reason enough to permit a third term.

It is possible to argue that intraparty politics and electoral politics are at times played out in parallel universes. The Labour Party during the 1980s, and the Conservatives from the mid-1990s to 2006, fought internal ideological battles that, electorally, proved disastrous. Moreover, the newsprint media have had at times a disproportionate effect on the prioritization of party political issues, the assumption being that the press universe is the same as the electorate's. In consequence, there are some issues to which the press and parties give prominence that bear little resemblance to the predilections of the electorate. Thus immigration and asylum in the 2005 election were high on the list of issues for the Conservative core vote and also issues capable of press sensationalism. However, for the electorate at large these issues "did not swing voters" (Kavanagh and Butler 2006: 185). As we have suggested, the euro featured significantly in the 2001 elections; but once again it was simply not a swing vote issue (Geddes 2005: 282 and below). Both immigration and the EU have been political issues at party level and in the media for many years. Both may be perceived as contributing to the "valence vote," in that they are associated with the broader debate on national integrity and the competence of governments to protect and/or enhance that integrity. Indeed the two issues have, for some, become conflated—given the EU open-borders labor policy of the government between 2004 and 2006.

Immigration is an issue around which the Conservative Party has united and, while the electoral advantages of taking a strong line are debateable, it remains one that is more tactically problematic for the Labour Party. It is, however, an arena that has been recently open to public debate, either directly or indirectly, through discussion of multiculturalism, social inclusiveness, Britishness, internal security, and the distribution of public services. The EU, however, is an equally pernicious issue for political parties and the electorate.

PARTIES AND THE STRANGE EFFECT OF THE EU

Until the early 1980s the EU (then the EC) was an issue of secondary importance for the party divide. Once the 1960s Labour governments had accepted that national economic interests were best served by joining the Community, and once the ideological arguments of the left (about joining a "capitalist club") were derailed by the 1975 referendum, the subject was of only irritant value for the Wilson/Callaghan governments as they struggled for domestic economic survival. Similarly, Edward Heath, who had finally led Britain into the Community in 1973, was able to marginalize the Eurosceptic right of his party that perceived "Europe" as a threat to national and parliamentary sovereignty. The referendum debate (1975), temporarily as it turned out, also deflected this critique. A cross-party position existed until 1981, when the Labour left took control of the party's election agenda, returning to its neo-Marxist view of the Community as a capitalist cartel, and campaigned for British withdrawal. Divided and massively defeated in 1983, Labour returned to a more positive stance on the EU for the 1987 election. This was in part associated with those social aspects of the SEA that were perceived as a lifeline to a trade union movement battered by the Thatcherite neoliberal agenda: conversely the SEA was, for Thatcherite Conservatives, the driving factor of a movement in the opposite direction, culminating in divisions within the party after the 1989 election and contributing to the demise of Mrs. Thatcher's leadership in 1990.

Internal party divisions over Britain's EU relationship have been of major significance for both parties, contributing to Labour's electoral malaise during the 1980s and the Conservatives' divisions during the 1990s. Only the Liberal Democrats have held a consistent pro-EU line, though this has presented them with some regional electoral headaches in southwest England, a historic source of Liberal strength, where there has emerged an increasingly Eurosceptic electorate concerned with the local impact of the EU's common fisheries and agricultural policies. We may analyze the EU effect on Britain's parties in terms of an EU impact on party ideology and on party electoral strategy and, finally, on party organization.

Ideas about the EU

"Ideas, subjectivity and meanings are integral components of the debates about the EU," suggests Andrew Geddes, because the notion of EU integration collides with "broader debates about the state, nation and sovereignty within and between the parties" (Geddes 2006: 119). For Labour and Conservative parties, Britain's relationship with the EU has played a significant part in how each has interpreted Britain's external and domestic priorities. And as the parties have shifted their ideological perspectives, their stances on the issue of "Europe" have adjusted. Thus, in the late 1950s and early 1960s Labour grappled with its internationalist conscience by rejecting EU membership, partly on the grounds that it would damage British responsibilities for its African Commonwealth partners.

A similar stance was taken by many Conservatives, who saw prioriti-zation of Commonwealth interests as a mix of modernity and tradition, as a positive response to colonialism, a means of sustaining cherished links with an imperial past, and as a bulwark against world Communism. Another perspective shared by both Labour and Conservative Euroscep-tics was the importance of the English-speaking diaspora to include the "white" Commonwealth *and* the United States that was perceived as "far closer to Britain in language, trade, population, investment and sentiment than the EEC" (Shore 1973: 27). For the left, the EU was no more than a capitalist trap and, later, for the Conservative neoliberal right, a socialist plot. Finally, the issue of parliamentary sovereignty united Eurosceptics of both the left and right, never more obviously than in the 1975 referen-dum, when the English nationalist Tory Enoch Powell and intellectual so-cialist Michael Foot, parliamentarians to their core, campaigned side by side in Eurosceptic solidarity. Since the early 1990s, the Labour party in the Commons, together with the Liberal Democrats, has presented a con-sistent if pragmatic pro-EU front when compared with the Conservative Party, which has adopted a semidetached perspective in opposition that, on occasion, has bordered on the Europhobic.

There is no doubt that to utilize the concept of European integration in electoral debate is fraught with problems. Since the EU is a fiercely con-tested concept, debate about it is shaped not by any objective and gener-ally accepted view but by what one writer suggests is "the distorted lens" of party politics (Geddes 2006: 121). One cannot, therefore, ignore the ide-ological implications of particular interpretations of what European inte-gration means to the main parties. Since returning to opposition in 1997, Conservative Eurosceptic opinion has been consolidated by the election of MPs and leadership that has moved the party progressively toward what might be termed EU detachment. A neoliberal perspective includes glob-alist views of Britain's economic destiny that fit uncomfortably with their view of European integration as protectionist and interventionist. While the majority of Eurosceptic Conservative MPs are of the economic right, other factors, particularly adherence to traditional notions of state and par-liamentary independence, must also be recognized in explaining why the party is now identified as predominantly Eurosceptic in outlook. For one writer "the question of European integration *was* the ideological deter-minant of Conservatism" during the 1990s (Heppell 2002: 320).

While this cannot be said of New Labour during the ideological jour-ney that the party has made since the late 1980s, it has created conditions for an engagement with the EU not possible a few years earlier. We can identify three periods of their ideological (and tactical) adjustment. Between 1987 and 1994 there was a search for renewal that sought electoral salva-tion in the European social model long established in Swedish politics, in

French president Mitterrand's mostly successful reinvention of the *Partie Socialiste*, or in 1990s German social democracy. This ideological reconfiguration of the party toward the European mainstream was enhanced by a shift in the position of the British trade union movement, which abandoned its traditional Eurosceptic glowering to embrace the lifeline of "social solidarity" and "social cohesion" associated with Single Market legislation. This partial Europeanization of the British trade union movement gave a modernizing Labour party political freedom to pursue Continental alliances and present an alternative to the strident anti-European stance of Thatcherite Conservatives, especially after the 1992 election that reduced the Eurosceptic left to around thirty MPs.

The advent of Blair-led "New Labour" resulted in a further ideological shift and a revised EU policy perspective. Rather than learn from the European social market, Labour's "Third Way" implied that Britain's reengagement with the EU would involve the reeducation of other member states with regard to at least some aspects of labor and market reform. Both before and after the 1997 election, Tony Blair made himself unpopular with several fellow social democrat leaders in pushing too zealously for an EU Third Way agenda. In particular, one aspect of the Third Way mantra fitted uncomfortably with the domestic agendas of some EU partners: the stress on preparing the EU for globalized market competition was pushed enthusiastically by both PM Blair and his then chancellor, Gordon Brown. This was to present difficulties with other EU leaders, especially in France and Germany.

While New Labour in government had embraced several aspects of the EU post-Maastricht agenda, its conversion to integration was hedged by many of the doubts expressed by Conservative Eurosceptics. Thus, membership in the Single Currency, reluctance to accept a developed European foreign and security policy, and opt-outs from restrictive legislation relating to the labor market suggest limitations to any claims to a radical, ideologically based repositioning of the party's European policy. Subsequently, Labours "red lines" in the 2007 negotiations over a reshaped constitutional treaty (now Lisbon Treaty) led to British opt-outs, not least with regard to the Charter of Fundamental Rights, seen as a possible challenge to labor-market flexibility and the English legal process.

Initially the Brown premiership adopted a more distant EU tone, reflecting the PM's global and US perspectives on Britain's economic future. But in his speech to the European Parliament prior to the critical G20 Conference in 2009, Brown produced the most positive statement of EU-British relationships in his public career. The need to establish support for vital international agreements may have been a contributing factor for this show of Europhilia. Labour's more pro-European policies are not, it seems, shaped by any marked ideological shift but fit within a pragmatic, intergovernmentalist perspective, constructed by national interest and electoral considerations. Thus, the parameters of interparty debate, and the debate that the main parties have with their electorates, are persistently delimited by issues of nationhood and sovereignty. These, of course, have ideological overtones that the British press has debated with relish (see chapter 7).

European Integration, Party Competition, and the Electorate

When asked about "Europe," the British electorate tend to produce defensive or negative opinions. Eurobarometer surveys over time indicate this negativity. In 2006 Britons were highest in viewing the EU negatively (35%). Only 26 percent "trusted" the EU, the lowest in the EU. Britain also had the highest percentage of people disinterested in the EU (27%) and the lowest who thought it was "a good thing" (36%) (further opinions are compared in table 6.5). As we have seen, as an electoral issue the EU has consistently scored well below other voter concerns. Yet both Labour and Conservative parties have damaged their electoral credibility by periodically dividing over matters European. The intraparty debates on the issue are bitter, yet the electoral return for expending political effort on this issue looks limited. How does the EU affect party competition for the ear of the electorate?

The EU is unusual for party competition for a number of reasons, first because of its ability to cause division across party lines. Second, politicians perceive that the issue touches on electoral sensitivities directly, given its encapsulation in the debate about national sovereignty (Geddes 2006). This is reinforced by a third factor: the salience of much of the print media in representing the EU in a stark positive/negative light (Carey and Burton 2004; Anderson and Weymouth, 1999). In effect, perhaps more than any other political issue, Britain's relationship with the EU is forced onto the political agenda by the combination of deep-seated attitudes of part of the political elite toward the EU and a print media that may be described as bipolar. As we shall argue, the optimum party campaign strategy may thus be to keep the EU off the political agenda; and here recent Labour tactics have been quite successful (see the book's website).

For both the Conservative and Labour parties, issues of European integration are currently treated like the "elephant in the room," with great caution and best left alone. Should the beast be stirred, fundamental questions concerning nation, identity, and sovereignty are easily raised that, in the recent history of both parties, have contributed to periods of disunity. With one eye on a mainly Eurosceptic electorate, both parties have adopted tactical positioning that seeks to preserve hard-won party unity—the Conservatives through a generally negative neoliberal/neoconservative perspective and Labour with a pragmatic but, where tactically necessary, soft Eurosceptic line. Both positions aim to placate respective core electorates.

Table 6.5.   Public Opinions about the EU

Has your country benefitted from the EU?

Highest	Ireland	87%
	Lithuania	77%
	Denmark	74%
Lowest	Sweden	41%
	Hungary	41%
	Britain	*39%*

Do you understand how the EU works?

Highest	Luxembourg	65%
	Poland	59%
	Cyprus	58%
	Britain	*40%*
Lowest	Italy	36%
	Czech Rep	34%
	Spain	31%

Do you trust (a) EU institutions and (b) Parliament

	(a)		(b)	
Highest	Slovenia	70%	Denmark	72%
	Greece	65%	Finland	65%
	Czech Rep	62%	Sweden	61%
			Britain	*29%*
Lowest	Germany	38%	Czech Rep	19%
	Sweden	38%	Lithuania	16%
	Britain	*26%*	Poland	11%

Source: Eurobarometer 2006a.

But what frequently disturbs these now distinctive positions is the need for the government to respond to its member-state responsibilities. Consequently decisions agreed to in the Council of Ministers produce powerful responses from the press, UKIP, and elements of Conservative Party opinion. Thus, the Brown government was faced, at an early stage, with the issue of the Reform Treaty and calls by the opposition for a referendum at the time—"the thorniest problem on Mr Brown's foreign policy in-tray" (Richards 2007: 29). Issues of EU integration are therefore periodically, and sometimes unpredictably, thrown into public debate. In this negative sense, EU issues have "Europeanized" party political agendas since the mid-1980s (Geddes 2006).

There are two consequences of significance for the British political process. The first is that evidently principled divisions between party elites over the nature of the EU produce opportunities for often unprincipled and crude opinion to be articulated. UKIP's entry into electoral competition, together with the unsophisticated stances taken by large sectors of the British press, at best oversimplifies and at worst destroys opportunities for cool consideration of complex issues. Second, since the tendency of both the Conservative and Labour parties has been to fight, lacking more sophisticated explanations of British-EU association, one major source of communication and education for the general public on EU matters is undermined. The result is that the British public are underinformed and therefore sceptical and/or disinterested bystanders, as their elites attempt to avoid discussion about fundamental issues of direct electoral concern. For students of British politics, however, to avoid grappling with this complex issue of the Europeanization of political parties in Britain would result in "a strange reading of political history" (Geddes 2006: 133).

The EU and Party Organization

Previous and subsequent chapters identify the ways in which membership in the EU has changed the structure and processes of political and bureaucratic organizations. In the case of political parties, there have been several effects, the most evident of which is the creation of a layer of organization to interact with the European Parliament, which has entailed an interaction between the domestic and EP party structures. This would seem natural enough, given the impact of the EU on domestic policies and the fact that, other than ministers in attendance at the Council of Ministers and the PM at the European Council, MEPs are the only elected representatives from Britain within the EU political process. But the extent to which British political parties have adapted to these processes, that is, Europeanized, is limited. This is, in part, a result of the internal organization of the EP, where member state representatives sit in supranational groupings, for example the Party of European Socialists (PES), in order to gain access to EP committees and resources. Together with a general lack of interest in the activities of the EP by party bureaucrats and elites, this situation has led to MEPs occupying a space largely detached from their domestic party organizations.

The Labour Party has gone further in integrating its MEPs within its domestic activities. MEPs, together with MPs, make up one-third of the votes of the electoral college for leadership contests and are also represented on the NEC. Since 1999, each of the spokespersons on EP committees from the Labour Party has been invited to attend relevant (domestic) ministerial committees. It was hoped that this linkage would establish loyalty to the government line on policy issues as they appeared in EP deliberations (Carter and Ladrech 2007). The input of Conservative and Liberal Democrat MEPs to domestic policy making is less institutionalized.

There is little evidence that domestic parties, other than UKIP, devote more than a small proportion of their resources toward EU-related party activities. MEPs fund their own activities from their salaries and EP resources. Domestic central-party organizations have only tiny European affairs departments, whose influence has become less significant because many of their activities have been incorporated under international rather than specifically EU affairs (Carter and Ladrech 2007: 144). Specialist advice, whether from MEPs or from European specialists, is limited "and tends only to be sought if it is in line with national party leadership's policy preferences or only if it is likely to help party strategy" (Geddes 2006: 140).

One other arena for domestic party interaction with the EU is through association with European transnational parties, of which the PES, founded in 1992, is the best established (Lightfoot 2005). Socialism has had a historical internationalist dimension, and the Labour Party pursued briefly a close relationship with European social democrat parties during its early modernization period (1987–1994). During the 1990s Robin Cook, who was foreign secretary between 1997 and 2001, played an active role in the PES and was its president from 2001 to 2004. However, New Labour's market-oriented approaches did not sit well with more traditional social democratic values, and Tony Blair's attendance at PES party leaders' meetings was often an uncomfortable affair (Lightfoot 2005: 68–69). The Conservative association with the European People's Party (EPP) has been even more uncomfortable, given the Christian Democrat and federalist character of the party grouping. Conservative Eurosceptics have called for their party's withdrawal from the EPP, and as part of his leadership manifesto David Cameron signalled his intention to seek new alliances for Conservative MEPs in the EP. This led to inconclusive negotiations with somewhat unsavory right-wing groupings, and many Conservative MEPs have deplored these maneuverings as likely to jeopardize their contribution to EU policy making within the EP's largest political group. While transnational parties are significant contributors to the search for policy consensus within the EP's legislative process, they are in general perceived as less relevant than the activities of national party elites as members of the Council of Ministers.

To summarize, British party organizations have adapted to the EU arena minimally. There has been very little attempt to incorporate the EP activities of their MEPs into elite policy activity and little in the way of resource allocation for the EU policy agenda. The result is what Carter and Ladrech refer to as "the high autonomy and low accountability" of MEPs to their respective domestic parties (Carter and Ladrech 2007: 161). As with the failure of domestic parties to include EU issues in electoral debate, the disjuncture between domestic and EP parties underscores the existence of parallel political universes, EU and national, in British politics today.

CONCLUSION

Much has changed in the nature of the British party system since it was cited confidently as an example of a two-party system during the 1950s (Duverger 1954). Coalition or minority-party systems are a feature of devolved and local government, and in EP elections, seven parties represent British interests. At the national level, only six out of ten electors voted for the two major parties in 2005—and this from a diminishing sector of citizens who exercised their right to vote. Conservative and Labour parties face a dual challenge: from minor parties that seek to break the winner-take-all system associated with FPTP; and from a voter base no longer so clearly aligned through class-based perspectives on politics. What remains of the two-party model, the party structure of the House of Commons, it can be argued, is only kept alive by the perversity of the FPTP voting system (Childs 2006; Curtice et al. 2005).

We can also note changes to the composition of political parties that reflect the dynamics of British political culture. Women candidates, at least in devolved politics and in Labour's Commons representation, have achieved significant electoral success. There is, however, little sign that ethnic groups are obtaining party candidacies commensurate with their increasing demographic presence. Well under a million people are members of a political party, a decline of 75 percent since the 1950s. This decline in party activism brings with it a resource crisis, especially as the addition of elections to devolved assemblies has led to the need for annual campaigning activities in multilevel competitions.

Ideologically, the left/right polarization that encouraged high levels of class-based partisanship has been mitigated by a battle for the middle ground. New Labour's shift in the 1990s to embrace the market and social justice was now matched by the Social Conservatism of David Cameron's party. Within this crowded middle ground, campaigning has vigorously embraced media presentation and, through the deification/demonization of leadership, parties seek to differentiate their qualities to an electorate that judges political capability by mediated images of competence. In consequence, professional cadres marshal party machinery and resources, challenging the role of the membership in policy choices and candidate selection. This centralization of party organization is, however, crosscut by phenomena not evident in the 1950s. Subnationalism and devolution have caused tensions, especially for the governing Labour Party, as the very different complexion of subnational politics has led to disputes between central and devolved governments over policy requirements.

The chapter has also stressed the complex and generally underresearched impact of European integration on party politics. We have noted the cross-party divisions that the issue creates and the periods of turmoil that disagreement over the fundamentals of European integration has produced. Both parties in government have, on the one hand, acquiesced to further European integration but have negotiated opt-outs that placate anti-EU opinion at party and electoral levels. A mainly Eurosceptic press has watched, hawk-like, over major EU developments, helping to confirm a Eurosceptic public opinion, which in turn produces media-driven party responses rather than an optimal European policy. Much of the discussion, whether in the Commons, in newspapers, or on the campaign trail, involves broad and emotive stances on issues associated with national independence, parliamentary sovereignty, or Britain's global positioning. In the meantime, EU policies, especially since the implementation of the Single European Act, have made a substantial impact on the lives of British citizens, yet mainstream parties, whether in government or opposition, have failed to inform and educate the electorate of the integral role of the EU in Britain's domestic affairs. As a consequence, the EU elephant in the room waits to be discussed by a currently disinterested and often bewildered public, while party elites squabble disingenuously about whether its very existence should be accepted—or not.

FURTHER READING

Paul Webb's *The Modern British Party System* (2000) is a starting point for a study of British party politics. The ideological roots of the party system are described in *British Political Ideologies* by Robert Leach (2002). Patrick Dunleavy et al. point to the weakness of the idea of a two-party system in *Developments in British Politics* (2006). Thomas Quinn examines the emergence of New Labour in *Modernizing the Labour Party: Organizational Change since 1983* (2004). Liberal Democrat fortunes are traced in Andrew Russell's *Neither Left nor Right* (2005). Anthony Seldon and Peter Snowden's *The Conservative Party* (2004) and *After Blair: David Cameron and the Conservative Tradition* by Kieron O'Hara (2007) give historical and contemporary background. Denver (2007) in *Elections and Voters in Britain* (2nd ed.) presents reasons why citizens vote. Dennis Kavanagh and David Butler (2006) and Andrew Geddes and Jon Tonge, eds. (2005), show how they did, in the 2005 general elections. Geddes sums up the factors that make the EU a problematic electoral issue (2006). The "problem of Europe" for the Conservatives is documented in *The Conservative Party and European Integration since 1945* by Neill Crowson (2006). Robert Ladrech and Elizabeth Carter reveal limited political and organizational connection between domestic parties and the European level of party activity in Poguntke et al. (2007).

Participation, Pressure Groups, and the Media

CIVIL SOCIETY IN BRITAIN

In its fourth annual report on political engagement, in 2007, the Electoral Commission found mixed blessings for the health of Britain's political participation. On the one hand, the report showed that, though many people show an interest in political issues, "few are willing to be potentially active. However there is no evidence of any decline in political engagement in recent years" (Electoral Commission 2007: 7). Placed in a comparative perspective, political participation in Britain is not much different from other European countries. A 2006 Eurobarometer survey reported that in EU15, 78 percent of respondents had voted in a previous election or referendum (74% Britain); that 23 percent has contacted a politician or government official (27% Britain); that 9 percent had worked for a party or "action group" (6% Britain); and 32 percent had signed a petition (41% Britain). Rather less Britons (10%) had taken part in demonstrations than in EU15 (22%) (Eurobarometer 2006b). While the last is illustrative of a difference in political behavior (39% of Spanish respondents had recently demonstrated), similarities rather than differences are more significant: in general terms turnout at elections, membership of and trust in political parties, and trust in national institutions and politicians, though varying between countries, declined across Europe during the five years before and after the turn of the century (see table 7.1 and Bale 2005; Eurobarometer 2006b; Franklin 2004).

Britons—Still Participating

However, the notion of civil society takes us beyond the view of "politics" that British and other European peoples seem to reject. As part of a research

Table 7.1.   Political Participation in the EU: Some Similarities—and Differences (by percentage)

In the last three years have you . . . ?

	Voted in an election/ referendum?	Contacted a politician or gov. official	Worked in a party or action group	Worked for another civic association	Signed a petition	Presented your view online	Demon- strated publically
Britain	74	27	6	8	42	12	10
EU15	78	22	9	17	32	14	22
Germany	75	18	11	16	20	14	15
France	83	30	7	28	53	12	32
Italy	85	24	9	15	25	11	27
Luxembourg	70	27	9	21	39	18	22
Sweden	87	24	9	24	28	15	15

Source: Eurobarometer (2006a), Flash Barometer Series 189a (percentages rounded).

program on democracy and participation, the Economic and Social Research Council presented a Citizens Audit to find "'what it meant to be a citizen at the beginning of the twenty-first century" (Pattie et al. 2003: 616). In an initial analysis, the authors found a strong sense of civic obligation in terms of obeying the law, paying taxes, jury service, voting or giving blood: three out of four citizens perceived these as civic duties. There were also high civic expectations of government—to reduce poverty extremes and to provide cheap housing for the poor (around seven out of ten respondents). Rather less than half, however, thought government was obliged to create jobs or encourage private medicine or that people should rely on a state pension. The impact of recession in 2009 has led to a reversal of this noninterventionist perspective.

When contrasting behavior in 1981 and 2001, more citizens in 1981 voted in national and local elections, belonged to parties, and contacted politicians, whereas in 2001 more were boycotting products and contacting the media directly. Many more were donating to pressure groups or buying certain products for ethical or environmental reasons (28%). Thus, on the basis of the audit, at the turn of the century out of an adult population of 44 million, "in order to influence political outcomes," 27 million gave money to an organization, 18 million signed a petition, 13 million shopped with political objectives in mind, and 2 million took part in a public demonstration (Pattie et al. 2003: 623).

Inevitably the more politically active segments of the population are found in middle-class socioeconomic groups who are educated to above high school level and are middle aged and who watch little television. But for most of the British population who engage in politics, it is a spectator sport, wherein one pays money for a professional to engage with political decision makers in order to represent the individual and civic good (Putnam 2002: 412). As we entered the twenty-first century, civic participation was analyzed as more individual than collective and purchased rather than participated in, fitting, as we suggested in chapter 2, an atomized or modular postindustrial society (Krieger 1999). So while it can safely be argued that conventional political activism and belief in its efficiency has declined over twenty years, participation in what Pattie et al. call "consumption and contact politics" has increased significantly, evidencing a good deal of civic vitality (Pattie et al. 2003: 632).

As against this cynicism for party politics, the decline in trade unionism and an evident public expression of negativity toward the role of representative institutions and the people in them are, as we have noted, of concern—especially to politicians (see the book's website). While we may note a certain health in the civic activities of better educated, wealthier consumer/participators, there would seem less opportunity for those whose need for interest representation—the unhealthy, the unhoused, the young and old, poor and uneducated—is highest, as "working-class" organizations decline (Pattie, et al. 2004).

So what may we conclude about the level of *social capital* within Britain's civil society? This is evidenced in the quantity and range of voluntary associations that are not public or for-profit organizations. Social capital develops from the social networks encouraged by voluntary association and the inclination of people to do things for each other. From this emanates a civil society based on tendencies of trust and reciprocity (Putnam 2000). In contrast to membership in political organizations, membership in social organizations and willingness to be involved in "'civic commitments" is high and has increased in the past thirty years. On such evidence we might conclude that groups may be replacing political parties as the more trusted association to achieve particular outcomes and, as one commentator suggests, unlike the United States "the British appear not to be Bowling Alone" (Maloney 2006: 114). We shall return later, however, from examining the paradox of this relatively healthy assessment of Britain's social capital to the much more negative perception and involvements of British people in their formal democratic institutions.

ORGANIZED INTERESTS AND PRESSURE POLITICS

The Directory of British Associations lists over 7,000 entries in its 2007 edition. Since its first publication in 1965 the number of listed groups has doubled. Of these, over 1,500 are trade associations, 1,350 are professional bodies, and over 800 are learned societies. Of the rest, over 3,000 listings, there are nineteen categories in such fields as the arts, education, medical interests, sports, and hobbies. The National Trust claims a membership of 2.7 million, the Consumer Association has over a million subscribers, many groups number under a hundred, and the UK Flat Glass Manufacturers Association has a membership of one! It does, however, represent the British division of one of the world's largest glass manufacturers that turns itself into a trade association when politically prudent to do so. The motives for joining or organizing associations vary: material interests such as the tangible economic benefits that might accrue from a trade union or employers' association; for purposive or cause reasons—such as promoting human rights (Amnesty International) or to change the law (Fathers 4 Justice); or for social reasons—any hobby, sporting, or social club one cares to think of.

Groups that have general interests to share can join together into confederations either at national or international levels. These "peak groups" come to represent sectoral or sectional interests with some considerable effect. The Confederation of British Industry (CBI) and the Trades Union Congress (TUC) are the most obvious; these in turn have joined EU-wide peak groups of which the Union of Industrial and Employers' Confederations of Europe (UNICE—now called BusinessEurope) and the European Trade Union Confederation (ETUC) are significant Brussels players. Many groups are both domestic and international in perspective and organization—Oxfam, Greenpeace, Amnesty International—or are affiliated with international federations such as the International Transport Federation, the International Federation of Business and Professional Women, or the International Federation of Pharmaceutical Manufacturers Associations. British Sports Federations are represented, either directly or indirectly, in myriad regional and international associations. Thus the English, Welsh, and Scottish Football Associations are members of the European Football Association (UEFA) and are also members of the International Federation of Football Associations (FIFA); FIFA is also a member of the Association of International Sports Federations. Each of these associations has its headquarters in Europe. Domestic interests and their representation can stretch beyond national targets and, as we shall argue below, the organization of interests in Britain as a member state of the EU has been profoundly affected by the opportunities that have emerged in dealing with a multilevel policy process in so many interest sectors.

Academics over many years have defined and categorized interest groups in many different ways (Almond 1958; Eckstein 1960; La Palombara 1961; Richardson 1993; Grant 1999). And the distinction between an interest and pressure group is not particularly clear, for, as one author suggests, the term *interest group* in the United States is used to refer to all organized interests; whereas in Britain it is more likely to be used for those groups whose aim is to promote the interests of their members. "The term pressure group is preferred in the UK [with] interest group tending to be used as a subcategory of the broader classification" (Heywood 2002: 270).

More recently, many authors have adapted a dual distinction and categorize in terms of group objectives: thus *sectional groups* are primarily self-regarding organizations that promote the welfare of their members; and *cause groups* (or attitude or promotional groups) have values, principles, and ideals to advance. We shall, however, introduce a third category here—*the institutional group*. These are civic and public organizations, such as churches, the police, or components of the machinery of governance, and they are of growing significance, it is suggested, because of the multilevel nature of Britain's policy-making process. As we shall argue below, this is evident in the role of some institutions, for instance, local and regional governments, as pressure groups at EU level. Examples of each of these categorizations are contained in table 7.2.

Another form of categorization applies to the strategies adopted and the relationship between groups and government. Here, the distinction is between *insider* and *outsider* status. Thus some authors distinguish between the strategies and opportunities of groups, which lead to their status as part of a policy community, issues network, or policy network (Jordan and Richardson 1987; Baggott 1995; Grant 1999 and 2004). The concept of insider and outsider groups recognizes the significance of a group's status in relation to government; thus an insider group may be low profile and covert in its dealings with government—the various food and drink trade associations, for instance; or high profile in that it seeks to supplement its achieved government access by "going public."

The British Medical Association (BMA), an insider group, is not shy in seeking media support for its opinions on health policy. Other groups may not have this opportunity, being prisoners to government—the hand that

Table 7.2.   A Categorization of British Pressure Groups

	Insider Status	Outsider Status
Associational	National Farmers Union	Farmers for Action
	Confederation of British Industry	British Field Sports Society
	British Medical Association	Fire Brigades Union
Promotional	Parents for Equality	Fathers 4 Justice
	Stonewall (Gay Rights)	Outrage (Gay Rights)
	Greenpeace (in business suits)	Greenpeace (in wetsuits)
Institutional*	The Church of England	The Church of England (1980s)
	British Broadcasting Corporation	British Broadcasting
	(pre–Iraq War)	Corporation (post–Iraq War)
	Devolved Assemblies	Greater London Council
		(1980s)

* Some institutional groups fall out with government. The Church of England was critical of the consequences of 1980s Conservative economic policies for the inner cities; the BBC had a checkered relationship with the Blair government. However being an institution of the state gives some insider status by definition, even in the most uncomfortable times.

feeds them—such as Research Councils or local authority associations. Outsider groups may seek insider status: the pro-hunting Countryside Alliance would undoubtedly seek insider status with a more sympathetic Conservative government. Some have no choice in their outsider status, for instance, the forthright gay rights organization Outrage, or have no wish to compromise ideological aims that can only be achieved by what amounts to a major policy or system change (the Campaign for Nuclear Disarmament or a radical Islamist group). Grant's categorization (2004) cuts across the sectoral/issue group division but also recognizes that the line between an insider and an outsider is thin. Thus the Trades Union Congress (TUC) enjoyed insider status as peak group in the period of corporatism during the 1960s and 1970s; by the 1980s it was turned into a de facto outsider group, campaigning and promoting the cause of its members to inattentive Thatcher-Major administrations (see the book's website).

A number of other factors allow the insider/outsider perspective powerful explanatory characteristics. We have already referred to the professionalization of organized interests in Britain and the growth of sophisticated lobbying processes and services. The cultivation of access through networking and the establishment of networks of influence, together with the increase in access points through MLG, have revolutionized the world of pressure group activity. The EU presents not just new opportunities for interest group lobbying but has itself "downloaded" policies and processes that, through notions of institutionalized pluralism, have favored certain interests and interest practices (see below). Globalized economic production and political phenomena have created a multinational and international network of interest organizations capable of canvassing the UN in New York, the WTO in Geneva, the EU in Brussels or Strasbourg, or the DTI or DEFRA in London. Greenpeace is thus both an international and national pressure group with potential for both insider and outsider group status, depending whether it is adopting "wet suit" or "dry suit" tactics (Grant 2004).

There are also international ramifications for national pressure group activities, as the consequences of the intimidating tactics of an animal rights group Stop Huntingdon Animal Cruelty (SHAC) illustrate. Their threatening actions in the early years of this century produced not only reaction from the British bioindustry but changes to public order legislation and protests from Japanese multinational companies associated with SHAC's target, Huntingdon Life Sciences. Other actions against Oxford and Cambridge research organizations prompted the chairman of Glaxo Smith Kline and AstraZeneca, in a meeting with Prime Minister Blair, to threaten withdrawal of research investment from Britain (Grant 2004). All this, suggests Grant, "achieved by no more than 20 core activists, backed up by a network of over one thousand supporters in the UK and overseas" (Grant 2004: 414).

So we might summarize the character of British interest group activity under a Labour centrist government in the first decade of the twenty-first century as follows:

- a general growth in the number and membership range of organized interests
- a growing professionalization of pressure group organization and media utilization
- multilevel lobbying directed toward relevant local, national, and international governmental gatekeepers
- the growth of direct action and the emergence of new social movements
- varied pathways of interest articulation reflecting interest group objectives
- a decline in corporatist tripartism, more at the expense of trade unionism than business.

As Grant opined, while traditional forms of pressure group activity are still evident, that is, pressure directed toward Whitehall or Westminster, many contemporary issues, such as animal rights, policies towards climate change and international poverty, and indeed the unpopular wars in Iraq and Afghanistan "involve fundamental differences of principle that cannot be resolved through negotiation and compromise" (Grant 2004: 418 and see the book's website). A further challenge to traditional Whitehall/Parliament-focused pressure group activity is the significance of the EU for many previously nationally based policy arenas, a subject we now examine.

THE EU AND INTEREST GROUP ACTIVITY

Since its formation, but especially as the Single European Act (SEA) was implemented, pressures by member state domestic interest groups have been directed toward EU institutions. While this varies between and within policy arenas, as we shall examine below, one count of EU-level interest groups in 1959 gave a figure of "more than 100," but by 2000, they totalled between around 1,300 to 5,000 according to definition and mode of counting (Greenwood 2007: 12). The key growth period was the early 1990s as the SEA and the Treaty on European Union (TEU) radically changed the EU's policy competences and mode of decision making. By 2007 over half of these groups were business- and trade-oriented organizations, but a striking increase in citizen-interest organizations had occurred from 2000 to 2007, to around 33 percent (Greenwood 2007: 12). One other trend is the growth in groups representing EU regions and local governments (institutional groups), reflecting both local and regional interest in EU cohesion policies as well as the notion of "social partnership" fostered by the Commission. In effect, there are British associational, promotional, and institutional interest groupings in Brussels as well as a supranational and multinational corporation presence. Estimates of those employed in what amounts to a lobby industry vary from a conservative EP register of lobbyists of around 4,500 to a more expansive Commission estimate of 15,000.

A description of the Brussels interest group arena might be as follows: though the EP has enjoyed a greater role in legislative processes since the SEA and TEU, the Commission and its directorates general (DGs) are the main target for interest groups. The EP, however, with increased powers of co-decision, has become a target for groups, especially citizen-interest organizations. There has also been some attempt to register and regulate lobby activity in the EP. The ECJ delivers judgments on a range of issues that make it a target for interest group legal action. Equality-of-opportunity cases have been successfully brought before the Court. Infringement of environmental legislation has also been successfully resolved after interest group legal intervention. The British Equal Opportunities Commission has funded several cases that needed legal clarification (Greenwood 2007). As a recent example in 2009, Heyday, a branch of Age Concern, challenged existing British government legislation on compulsory retirement at age sixty-five; the issue was also being taken up by other EU pensioner lobbies. Lobby access to the Council of Ministers is inevitably indirect, via pressure brought on national ministries and the politicians who attend Council meetings. Finally, neither the Economic and Social Committee nor the Committee of Regions has been seen as an important target, given their relatively weak position within the EU's institutional structure.

The ease of access to the DGs and EP that interest groups can experience is in large part a reflection of a political quest for information and for legitimacy—by both institutions. In the case of the Commission, a staff of only 27,000 means a reliance on stakeholders for information, opinion, and the monitoring of implementation of policy—which is undertaken not by Commission bureaucrats, but by the member states. As such, civil-society organizations provide a conduit through which the Commission fulfills its role as guardian of the EU Treaties. For the EP, and the Commission also, interaction with civil society provides the opportunity for social dialogue to complement a relatively weak political legitimacy. While there is a need to establish a balance between its representative and participative democratic functions, most MEPs recognize that an open social dialogue is one means of overcoming its democratic dilemma. "Taken as a whole," opines Greenwood, "the EU is highly accessible to civil society interests because its multi level nature provides for easy access, and because of its need for political participation" (Greenwood 2007: 5).

The EU's most evident characteristic in terms of interest representation is its institutionalized nature. The Commission, especially, has sought dialogue with social partners, funding the establishment of Brussels-based groupings if necessary. ETUC, women's lobby organizations, and environmental groups such as the European Environmental Bureau (EEB) are in receipt of Commission financial support (Eising 2007). These and other peak organizations, together with special-interest groups, national associations, large companies, and citizen-interest groups such as Social Platform, form contact groups and DG partnerships, or are heavily institutionalized into DG bureaucracies in pursuit of the Commission's wish for economic, electoral, social, and civic dialogue.

A EUROPEANIZATION OF BRITISH INTEREST GROUPS?

British pressure groups have not been shy in taking advantage of the access to EU policy-making machinery affecting their members' interests or the ideas and values that they seek to promote. This fits within the *neofunctionalist* perspective on European integration that envisaged that domestic interests would naturally shift their activities to the EU as it became a main source of legislation and regulation. Nevertheless, the character of EU pressure group engagement is majorly shaped by domestic political culture and, as we shall argue below, the particular sector involved. Thus the EU effect may be observed in "downloading" of EU legislation and policy objectives and "uploading" of particular group interests. As such, any assessment of the Europeanization of British interest-group activity is complex and nuanced.

We can, however, make several general points. First, the character of pressure group involvement is affected by the objectives of the group: do they seek EU regulation or deregulation; are aims broadly in line with EU policy or do they seek protection from its impact? Thus Fairbrass contrasts the objectives and tactics of many British companies that seek market liberalization with the interests of environmental campaigners whose interests are in environmental regulation (Fairbrass 2003). Are the aims of the group in line with EU policy or at variance; is the government in support of EU policy—or not? Are similar groups from member states allied to a particular cause, or is there a likelihood of dissension between national groups? In effect, where are political allies—in Brussels or in Westminster; at the national or international level? Answers to these questions are likely to shape the routes that organized interests will take in pursuit of achieving their objectives. As figure 7.1 illustrates, there are two Brussels routes that may be chosen—a route *direct* to the Commission and an *indirect* route via Brussels intermediaries (Eurogroups or professional lobbyists).

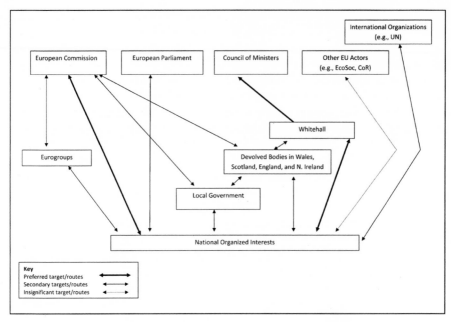

Figure 7.1. Patterns of Organized Interests (after Fairbrass 2006)

There remains, of course, a *national* route via Whitehall and thus through to the Council of Ministers as a more traditional option (Fairbrass 2006).

The use of these routes by British groups has changed over time. Of note is the striking difference in perspective of sections of the British Trade Union movement during the late 1980s and early 1990s as it sought allies through the EU's Social Dialogue that was manifestly absent in its domestic setting. Environmentalists also perceived Brussels as a more favorable political environment during the 1990s, when EU competences increased in that arena and the "European Commission and the EP supplied some influential allies" and resources to assist in the development of biodiversity legislation (Fairbrass 2003: 24). In both cases the then Conservative government was perceived as an opponent to trade union and environmental interests. What follows is a brief assessment of the concept of Europeanization in the behaviors and organization of three interest group sectors today.

Business Interests

The business sector is powerfully represented in British government networks. The CBI continues to be the largest peak organization, with a membership of around 15,000 and an available budget of more than £5 million. It represents larger companies and, as such, fitted comfortably into the tripartite system of the 1960s–1970s. New Labour courted the organization and, despite periods of disagreement, a reasonably mutually supportive relationship has been sustained. Under Gordon Brown's premiership, the ex-director of the CBI, Sir Digby-Jones, was elevated to the peerage to become minister for trade in 2007. Less comfortable relationships exist with the Institute of Directors, whose policies sit more on the neoliberal right. A plethora of trade associations and industry federations such as the Society for Motor Manufacturers or the British Retail Consortium, represent sectoral interests. Large companies such as British Telecom, Tesco, or Barclays Bank have enjoyed, especially during the Blair administration, direct access to Whitehall departments and, in some cases, the prime minister (Grant 2004: 376–77).

Within Britain there now exists what has been called an elite pluralist model of business representation within a fairly business-friendly government environment compared with the more corporatist situation that had existed until 1979. Deregulation during the 1980s and 1990s, together with labor flexibility, coincided (indeed was in advance of) EU market liberalization and, until the late 1980s, much business pressure was directed to Whitehall to sustain the deregulatory policies emanating from the SEA.

Since the Single Market Act also included "compensatory measures" in such fields as environmental impact, or training and labor mobility rights, there emerged an increasing tendency for business interests to switch their lobbying activity toward the EU as large number of directives impacted on the market place (Fairbrass 2004). Thus direct and indirect lobby routes to Brussels are increasingly evident in business pressure activity alongside the more familiar national route. The Institute of Directors has fought vigorously to mitigate EU social market regulations and against Britain's entry to the Single Currency, utilizing the Commons, Whitehall, and the media as means of influence. The telecommunications and energy industries, dominated by a few large players, lobby directly for further deregulation to the relevant directorate general in Brussels (Fairbrass 2003).

Having a Brussels office is perceived to be important in some companies for sustained contact with EU officials and politicians. Smaller companies utilize their trade associations, which may establish a Brussels office and would certainly establish links with European-wide trade federations (see the book's website). In general, whether seeking to protect sectoral interests from unwelcome regulations or promote deregulation of utilities, British business interests now pursue strategies that involve lobbying EU institutions. They also seek international sectoral alliances at the EU level. As one researcher points out, however, for most business actors the EU represents an *additional* range of targets, lobbying routes, and allies as, for the most part, recent British governments have broadly shared the objectives of business interests and the Commission "in relation to the core objectives of the EU's market liberalization strategy" (Fairbrass 2006: 149).

Trade Unions

British trade unionism has a number of features that are said to mark it out from its Continental counterparts. Trade unions predated the emergence of the Labour Party and performed a vital role in creating a parliamentary party in the 1900s. As such, both were shaped by the reformist conventions of parliamentary democracy and for the most part lacked, or managed to contain, the Marxist radicalism of parties and labor movements in parts of Continental Europe. The role of individual trade unions was to protect the interests of members through collective bargaining. The link between collective economic interests and the political system within which individual unions operated was via the direct sponsorship of individual MPs and through membership in Labour's National Executive Committee (NEC). The TUC, through unofficial linkages with the Labour Party, attempted to frame congruent union/party objectives. For many years the principal objective was to sustain a legal framework within which the activity of collective bargaining would take place.

There is a broad range of trade unions, with craft, public sector, industrial, and general unions existing together "each with different ideas of how to balance participating vs representative forms of organization" (Van der Mass 2004: 10). Union organization is centralist, both legally and in self-regulation, and it has thrown up strong and influential leadership figures who have played a crucial role in shaping their union's strategic position on "external" issues, one of which is the European Union. The TUC, as the union's peak organization, has a membership of sixty unions representing around 7 million members. While only sixteen of those unions are affiliated with the Labour Party, those that are, like UNITE and the GMB, represent a considerable proportion of Britain's union members.

Apart from short periods in its history, such as the events surrounding the general strike in 1926 and the miners' strikes of 1984–1985, trade unionists worked within a culture of *voluntarism* and individual union collective bargaining, and within largely separate industrial and political spheres, "each area jealously guarded by the two components of the British Labour movement" (Van der Mass 2004: 13). Britain's unions seek to improve the wages and working conditions of British citizens and, as such, reflect a somewhat suspicious view of "externalities" that, through to the late 1980s, included negative perspectives on the European Union. In the 1945–1979 period the domestic conditions of a mixed economy, a welfare state, and Keynesian economic solutions, with a stress on full employment and, in the later period, the tripartism of political decision making, were all fundamentally challenged by Conservative administrations after 1979. Their neoliberal, market-driven policies of the 1980s were, to some considerable extent, a response to the external forces of globalized business and capital formation, competition, and market deregulation. Britain's already declining manufacturing sectors could no longer anticipate the direct and indirect subsidies of an interventionist state, and unions were politically and legally battered in the new climate of a low-waged, low-cost, flexible-labor-market economy.

The impact on trade unionism was great, and unemployment contributed to a reduction in union membership between 1979 and 1989 by around 25 percent, to 3 million, as the labor force adjusted to accommodate "flexibility"—which became a euphemism for part-time, temporary employment. It was thus somewhat ironic that British trade unions in search of protection from the vicissitudes of Thatcherite policies looked for protection to the EU and aspects of the Single European Act that Mrs. Thatcher had earnestly promoted as part of her domestic market reforms in 1980s Britain. The compensatory elements to achieve "social solidarity," as the EU liberalized its market, were a social dialogue and, later, a commitment to workers' rights in the shape of a Social Chapter. When offered this opportunity in an address by Jacques Delors at the TUC in 1988, the delegates offered in turn a standing ovation and a chorus of "Frère Jacques"!

In the absence of Labour victories (1989 and 1992) Brussels was "the only card game in town" for Ron Todd, then general secretary of the TUC. Todd, who had openly admitted his Euroscepticism, was to oversee an "astonishing conversion" of the TUC to a pro-EU position (Rosamund 1993: 20; Van der Mass 2006: 150). This entailed the creation of a Network Europe (NE) that was to ensure TUC representation of British TU interests and to educate the TU audience in Britain. A Brussels TUC office was opened in 1993. The office serves a subcommittee of the General Council, the Europe Monitoring Group, and meets regularly with Labour MEPs and socialist MEPs from other member states. Through its NE contact point, the TUC informs its members of its activities in ETUC, the EP, and its discussions with British representatives on the Council of Ministers and Commission officials.

Despite a thawing of TUC/government relations once Labour returned to power in 1997, the TUC has been disappointed with what it sees as the government's reluctance to enter the full spirit of EU social dialogue, especially after the hopes engendered by New Labour's signature of the Social Chapter in 1998. The TUC has also argued for Britain's entry to the euro and for greater government clarity on the issue. More recently, at its 2007 conference, delegates voted for a referendum on the

Reform Treaty mainly in an attempt to force the Brown government to reconsider its opt-out from a proposed Charter of Fundamental Rights. For one commentator, the TUC has reinvented itself by adopting a proactive role in EU affairs, thus saving itself from "a limited future as an arbiter of inter-union squabbles" (Van der Mass 2006: 160). In doing so, it may have reactivated its significance in TU politics as a peak organization, capable of sustaining the cohesion of a movement still adjusting to a postindustrial environment.

There are, however, mixed reactions to the salience of the EU as a positive force among TUC affiliates. Individual trade unions represent men and women in various economic sectors and therefore encounter and reflect various rank-and-file opinions; in addition they evaluate the salience of EU policy making to the particular employment interest the union represents. For example, the giant Transport and General Workers Union (TGWU) took an anti-euro position because the euro was seen as not only consolidating an Anglo-American business model at the heart of the EU, but also threatening national identity and sovereignty. Other unions, particularly the GMB, were pro-euro because of the protection it was believed euro membership would give *against* the Anglo-American model.

In so far as a pattern emerged, manufacturing unions, aware of the dangers of global capital movements, are more likely to support the euro as potentially offering some protection, whereas public-sector unions fear the loss of national control over the economy that adopting the euro would entail. However, Van der Mass (2006) suggests that other factors are necessary to explain the divergent stances of the two largest unions (TGWU and GMB), who represent workers in both sheltered and exposed sectors of the economy, including leadership and available resources (see the book's website).

Trade unions represent a declining but still significant proportion of Britain's working population and, until comparatively recently in their long history, have operated within a national environment of collective bargaining for working conditions and pay improvements. Since the 1980s, the impact of global markets and the pressure of technological change have burst this domestic bubble. The EU has presented both challenges and opportunities for unions seeking protection from the market-driven policies of companies and governments. With the implementation of the Single European Act, there has been a "structural bias in the EU integration process towards market liberalization" (Van der Mass 2006: 166). On the other hand, in search of solidarity and indeed legitimacy, EU objectives and policies such as social dialogue, protections within the Social Chapter, and opportunities for social partnership—a European social model—offered opportunities for British trade unions to recover some of the influence lost during the 1980s.

The Interests of Citizens

We have noted the increase in citizen group numbers and activities at both British and EU levels. This, we suggested, is a result of a number of factors: the emergence of a consumerist culture, the segmentation of social interests, a decline in membership of political parties, and a skeptical view of formal representative institutions. The EU's competences in the concerns of this "third sector" (Chapman 2006) and the Commission's seeking legitimacy through social dialogue have led to a significant increase in groups setting up operations in Brussels, many of them at least partially supported by EU funds.

Third-sector groups are mainly promotional and represent a wide range of citizen interests. They operate at community, regional, national, and international levels depending on their aims and perspectives. Included in these groupings are women's organizations; consumer groups; single-issue or special interest groups; and, as part of this phenomenon, institutional pressure groups of regional and local governments, which are a major growth area in Brussels. A further growth area in both domestic and EU-level pressure-group activities is in the field of environmental politics, a subject discussed in detail in chapter 11. Since so much of domestic environmental policy emanates from EU directives, DG Environment has been active in seeking specialist information from both Brussels and MS-based groups, including British organizations such as the Royal Society for the Protection of Birds or the World Wildlife Fund. Funding for research or consultancy, and in some cases to assist group organization, has also emanated from Brussels.

Since the mid-1990s, British governments have "greened" their policies, mainstreaming concepts such as sustainability and environmental impact. However the EU Commission and EP have often presented a sympathy, enthusiasm, and ease of access that ran ahead of Whitehall's environmental commitment. As such, both the direct and indirect (via peak group or group alliances) Brussels routes are routinely utilized, as the EU is perceived as a major and "alternative set of venues, conduits and coalitions" (Fairbrass 2004).

As with environmental policy, the development of EU consumer policy has encouraged nationally based organizations to utilize Brussels institutions. In common with environmental policy, consumer policy is now mainstreamed (Article 153: Amsterdam Treaty) and has its own DG (Health and Consumer Protection) (see the book's website).

Also, we can point to the linkage between social and community groups' local and regional structures, and EU cohesion policy. This "third sector" of pressure group activity engages in "a diverse range of activities, from service provision, self help and mutual aid of communities' development, advocacy and representation" (Chapman 2006: 168). Thus the growth of third-sector activities in Britain is paralleled by the recognition given to such organizations by EU institutions seeking social dialogue, which raises "'the intriguing possibility that domestic third sector activity in Brit[ain] might have been Europeanized by EU-level policies and law making activities (Chapman 2006: 168).

The concern to develop a social dialogue is also evident in policies associated with the distribution of EU structural funding. The Commission's insistence on the involvement of social partners in its structural funding programs has resulted in the involvement of third-sector groups in the planning, implementation, and monitoring of regional programs. Between 2000 and 2006 Britain's involvement in Objective I and II programs evidenced partnerships between local and regional governance, business, trade unions, and community organizations in an institutionalized process. As examples, a variety of models of partnership were evident in South Yorkshire, West Wales, and Merseyside Objective I programs. Merseyside's Pathways Area initiative, established in the mid-1990s and based on principles of community-led economic development "informed the development of the European Commission's own model . . . indicating a degree of 'uploading' to the EU" (Chapman 2006:180). While the impact of structural funding is selective and territorial, it is interesting to note that British regional and local representation in Brussels is the largest among member states. As *institutional* pressure groups, they provide organization, coordination, and a gateway to EU networks for multilevel social partners of which, of course, they are part.

A EUROPEANIZATION OF INTERESTS?

The examples above have emphasized the shifts made by many pressure groups toward an EU dimension in their strategy and tactics. A burgeoning set of policy competences have made the EU a main target in such policy arenas as the environment, competition regulation, equal opportunities, and food standards. The EU, especially the Commission and EP, have sought out interest-group participation to inform, legitimate, and in some cases implement and monitor EU policies. Peak interest groups have been institutionalized as Brussels players and, where member states have lagged behind EU policy formulation, Brussels has been perceived as an ally. In these situations some British groups like the GMB or Consumer Association have fulfilled the predictions of neofunctionalists in uploading their expectations to the supranational level. One factor that has favored British interests is a relatively good fit between contemporary British elite pluralist group culture and the requirements of the EU. That is less evident in the state-dominated pattern of organized interests in France (Fairbrass 2006).

However, the importance of an EU dimension to domestic pressure-group activity is variable, and the tactics of groups are complex. The significance of the Council of Ministers as the legislative fulcrum of the EU, and therefore the continuing importance of British ministers in the policy process, has sustained Whitehall as a target for interest pressure, while Parliament remains a target for environmental interests who also "find themselves drawn into the transnational and global activities of organizations such as the UN and the OECD" (Fairbrass 2006: 149). While a social platform for citizen and minority groups is offered by the EU, the "third sector" of social interests, composed of many locally based groups, has neither the necessary resources nor the consciousness of the EU's relevance to their interests, and they continue to focus on local and national targets. Thus, for local women's groups, the perceived remoteness of Brussels and lack of understanding of the EU's relevance to their interests contrasted with the sophisticated networking of a European Women's Lobby that, despite the activity of British intermediaries, was not appreciated at the grass-roots level (Bretherton and Sperling 1996). As with the general public, the EU is perceived by many local activists as elitist and inaccessible.

However, the contrasts between available interest group paths and networks in Britain in the 1970s and those of today are vivid; for many groups, the EU is an alternative route; for others it is supplementary to domestic paths. As such we must acknowledge a Europeanization of much of British interest-group activity. We must also acknowledge the changes in political communication through which interest groups articulate their desires, and it is to this that we now turn.

COMMUNICATING INTERESTS AND IDEAS—
THE BRITISH MEDIA

Here we examine the particular role of the media in communicating political interests. We start with a brief examination of the structure of the media industry in Britain and then the responses of political actors to what one author describes as a "media rich and media dependent society" (Kuhn 2007: 1). We shall also examine the contention that Britain is now a public relations democracy (Davis 2002).

Television and Radio

Technological advances in the broadcasting industry have helped produce some marked changes since the 1950s, when the BBC monopolized output in both radio and TV. Fifty years later, in excess of 400 TV channels exist, and community, local, regional, and national radio offer, alongside an expanded BBC service, listening for almost every taste. The viewer/listener accesses this broadcasting cornucopia through a variety of "platforms" that include cable, satellite, cell phone, and Internet, as well as "free-to-air" terrestrial modes. Commercial interests fund programming alongside the public subscription (licence fees) that pays for the vast array of BBC output. But if these changes in the organization, funding, variety, and delivery of broadcasting are significant, so also is the legacy of thirty years of public monopoly broadcasting from 1922 to 1957 that is at the core of a British media culture. Public service broadcasting has emerged as a social value with iconic, indeed international, status. Textbox 7.1 contrasts the characteristics of British public broadcasting against free market values that are also manifest in the development of the British press.

Since the second half of the twentieth century, there has emerged a contested framework of broadcasting that reflects both sets of values. Though the BBC has attracted some criticism—indeed every government

---

**Textbox 7.1. Public Service Broadcasting (PSB)
or Consumer Sovereignty?**

The main features of British PSB are:

- One nationwide service
- Funded by citizens through a flat tax (the annual licence)
- Provided by an independent public corporation (BBC)
- Working within a charter of public service
- Providing a universal and diverse range of programs
- Reflecting social norms and values
- Operating at a distance from vested political or government interests
- Contributing to an informed citizenship through unbiased/balanced news and information coverage

Free market broadcasting consists of:

- Open Skys entrepreneurial access to the broadcasting market
- Freedom to provide consumers with programs they desire
- Sources of funding based on commercial principles and needs
- Unfettered freedom to present views, including political positions, commensurate with perceived audience interests
- Regulation within minimal legal protections
- Choice for providers and consumers in program content and frequency

from the 1970s onwards has complained about its treatment by the BBC—"Auntie" or the "Beeb," as it is popularly known, continues to profess political independence and public-sector and social responsibility as its core values. This, in turn, has affected the culture of its competitors, themselves subject to regulatory conditions that encourage at least elements of corporate responsibility toward their citizen viewers. Thus commercial television news and documentaries were set within both an already established BBC public service culture and their own formal regulatory frameworks and were seen by many as an extension of public service broadcasting (Kuhn 2007: 44). As such, up until the 1980s, there seemed to be a balance between the public service ethic and the needs of a commercial broadcasting market.

Two forces challenged this British public/market compromise. The first was the rapid technological change that produced delivery platforms for broadcasting allowing an almost unlimited range of programs by global as well as national providers. The second factor was ideological and intellectual, as New Right ideas challenged the basis of public broadcasting values and promoted consumer sovereignty as an alternative perspective. A Broadcasting Act (1990) created the legal and political framework for British media in a new consumerist and digital age. In effect, commercial television became more commercial, the BBC more varied in its output, and both sectors faced competition from global media organizations such as Rupert Murdoch's News International and Sky.

Competition between channels and between broadcasting media and the press has been complicated by looser restrictions on the ownership of terrestrial broadcasting companies and newspapers. The Communications Act (2003) permits cross-media ownership (up to 20% of each sector). For News International, already a major player in satellite broadcasting through BSkyB and the owner of the Sun and Times group of newspapers, this gave the possibility of investing in terrestrial commercial channels. The 2003 Act also opened up the broadcasting market to non-EU companies such as Disney or Viacom (Kuhn 2007). These developments, along with interventions in the broadcast market by Internet providers and cell phone companies, make for a dynamic and increasingly competitive broadcast scenario.

The Newspapers

A snapshot of the British newspaper industry reveals characteristics that, to an external observer, may be seen as exceptional. First the industry has a mainly national market. With the caveat of the Scottish press, readers will be buying the same brand newspaper throughout the Isles. But while newspapers may sell in a national market they sell to stratified elements within that market. Thus there are mass-selling tabloids (red tops), middle-market (blue tops), and "quality papers" catering and competing for "classes" of readership. Newspaper content is less regulated than the broadcast media and there is an oligopoly of ownership that has been, traditionally, closely involved with the political stances taken by their newspapers (see table 7.3).

These features have been fairly consistent from the post–World War II period. Thus, in 1955, the total daily sales of newspapers averaged around 16.2 million; by 2007 this had declined to 11.5 million. However, since each newspaper is available, on average, to three people, the potential daily newspaper readership in Britain is still in the order of 34 million—over half the population. The number of daily newspaper titles in circulation today is the same as it was in 1961, and the spread of "quality" to popular papers is as broad. Ownership is concentrated among a small number of press groups, of which one, News International, commands 33 percent of national circulation. Five groups command 90 percent of the daily and Sunday circulation. One marked change is in the spread of readership. Thus, in 1955, only 8 percent of circulation was in quality market; by 2005, 22 percent of sales were in this segment; in the same period, however, sales of red tops had increased by 26 percent to 51 percent, with the middle-market down to 27 percent, losing half its share of total sales.

Table 7.3.   Weekday Newspapers in Britain (2007)

	Title	Ownership	Circulation (Millions)	Electoral Support 2001	2005
Red Tops (popular press)	Sun	News Int.	3.1	Labour	Labour
	Mirror/Record*	Trinity	2.1	Labour	Labour
	Star	Northern/Shell	0.8	Labour	no preference
Blue Tops (middle-market)	Mail	Mail Trust	2.4	Conservative	Anti-Blair
	Express	Northern/Shell	0.8	Labour	Conservative
	Standard**	Mail Trust	0.3		
Quality Press	Times	News Int.	0.6	Labour	Labour
	Guardian	Guardian	0.3	Weak Labour	Labour
	Independent	Independent	0.2	Not Conservative	Liberal Dem
	Financial Times	Pearson	0.4	Labour	Labour
	Telegraph	Telegraph	0.8	Conservative	Conservative

All newspapers publish Sunday sister papers that have similar market shares and, with the exception of the *Sunday Times* in 2005, which supported the Conservatives, followed the same political line as their respective dailies.
* *Daily Record* is a Scottish-based newspaper.
** London evening daily
Source: *Media Guardian* 13 August 2007.

Despite the decline in readership, Britain remains exceptional in the EU in that its mainly national press reaches a high proportion of citizens. Reading a daily newspaper "is for many still part of a well ingrained daily ritual which is why the impact of television and the media has been gradual rather than sudden" (Kuhn 2007: 8). In consequence, it is not surprising that interventions in editorial policy and sometimes content have been, historically, a feature of the British press. The extent of proprietary intervention varies between newspapers, and the motives for intervention may be commercial, political, or idiosyncratic. Examples of direct intervention abound and, while there is some difficulty in distinguishing between the two, commercial rather than political motivation would seem rather more evident in recent years (see the book's website).

It is equally unsurprising that, with such tough competition for a declining readership and between media sectors, one set of criticisms of much of the British press relates to its sensationalism and tendency to "hurry on down" the cultural/intellectual scale. Much of this critique has also been applied to television programming, and indeed has a certain historical ring to it: similar criticisms were hurled at the press in the late nineteenth century and in the 1920s. There is, however, little doubt that sleaze, division, personality, revelation, disasters, all preferably accompanied by good photos, sell tabloid (and indeed other) newspapers. The result for political reportage, according to some political journalists, is an assumption that British politics is a dirty game played by devious people. Exposure, therefore, is the major task of the press. The result of this assumption is aggressive reporting and defensive stances by politicians that seem only to confirm such assumptions. This, in turn, may feed into the mood of public apathy and alienation about which politicians have become concerned. Whether "the British press is the most reptilian in the world" as a *Times* journalist opined in 2004 is debatable.

New Media Challenges

We have mentioned above the impact of first cable, then satellite, and now digital technology on the structure and content of the broadcast industry. Web and cell phone technology has also created challenges and opportunities for both broadcast and newspaper sectors. Cell phone ownership is in excess of 80 percent of the population; Internet connection has increased from around 5 percent in 1995 to around 60 percent in 2007.

There has been, in effect, an exponential growth in personal communication in the first years of the twenty-first century. The media industry, government, political parties, and interest groups have responded to the potential of this phenomenon. Within a regulatory framework that has struggled to keep pace with the consequences of technological change, cross-media ownership has become a feature of Britain's technological environment, with companies such as British Telecom offering "all service solutions" to a consumer's communication desires. The BBC, notwithstanding its increased TV and radio network coverage, provides an online platform that has extended its audience reach both nationally and globally. Newspapers have also offered online access to their content. In particular The Guardian and Telegraph media groups provide an extensive news and information online platform that has a bigger daily Web audience than their print editions. It goes without saying that "the Net" presents an almost unlimited source of information, comment, and opinion that challenges the traditional bases of media communication—to which political actors have inevitably had to respond.

The Government and the Media: Regulation and Rapid Response

In conditions of a globalized media market and almost hyper change in its technology, how does a government relate to this complex communication process? Here we examine two aspects of this relationship: regulation and government/media access.

With regard to regulatory control, the violent events of autumn 2007 and June 2008 in Burma illustrate the difficulties of even a secretive military junta in containing media coverage in a Web-connected world. Instant cell phone coverage of events by individuals present is testimony to the potential democratization and deprofessionalization of news reportage on a global scale. Regulation of information flows would seem an impossible task and, from a neoliberal perspective, this is not necessarily unwelcome. However, cultural values, individual and collective interests, and political expediency combine to create a raison d être for government intervention.

Textbox 7.2 details the current regulatory structures for broadcasting and the press. It can be seen that, while the press has managed to sustain its self-regulation as a significant pillar of press independence, the broadcasting industry since its inception (the 1926 BBC Charter) has been subject to statutory external regulation. In both media sectors, however, the trend has been toward light-touch regulation in favor of consumer choice and competition for audiences in a varied market place. When one adds to this mix the impact of the Internet, whose regulation is currently (in Western liberal societies) by the consumers themselves, national regulation has its problems.

Yet it is demanded. Competition for declining market share in press and broadcasting has produced a propensity for sensationalism and an interest in the personal lives of celebrities and political figures that has involved invasions of privacy and questionable levels of accurate reportage.

Textbox 7.2. Regulating the Media in Britain

The Broadcasting Media

Ofcom

The Office of Communications (2003) replaced several regulatory bodies in relation to economic, content, and spectrum regulation. It is an independent commission whose task is to protect consumer interests by promoting competition alongside content quality, broad programming, fairness, and privacy, all through a light-touch ethos. Its remit includes all telecommunication, terrestrial, and satellite channels including certain activities of the BBC such as "balance" in religious or children's broadcasts, and the BBC's commercial activities. Its creation followed the tenets of the EU's Directive Television without Frontiers (1997), which was liberal and sought to enhance a single market in European Broadcasting. Ofcom can decide and fine when it considers appropriate.

The BBC Trust

The Trust replaced the BBC Board of Governors in 2007. This reform owed much to the debates regarding BBC independence in reporting and its financial status emanating from government/BBC disputes over coverage of the Iraq War (see the book's website). A 2006 White Paper recommended a BBC Trust whose task was to represent license payers rather than the BBC's interests. In effect, the trust is both independent of government and of the BBC executive. Its tasks are to set BBC strategic objectives and priorities and to oversee the work of the BBC executive.

The Press

Press Complaints Commission

In keeping with the self-regulatory tradition of the British press the PCC is a seventeen-member body whose chairman is appointed by the newspaper and publishing industry. There is an independent appointments board that selects the remaining sixteen members, a majority of whom come from outside the industry. The PCC administers a code of conduct for newspaper and journal content and work processes and receives and adjudicates on public complaints of malpractice. The code is set by editors and includes reporting practice and privacy intrusion. A newspaper or journal is bound to accept the PCC's decision and the PCC will negotiate an acceptable outcome between the complainant and the newspaper that may involve published retraction or compensation.

(Continued)

Textbox 7.2. Regulating the Media in Britain (*continued*)

The EU

Directives   Particularly after the development of transnational satellite television, there has emerged an EU interest and competence in
the broadcasting market. This concentrated initially on the harmonization of member states' broadcast regulations, preventing
member states from interfering with the retransmission of programs from other member states and protectionist measures
such as "European content quotas" to contain especially US incursions into the market, as well as rules on quantities of advertising and their limitation in children's and news programs.
By 2007 the previously titled Television without Frontiers Directive (1989–1997) was revised to become a proposed Audio
Visual without Frontiers Directive to include other industries,
for example, the telephone, cell phone, and Web sectors, which
were now involved in commercial broadcasting. Within this expanded sector the directive will set standards for product place-
ment in advertising, require member states to protect minors,
promote European works and independent productions, and inhibit contentious religious or racial broadcasting. Once agreed,
Britain like other member states will have two years to trans-
pose the directive into national law (Europa 2007). In 1997 the
Commission intervened to preclude the Murdoch company
BSkyB from joining a terrestrial digital consortium, ITV Digital.
The Commission also intervened in the bidding process that has
established live Premier League soccer TV broadcasting.

The royal family throughout the 1990s provided a wealth of copy: the rise
and fall of the Charles/Diana marriage, her death and the debates surrounding its circumstances, and the Prince of Wales's eventual remarriage
(as well as the toe-sucking activities of minor royals) all sold newspapers
and produced reactions from the offended parties and offended citizens.
Political elites have also provided fodder, from the mawkish press interest in the wife of Tony Blair, Cherie Booth, to the resignations of David
Blunkett, a minister, over minor ministerial and sexual indiscretions; see
also David Mellor, Paddy Ashdown, Tim Yeo, John Major, Ron Davies, Peter Mandelson, John Prescott, and other politicians, all victims of "attack
journalism" (Sabato 1991). Inevitably such reportage may be countered by
defensive tactics and reinforced by the professionalization of party and
government media relations; this in turn has been criticized as "control
freakery." In such an abrasive, evasive, and high-profile environment of

spin and counter-spin, issues such as privacy and public access, press and broadcast freedom, balanced reportage, and commercial versus public interest, continue to be juxtaposed in contemporary political debate.

If there are political elite and public dissatisfactions with the media industry, the other side of the coin is the critique of government communications techniques that has contributed to the notion of Britain as a "public relations democracy." In the climate of an ever-intrusive media, no organization involved in the decision-making process can expect success without the professionalization of its public relations. Trade unions, political parties, businesses, and pressure groups, as well as government, now utilize PR techniques to achieve their ends. The result is the world of spin and its "doctors" (Davis 2002).

While the emergence of a sophisticated government media organization is not new, it is particularly during the Blair government that the art of media management was most evident—indeed for some the media was the message of the Blair years. Prior to this period, Bernard Ingham, the No. 10 Downing Street press secretary, had enjoyed notoriety as Mrs. Thatcher's media mouthpiece. For twelve years, save for a short period when an adept Ministry of Defence official publically monotoned government information output during the Falklands War, Ingham dominated, cajoled, and, it was suggested, manipulated the press and broadcasting lobby on behalf of the prime minister (Harris 1990). This lesson, together with the fact that the press throughout the twentieth century had been predominantly Tory supporting, set the scene for New Labour's calculated public relations (PR) strategy to effectively control representation of the Labour message as well as to win over the large Murdoch press. The latter became possible as Murdoch's support for John Major declined alongside that of the public. This also meant that the Eurosceptic section of the Tory party was able to project its position relatively easily to a mostly sympathetic news media.

A media-friendly strategy assisted Labour's victory in 1997 and, on coming to power, a centralized communications network was placed across Whitehall Departments under the direction of Alistair Campbell, an experienced professional journalist. As his predecessor, Bernard Ingham, had done, Campbell gave favorable access to certain lobby journalists, especially *Sun* employees. While PR manipulation was successful in some areas, media relations proved problematic as the Blair administration aged and as the popularity of the prime minister diminished. Divisions between Blair and Brown, the Iraq war, some minor sleaze, and ministerial indiscretions were tempting press targets. Campbell's resignation after the Hutton Report led to a less aggressive media strategy. On Blair's resignation, one of Gordon Brown's first regime changes was to restore the status of permanent civil servants over political appointees. But, while the tone of the early Brown premiership veered toward a less public media involvement, there is little reason to suggest that a new understated image is professionally managed. Brown's less than media-friendly persona was exposed in 2009 when a badly advised prime minister made an uncomfortable appearance on YouTube. His plans for MPs' expenses were announced and, later, mauled in the Commons—a media management disaster! Of note also was the appointment of a previous professional journalist, David Coulson, to David Cameron's Conservative opposition strike force in 2007. All of this implies the continuation of the "mediatization" of politics; the emergence of PR policy communities; and, indeed, the case for the existence of a public relations democracy in Britain today (Davis 2002).

THE PRESS, THE POLITICIAN, WORCESTER WOMAN, AND THE EU

One aim of this text is to examine British politics in the light of EU membership. Inevitably, therefore, how the EU is portrayed in the media needs our attention. Before dealing with the role of the press, it is worth mentioning the nature of especially terrestrial broadcast coverage of the EU.

Despite the fact that so much British law and public policy has EU origins, the informative and educative coverage of the EU is limited when compared to national politics. While keen Britons can tune to an EU satellite/Web-based audio-visual information service, direct coverage of EP, Council, and Commission day-to-day activities is virtually nonexistent on British terrestrial channels. By contrast, the BBC provides televised and audio coverage of British parliamentary business as well as a daily synopsis. Similarly, the Scottish and Welsh Parliament/Assembly, enjoy broadcast and news coverage on regional channels. British MEPs have no such broadcast. Of equal significance is the limited coverage of EU business in news broadcasts. EU newsworthiness is mostly evaluated, it seems, with regard to headline issues over the euro membership, treaty reform, or worker migration that, it could be argued, present the EU as a contentious and problematic externality rather than an integral aspect of policy and politics (Anderson 2004). It is, however, British press coverage of the EU, and the attitudes of the political elite to the press, that prove most intriguing in explaining public perspectives of the EU.

The British press is infamous for its biased coverage of EU matters. Of around 11 million newspapers sold each weekday, on almost any EU news item over 8 million will take a Eurosceptical stance. The tabloids *Mail*, *Express*, and *Sun* are most extreme in this positioning, with the *Times* and *Telegraph* presenting more informed Eurosceptical opinion. In contrast, the *Mirror* (tabloid) and *Guardian*, *Financial Times*, and *Independent* (qualities) present often critical support (see textbox 7.3). The *Sun*, espe-

> **Textbox 7.3. The EU Reform Treaty and Britain's Eurosceptical Press (June 2007)**
>
> In the days shortly before the Brussels Summit (June 2007) the following headline or editorial titles were published by the five most Eurosceptical daily newspapers:
>
> | | | |
> |---|---|---|
> | *Express* | 20 June | EU Superstate: 8% of US Want a Referendum |
> | *Times* | 18 June | Angela Merkl's Dream: Britain's Nightmare |
> | *Mail* | 19 June | Germany Unveils Latest Version of "Backdoor" Constitution |
> | *Sun* | 19 June | EU's Plot to Shackle Britain |
> | *Telegraph* | 19 June | EU Reform Chaos as Blair and Brown Disagree |
>
> The Europsceptical press was considered sufficiently influential for the European Commission to set up a "rebuttal" bureau whose task was to provide interpretation in the press of EU directives, "Franco-German plots," and the constant threat to the British way of life.

cially, is renowned for its crudely nationalistic headlines and opinion—no more evident than in its exhortation to its readers to resist British acceptance of the 1990 Maastricht Treaty proposals; they were invited to stand facing southeast and, with raised index fingers, shout across the channel to the then French Commission president "Up yours Delors!" This, interestingly, contrasted with the *Sun* in 1975, under a different ownership, exhorting its readership to "vote YES—for a future together or, NO for a future alone" in the upcoming referendum on Common Market membership. This "yes" stance was replicated in nearly all the British press at the time (see also the book's website).

Their stance in 1975 may be explained in a number of ways: that the press followed business opinion; that membership in an economic market was a "good thing"; that predominately Tory press had supported the Heath government in joining in 1973 and needed to bolster a Labour government in maintaining a Conservative policy; and that opinion polls confirmed a generally favorable attitude toward continued membership by the electorate. By 2007 the majority of the press strongly supported calls by the mainly Eurosceptic Conservatives for a referendum on the Reform Treaty, which was represented as a massive step toward political union and a federal state. In doing so, they looked once again to be mirroring public opinion, now mainly Eurosceptical in its stance on EU issues.

Discourse analysis (Anderson and Weymouth 1999; Daddow 2006) explores use made by the Eurosceptical press of a crude style based on a Whig-imperial or "school textbook" version of British history (Daddow 2006: 1). Thus "the historical backdrop to both tabloid and broadsheet Euroscepticism is the island story every British citizen supposedly knows, one that tells the irredeemable differences between Britain and the continent: one that adapts Shakespeare's tale of a 'Sceptr'd isle set in a silver sea' fighting off the pernicious effects of continental intrusions into British affairs" (Daddow 2006: 12). Add to this myths of Victorian imperial glories and more recent World War II triumphalism and the climate is conducive, by use of carefully chosen words, to push cultural buttons for a depiction of Continental Europe as "the other" and Britain as "us."

The impact on the opinions of readers is not so simply interpreted. One study suggests that the major effect is to reinforce already existing prejudices, especially when they are further reinforced by a political party. Thus, if individuals receive the same messages from their party of preference and the newspaper they read, then the combined influence can be considerable (Carey and Burton 2004). Ironically, for readers of the *Sun* and *Times*, the impact of a virulently Eurosceptic position was confused by pro-Blair electoral support. However, the influence of newspapers on public opinion is of less significance than the influence that newspapers have had on political elites.

A number of factors conspire to create this elite sensitivity. Communication with large sections of the British voting population is available through newspapers, which have had historically a Conservative bias. The Conservative Party has moved, since the 1980s, from a position of general support for a single market to a sceptical stance on a European Union. The press, especially much of the popular press, reflects this view, which seems to concur with the opinions of its readers. More than this, there seems little of commercial advantage to an industry dependent on the use of English (or something like it) in a Continental market of "foreign" languages. EU regulation, through the Social Charter or a Charter of Fundamental Human Rights, is perceived as costly and interfering. For the industry as a whole, and for some media groups such as News International, investment in the United States is more significant than in Continental Europe. In particular, News International has failed to make inroads into the EU media sector—a factor only reinforcing the antiregulatory globalist vision of its proprietor, Rupert Murdoch. The dilemma of a party with sympathetic EU policies, or indeed a government making pragmatic day-to-day decisions as a part of the EU system, is evident enough.

In its search for the support of the middle-England vote (termed "Worcester woman") the current Labour government has sought to avoid confrontation with the press by representing its EU dealings as a defense of

British interests; thus the opt-outs from the EU Lisbon Treaty (2007) were presented as both a national achievement and a reason not to hold a referendum on the issue. The electoral incentive to keep EU matters off the public agenda and below the sightlines of the Eurosceptical press seems high. The result of this is to inhibit any challenge to this "skewed coverage of the European Union" . . . and "a coverage of the European issues [that] has been overwhelmingly framed within the context of a *domestic* political debate . . . which makes it stand out in comparison with press coverage" in other member states (Kuhn 2007: 161). As such, press, parties, and government form a curious alliance in mis- and underinforming the British public about the EU, which, suggested one analysis, is an "insult" (Anderson and Weymouth 1999).

CONCLUSION

Civil society in Britain is characterized by quite high levels of voluntary participation that would seem to demonstrate a positive view of Britain's social capital. This, however, contrasts vividly with a declining interest in more traditional forms of political participation through trade unions or political parties and a mood of cynicism over the efficiency of the political system in general. With regard to organized interests, this has translated into "check book participation" by the public and an expanding number of organizations whose professional staffs attempt to represent their supporters at arm's length. In particular, we have noted two contemporary trends in interest representation: a consciousness of the need for effective public relations strategies as part of campaign activities and, in some sectors, the need to campaign at EU level, or at least to focus on British government as a mouthpiece for interests in Brussels corridors. The EU has fostered a multilayered pattern of pressure-group activity, much of which is conducted and can only be explained through complex networks that now extend beyond British borders.

The paradox, however, is that much of the media—and especially the print media—are not prepared to recognize this complexity. As a vital link between civil society, organized interests, and government, there must be concern over the media's role in constructing an informed and healthy demos for British politics. Whether perceived as an elite pluralist, consumer or PR democracy, the media's role in constructing "realities" for a still-involved but cynical civil society would seem vital; and it is no more important than in the representation of the process of domestic politics and the multilevel nature of British public affairs as a result of EU membership. Whatever its strengths, in this respect we find the contemporary British media deficient in helping to achieve a healthy pluralist society in the twenty-first century.

FURTHER READING

Harold Clarke and others review factors contributing to *Political Choice in Britain* (2004). Charles Pattie and others investigate the notion of participation in *Citizenship in Britain* (2004). Eurobarometer's periodic national reports on attitudes toward the EU give a comparative temporal perspective. Joel Krieger's conclusions that Britain is an "atomized" society are presented in his book *British Politics in the Global Age* (1999). Wyn Grant in a monograph (1999) and later a *Parliamentary Affairs* article (2004) applies the notion of insider/outsider pressure group politics to Britain. Justin Greenwood examines the processes of interest-group activity at EU level (2007), and Jenny Fairbrass analyzes how British interests have adopted to the EU, in Bache and Jordan (2006). With regard to the media an excellent examination called *Politics and the Media in Britain* is undertaken by Raymond Kuhn (2007). The significance of the growth of the public relations industry is explored by Davis (2002). The particular position of the British press is contained in *Power without Responsibility: The Press and Broadcasting in Britain* by James Curran and Jean Seaton (2003). More specifically, Peter Anderson and Anthony Weymouth brilliantly deconstruct the cultural bias of the print media in their book *Insulting the Public? The British Press and the European Union* (1999).

8

The Executive
Managing Decline in a Shrinking World?

The executive in a political system has, in its broadest sense, the task of both directing and managing the implementation of policies and therefore could be said to include much of the "output" side of government. More commonly, the executive refers to the "political executive" whose task it is to direct and coordinate governance and to take political and constitutional responsibility for that task. The actors involved therefore are politicians—elected for the most part—and those involved with them in this directional/coordinative task. They rely on advisors and senior bureaucrats who provide the political and expert linkage between the determination of policy and its implementation.

Within the Westminster model, the mix of the political-bureaucratic aspects of policy execution is as significant to the working of the model as the notion of a legislative-executive mix to provide the link between representation and policy creation. Thus, through the ballot box, the British people are linked to their MPs, who are linked to a parliamentary majority that is linked to the cabinet, which is linked to ministers and their civil servants: an electoral chain of command held together by the conventions of cabinet (collective) and ministerial (individual) responsibility to Parliament and thus the people (see textbox 8.1).

As is apparent in previous chapters, the strength of the analysis provided by the Westminster model is its baseline status. Conventionally, and thus constitutionally in the British case, the term *cabinet government* describes the British executive in a formal shorthand, differentiating it from the executive presidential model of the US Constitution or the shared-executive model of Fifth Republic France. It acts as a baseline in other contexts: for traditionalists, together with parliamentary sovereignty, it is the hallmark of a very British way of policy making, allowing for a

Textbox 8.1. Collective Responsibility

In collective responsibility, all cabinet ministers and, by implication, all other government ministers, are bound to support the decisions of the cabinet, in Parliament and in public. This reinforces the most powerful in cabinet discussions, and in most situations, this means the authority of the prime minister who, at minimum, is first-among-equals within the collegiate structure. Collective responsibility is seen as a powerful political weapon. First, it stretches beyond the twenty-two or so cabinet members to all those MPs who are ministers or parliamentary private secretaries, around one-third of the governing parliamentary party. Since senior ministers also have cabals of supporters in Parliament, the web of "collectivity" extends deep into the government backbench—or it should if the convention works effectively. If a government member cannot accept the decisions of the cabinet, he/she must resign—or shut up. Famous resignations include the Conservative rival to Mrs. Thatcher, Michael Heseltine, over defense procurement (1986), Geoffrey Howe over European policy, contributing to Mrs. Thatcher's downfall later (1990), and Robin Cook and Claire Short from the Blair government over Iraq (2003). Gordon Brown faced a "crisis" of resignations in June 2009. On two occasions, over the Common Market Referendum (1975) and on the issue of European Assembly elections (1977), collective responsibility was suspended as the cabinet was openly divided. Periodic leaking of cabinet details has undermined the show of unity in recent years and its use as evidence of political unity is questionable.

process of collective responsibility for decision making and, through the chairing leadership of the prime minister, the effective dispatch of a decision once taken. Thereafter, responsibility for a decision is shared by all involved, and a clear line of individual responsibility for the administration of the decisions leads back to the particular ministers associated with the policy area in Parliament. There is both an elegance and order in the process, as well as coincidence of political responsibility and responsiveness to Parliament as the general accountant for executive performance. Questions to the PM, ministers, and parliamentary committee allow for both the collective and individual actions of the executive to be evaluated and judged openly (see textbox 8.2).

As part of the Westminster model, cabinet government can be seen as an act of faith in this notion of British government, as a validated and customary process of decision making. Thus, for a former senior civil servant, Cabinet Secretary Lord Armstrong (1979–1987), the concept of cabinet government is a Platonic ideal, for "we have a system of Cabinet Government, not a system of Presidential or Chief Executive government . . . virtually no powers are formally invested in the office of Prime Minister and those formal powers the Prime Minister does have are those of patronage, not of policy. He is the chairman of a collective . . . and unless

> **Textbox 8.2. Ministerial Responsibility**
>
> *Ministerial responsibility* is the practice by which individual ministers take personal/constitutional responsibility for failures in the administration of policy or its outcomes that Parliament criticizes, or any injustice to individuals affected by policies—whether they are directly involved or not. In practice, ministers have long since avoided resignation when their civil servants make mistakes, as Sir Thomas Dugdale, minister of agriculture, did in the Crichel Down Affair (1954), though he knew nothing of the bureaucratic maladministration in the situation. More recently, ministers have resigned over personal and financial discretions or because they or their advisors have caused the government political embarrassment. Edwina Currie, undersecretary of state for health, was forced to resign over claims that British eggs were infected by salmonella (1988); Neil Hamilton, undersecretary of state for corporate affairs resigned over accepting cash for parliamentary questions; another minister, Peter Mandelson, resigned twice—over personal loans (1998) and the Hinduja passport affair (2001); David Blunkett, the home secretary, over a personal affair and paternity issues (2005). The allowances scandals (2009) produced a spate of resignations. In these and other cases resignation came only after political support from the cabinet and in particular, the prime minister, was withdrawn as the issue became overly controversial, generally because of persistent media pressure. An emerging operational convention seems to be, *hang on as long as you can until all political capital is exhausted.* Then resign if asked to by the PM.

and until he fires them—his own strength lies essentially in being the Chairman of the Cabinet" (Lord Armstrong 1999, in Hennessy 2001: 3). But, as Hennessy points out, Lord Armstrong, as Mrs. Thatcher's cabinet secretary, was not unaware of how the ideal can give way to the pragmatic in "real life." Much of the discussion in this chapter will be about the tension between this "Platonic" idea of the executive and the more realist view of a political deal between voter, prime minister, and his/her cabinet, that allows for such other views of the British executive as presidential, prime ministerial, command, and core (Foley 2000; Rose 2001). "For the debate is a running commentary. It is about a governing state of mind, about process as much as policy, about the nature of political power and arbitration at the epicenter of British government" (Hennessy 2001: 11).

THE EXECUTIVE: FUNCTIONS AND POWERS

We may start by comparing the responsibilities of the US and British executives against a notional set of executive functions. Table 8.1 lists a generic range of executive activities and what/who formally operates them in each political system. In doing so it is immediately evident that the US

Table 8.1.   The Functions of the Executive

Function	Main Actors Involved	
	USA	Britain
External Leadership		
Ceremonial Representation	President	**Monarchy**
Political/Diplomatic Representation	President	**Prime Minister**, EU
Military Command	President	**Prime Minister, War Cabinet**
The Policy Process		
Initiation	President-Congress	Prime Minister-EU; Ministries
Coordination	President	Prime Minister-Cabinet
Implementation	President-Depts. of State	Ministers-bureaucracy-EU
Popular Leadership		
National Figurehead	President	**Monarchy-Prime Minister**
Political Command	President	Prime Minister
Political Appointment	President	Prime Minister
Political Cohesion		
Integration; Preservation of Constitutional Values	President-Supreme Court	Monarchy/Parliament; ECHR
Change Agenda Leadership	President	Prime Minister-Cabinet, EU
Crisis Leadership/Management	President	**Prime Minister**

Bold Type gives main agent.
EU refers to EU institutions, especially the European Council, Council of Ministers, and European Commission

presidential system is more constitutionally defined than the British executive, which emanates from the conventions of British executive-legislative arrangements and Crown prerogative. Politically and constitutionally, the representation of US executive power is more obviously located in the office of the presidency itself.

Also apparent is the range of functions that are shared by institutions/ actors in Britain. There is clearly more room for debate about who or what has power than in the United States case. This is not to conclude that US presidential powers are stronger than prime ministerial powers—for in the best of circumstances the prime minister enjoys considerably more powers than a US president. It does, however, illustrate the importance of a dynamic approach to the analysis of the British executive. Also significant is the presence of the monarchy—the dignified ceremonial element of the executive equation. As indicated in chapter 3, the monarchy is constitutionally limited and precluded from proactive political engagement. However, the existence of the institution of monarchy has been criticized as a weight on the modernization agenda, "a comfortable palliative to the loss of world power status" (Cannadine, in Harrison 1996: 340).

One factor here, apart from the public support for the monarchy, is the particular advantage that accrues to political executives from the convention of exercising royal prerogative as a constitutional basis for executive action. The government, mainly the prime minister, exercises powers that once were the monarch's. For instance, the PM gained the right to dissolve Parliament and thus choose the date of a general election; make treaties, including treaties that limit the executive's powers; and declare war. Inevitably there are considerable political constraints on the application of these powers: thus in 2003 Prime Minister Blair sought Commons' approval for the incursion into Iraq; both the Blair and Brown governments committed the issue of Britain's membership in the eurozone to a referendum; and one of Gordon Brown's first steps to make Parliament more evidently involved in major decision making was to make several prerogative powers subject to parliamentary scrutiny and approval, including parliamentary dissolution, going to war, and treaty making.

But, despite these reforms, the executive function remains constitutionally uncodified and the formal source of prime ministerial powers still remains through the exercise of royal prerogatives. The PM's power of appointment (patronage) includes the appointment of cabinet and other ministers. Though on occasions restricted by considerations of party stability, he/she can also reshuffle the pack or sack individual ministers. With the assistance of several secretariats the PM appoints senior public administrators and managers, and dispenses public honors. Textbox 8.3 summarizes the tasks of the PM.

One other feature of this traditional base for political power is that ministers continue to perform functions—as do civil servants, judges, the police, military personnel, and postal workers—as servants of the Crown, not for the state or the public. In effect there is no formal duty of public service in the interests of the people. Crown interests may run counter to public interests—and there are many examples of Crown servants being prosecuted for revealing information that, in their judgment, has been in the public interest. This monarch/subject, rather than politician/citizen, relationship is also a consideration in exploring the nature of prime ministerial power and authority over cabinet and Parliament.

One other factor evident from table 8.1 is the presence of the EU as an externally generated intrusion into the activities of the British executive. This is manifest in several forms: as an opportunity for the prime minister and ministers to shape the nature of EU policies that affect both Britain and other member states—for example the "Blair/Brown agenda" for labor flexibility within the European economy; as a constraint on policy choices—when EU regulations preclude actions to deal with domestic problems—so the EU Common Fisheries Policy precludes policies for Scottish and English fishing communities that would run counter to EU stock

---

Textbox 8.3. The Tasks of the Prime Minister

- Managing the parliamentary majority
- Appointing the political and administrative executive*
- Ordering and prioritizing the policy agenda
- Organizing the institutions of government
- Leading and directing foreign relations/policy
- Chief communicator of government policy
- Chairing the cabinet and its important committees
- Responding to parliamentary inquisition
- Representing the public face of party government
- Leading crisis response, both domestic and external
- Dissolving Parliament* and leading the party electoral machine.
- Dispensing public honors*

* In a Green Paper *The Governance of Britain*, Gordon Brown signaled his intention to move the source of executive power away from prerogative authority "no longer considered appropriate in a modern democracy" toward powers drawn "from the people, through parliament" (CM7170 2007: 15).

---

preservation regulations; as agenda setting—when "EU matters" force their way to the top of political agendas with consequences for the timetable of usual domestic business. Periodic attention to issues like the Single Currency and European constitutional reform has, said one politician, the "unnerving ability to turn British politics inside out" (Baker 2005: 35). It is in the light of these exceptions that we will explore the contemporary role of the British executive.

THE EXECUTIVE AND THE DOMESTIC POLICY PROCESS

It is in the domestic political arena that we might anticipate cabinet and ministerial power being clearly evident in policy execution. Once elected with a working majority (see table 8.2), a prime minister, a cabinet, and ministers enjoy considerable political authority to get on with the job of governing: implementing manifesto commitments; dealing with events that need policy responses; and trying out policy ideas that may come from advisors, pressure groups, or indeed, personal agendas. The cabinet also arbitrates between ministerial differences and should present a concerted political leadership to Parliament, party, electors, and vitally, the media. Figure 8.1 illustrates the connectivity between the several structures that compose the political executive in domestic policy making.

Table 8.2.   British Government Majorities (1945–2009)

Election	Governing Party	Parliamentary Majority	Prime minister	Time in Office (years)
1945	Labour	147	Clement Attlee	5
1950	Labour	6	Clement Attlee	1
1951	Conservative	16	Winston Churchill	5
1955	Conservative	59	Anthony Eden (to 1957)	
			Harold Macmillan	4
1959	Conservative	99	Harold Macmillan (to 1963)	
			Sir Alec Douglas Home	4
1964	Labour	5	Harold Wilson	2
1966	Labour	97	Harold Wilson	4
1970	Conservative	31	Edward Heath	4
1974 (Feb)	Labour	None	Harold Wilson	8 months
1974 (Oct)	Labour	4	Harold Wilson (to 1976)	6
			Jim Callaghan*	3
1979	Conservative	4	Margaret Thatcher	4
1983	Conservative	144	Margaret Thatcher	4
1987	Conservative	102	Margaret Thatcher (to 1990)	4
			John Major	2
1992	Conservative	21	John Major	5
1997	Labour	179	Tony Blair	4
2001	Labour	167	Tony Blair	4
2005	Labour	66	Tony Blair (to 2007)	4
2007	Labour	66	Gordon Brown	

*With Liberal Democratic support in Parliament for agreed policies—a Parliamentary Accord (1978–1979).

Structuring the Cabinet

The cabinet formally registers, and approves, major policy decisions and initiates policy through its specialist and ad hoc committees, the importance of which was only officially acknowledged in 1992, when John Major made available the detail of cabinet committees. This allows an opportunity to examine the contemporary pecking order of policy priorities through the personnel of the committees (Dunleavy 2003). This will vary between administrations and also within a government's time in office. There were around fifty-sixty committees during Blair's last government; under Gordon Brown the number was more than halved to twenty-nine. Who chairs them and the content of their terms of reference give a pretty good guide to prime ministerial priorities. For the most part the prime minister will chair external-relations committees, those associated with intelligence and security, and selected committees that he/she perceives as important in terms of current government policy. The chancellor of the exchequer chairs major economic and domestic committees

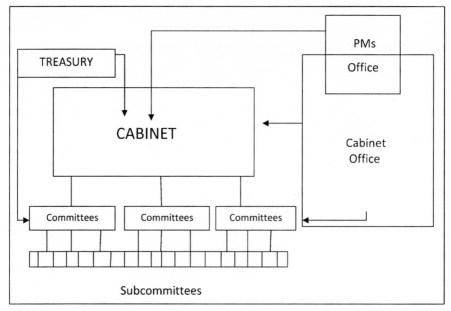

Figure 8.1.   Executive Connections

and use is also made of cabinet ministers without portfolio (i.e., without specific duties) who are close to the prime minister's ear. The relevant secretary or minister of state generally chairs the subcommittees. Since the majority of committees concern themselves with domestic policy, the power of the PM to control the policy process would seem limited. He simply cannot be involved in all government policy outcomes and must make use of the skills and loyalty of his senior colleagues to see through effective, politically acceptable, and coordinated decisions. The nomination and composition of the various cabinet committees is a significant component of what the Blair administration called "joined-up government."

The first Gordon Brown Cabinet (July 2007) and its subcommittees reflected his attempt to stamp a new direction on policy making. His cabinet of twenty-one consisted of only eleven ministers that had held office under Tony Blair. Only one, the minister of defense, held the same position. Apart from the reduction in committees and subcommittees, the Brown cabinet organization mirrored a departmental reconfiguration in Whitehall that also reflected a new prioritization of policies. Thus, there is a cabinet subcommittee on families, children, and young people; another on migration; and three committees, each chaired by the prime minister, on "Life Chances." The PM also chairs the committee on national security, international relations, and development as well as its subcommittees on

---

Textbox 8.4. The Cabinet Office

The Cabinet Office is the secretariat to the cabinet, whose head civil servant, the cabinet secretary, is the most senior official in British government. He is in close liaison with the prime minister and attends cabinet and some cabinet committee meetings. He is also in close contact with the treasury officials and the Prime Minister's Office. The strategic support offered to the government thus supports the leadership role of the prime minister and coordinates policies across the departmental spectrum; promotes administrative capacity (i.e., efficiency), and oversees standards in government; and provides intelligence assessment for internal and external security. Several subunits reflect the government's policy prioritization of such areas as social exclusion; government transformation; and, jointly with the Treasury, effective policy delivery. Overall, the Cabinet Office is politically headed by two cabinet ministers assisted by around forty senior civil servants and 2,000 other grades.

---

defense, foreign policy, and development. He chose not to chair a subcommittee on Europe, leaving its conduct to the foreign secretary. In contrast to his predecessor, the PM chaired only eight out of thirty-six committees compared with the chancellor of the exchequer, who chairs seven (November 2008). The Cabinet Office services both the full cabinet and its committees (see textbox 8.4).

THE PRIME MINISTER'S OFFICE

In recent years, and especially since the Blair government of 1997, the importance of the Prime Minister's Office as a center for policy discussion, initiation, and coordination has been the basis of much debate. Though prime ministers had the opportunity to create "kitchen cabinets" at No. 10 Downing Street (the prime minister's residence and office) and make use of academic or political advisors, it was not until 1974 that a Policy Unit was institutionalized under the Wilson administration. It remained relatively small in staff but, under Mrs. Thatcher, was strengthened to become a vehicle for her forceful intervention in domestic policy, ranging from local government reform to the school curriculum. It was, however, one of only several sources of supportive information that she sought; others included personal advisors such as the Conservative political guru Sir Keith Joseph and the academic economist Alan Walters, as well as neoliberal think tanks. She made no use of the slower and more public and formal Royal Commission, seeking in-house and instantaneous analysis and consultation.

Her successor, John Major, maintained the Policy Unit and called only one Royal Commission in his period of office. He also focused his attention on selected issues, notably Northern Ireland and a "back-to-basics" morality campaign. His collegiate style of leadership, together with political problems with his Conservative backbench and cabinet colleagues, contrasted vividly with Mrs. Thatcher's direct and often abrasive leadership style, leading a Treasury official to compare ministerial and civil service reactions to prime ministerial instruction. "A memo from No. 10 stating that the 'Prime Minister's wishes' . . . made people sit up in Whitehall under Mrs. Thatcher, but had little effect under John Major" (quoted in Kavanagh 1997: 115). Similar comments were also made about civil servants' lack of attention to No. 10 memos in the Wilson and Callaghan government of the 1970s.

In effect, the existence of a prime minister's office is not necessarily evidence of a countervailing or dominating feature of prime ministerial rather than cabinet government, unless accompanied by leadership that achieves real political effect. The Blair administrations 1997–2005 are interesting in that, not only was Tony Blair a powerful interventionist in domestic policy, but he reconstituted the Prime Minister's Office to assure both political *and* process intervention at Whitehall level. Personal intervention was institutionalized in Blair's Prime Minister's Office by the appointment of special advisors to exercise considerable authority over permanent officials and head three divisions—Communications; the Policy Unit, with overlapping membership and organization between the PM's Office and the Cabinet Office; and the Delivery Unit based in No. 10. These appointments were especially significant in allowing the prime minister an oversight on effective policy delivery by ministers and departments.

On finally achieving power in 2007, Gordon Brown indicated his wish to instigate a change in prime ministerial style. One manifestation of this was a reconfiguration of his office. First, in revoking the powers given by Tony Blair to his special (political) advisors to instruct permanent civil servants, the distinction between advice and the execution of policy was reestablished. Though there remained five special advisors, two had previously been senior civil servants, and of a total of ten senior staff, six had worked with Gordon Brown at the Treasury. The Delivery Unit is now located in the Treasury. Four of the team formed part of the Policy and Coordination section of the Cabinet Office, its steering group. So, while removing the intervening powers of political appointees over permanent civil servants and relying on advisors with civil service backgrounds, the new prime minister's immediate circle were a loyal and trusted group of mainly ex-Treasury staff whose interaction with the Cabinet Office was firmly maintained.

Staffing numbers remain tiny compared with the Oval Office and are lower than for the French prime minister or the German chancellor. Nevertheless, this institutionalization of prime ministerial access to Whitehall departmental networks has allowed the emergence of top-down policy interventions in selected areas such as, for Blair: social exclusion, policies for women, and e-governance, as well as public service reform and service delivery. For Brown the key issues were "Life Chances" and the national and international eradication of poverty, until the 2008 recession became a matter of political survival for him and the Labour project. Two ministers of cabinet rank move between the Prime Minister's Office and the Cabinet Office, as extra prime-ministerial eyes in what might be seen as the de facto combination of the two offices. The implications for the traditional role of departmental civil servants with regard to policy advice are discussed in the next chapter. What is evident here is that the role of the full cabinet and its committees can be challenged by this prime ministerial capability at the center.

A Symbolic Cabinet System?

Is the cabinet now only a "symbolic" part of the Constitution? If this is so, then the lines of political responsibility for policy execution to Parliament (as in the Westminster model) are challenged by the plethora of advisory and oversight sources, policy units, and task forces that are the stuff of the contemporary core executive (Smith 1999). Inevitably criticism has emerged of the prime minister's executive reach, the poor quality of advice, and the inherent danger of too rapid policy creation. This has been part of the price for clear and powerful PM leadership for many years. Mrs. Thatcher's ill-thought-out metropolitan government reforms in the 1980s were not fatal; however her insistence on a new local (poll) tax in 1990 was one factor in her political demise. Short-lived plans for immediate police-enforced fines for drunken behavior in 2000 caused only temporary embarrassment to Mr. Blair; much more serious were plans for House of Lords reform, "top-up fees" for the funding of undergraduate education, and the emergence of Foundation Hospitals as an element of National Health Service reform—all to be seriously contested as "ill conceived" in his second term, 2001–2005 (Seldon 2004). Conflicting advice about whether to hold a snap election in autumn 2007 and publicly revealed indecisiveness was to undermine Gordon Brown's credibility for firm decision making. In 2009 the Brown/Darling recession strategy also brought reports of major cabinet divisions over the effectiveness of recession-busting policies.

Structuring Whitehall

The prime minister's influence on the prioritization of policy extends further than the organization of her/his own resources. S/he is able not only to appoint ministers to head up departments but also to set the organizational structure of government for a parliamentary term. Both are powerful statements of prime ministerial priorities.

Blair led organizational restructuring that included the dismantling of the departments of the Environment and Agriculture and the emergence of the Department for Environment, Food and Rural Affairs (DEFRA), and the creation of a new Department for Constitutional Affairs, which involved the abolition of the historic Lord Chancellor's Department (and a botched attempt to abolish the post of lord chancellor). Each of these organizational changes was in response to a policy redirection for DEFRA, criticism of the work of the Ministry of Agriculture, Fisheries and Food (MAFF), and the need to respond to a constitutional agenda championed by the prime minister himself. Subsequently, in 2006, the responsibilities of the Home Office were split between a new Department for Justice that included responsibility for constitutional reform and a slimmed-down Home Office. Gordon Brown sustained this redistribution, appointing the first woman to the post of home secretary. A further Brown innovation was the appointment of ministers for each of the English regions and London. The PM's power to appoint not only ministers to their posts but to allocate the departmental functions for which they have responsibility sets the tone, prioritizes, and indeed personifies an administration. It may also create the framework for a successful leadership, or prove a lead weight if prioritized policies fall short (see the book's website).

TREASURY POLITICS: THE DUAL EXECUTIVE

Since 1945 several factors have expanded the scope of chancellor/Treasury involvement in domestic policy. First, massive growth in public expenditures on public welfare and support for the economy in Keynesian-style intervention emphasized the role of the Treasury as an integrally interested party in both the direction and detail of domestic policies and their implementation. Second, the weaknesses of the economy during the second half of the twentieth century, especially its vulnerability to international pressures, meant that the Treasury has been in the frontline of crisis management. This became more than evident starting in 2008 as global recession produced unprecedented Treasury and Bank of England responses to ward off the worst features of the dire economic and financial scenario. Both factors have tended to increase the profile of the chancellor and Treasury in policy creation as well as the more familiar role of the finance department as a naysayer for spending.

PM/Chancellor Relations

The extent to which the chancellor and Treasury enjoy political clout is dependent on the extent to which the prime minister involves him/herself with the economy. This has varied since 1945, with prime ministers such as Churchill, Eden, and Douglas-Home taking a comparatively backseat position on economic matters. This contrasts with PMs Attlee, Major, and Blair, whose level of involvement is perceived as moderate (Grant 2002: 184). Much more evident high-level involvement is attributed to Wilson (1966–1970), who sought to introduce "the white heat of technological change" to the economy; Callaghan (1976–1979), battling with economic crisis after IMF intervention; and, famously, Mrs. Thatcher, whose neoliberal policies, the antithesis of Keynesian interventionism, were to radically reshape the British economy. This was not without pain and protest as the impact of deregulation, the privatization of public utilities, and denationalization confronted various sectors of the economic community. These difficulties led inevitably to disagreement between the strong leadership that Mrs. Thatcher demonstrated and the equally strong-minded Nigel Lawson, her chancellor of the exchequer, who was eventually removed from office because of disputes over the European Exchange Rate mechanism. Others like Peter Thornycroft (1958) or Norman Lamont (1993) came to bad ends after economic crises. Given the general concern for the appearance of economic continuity, however, PMs are reluctant to move chancellors unless political pressure to do so becomes too great to resist.

The relationship between Tony Blair and Gordon Brown is illustrative of what seems to have emerged as an almost symbiotic connection between the two offices. If all governments need to modernize, to ride out international economic downturn, and to effectively oversee the huge arena of domestic policy, then the Blair/Brown axis represented one of the most long-lived and effective political tandems in postwar British politics. Their early and close personal relationship changed to one of political codependency, as Blair's popularity declined during his second administration. Brown's influence over domestic policy was seen as extensive, leading to conflict between him and Blair over such issues as the merits of joining the euro, the nature of National Health Service reform, and the timing of increased public spending—which were reported as serious rifts between two powerful politicians.

Brown's ambition to eventually become prime minister was the subject of considerable press speculation, and in the 2005 elections, with Blair's unpopularity impacting on the opinion polls, a Blair/Brown appearance was itself a commentary on the codependency that some observers saw as a dual executive. Despite its tensions, the relationship was key to Labour's three election victories. It was vital that the Treasury played a strong role in changing priorities of public expenditure, squeezing more out of existing resources and thus intervening in the processes of the domestic policy agenda. The chancellor chaired key economic cabinet committees and, despite his interest in the subject, it was not Blair but Brown who insisted that he was to make the final decision on Britain's adoption of the euro (House of Commons 2005). Whatever the veracity of this statement, there is no doubt that the Blair administrations were characterized by an often fractious close relationship between the two.

The appointment of Alistair Darling to act as Gordon Brown's chancellor of the exchequer was greeted by both political and press speculation concerning the extent to which he would enjoy independence of action from the self-nominated most successful chancellor in recent history—his boss! Chancellor Darling was given all economic cabinet committees to chair and in a first public test of crisis management took the lead in calming public and banking nerves when in October 2007 a British bank, Northern Rock, suffered a liquidity difficulty. Subsequently the new chancellor, in addressing the most difficult economic scenario since the 1930s, received both praise and blame for the decisions he was forced to take. Though the prime minister took maximum credit on a G20 international stage in 2009, his chancellor was praised as an asset to the government. Their opponents criticize both of them for causing Britain's economic woes. In adversity prime minister and chancellor are seen both as partners and their own men.

THE EXECUTIVE AND EU INTEGRATION

As the European Single Market legislation began to bite into British domestic policy, the international and domestic roles of the British executive, and especially the prime minister, have become deeply enmeshed. The term *intermestic* encapsulates this phenomenon. Attendance at Council of Ministers meetings takes up a considerable amount of ministerial time. For the prime minister, European councils, intergovernmental conferences, and bilateral meetings with other member-state colleagues often result in tough negotiations that involve the use of much political capital. On the one hand, a minister or prime minister will be expected to reach collegiate agreement over vital sectoral interests in such vexed fields as agricultural reform, environmental standards, or working conditions. Standing with European colleagues will be diminished if there is not a degree of give and take to produce an acceptable consensus. But British ministers, and especially the prime minister, face a rough ride if what is brought home from the negotiation table is not defensible in terms of "national interest." Mrs. Thatcher's demand for a rebate of Britain's EU budget contribution (1984) and John Major's defensive stance during the Maastricht Treaty of Union negotiations over the EMU and Social Chapter opt-outs won political applause at home but met with negative responses in Brussels. When political capital was needed later over Britain's defense of the value of the pound (1992) and solving the BSE (mad cow) crisis, there was little available from fellow EU leaders; Tony Blair's last major act as PM was to establish "red lines" when agreeing to an EU Reform Treaty (June 2007) to placate domestic accusations of sellout to "Brussels."

EU "intermestic" politics, therefore, needs three levels of response from the British executive: at EU level being at the "heart of Europe" by shaping and initiating EU policies; at domestic political level, invariably meaning a robust defense of actions from media and opposition criticism; and at Whitehall level in terms of coordination and implementation, as EU policies have impacted on British governance since the 1980s.

Organizing for EU Participation

Prior to 1997 the coordination of European policy making involved the European Secretariat of the Cabinet Office alongside prime ministerial advisors in the PM's Office. These together with European officers within the Foreign and Commonwealth Office (FCO) and Britain's permanent representation in Brussels (UKRep) are the key players in the government's European policy-making network. Gradually, as the EU's interface with its member states increased, the core implementing ministries (agriculture, trade, industry, and customs) were joined by other ministries. Thus inclusion in the SEA and TEU expanded EC policy competences for the environment, regional policy, justice, and home affairs, necessitating the incorporation of such departments as the Home Office and the environment ministry into the "inner core" of EU-active departments. This expansion meant closer prime ministerial attention to European policy and, since the creation of the European Council (1973), regular summit meetings have drawn the PM into European business at strategic and tactical levels. There is no single Department of European Affairs, though there is a minister for Europe within the Foreign Office (Bulmer and Burch 2004). Institutional adjustment was limited, reflecting the political limitations, and indeed attitudes, of the dominant Conservative governments since 1979.

The advent of a New Labour Government in 1997, with an avowedly positive view of Britain in Europe, brought with it some significant changes to the organization of the executive. In an attempt to enhance its *projection* (rather than just *reception*) of matters European, there was a greater effort to centralize the coordination of EU policy by integrating the work of the Cabinet Office European Secretariat and the Prime Minister's Office. The Head of the European Secretariat is also the prime minister's advisor and has an office in No. 10. Blair administrations since 1997 built upon already existing trends toward EU heads of government by taking a much greater interest in EU policy making—as regular European Council meetings came to play an increasing role in EU governance. Other changes included the creation of a cabinet committee on European Strategy (2003) and an ambitious ten-year Step Change program aimed at achieving a more proactive role in shaping the EU policy agenda. From this emerged a series of institutional and process changes aimed at achieving an effective European engagement.

In organizational terms, Gordon Brown seems to have demoted European policy issues. While maintaining the position of a European policy advisor and a Cabinet Office European bureau, the Cabinet European Secretariat is now only part of a broader organization providing international policy advice. The European Strategy Committee of the cabinet, which was previously chaired by PM Blair, no longer exists. However a subcommittee on Europe continues, now chaired by the foreign secretary.

Other changes have challenged the central coordination of European policy. The Treasury is especially jealous of controlling the economic aspects of European policy; thus the *"Europes"* system of financial accounting (see chapter 9) and issues associated with the Stabilization and Employment Pact and the Single Currency have given the Treasury a significant veto point in initiation and implementation of EU policy. Devolved powers to Scotland and Wales have also resulted in challenges to PM/Whitehall control and coordination (see chapter 10). So, while it can be argued that recent institutional and organizational changes have, for the most part, centralized the process of EU policy within the constellation of the prime minister, it is possible to argue that the ability of the PM to control the domestic agenda is challenged by the embrace of the EU's own policy agenda and the supremacy of EU law in the arena of British domestic governance. So while the PM's power may be enhanced, it is over a smaller and smaller decision-making arena (Rose 2001).

The Prime Minister and International Leadership

The term *intermestic* also applies to the role a prime minister plays in the international arena. Popular leadership has an international dimension, and a PM can benefit domestically from the representative and decision-making role he/she plays in international affairs. As table 8.1 shows, unlike the US president, the PM shares aspects of external representation with the monarch. The office of the US presidency has a dignified aspect to it that is not shared to such an extent by the PM. Much of the pomp and ceremony, glitz and glamour of being a British head of state goes to the institution of the monarchy, and as such the PM does not easily receive the traditional authority afforded to the monarchy or presidency. International ceremonial representation of the British state falls to the monarch and is fiercely guarded.

But if entertaining the presidents and monarchs of other countries and undertaking government-approved state visits is the monarch's preserve, the PM enjoys massive political opportunity to represent the state at the sharp end of diplomatic affairs. Travel to other countries, meeting incoming governmental heads, and representing Britain in regular international meetings (the G8/20, Commonwealth heads of government, and European councils and intergovernmental conferences) are minimum prime ministerial international duties. Bilateral meetings with, for example, the Irish prime minister, the German chancellor and US and French presidents, takes up more time. Occasional international conferences—on climate change, poverty, world debt, and other global issues—ensure that the PM enjoys an international (and thus also domestic) profile vastly more evident than all but the monarchy, whose international activities are also carefully managed to maximum domestic effect.

The responsibility for leading and organizing the national response to international crises is also that of the prime minister. "Events dear boy, events" were the most problematic aspect for any prime minister, suggested Harold Macmillan to a young reporter, meaning that the unforeseen can cut across the best laid plans in politics. International events have indeed undermined the plans of many PMs, sometimes with positive but often with negative domestic effect. Famously, the Anglo-French invasion of Suez, Egypt, in October 1956, secretive in its planning, produced a run on the pound, and US criticism ended the incursion sooner than had been anticipated. Eden resigned in January 1957, sick and in low political esteem. Another famous Macmillan reflection concerned the "wind of change" in Africa (1960) that was followed by Britain's attempt to decolonize in several parts of the continent. Elements in Southern Rhodesia (now Zimbabwe) resisted the move toward majority black rule, and led by a white minority declared unilateral independence. A racist white minority ruled the country until 1980, causing major international embarrassment to four successive British governments. For the current Labour government, the Zimbabwe legacy remains—in the dilemma of how to respond to a now black-ruled "failed state" that has shown similarly scant regard for the rule of law.

In the 1982 Falklands/Malvinas war, when Argentina invaded this British colony, a measured counterinvasion was organized and led by Mrs. Thatcher. Military success saw her preeminent in the polls, which became a major factor in her landslide electoral victory in 1983. Mrs. Thatcher's international prestige and friendship with President Reagan was, however, unable to preclude a unilateral move by the United States to invade Grenada, a Commonwealth member state, despite her pleas to the contrary—a minor but humiliating defeat. More significantly, her growing Euroscepticism, publicly articulated at EU summits and internally, was a significant factor in her political isolation and eventual demise in 1990. For John Major, the first

Gulf War and support for President Bush enhanced his domestic profile. A few months later Britain was forced to leave the European Exchange Rate Mechanism (ERM), a humiliation that impacted on Major's future leadership and the Conservative Party's stance on the EU for the rest of their administration to 1997.

Prime Minister Blair's successes and failures as an international leader are dealt with in the concluding discussion of this chapter. Suffice it to say that, as a new incumbent in 1997, he traveled 26,800 miles in eight weeks from Amsterdam to Hong Kong, from Paris to Denver. His subsequent attention to both the UK/US "special relationship" and his more inconsistent drive to be "at the heart of Europe" made him the most traveled of prime ministers. Gordon Brown, in contrast, spent the first weeks of his premiership mostly at home, dealing successfully with a succession of domestic crises. By 2008 however, the "subprime" mortgage crisis in the United States and the subsequent "credit crunch" gave him ample opportunity to offer his solutions to the world recession to an international audience.

Ironically, as Britain's world role diminishes, successive PMs "continue to define their role in global terms" suggests Richard Rose (2001). Coming to terms with this diminished role has been a significant problem for British leaders, who face, on the one hand, difficulties in achieving external goals without building consensual alliances and, on the other, the opprobrium of the opposition and parts of the electorate if their behavior suggests "selling Britain short." So, while PMs enjoy the "photo opportunity" of rubbing shoulders with presidents and PM colleagues, the management of Britain's diminished role involves risk taking that can lead to diminished domestic popularity—witness the electoral impact of Blair's support for the United States over the invasion of Iraq in 2003.

The EU as a Special Arena

As we suggest above, EU membership has created special difficulties for the British executive and its lead player in external affairs—the prime minister. First, in a small set of external arenas, especially in environmental and trade policy, the prime minister and relevant ministerial colleagues have the chance to contribute to the EU negotiating position in premeetings of the European Council and Council of Ministers respectively; however, actual negotiations are the preserve of the European Commission's negotiating team. Second, in some areas of external policy the EU depends on achieving a consensus in order to impose its often binding decisions on member states. Power sharing, as Richard Rose points out, is "a doctrine antithetical to the doctrine of parliamentary sovereignty" and also to the de facto centralizing tendency of prime ministerial leadership and Whitehall decision making. Power sharing, therefore, goes against the grain of No. 10 culture (Rose 2001: 213).

Third, decisions, once agreed in Brussels, have binding consequences for member states, often in areas of "low politics" that have direct effects on the lives of British and other EU citizens. John Major's problem with adopting the Social Chapter and euro, and Tony Blair's equivocation over the euro and the European Constitution, are evidence of the limitations that membership in the EU imposes on executive action. The outcomes of a Commonwealth conference or bilateral statements of good intent do not have the weight of EU decisions that are binding and may be enforced by EU law. While the executive leadership of most member states fits politically and culturally within a consensual and Europhile domestic framework, British decision makers, whether by conviction or consciousness of electoral agnosticism toward things European, struggle with the management of their EU role.

The tendency has therefore been to either play up the "battling for Britain" persona, so as to win game, set, and match for the national cause, or play down decisions in the hope of not disturbing the anti-EU beast that is perceived to exist within the British electorate. The first causes damage when trying to negotiate with EU partners; the second may end in exposure as issues are "revealed" in the media by political opponents as sell-out politics. Thus, in October 2007 Gordon Brown missed the champagne toast of the successful negotiation of the Reform Treaty with fellow leaders in what became seen as an attempt to play down the agreement's impact on British "sovereignty," and therefore avoid the wrath of the British Eurosceptic press. In 2009, when addressing the EP and perhaps emboldened by the depth of economic crisis, he was to make one of the most pro-EU speeches made by a British prime minister. As Britain's senior EU political representative, the PM is closely evaluated in her/his performance by both allies and enemies at home. Lack of adequate performance, as interpreted by Parliament, party, and the media, means a loss of political capital. Similarly, domestic politics and especially political storms and public crises also need leadership and the semblance of successful resolution.

LEADING PARTY AND PEOPLE

In times of crisis the PM, more than any other cabinet minister, needs to show leadership presence. As such, maintaining control over party, performing well in confrontational set pieces in the House of Commons, especially during Question Time, and communicating with the public through a friendly media are important factors in sustaining leadership.

Failure to control, perform, or communicate well has broken the careers of several prime ministers. Edward Heath's confrontation with mining unions and the government response to power cuts (the three-day week) lost him parliamentary and media credibility and eventually the 1974 election. A similar confrontation with unions after a period of economic instability led to a gradual erosion of parliamentary support for Jim Callaghan. In 1979, after the loss of several by-elections and a "winter of discontent," the Callaghan government was defeated on a vote of no confidence in the House of Commons and lost the resulting general election to Mrs. Thatcher.

We have already mentioned the growing dissatisfaction on the Tory backbenches with Mrs. Thatcher's leadership in 1989–1990. The much-hated reform of local taxation (the poll tax) produced public demonstrations, some of which were violent, and this, together with her strident anti-Europeanism, led to her downfall in 1990. In 1995, having lost the esteem of at least part of his backbench over European issues and his inconsequential leadership style, John Major forced an internal party election to reestablish backbench support. Though winning the vote, eighty-nine Conservative MPs voted against him. His lack of authority within the party was exposed, and in 1997 the Conservatives were defeated by a New Labour landslide victory.

More successfully, Tony Blair intervened in the slow process of solving a national foot-and-mouth (sheep disease) infection in 2001, but his concern for being identified with a failed outcome led him to postpone the election by two months. While this election was won by another landslide to New Labour, his support for the Bush government's intervention in Iraq alienated media and public support. The decline in Labour's majority to 66 seats in 2005 was, for many, the direct result of the loss of Blair's authority compared to previous periods of his administration. In the first few months of his premiership Gordon Brown benefitted from his handling of a flood in several parts of England, a terrorist attack at Glasgow Airport, and another foot-and-mouth outbreak. This popularity was dented when he was seen to dither over deciding whether to seek an early election and thus mandate for his new government.

Since then, his popularity recovered when he was seen to be taking decisive action in relation to global recession in the autumn of 2008 and as host to the G20 conference in London in April 2009. Parallel domestic calamities, including embarrassing expenses claims by Labour MPs, backbench rebellions, a Commons defeat on Gurkha migration rights, and an ill-judged Internet smear campaign recommended by a personal aide all undermined his leadership profile and potential political recovery. A hungry media seeks heroes or villains; anything in between, it seems, is not newsworthy.

The PM: Managing a Change Agenda?

Since the overarching political strategy of the prime minister is to retain power for his party, in effect to lead his government to election victory, a major personal attribute would seem to be management—of cabinet and party; of domestic and international image; and of "events," planned or otherwise. In the last thirty years several factors have conspired to give the office of the PM salience, authority, and preeminence over the formal collegiate model of the British executive process.

Managing decline in a shrinking world, suggests one commentator, has intensified visibility of the PM, who must manage change in so many political circumstances (Rose 2001). Dean Acheson's oft-quoted comment that Britain had lost an empire but not yet found an alternative role has been reinforced by the end of the Cold War. Until the early 1990s the transatlantic community, in the formal shape of NATO, was the anchor point around which British leaders could articulate national interest and international ideals. The emergence of the United States as the contemporary hegemon has presented alternative international strategies to the British government—exemplified through Tony Blair's hot pursuit of a special relationship with the United States. Much is made, therefore, of the closeness—or lack of rapport—that British prime ministers have achieved in recent years with US presidents.

The Labour government publicity machine made much of Gordon Brown's visit to Washington to meet President Obama, billed as the first *European* leadership visit (the president had already been visited by the Japanese prime minister). The nature of the special relationship is dealt with in chapter 13. We note here that perspectives on the Anglo-American relationship and the extent to which Britain is integrally involved with the EU have come to define the external choices of the PM, most vividly during the Blair administration, after his choice of fulsome support for the US invasion of Iraq in 2003.

Changes in Britain's external agenda since the 1980s have been one part of a response to globalization. Economic interdependence, assisted by rapid technological change, has impacted on British domestic politics and, inevitably, the shape of executive decision making and national leadership. The British economy, with its sectoral strength in international finance and financial services, has both taken advantage of and been subject to the vicissitudes of global economic forces. Both Conservative and Labour governments sought to rebalance the British economy toward market efficiency and flexibility to cope with globalization. Mrs. Thatcher, especially, led that drive with her brand of "conviction politics," riding often roughshod over opposition from outside and also within her party. Leading this tilt toward a reformed economy and political culture gave the premiership an authoritative and interventionist reputation. John Major, while not relinquishing the economic message, did not share her style of conviction leadership, but found little political thanks for his more traditional, collegiate style of executive leadership.

Blair's New Labour policies and style of leadership were honed from these factors and contributed significantly to what some have seen as presidential-style politics in the twenty-first century (Foley 2000); subsequently Gordon Brown has sought to sustain a "safe hands" reputation and a domestic and external change agenda against the backdrop of economic downturn and global uncertainties. As discussed in chapter 6, the emergence of market-based consumer politics in Britain has contributed to a more fluid rational choice base to voting behavior, enhancing the pivotal role of party leadership in convincing electors of effective change management.

The British President?

A danger in writing any political commentary is the exaggeration of contemporary circumstances. As early as 1963 the Labour politician and intellectual Richard Crossman was referring to the advent of "prime ministerial government" in the light of Harold Macmillan's premiership (1957–1962). Lord Hailsham was referring to Harold Wilson when he described the premier as an "elected dictator" in 1976 (Hailsham 1976). Mrs. Thatcher was "the nearest thing to a demagogue the leadership of the Conservative Party has ever produced" (Harris 1988: 62) giving her name, Thatcherism, to the period of her administrations. After one year in power, the *Sunday Times* concluded that the first Blair government had brought the British political process "as close to having a presidential system as is possible" (*Sunday Times*, April 26, 1998). And according to one political commentator and prior to taking over the premiership, a joke was doing the ministerial and Whitehall round: "What's the difference between Gordon Brown and Stalin? One is a ruthless dictator who murders his opponents and rules by absolute terror. The other was leader of the Soviet Union" (*Observer*, September 9, 2007).

Is this evidence of a slow drift toward a British system of presidential government? Or is it the instant assessment of a contemporary situation, dependent on a mix of personal characteristics and political advantages of the incumbent? The early admiration of the "Blair presidency" was replaced, even before the 2005 election, by more sober discussion of the prime ministerial/cabinet/parliamentary relationship (Seldon 2001; Rose 2001; Smith 2006) with much emphasis upon the notion of a dynamic core executive (Hennessy 2001; and see the book's website).

The character of Blair premiership was apparent in his leadership of the Labour Party in opposition (1993–1997). His rebranding of the national party as "New Labour" and reshaping of its values and priorities in the shape of a "Third Way" were designed to win power. The party's redirection was a Blair "project" that was dependent on his leadership qualities and personal alliances with colleagues who shared his vision and purpose. Also, Blair's vision reached out to the electoral center, and a brand of middle-ground "populism" emerged with which Blair freely identified himself. Business and media interests were courted and successfully seduced by what rapidly emerged as "Blairism." The promise of "renewal" led to his initial and, as it was portrayed, personal landslide victory in 1997.

Subsequently this personalization was translated into a cultivated identification with carefully chosen policy arenas; these ranged from education; European labor-market reform; the war on drugs; hospital waiting lists; immigration and asylum; poverty in Africa; and, almost fatally, intervention in Iraq. Even after what some perceived as a limited victory in his third election (2005), Blair sought personal identification with radical policies. This identification was, to some extent, institutionalized in his search for effective control of the process of government. It is this aspect of Blair's premiership that may have accelerated an incremental process toward a presidential core to the British executive. Thus greater use of party-appointed advisors for the prime minister (and other ministers) has demoted the initiating role of the senior civil servant. This, together with PM-appointed or -approved task forces and special units in an expanded Office of the Prime Minister, went some way to detaching policy initiative from Whitehall and the Labour Party. Thus the formality of the oval cabinet table was replaced by the settee in the PM's office, from which the PM initiated and oversaw policy.

Accompanying these oversight units was, from the beginning of Blair's premiership, a communications machine that, under his first director of communications, Alistair Campbell, gained a reputation for manipulation and spin in its attempt to control the presentation of the PM, and indeed all government policy. More resources than any previous British government have been directed toward the favorable communication of government policy to the media, and no British prime minister spent so much time in media cultivation. Prime Minister Blair also attended Parliament less than any premier since 1945 and reduced the famous prime minister's Question Time to one period (Wednesday, 3:00–3:30 in the afternoon) from two periods a week. The cabinet met for less than one hour per week, and commentators began to argue that its role occupied the dignified parts of the constitution rather than playing any formal role in the political process.

In the consolidation of his command position, PM Blair was assisted, at least until 2003 and the Iraq war, by a considerable party majority in the Commons and a degree of popularity with the voters that, though gradually waning, proved remarkably durable for such a long-lived period in office. He was the "command premier" (Hennessy 2001). For Michael Foley (2000: 323) the "usage of presidential terminology has become an almost prosaic form of descriptive license." One argument was that the subsequent incumbents of the office would benefit incrementally from Blair's institutionalization of his personal power. More than this, not to adopt a presidential persona flies in the face of the changed political environment and consequently the expectations of the electorate—the final arbiter of prime ministerial success.

BUT STILL A CABINET SYSTEM?

The Blair governments were seen as a continuation of the process of power concentration during the Thatcher years, as the PM's responsibilities to appoint and dismiss ministers, to control government information, to choose policy priorities, and to induce economic and social change—and thus achieve successful reelection—made her/him a domestic political giant. The nature of party leadership and the diminished role of the parties also facilitated top-down, personified policy innovation. Finally, the changing commercial and technological base of the media also created conditions by which a presidential presence could be enhanced, as it was for long periods of the Blair premiership.

Several factors combine to balance the presidential view of the British executive. The first is that Britain remains a parliamentary not a presidential system. The PM is not elected directly by all the people. Her/his legitimacy remains with Commons assent and party leadership. Carrying the cabinet with the PM still matters. Mrs. Thatcher was eventually ousted because of her inability to maintain cabinet support. The particularly powerful political position of Blair's chancellor, Gordon Brown, and resultant cabinet alliances over certain issues—the euro especially—curtailed Blairist policy initiatives. A greatly reduced parliamentary majority after the 2005 election also reduced opportunities for party bypass and altered the political position of the PM from the presidential toward a more collegiate persona. In the period of his current prime ministerial tenure, 2007 to 2009, Gordon Brown has enjoyed both a reputation as world leader and broken political reed. The PM is also not the head of state—in effect s/he is a mere mortal—worse, a political animal. Traditional authority is therefore not available, and this detracts from a PM's ability to build up a mystique or rely on dignified and ceremonial characteristics of statehood available to the queen, the US president, or the president of France.

The tendency to overstate prime ministerial power is evident, especially when examining the scope for other executive actors to create, implement, and control policies. There remains only so much time in a day, and prime ministerial attachment to "vanguard" policies is limited to a few issues. Senior ministers tasked to initiate policy are expected to achieve results. In particular, the chancellor of the exchequer and the Treasury can provide potential antidotes to the presidential thesis. Cabinet subcommittees remain important centers for policy process, a factor underscored by PM Blair, who pointed to a doubling of the number of these committees as an indication of the strength of collegiate government under his administrations (Smith 2003: 76).

For his successor, cabinet committees are also significant policy centers; however his approach was to reduce their number and chair committees in a narrower set of policy areas. It was interesting to observe Gordon Brown's initial actions when becoming prime minister. In the space of a few days he announced a series of measures that were designed to enhance the role of parliament and cabinet government (see above). A Green Paper underscored this desire for a more accountable and listening style of government (CM7170 2007). In effect, the new PM attempted to draw a clear line between Blair's presidential style and his collegiate intentions.

Finally, the semblance of a presidential executive must be examined in the context of the shrinking world of British central government. Rose (2001) makes the potent argument that a British premier in the twenty-first century has more power, but within a shrinking policy arena. Economic and political globalization, together with the Europeanization of many policy arenas, has tended to raise the profile of the PM as a leading policy actor without necessarily offering the opportunity for independent action. Domestically, since the Thatcher governments of the 1980s, the organization of public services shifted away from Whitehall as privatization, agency provision, and devolution have taken place. Thus the PM and other ministers had less opportunity for intervention in domestic policy than previously.

The extra resources that successive prime ministers have utilized are recognition of the new environment of executive leadership The "hollowing of the state," especially as a consequence of EU integration and more latterly devolution; the demands of the consumer-elector; and the media opportunities for a presidential form of leadership are all factors that have altered the character of the British executive. While examples of "presidentialism" are, on the surface, easy to identify, the British policy-making system is now a complex of layered systems—of multilevel governance. As such, a focus upon the emergence of a dynamic core executive is a more fruitful approach for an analysis of governance in Britain than a presidential/collegiate dichotomy. The next chapter seeks to examine this policy-making complex.

FURTHER READING

For a classic account of British cabinet government see John Mackintosh *The British Cabinet* (1962). Richard Crossman in an introduction to Bagehot's *The English Constitution* presents the case of prime ministerial government (1963). Anthony King brings these discussions together in an edited volume (1985). Peter Hennessy (2001) provides a historical review of prime ministers since 1945 and Michael Foley presents the case for *The British Presidency* (2000). The notion of a *Core Executive in Britain* is presented by Martin J. Smith (1999 and 2003). Richard Rose proposes the strengths of a *Prime Minister in a Shrinking World* (2001). Books by Seldon on *Blair* (2004) and *The Blair Effect* (2001), an edited volume, examine the era (1997–2005). PM/chancellor relations are traced in Wyn Grant's *Economic Policy in Britain*, chapter 8 (2002). Prime ministerial attitudes to the EU may be gleaned from Stephen Wall's account of his service as a diplomat and advisor in *A Stranger in Europe: Britain and the EU from Thatcher to Blair* (2008). Andrew Rawnsley presents a journalist view of the Blair-Brown tandem in *Servants of the People* (2001), and biographies of Gordon Brown by Paul Routledge (1998) and Tom Bower (2003) gave background to Britain's current prime minister.

9

The British State and the Policy Process

How is British public policy shaped in the twenty-first century? From the discussion of leadership and executive power in chapter 8 and elsewhere, one may discern a few general pointers to answering this question. Three different perspectives for viewing the British political system were introduced, each having its normative assumptions and structural characteristics: the Westminster model, the core executive, and MLG. Each prioritizes different elements within the policy system that are considered to be vital explanatory factors, and each of these perspectives grapples with how political solutions to societal demands are shaped by factors that are external to the "normal" political process. Also, technological change, especially in relation to information and communication; manifestations of globalization; and, in the case of Britain and other member states, Europeanization, needs accounting for in any analysis of the nature of the political process. Finally, for Britain's medium-term policy choices, the 2008–2009 recession, the measures taken to overcome its impact, and its consequences all have to be factored into any contemporary assessment of the policy process. We shall commence with an examination of the characteristics of the contemporary British state and the domestic political changes that have affected the public-policy process.

THE BRITISH STATE AND POLICY CONSENSUS

We start by viewing what we have called the default perspective of the British state. Policy emerges from the particular institutions of the British political system, with "Westminster" for debate and representation, PM and cabinet for policy execution, and Whitehall for implementation—with

225

the assistance of other public agencies including local governments. The British state also has a set of traditional checks and balances that differentiate it from other political systems and their policy processes and that act as a political yardstick to judge the activities of policy makers. Thus, for newspapers, opposition MPs, and pressure groups, a particular minister, as the public face of his/her department, is directly accountable for public policies pertinent to that department. Civil servants support this notion of political accountability in official documentation and when making their limited appearances in public. Their job is to advise and support their ministers and, if necessary, implement "ordained error." A variant of this Westminster view of policy making accepts the salience of bureaucratic Whitehall politics, and thus the importance of the professional civil servant—if not in originating, then in reworking policies to enhance political and administrative efficacy.

Civil Servants and Silos

The personnel of this Westminster/Whitehall policy tandem operate formally within a set of codes and practices and within the limits of their responsibilities and expertise. For ministers, appointed mainly for political rather than technical skills, their major concerns are the sound management of departmental responsibilities and the external projection of their department's effectiveness. The skills necessary are primarily political and evaluative. First, they strive to win internal recognition of their department's worth against other departmental aspirations, as well as perform the vital task of promoting the department's agenda within the cabinet and to the public. Second, judging the value and political consequences of the advice of senior civil servants may be vital for a minister's survival. Advice will come from departmental policy communities, who might well be close knit and clientalist in their nature, or from external sources— party, Parliament, press, and public.

In the context of this default perspective of the state, the senior civil servant is an expert administrator, not a technical advisor, who broadly guides and facilitates the leadership of a temporary, politically ambitious boss. The British civil servant's permanent status might present obstacles to an incoming reforming minister, as continuity and only necessary incremental change easily become the department's overriding objectives. In a sense, this "British policy style," based on a culture of continuity, consultation, and negotiated order, reflected the consensus politics evident in the third quarter of the twentieth century (Jordan and Richardson 1982; Dorey 2005a). After World War II, the British civil service loyally adapted itself to facilitate the new welfare state, alongside maintaining the character of British central bureaucracy encapsulated in mid-nineteenth-century

Northcote-Trevelyan reforms (see the book's website). Thus, a permanent nonparty, nonspecialist public service was sustained despite its massive increase in function, size, and technical output.

There emerged a number of consequences for the capability of the British state to facilitate this vast public policy. Within each ever-larger department there developed a departmental culture of continuity and limited incremental expansion. Client groups in such areas as agriculture, transportation, and health, or party consensus over programs such as universal retirement pensions, alongside a private sector supported by tax incentives, helped sustain "departmentalism, whereby particular ministries evinced a discernable philosophy or ethos [and thus] sustained an institutional agenda frequently sceptical of new ideas or policy initiatives" (Dorey 2005a: 210). The permanence of senior civil servants, often in one departmental silo for many years, together with the willingness of younger staff to absorb departmental values, mitigated the change agenda that, at least initially, may have informed a new minister's aspirations. As Dorey points out, the result was that many ministers "went native" and accepted the views and agendas of the departmental officials—thus managing rather than leading their departments (see the book's website).

FROM CONSENSUS TO REGULATION

The Thatcher and Major governments not only disturbed and attempted to break the social and political consensus of the previous twenty-five years, but they also attempted to dismantle the policy process, moving to reduce the size of the state in terms not only of its functions and personnel, but also its cost. An ideological commitment to a New Right agenda, enjoying considerable electoral support and thus parliamentary majorities, gave legitimacy to the task of "rolling back the state" and, as a corollary, utilizing market-based solutions for public-policy requirements. The implications for the consensus state were great. In effect "the 1980s and 1990s witnessed an increasing emphasis on deregulation, liberalization and privatization . . . coupled with the promotion of consumer choice in the conduct of public services" (Dorey 2005b: 215). The sale of state-run services and energy utilities on the open market, for example British Gas, Airways, and Rail; the opening of previously state monopolies to competition (British Telecoms and the Post Office); and the introduction of competition in the supply and delivery of public services (at the local level in school supplies and refuse collection) were among the changes. In addition there were moves to decentralize government departments through a series of geographical and functional reorganizations and, inevitably, cuts in public services and thus civil service employment levels (see textbox 9.1).

**Textbox 9.1. The Transformation
of Central Governance (1979–2005)**

1979	Raynor Report: Cabinet Office Efficiency Unit Report on reducing costs and removing waste.
1981	Abolition of Civil Service Department
1982	Financial Management Initiative: attempts to set clear policy objectives and measures performance
1983	Privatization of public utilities, nationalized industries et seq.
1988	Next Steps Report: application of New Public Management principles to civil service
1991	White Paper: Competing for Quality—market testing
1991	Citizens Charter: citizens become customers
1992	Private Finance Initiative introduced
1994	White Paper: Civil Service—Continuity and Change further moves to executive agencies
1994	Regional Government Offices establishment
1995	Office of Public Service set up within Cabinet Office
1996	Nolan Report: standards in public life
1997	Next Steps Review: New Labour reinforces previous policies with "joined-up government"; IT revolution: ministers as change champions
1998	Service First Charter: reinforces Citizens Charter
	Step Change Programme to insert EU consciousness into British political administration
1998	Regional Development Agencies set up
1999	White Paper: Modernizing Government: reinforces "joined-up government" through policies that are group/area focused
	Scottish/Welsh devolution commences
2000	Treasury Comprehensive Spending Reviews/Public Service Agreements
	Office of Government Commerce (to promote best value)
2001	Office of Public Sector Reform and Delivery Unit in Cabinet Office
	Endorsement of PPI and its extension to PPP
2004	Gershon Review: to reduce numbers of civil servants
2005	Departmental Capability Reviews to achieve/assess open "public" targets.
2007	Green Paper: Civil Service Code recommended.

This radical shift in the role of the state had wider ideological and political implications. First, "old" policy communities that had held considerable sway within a number of policy areas lost their traditional access to the decision process. Trade unions were the most evidently affected, not only in their loss of legal position, particularly in relation to the range of industrial action they could take, but also through the demise of most of the formal corporate bodies that gave them an institutional legitimacy.

The National Economic Development Council was abolished by 1992, and the Manpower Services Commission, which had a 50 percent union representation, was replaced by several Training and Enterprise Councils that had only 5 percent union membership (Dorey 2005b: 154). The "tripartism" of the 1960s and 1970s was well and truly buried. The teaching unions, represented in many formal bodies, as well as the powerful British Medical Association, found their influence diminished and advice ignored when radical changes to education and health policies were considered and implemented.

Sources of advice and the search for blue-skies ideas to fit a neoliberal paradigm for public policy now came from outside the "usual channels." Right-leaning US-style think tanks such as the Adam Smith Institute and the Centre for Economic Affairs produced a stream of reports, especially during the Thatcher premierships. The more traditional sources of policy investigation, through royal commissions and official departmental inquiries, together with the use of (especially) Oxbridge "dons," were spurned. Political advisors sympathetic to Thatcherite political values and perspectives became closely associated with PM and ministerial policy positions. While this was not a new phenomenon, special advice from publicly vocal appointees such as Alan Walters, an academic economist, or Sir Derek Rayner, a retail entrepreneur, cut across civil service/ministerial channels and politicized what was previously a closed and thus depoliticized set of policy communities. It also transformed the traditional status of senior bureaucrats as the right hand of their ministers.

The implication for ambitious ministers, in a government dedicated to radical change, was that they should play a proactive rather than managerial role, which may well rely on external policy transfer. As we indicate in subsequent chapters, transfer from US experiences in economic, education, and social policy is evident in both Conservative and New Labour administrations, as is, for different reasons, a downloading of policies that emanate from EU directives and regulations, especially after the SEA. (See the book's website.) In effect, the potential failure of the state due to overstretched government was addressed not just through the introduction of new policies, but also through radical changes to the policy process itself.

FROM NEXT STEPS TO STEP CHANGE

A new public management (NPM) ethos, to provide effective accountability, value for money, increased efficiency, and improved consumer satisfaction, became the hallmark of the Thatcher/Major governments. It also set the pace and direction of public sector renewal under New Labour. The result has been a series of incremental changes in British public service and the policy process that in several respects comprised a managerial revolution (see the book's website).

The most significant manifestations of the NPM doctrine were the ideas contained in a Thatcher government Efficiency Unit Report "Improving Management in Government: The Next Steps" (February 1988). The report advocated management to achieve clearly stipulated public policy objectives in place of the traditional civil service consensus process that fitted change around existing policy practices. Much of the doctrine of NPM was applied with great enthusiasm. Within the space of five years a mainly centralized collection of civil service departments had been restructured, with a clear separation between small, central policy directorates and various forms of executive agencies, with contractual relationships to achieve specified outputs within central departmental guidelines. The chief executives of these new executive agencies were also to be employed on a contractual basis with a negotiated business plan and targets that, if met, would bring rewards. In general, much more flexible conditions of service allowed what was left of the central civil service and the various agencies to recruit and pay commensurate with the achievement of contractual goals. The opportunity for temporary short-term employment, especially in "managing change," has led to an expensive influx of executive consultants and has given private consulting companies access to valuable public contracts, especially in the field of IT (Craig and Brooks 2006).

By the mid-1990s around 100 executive agencies with varying degrees of independence had been set up. Six out of ten civil servants were now working in agencies. By 2006 around 75 percent of staff working for government departments worked in approximately 127 executive agencies. Other initiatives sought to make use of market solutions for public service delivery. Market testing, to evaluate whether provision of services might be better delivered by commercial contractors, was established for all government departments in 1991, as was the launch of the Private Finance Initiative (PFI) to develop capital investment in public facilities such as hospitals. Through long-term government contracts, this would allow private consortia an income on their investment over time. Other initiatives involved the sale of government service agencies to private companies—HMSO publications were sold at a price of £54 million in 1996, and the London Dartford and Scottish Isle of Skye toll bridges were early examples of PFI (1991 and 1995). Attempts to introduce an internal market, particularly within the NHS, were less successful and abandoned, temporarily at least, by the 1997 New Labour government. As we argue below, the future of PFI during a period of massive economic downturn (2008) onward is now in question.

The Quango Jungle

A further characteristic of the Thatcher-Major period was the increase in "quasi-government." Quangos (quasi-autonomous nongovernmental agencies) are financed by government, and their boards are appointed through central government procedures. However, they operate at arms length from Whitehall or Westminster in their performance of a variety of public service functions. The BBC is an established quango, as was the Commission for Racial Equality (now Equality and Human Rights Commission). Newer examples are Ofgem (Office of Gas and Electricity Markets) and Ofcom (Office of Communications), which are the public regulatory bureaus for their industries. The Electoral Commission both regulates electoral processes and advises government on electoral reform. NHS trusts and administrative tribunals are also part of the quango family. The Thatcher government, in 1979, promised to reduce their numbers, but they actually increased to around 6,700 by 1994. They had proved a useful tool for bypassing Labour-dominated local governments, and they were needed to regulate privatized public utilities and respond to regulatory codes demanded by the 1986 SEA. The Parliamentary Select Committee on Public Administration (PAC) located approximately 8,470 quangos, of which around 5,200 were territorially local in their activities. Despite pledges by the Labour government to broaden access for appointments to quangos, both academic and official bodies have periodically raised questions of accountability, cost, and openness (e.g., Democratic Audit 1994; PAC 2001).

New Labour governments have sustained much of the radical thrust of 1980s–1990s public-sector restructuring. Their philosophy of reform is reflected in the White Paper, *Modernising Government*, which promised 24/7 customer service with a continued focus on delivery; joined-up strategy and implementation for users, not providers; high-quality efficiency; a reduction in unnecessary regulation; and, significantly, investment in electronic solutions (e-government) with a 2008 target for total electronic central government "dealings." This last objective, information-age government, was to prove expensive, ambitious, vexatious, and not achieved by its target date (see the book's website).

Joined-Up Performance

A number of distinctions can be made between Conservative and Labour modernization reforms. NPM and market-led policies and processes are evidently shared factors for change, as is a concern to reduce the size of the Whitehall (central) bureaucracy. Rather than reduction in size and scope, however, Labour emphasized better service delivery and public consultation as part of their policy process in several arenas. This attempted openness is also evident from the availability of "league tables" (i.e., ratings) of performance—in health and education, local government services, policing, and many other public services in England. Consumer "choice" was to be enhanced by open information regarding performance. The Conservative idea of a Citizens' Charter was reinforced by Labour's "Services First" campaign, which spread the adoption of standard-setting charters to all key public services.

Other refinements to the Conservative modernization have been not always successful attempts to "join up government" by establishing centralized coordinating units to tackle problems within related contexts in such areas as child poverty; social exclusion; and, rather unsuccessfully, antidrug policy. This has involved centrally established units or task forces in the Cabinet Office and Treasury, for example a Social Exclusion Task Force, or lead departments (The Women's and Equality Unit in the Department for Works and Pensions). In each case the lead has been political, with PM, chancellor, or minister attempting to force through "silo-busting" programs to solve problems. Efforts to produce joined-up government have entailed a high level of political direction, "control freakery" as it became termed, running diametrically against the New Labour objective of governmental decentralization (Bogdanor 2005b).

As we discuss in the following chapter, Treasury control, historically a feature of British public policy, took new directions as (then) chancellor, Gordon Brown, who held the position throughout the Blair years, forced through modernization of service delivery, demanded specifically detailed efficiency standards, and pursued a redistributive objective in social fields that are aimed at improving labor-market flexibility and reducing child poverty. The Treasury encouraged the use of PFI, involving private funding to finance public capital expenditure, and expanded the concept to public/private partnerships (PPPs) that involve business and voluntary associations managing and delivering public services, for example the urban academy schools. PFI received considerable criticism for its use in transportation policy; the London Underground (subway system) received PFI despite the bitter opposition of London's then mayor, Ken Livingstone. And some projects to run prisons through PPP have also been criticized. The recession has added to these problems. Finally, triennial comprehensive spending reviews aligned spending with Treasury policy objectives and annual departmental "capability reviews."

One further Labour initiative needs mentioning. In 1998, as an aspect of lessons learned from the British presidency of the EU, Prime Minister Blair ordered a "step change" in ministerial and official departmental contacts with their counterparts in other EU member states. While the strategic aim of this initiative was to position Britain as a leader rather than outsider in EU affairs, it also recognized the multilevel nature of contemporary British governance and the importance of "mainstreaming Europe" across Britain's central government (Bulmer and Burch 2004). This was a significant shift from the, at best neutral, but often obstructive stance expected from civil servants in their dealings with the EU under Conservative administrations. The impact of this extensive period of piecemeal modernization of the British state is discussed in the conclusion to this chapter.

EXTERNAL PRESSURES: THE NUTCRACKER EFFECT

Most of the discussion above has concentrated on internal factors of policy and process modernization directed toward improving service quality. The broader motivations for radical change are external and place the British state in its global and regional context. These factors and, in a somewhat different sense of externality, devolution for Scotland and Wales, have created pressures on the integrity of the state as described in chapter 3. This "nutcracker effect" of external and internal pressures on a central government resulting in the need for political and administrative change is not new. James Cornford argued shortly after Britain joined the European Union that the failure of the centralized state to cope with economic and welfare demands was propelling European states to seek solutions that necessitated the ceding of power to supranational and subnational levels, resulting in political and administrative decentralization of European political systems (Cornford 1975). This "hollowing of the state" was reinforced as treaty provisions that increased the EU's competences, beginning in the late 1980s, impacted on all member states (see figure 9.1). But external pressures were of a global as well as regional nature—and it is to this phenomenon that we now turn.

Globalization, the State, and the Policy Process

Here we focus briefly on two factors emanating from the generic characteristics of globalization: the response of the British state to the advantages and fears of a global market; and resulting from these phenomena, the evidence of policy transfer from other states' experiences in solving shared societal problems.

We have already pointed out the Treasury's interest in the modernization of most aspects of the domestic policy-making process. This interest goes much further than the traditional concerns for controlling departmental money. As is evident in the following chapters, New

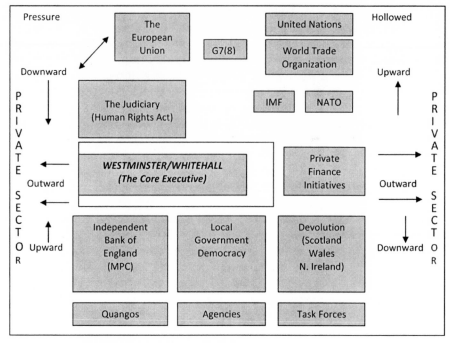

Figure 9.1.   The Hollowing of the British State

Labour's Third Way vision was of *the enabling state,* the purpose of which is to "strengthen Britain for global opportunities." A flexible and skilled labor force; investment in human capital, especially children's futures; and playing a full part in meeting environmental challenges necessitate public service reform to create a state infrastructure fit for its global purpose. From this follows concern for a central engagement with public-policy processes to ensure joined-up governance, best value for the public, and achievement of clearly stated objectives. A glance at any of the Whitehall departments' websites will illustrate this consciousness of making policy fit for "global purpose."

From a more general perspective, the perception of market globalization brought with it a neoliberal view of the state that permitted little room for much other than sound monetary policy and balanced budgets. Public expenditure in Britain, as in most states, has more than one international accountant in the cupboard, overseeing and commenting on the worth of public policy in the light of survival in the global market. Thus Conservative government, bitten badly by international financial speculation in 1992, was watched by, and sought international approval from, such bodies as the OECD; IMF; and, through EMU Stage Two Treaty obligations, the European Commission—to achieve domestic public-policy choices in keeping with international economic orthodoxy.

The first two years of New Labour's administration (1997–1999) sustained this financial orthodoxy but committed itself to a major renewal of public services and increased public spending from 36.3 percent (1999) to 41 percent (2002). As we point out in chapter 10, this was against a background of domestic economic growth and an expanding tax base. Though occasionally criticized from within and without, by the OECD and IMF, for the consumer, credit-led nature of this growth, Chancellor Brown presided over an expanding public sector and investment in health and education especially. Decisions to cut the NHS waiting list from eighteen months to eighteen weeks and to take 1 million pensioners and 500,000 children out of poverty resulted in an increase in public spending to nearly 48 percent, a third higher than when Labour came to power in 1997.

This structural increase in public spending, founded on an optimistic view of Britain's position in the global economy, has been confounded by the 2008–2009 global recession, and some international commentary has been less than complimentary on Britain's preparedness for recession and the solutions that the Brown/Darling administration have emphasized (see chapter 10).

Transferring Ideas

A further outcome of a globalization effect on public policy is the growth of policy transfer. While by no means a totally new phenomenon, the importing of public policy ideas has been a noticeable feature of both New Labour and previous Conservative governments. The Child Support Agency, Welfare to Work, Working Tax Credit, aspects of crime and penal policy, and policies in further and higher education all show close relationships with policies in existence in Australia and the United States. At one point the Blair government examined the Chilean experience as a possible route for the difficult task of pensions reform (Dolowitz et al. 2000). The role of the New Right agenda in both Britain and the United States was one important factor in accounting for these transatlantic policy transfers. Other factors include the emergence of international think tanks, consultancy organizations, and NGOs with global reach, which are a source of comparative data, experience, and strongly stated opinion, all of which are enhanced by the availability of information on the World Wide Web. The result is the possibility of a global dimension to policy networking across the gamut of public policy. This has widened debates on, for instance, welfare and labor market reform. The more direct, treaty-based impact of the EU on British policy is dealt with in depth below.

DEVOLUTION AND THE ENGLISH REGIONS

As Cornford argued in 1975, pressure on the central state is also internal. The implications of strong devolved governments and the emergence of English regional administration are considered below in the context of Britain's relationship with the EU. For, "when combined with the impact of Europeanization, devolution has conspired to transform British central government politically if not so obviously administratively, hollowing out the state into a differentiated polity where the writ of Whitehall is constrained and the desire of the constituent nations to obey a central authority is itself limited" (McMillan and Massey 2004: 232).

Devolved Administration

We have already mentioned several institutional changes that devolution has paralleled, notably the creation of a Department for Constitutional Affairs (subsequently Department of Justice) and the separation of higher judicial functions from Parliament (the Lords) into a quasi–supreme court. In 2002 the positions of secretary of state for Wales and secretary of state for Scotland were combined with other ministerial functions that in 2007 were Defence for Scotland and Work and Pensions for Wales. This reflects the substantial transfer of powers to the Welsh and Scottish devolved institutions. The post of Northern Ireland secretary is retained, but the incumbent receives no ministerial salary. The coordination of policy and any potential problems are dealt with as part of the remit of the Cabinet Committee on the Constitution.

Less known is the Joint Ministerial Committee (JMC), composed of the prime minister, the secretaries of state for the devolved governments, and "first" ministers from the devolved governments, whose task is to iron out difficulties that may arise between devolved and nondevolved responsibilities. Subcommittees of the JMC include poverty and health, the knowledge economy, and EU matters. Other ministerial committees that deal with matters of interest to devolved governments include the Committee on Domestic Affairs and its subcommittee on energy. "Concordats" between Whitehall and the devolved governments facilitate cooperation, especially where concurrent (joint) responsibilities exist and also where decisions made by one administration have an effect on another (Bulmer et al. 2002: 37). This situation can arise particularly in the area of European policy, for while the British government has retained overall control of EU policy—the devolved governments are crucially involved in its implementation.

Given the scale of devolved power for Wales and Scotland that took place in 2000 and was further developed for Wales in 2006, the changes in central government machinery have been relatively small and have not fundamentally altered traditional Whitehall-Westminster structures. On face value, a similar argument could be made regarding the impact on the British Home Civil Service. For Wales and Scotland, devolution did not bring with it a distinct and legally separate bureaucracy. Most Scottish and Welsh civil servants were transferred to the Scottish executive and Welsh Assembly respectively, to become arms of a still-British Home Civil Service. Scottish civil servants had for long felt a strong allegiance to Edinburgh, however, and this may well be enhanced by their closeness to a democratically elected executive and Parliament. A similar argument could be made for Wales (McMillan and Massey 2004: 241). However, the confirmed existence of a formally unified Home Civil Service, the coordinating concordats between devolved departments and their Whitehall counterparts, and the continued pressure from London for "joined-up government" are powerful centralizing factors against, or perhaps as a check on, devolved government.

As discussed earlier, Northern Ireland presents a somewhat different and contradictory perspective on devolved administration. While the potential for extensively devolved government exists, and indeed was experienced from 1921 to 1972, the imposition of periodic direct rule has compromised the independence of devolved government and the Northern Ireland Civil Service (NICS). In practice, however, the NICS has played an important integrating role with London government, and, as is the case for Scottish and Welsh bureaucracies, their practices and those of central government have been mutually reshaped by the common experience of public management reforms.

The English Regions

The issue of regional government for England was part of New Labour's commitment to open and decentralized governance during the 1990s. Adding a democratic element to the already existing regional administrative areas has proved much more contentious than the establishment of governments for the Celtic nations. The case for an "added" layer of democracy has not captured the imagination of the English public, and as we have mentioned in chapter 3, it was stopped dead in its tracks by a referendum on northeast regional government in 2004. As one writer argues, it is possible to observe both official and civic *regionalization* in England, but this is not strong enough to create *regionalism* (C. Stevens 2004: 254).

Some form of regional administration has existed since the 1940s, but it was not until 1994, when Government Offices for the Regions (GOR) were created, that a coherent and symmetrical pattern of regional administration was developed. GORs brought together the regional bureaus of Whitehall departments under one office and a regional director. This was an early Conservative attempt at joined-up government and was the result of a number of factors that included the need to focus and coordinate economic regeneration and to provide a focal point for local regional government and business interests. Moreover, as we shall see, it responded to the particular demands of applying for and utilizing EU structural funding support. In 2007, the Brown government appointed ministers for each of the English regions to act as "champions" for their particular areas and to account for regional policy in Parliament.

Whether as an intended consequence or not, the emergence of regional governance in England and devolution to Scotland, Wales, and Northern Ireland has created a more complex set of multilevel relationships for central government, especially within the EU. The conceptual framework of multilevel government and the application of policy networks analysis to policy making assist understanding of this complex period of institutional reform. This understanding is reinforced by the parallel impact of the EU on British domestic policy in the past twenty years. Britain's emergence as a multilevel polity is undeniable in this context (Rhodes 1988, 1997; Bulmer et al. 2002; Bache and Flinders 2004).

THE EUROPEANIZATION OF THE POLICY PROCESS?

British state adaptation to the demands and opportunities that the EU has offered have taken place against a shifting domestic landscape—of privatization, deconcentration, devolution, and new management techniques—as well as major shifts in the direction of economic and social policies (Bulmer and Burch 2004: 2). As outlined in the introduction, the concept of Europeanization may be focused in three ways: as a set of values; in considering the nature and extent of member state involvement in integration; and as a driver for member-state policy change. Here, we explore the ways in which British governmental institutions and processes have adapted to EU integration and the implications that EU policies have for the implementation of British public policy.

Some of the changes to the organization of the executive are discussed in chapter 8, within the PM's Office/Cabinet Office, and in chapter 12 regarding the European bureaucracy within the Foreign and Commonwealth Office (FCO) and the British permanent representation in Brussels (UKRep). These are the main agents of advice coordination and leadership for Britain's relations with the EU and other member states. Of note is the lack of a Ministry for Europe, and instead the existence of a minister for European affairs. We also note the increasing EU focus of Whitehall departments such as the DEFRA, the Home Office, DWP, and the Treasury. This focus on Europe has resulted from incremental policy changes in the wake of EU treaties from the 1987 SEA to the Treaty of Nice in 2000.

Thus Britain's organizational response to membership is characterized by two factors that have governed its depth and adaptive capacity: (1) the political will of successive governments to engage with the European dimension and (2) the veto strength of existing institutional arrangements. Political will on the part of British governments until 1997 involved, at best, guarded commitment to an EU perceived as a liberalized economic market. Thus, on accession in 1973, alongside the FCO, it was the Department of Trade and Industry, Customs and Excise, and the Ministry of Agriculture that were perceived as the core actors in this new experience. The idea of creating a Ministry for Europe, as existed in France, was rejected, as this would disturb the traditional division of departmental responsibilities. The transposition of EC legislation was to be undertaken by the lawyers of the Treasury Solicitor's Department (TSD), working in close cooperation with the Cabinet Office. The TSD has established an effective machinery for the incorporation of European legislation into British legal systems.

Accommodating the EU

The coordination of European policy making in terms of both the *reception* of externally derived "Brussels" policy and internally generated responses/initiatives (*projection*) was contained within the traditional Cabinet/Whitehall arrangements, represented in Brussels by UKRep. Westminster was engaged through the establishment of two select committees—for European legislation in the Commons and the more broadly referenced EU Committee of the House of Lords. Assurances by the Heath government that British accession to the EU would in no way affect parliamentary sovereignty buried some of the larger constitutional issues, despite attempts to raise them during the 1975 referendum campaign. Neither did the judiciary offer particular objection to a new external source of legislation, given its effective transposition through conventional and constitutionally acceptable processes.

As we shall see below, there are various "misfits" in the meshing of EU and British policy processes, but in the early years there was no constitutional revolution or organizational disturbance to Britain's Westminster-Whitehall tandem. In effect, the extent of institutional adjustment was limited and has been summarized by Bulmer and Burch (2004: 5–6) as:

- ministerial responsibility for evaluating substantive policy
- the use of traditional cabinet mechanisms of coordination
- an inner (core) and outer tier of ministerial involvement
- the FCO responsible for diplomatic engagement
- a stress on the importance of legal transposition

One factor in this relatively limited institutional response to EU membership was the undoubted strength of existing governmental practice, the baseline of the long-established Westminster/Whitehall tandem. This coupled with a second political factor—Britain's guarded engagement with an EU already up and running—produced an emphasis on *receiving* an existing limited set of supranational policies, rather than *projecting* or initiating new British policy demands on the EU. With the possible exception of regional policy (see below), it was agricultural and trade policy, together with the foreign policy implications of EC membership, that were of concern to British government (Geddes 2004: 163).

Adapting to the EU

The subsequent expansion of EU policy competences and the changes to the EU policy process have necessitated further and more radical adaptation for British governments. Since the emergence of the European Council in 1976, the prime minister has necessarily been involved in formal and regular meetings with other member-state leaders. The Council has now come "to sit at the apex of the EU's decision-making structure, a position dictated by both the authoritative positions held by its members and its particular functions in the EU decision-making system" (Gowland et al. 2006: 326). This is reflected, as we have seen, in the close relationship between the PM and his European policy advisors, located in both the PM's Office and the Cabinet Office European Secretariat. The direct election of MEPs and the gradual extension of EP influence over European legislation have increased the PM's involvement in EP party politics. Prime Minister Blair's exhortations to the Party of European Socialists (PES) in the 1990s to adopt New Labour values (Mannin 2004) and David Cameron's (as Conservative Opposition Leader) decision to dissolve the British Conservative association with the "too federalist" European Peoples' Party (EPP) in 2006, are testimony to a concern on behalf of British political leaders to shape EU parliamentary politics. Finally, the increased use of qualified majority voting (QMV) in both the European Council and the Council of Ministers has necessitated proactive alliance building and recourse to projection of British policy positions by a growing proportion of cabinet and non-cabinet ministers.

The projection of British policy interests is now a necessary aspect of ministerial and civil service activity in almost all areas of domestic policy. Inevitably, an increasing number of Whitehall departments have been drawn into the orbit of British-EU political processes. Initially it was a core group of ministries, but "by the time of John Major's government (1990–1992), all ministers had established European offices" (Bulmer and Burch 2004: 17). At the time of the first Blair government, the Home Office and DEFRA could be included in the initial core group of "intensely involved" Whitehall bureaucracies. In particular, the impact of the SEA has been significant in opening British domestic policy to EC-originated policies, as well as increasing the capacity of EU institutions to make decisions in these policy areas (see table 9.1).

The Impact of the Single Market

Much has been written about the decision by Margaret Thatcher to promote and support the idea of a Single Market—and whether or not she read the small print (Young 1991; Young 2000; Thatcher 1993). While enthusiastically supporting a European market without national frontiers for services, goods, and capital, the associated "social" policies designed to facilitate free movement of EU labor were less well received, especially when a Social Charter emerged that was perceived by Mrs. Thatcher as "socialism through the back door" (Thatcher 1988). Nevertheless, the SEA was transcribed into British law by the end of 1992 and, despite the political reservations of much of the Conservative Party, Whitehall responded positively to this considerable legal/administrative task. By 1993, 295 directives had been transcribed that amended British law and gave a supranational dimension to many areas of policy that were previously domestic matters. This was especially true of local government, whose task was to implement many EC regulations and directives in such fields as health and safety and environmental policy.

Table 9.1.   The Extent of EU Involvement in British Policy

Extensive EU policy involvement	Considerable EU policy involvement	Policy responsibility shared between the EU and the member states	Limited EU policy involvement	Virtually no EU policy involvement
Market regulations Environment Trade Agriculture Fisheries	Equal opportunities Health and safety Consumer protection	Regional competition Industrial Foreign Movement across external borders Energy Transport Cross-border crime	Health Education Defense Social welfare Monetary Macroeconomic	Housing Civil liberties Domestic crime

Source: Adapted from Nugent (2006).

In effect, the Single European Act created conditions for a major reconfiguration of much of the British policy process toward inter- and multilevel governmental modes. Inevitably this was to increase tension between Eurosceptic and Europhile opinion in an undoubted challenge to a sovereign Parliament. The SEA also set in motion a series of events that, from a neofunctionalist view of European integration, resulted in a spillover to further institutional reform and policy change. In this sense the SEA was a "Pandora's box" whose contents facilitated the changes contained in the Maastricht, Amsterdam, Nice, and Lisbon Reform Treaties. QMV, in areas mostly covered by the SEA, necessitated a more proactive role from all member states as they sought to project their national interests. This involved not just initiatives on behalf of political elites (ministers) but closer interaction between national bureaucracies and a proactive European Commission as well as a European Court of Justice (ECJ) with an expanded set of judicial responsibilities. As much as Mrs. Thatcher may have later wanted to do so, putting a lid back on the box was not an option for British policy makers (Thatcher 1993).

The SEA also facilitated a number of further developments in the EU's areas of policy competence (see textbox 9.2). These areas include foreign and security policy, social policy, economic policy, and environmental policy, all of which are discussed in following chapters. These and other developments have led to British policy makers closely engaging with EU institutions—supporting the claim that the British state can be most effectively analyzed within the framework of multilevel governance. Before examining the validity of this assertion we shall explore the adaptation of British governmental machinery to the projection and reception of EU policies.

The Projection of British Interests

We can point to a number of initiatives taken by successive governments to improve EU policy projection. At central government departmental level, all ministries now have European units or sections and, since Labour's Step Change initiative, they have engaged with European counterparts in member states and in Brussels in an attempt to alter the perception of Britain as an awkward partner in negotiations (Bulmer and Burch 2004; Massey 2004). Also, prior to Step Change, a European Fast Stream sought to provide a cadre of civil servants to deal with the considerable increase in EU business. A European staffing unit working with UKRep was also established to promote the employment of British nationals in the EU. Within the core executive we have already noted the integration of the work of the Cabinet Office Secretariat and the PM's Office and policy unit. A European Pol-

Textbox 9.2. The Single European Act (1986)

The Single European Act (SEA) came into force July 1, 1987, and provided the first modification of the foundational treaties of the 1950s. The SEA is recognized as a key turning point in the history of European integration. The treaty was stewarded by then president of the European Commission, Jacques Delors. It was an economic agreement, committed to free trade among EC states, but it also had important implications for EU procedures, institutional reform, and social and environmental policy.

The principle aim of the SEA was to complete a European common market. National constraints on movement of goods, labor, services, and capital flows were to be abolished, to which a deadline of December 31, 1992, was set. This ambitious goal was summarized in 282 detailed measures, outlined in Lord Cockfield's (then vice president of the European Commission) "White Paper on Completion of the Internal Market," of 1985.

Importantly, the SEA introduced qualified majority voting to the Council of Ministers, replacing the national veto in several important policy areas, thus reducing a commitment to unanimity established under the foundational treaties. The act granted greater powers to the European Parliament, including power to veto accession treaties and to be consulted through a cooperation procedure over certain legislation. It was initially rejected by Denmark, and signing was delayed until a referendum could be held (Italy and Greece were also reticent, and Ireland stalled for constitutional reasons).

The competencies of the European Council were also strengthened. The act formalized the concept of European Political Cooperation (EPC), which prioritizes intergovernmental decision making on foreign policy matters. This was developed in the later Common Foreign and Security Policy. Finally, a number of policy areas were reinforced, claiming formal status under the act. Research and technological development, environment, and "economic and social cohesion" were given priority, and a number of new agencies were established.

icy Committee of the Cabinet was augmented in 2003 by a subcommittee on European Strategy but was later removed by the Brown government. Also indicative of less prioritized attitude to matters EU, fast-stream recruitment was suspended by the Brown administration in 2007. At ministerial level an interdepartmental committee (Minecor) chaired by the Europe Minister has, since 1997, attempted to create awareness of policies in departments that have an EU dimension. The committee includes ministerial representation from the devolved administrations and, as well as its coordinating role, has the task of promoting the EU within Britain in support of the Step Change program.

These generally positive factors reflect the EU realist perspectives of successive New Labour administrations, as well as a longer-term trend of "increased involvement of government heads and ministers in

EU policy making" (Bulmer and Burch 2004: 12). But, as we point out in chapter 10, a more negative central control over European policy projection has emanated from the British Treasury that, under the political direction of Gordon Brown, the chancellor, between 1997 and 2007, has sent out more cautious messages regarding British-EU relations. The chancellor's controlling influence over when to recommend membership in the eurozone remained a considerable potential veto on Britain's commitment to European integration and involvement in related economic policies. Moreover, since the Treasury jealously guards departmental public expenditure, it has sought through its financial accounting system to reduce departmental receipts from European sources—in support of a long-established Treasury objective of limiting the EU budget. So departments are pressured not to be overly enthusiastic in seeking EU funding (Bulmer and Burch 1998). The Treasury may thus be considered a potential institutional "veto point" for British EU policy projection. Its role in shaping domestic policy in the post-recession period is considered below.

For the most part it can be concluded that the institutions and processes of the executive in Britain have successfully adapted to, rather than been transformed by, their interaction with the European Union. Existing structures such as the cabinet and its committees, the PM's Office, the FCO, and the coordinative and ambassadorial services of UKRep have been strengthened to cope with a growing pressure, initially for the reception but subsequently for the projection of British interests within EU forums. Since 1997 this strengthening has resulted in a more coherent and integrated approach to policy projection—as demanded by the pace of European integration and allowed by the more positive New Labour EU perspective—thus providing a more proactive British policy environment in the opening years of the twenty-first century in such new arenas as labor-market reform and aspects of European defense and internal security.

The Reception of EU Policies

Here we comment on the breadth and depth of public policy received from EU sources and the range of institutions involved with EU policy output. As can be deduced from the discussion so far, the extent to which policies can be accredited to EU sources varies considerably between, and in several cases within, policy arenas. For instance, within DEFRA, EU directives on waste management account for most British policy, whereas planning laws and regulations remain primarily a domestic responsibility. Personal healthcare is a member-state issue; however the regulation of drugs is an EU issue; in some areas of foreign and defense policy there is extensive member-state cooperation, in others—not the least over policy toward Iraq—British policy has been fiercely independent. As we have suggested, external trade policy and agricultural policy are predominantly shaped by Brussels-based procedures. To complicate matters, cutting across all policy arenas is the commonality of EU regulations and directives on working conditions in both public and private sectors—in health and safety, equal opportunity, and aspects of employer/employee contractual relations (see appendix). Aspects of environmental policy, especially environmental impact assessment, also cut across policy arenas. The EU procedures through which these policies have been processed are important in that they indicate the extent of flexibility that a member state has in implementing these externally derived policies (see also textbox 9.3).

Textbox 9.3. Main Instruments of EU Policy Implementation

EU Directives

The most utilized form of EU legislation. While detailing the end objective(s) it gives discretion to member states as to how to implement the legislation to achieve the end state. There is an agreed date for implementation. Then the declaration has direct effect; that is, it must be upheld in member-states' courts through the creation of new law(s) or legally recognized statutory instruments. Directives are utilized as examples in applying EU environmental policy or equal opportunity policies. In practice, directives may be drawn up in such detail that there is little difference between a directive and a regulation.

EU Regulations

Regulations are binding legal rules at the EU Community and national levels that once passed through the EU process apply immediately in national courts (direct effect). Laws must be passed that give direct effect to a regulation. Regulations are utilized in applying the details of agricultural or external trade policy.

The Open Method of Coordination (OMC)

Since the Lisbon Council (2000) member states have agreed to coordinate their domestic policies in some areas such as social exclusion or labor-market policies through OMC. This is achieved by agreeing to common objectives, establishing common indications, translating EU objectives into national/regional policies through national reports published regularly, encouraging policy cooperation, and transnational sharing of good practice.

Agricultural Policy (CAP)

The Common Agricultural Policy of the EU (CAP) is an illustration of how EU policy works. (Another on immigration and asylum policy is on the book's website.) Somewhat notoriously, the CAP is a historic expression of EU supranationalism—in that, since its inception in 1962, it has sought to command a protected supply of food at affordable prices while guaranteeing the farmer an adequate standard of living. Import tariffs protected EU farmers from world competition, and export subsidies protected prices received by farmers from unstable world prices. Common prices within the EU are decided on an annual basis by the Agricultural Council (of Ministers) on the basis of DG Agriculture recommendations. Farmers receive payments on the basis of this annual review. When Britain joined the EU in 1972, approximately 80 percent of the EU budget was devoted to the CAP, which reflected the particular national interests of France and Italy as two of the original member states. The policy process is intergovernmental in character, with agriculture ministers, pressurized by their farming interest groups, seeking best deals for their countries with DG Agriculture as formal policy initiator, conciliator, fixer, and eventually policeman of the policy process. The commission "has little choice but to anticipate both the wishes and reactions of the Council of Ministers" within a system "that has been vertically integrated through national and community mechanisms" (Rieger 2005: 172).

The problems associated with CAP throughout the 1980s are famous: of butter mountains and wine lakes, of production inefficiency; of world trade protection and its impact on developing countries; and overpayments to EU farmers (Grant 1997). Various factors, including the effect of impending enlargement, inclusion of agricultural products in the disciplines of the World Trade Organization, the considerable increase in EU structural funding, environmental issues, and the poor reputation of the existing CAP, have led to its extensive reform. Successive British governments, alongside the Danish and Dutch governments and later Sweden, were instrumental in pushing for change. The McSharry Reforms of 1992 "decoupled" arable farming production from farming support. In further reforms (2003) decoupling was extended to other food products, allowing subsidies to be paid for rural economic development and environmental management, reflecting the broad EU objectives of economic change, market efficiency, and environmental improvement.

The emergence of these new agendas has disturbed the relatively closed British agricultural policy community. An efficient agricultural sector, represented in the main by one organization, the National Farmers' Union (NFU), played a major role in both the articulation of British agricultural interests in Brussels through its close relationship with the then Ministry of Agriculture, Fisheries and Food (MAFF) and then in helping to deal with the complexities of an agreed farm payments system. This tight policy community was disturbed by a number of factors. Domestic food crises—salmonella in eggs (1988) the "mad cow" (BSE) crisis in the mid-1990s, and periodic outbreaks of cattle and sheep disease (foot-and-mouth)—led to both domestic and EU interventions. In particular, the 1996 ban on British beef exports by the Commission (only completely lifted in 2006) illustrated the supranational strength of CAP; it also represented a nadir in EU-British relations in the mid-1990s, only recovered by the election of a New Labour government. Food quality as a political issue weakened the reputation of MAFF. Despite the creation of an internal Food Quality Directorate (1993) and later an independent Food Standards Agency (1997), MAFF did not survive the criticism of its responses to the foot-and-mouth crisis in 2001 and was abolished, to be incorporated into a new department of the Environment, Food and Rural Affairs (DEFRA). In its creation, the government was both downgrading the influence of a dwindling and heavily subsidized agricultural industry and recognizing a shared set of objectives within the EU in relation to rural change and development and concerns with environmental protection.

DEFRA is still criticized as remaining heavily oriented toward an agricultural agenda (Grant 2004: 21), although it has been engaged since 2002 in "uploading" a market-based reform solution to a still heavily subsidized EU agricultural sector (Curry 2002). The Commission has put forward limited reforms of CAP (2008), but it remains an integral problem for British agriculture policy making (Geddes 2004).

Multilevel Governance in Practice: Britain, the EU, and Regional Policy

We have earlier discussed the regional dimensions to British society and economy. The recognition of deprivation and inequality of opportunity in especially traditional industrial and rural areas led to a series of initiatives, financial incentives, and redistributive policies that, from 1945 to 1979, were directed toward regions and subregions of Britain. Having joined the EU, one of the first important projections of British interests, along with those of Italy and Ireland, was an EU-wide regional policy that in part compensated Britain for its net loss from budgetary contributions. The first commissioner for regional policy was the ex-labour minister George Thompson, who was active between 1973 and 1977 in promoting the development of a regional dimension to the EU budget that was then so dominated by agriculture funding (CAP).

From 1979 throughout the 1980s, the neoliberal economic policies of Conservative governments placed little emphasis on redistributive regional "handouts" (as they saw it) and British domestic regional policies were drastically reduced or directed toward competition for limited central government funding. The second enlargement of the EU to include Greece (1981) and Portugal and Spain (1986) resulted in fresh demands for an increased regional dimension to the EU budget, in part to cushion the negative effects that implementation of the SEM might have on weaker parts of the European economy. So, as the British government was withdrawing from the notion of regional policy, a package of measures was being designed to help alleviate EU regional inequalities and to make the market work. The available structural funding from which the poorer British regions might benefit was to increase dramatically during the 1980s and 1990s—from 5 percent in 1975 to 34 percent of the EU budget during the period 2000–2006 (Mannin 2006b).

The 1988 reform of structural funds was significant for British regional policy in a number of ways. First, the changes were designed to coincide with Single Market legislation. A reluctant Conservative administration was drawn into an integrative EU policy arena that presented tangible benefits for deprived British regions, whose political and economic leaders pressured the central government to take full advantage of potential EU largesse. Second, the EU, in negotiation with member states, drew up the regional map of the EU on which funding opportunities were to be based.

For Britain, without a tradition of regional government, this meant an attention to regional administration that was to culminate in the creation of Integrated Regional Government Offices in England (IGO) in 1994 and an increased European dimension within the then Scottish and Welsh Offices of State. IGOs were established, in part, to sustain Whitehall control of this new phenomenon but also to assist various local bodies to prepare plans that conformed to rigorous Commission bidding requirements. This necessitated an integrated policy process that enabled access to "envelopes" of financial support from several previously separate EU funds. These envelopes included funding for infrastructural renewal (the ERDF), support for skills retraining and education for the labor force (the ESF), and particular support for diversification of rural and fishing economies. The policy process was to be subject to monitoring jointly by member states and the EU and must indicate clear evidence of good practice—in particular "principles" of multiannual programming; partnership (of those local and national actors involved); subsidiarity (which implied implementing policies at the most appropriate level); and additionality (clear evidence that extra matching funds had been made available to facilitate this EU source of domestic resources).

Accepting these principles was not without its difficulties for a Eurosceptic Conservative government. Indeed, some aspects of funding were not welcomed by a government seeking to produce market-based solutions for Britain's economy. Subregions such as Strathclyde and Merseyside were discouraged from maximizing their structural funding potential. There was a serious dispute over the "additionality" principle, with the Commission accusing the British Treasury of failing to match funding in an acceptably value-added manner. Trade unions found themselves excluded as social partners in the policy-planning process. In many cases, the Commission and regional and local actors found themselves in alliance in bringing central government to heel over what was perceived as obstructive tactics or, at worst, maladministration of EU policies. The creation of regional offices in 1994 helped mediate local-central tensions and provided a mechanism to improve the quality of applications for structural funding (Bache and Marshall 2004: 110).

A gradual change of heart on behalf of Westminster elites was evident prior to the election of the more pro-European Labour government from 1997. This was a result of the realization that structural funding was "serious money" and was worth accessing; the undoubted enthusiasm of subregions like Merseyside and Strathclyde, and cities like Birmingham and Glasgow, for achieving maximum benefit for their regeneration from this source; and the tangible role of the Commission Directorate-General for Regions in encouraging the integration of local, central, and EU development plans. Subregions and cities joined with already articulated Scottish and Welsh interests to establish offices in Brussels in order to facilitate their local/regional interests. Thus, local and regional administrations "do not merely administer structural funding; instead they reflect the internalization of the Commission principle of programming and the EU push for strategic and holistic approaches to regeneration," which has led to a voluntary Europeanization of this aspect of their public activity (Bache and Marshall 2004: 12).

The Labour government's acceptance of social partnership to include trade unions, and the reduction of ideological conflict between Britain and the EU, has facilitated a better "fit" between domestic and Brussels policy norms. Parallel decisions—to devolve powers to Scotland and Wales and to partly democratize regional government through the establishment of indirectly elected regional chambers—similarly facilitated closer accordance between the culture and ethos of British and EU regional policy norms. Local, regional, and central decision makers are involved in uploading and downloading policy, implying the emergence of multilevel governance in this policy arena. Nevertheless, "the center" is still capable of asserting powerful control in this most Europeanized of policy arenas.

CONCLUSION: BETWEEN THE CENTRALIZED STATE AND MULTILEVEL GOVERNANCE

If we perceive the state as both a legal *and* organic entity, its main objective is its own survival. For the British state, with its history as a world player, its dependence on world trade, and its peculiar geographic position, survival has involved a worldview perspective and a mixture of fiercely guarded independence; the external projection of British interests; and, where necessary, the acquisition of international alliances to bolster a powerful sense of sovereignty. As a metaphor, the Westminster model remains a "defiant" representation of the British state as a historic institutionalization of its identity.

We have argued that the phenomena of globalization and Europeanization have provided an external challenge to assumptions regarding the integrity of the British state. The survival responses of successive governments from the second half of the twentieth century have been necessarily complex and perhaps contradictory. As the British imperial and economic "reach" declined, so emerged eventually a global market capitalism that, coupled with the exponential growth of ICT, has called for corresponding changes to economic policy. The Keynesian welfare state was replaced by more open, market-based approaches to domestic problems. "Welfare to work" and education for economic change have become the watchwords for domestic policies—seen equally as social investment for the global market and as an individual citizen right. The state emerged as an "enabler," steering rather than rowing in potentially stormy global market seas. What also has emerged is the blurring of a public/private distinction in the provision of state resources, manifest in notions of NPM and PPP, and strong, centrally led government to force through radical change.

Policy Making in Recession

It is evident that dire economic circumstances strengthen the hands of central government, especially the Treasury. The state is back rowing the stormy seas. To deal with recession in 2009, the chancellor announced a rise in public expenditure by 2010 to 48 percent to be followed by a rapid fall by 2013 as, whether through taxation or cuts in public services, the level of public debt is addressed. This "austerity scenario," as David Cameron termed it, has implications for New Labour policies, including cuts in infrastructure in schools and road building. Proposed PFI projects such as the modernization of the London Tube network and motorway network together with public-private affordable home ventures were, in 2009, under threat as a Treasury-led review of their viability commenced. A proposed super prison program has been scaled back as has the progress toward a national ID program. The success of trimming expenditure is dependent on an early return to economic growth and thus a stronger tax take to assist in balancing public accounts. More surgical solutions, such as cuts in defense and domestic policy are available that would bring into question not only New Labour's renewal and modernization policies since 1999 but Britain's ability to play a role in international politics (see textbox 9.4 and the book's website).

The economic survival of the British state, however, is also marked by an ongoing search for regional security in the shape of the European Union. This, as we have illustrated, has meant a series of treaty-based agreements resulting in a variety of supranational and intergovernmental interventions across a range of what were previously state-based policy arenas. The concept of shared sovereignty, and EU-based solutions to external and domestic problems, is part of the fabric of the British policy process in the twenty-first century. As we point out, the impact on individual policy arenas varies, from the EU-dominated competence in external trade and agricultural policy to foreign, education, and health policies that remain under domestic control for the most part. The Europeanization of some policies is therefore extensive—in others less so. However, the breadth of EU influence is evident in the organization of Whitehall to both *project* and *receive* British/EU demands and policy, and also in the time and attention spent by ministers in "dealing with Brussels." New Labour's ten-year Step Change strategy to enhance British leadership in certain EU policy areas was a political statement recognizing the depth of EU involvement in British policy making.

Cornford, writing in 1975, discussed not only the external pressures on European states but also the political demands for decentralization. He argued that state survival must also take into account these internal dynamics. Devolution for Scotland and Wales and eventually Northern Ireland, and regional administration for England, are likely to alter not just domestic policy processes, but also British/EU relations. As one commentator suggests, both "devolution and independence for the Bank of England . . . have brought UK policies in closer

Textbox 9.4. Surgery for the New Age of Austerity

Can Britain afford . . .

New Schools Refurbishment	Under the program for building schools for the future (renewing every high school by 2020) a PFI scheme would cost up to £55 billion. Private funds are drying up. Are all schools in need of refurbishment in the medium term?
Surestart Centres	A key element of Labour's Children's Policy, over 3,500 locations give support to families as a way of creating a level social playing field for a child's life opportunities. Annual running costs are £1.3 billion by 2011.
Winter Fuel Allowance	Automatically paid to all people over the age of sixty, as are free drug prescriptions and bus travel passes. A means test for the Winter Fuel Allowance would reduce its £2.6 billion annual cost.
Student Grants/Loans	Available to 2 million undergraduates each year. Massive reductions in student numbers, paying commercial rates for student loans, and restricting university courses would cut into the £2 billion annual cost of Labour's policies to widen the availability of higher education.
Aircraft Carriers	And the F-35 planes to fly from them are due to enter Royal Navy service by 2018 at a cost of £16 billion.
Euro Fighter/Typhoon	Still not available after ten years of development at a cost of £20 billion for 232. But cancellation costs would be considerable.
A Nuclear Deterrent	For the twenty-first century; new submarines are to take up 6 percent of the total defense budget, excluding running costs over twenty-five years. Lifetime costs for Britain's nuclear "independence" are in the region of £70 billion. The system is totally reliant on a new US weapons system to replace existing Trident missiles.

Source: The *Guardian* 24 April 2009.

alignment with continental practice" (Bulmer and Burch 2004: 19). This, together with the adoption of the ECHR, has produced what is perhaps an unintended rationality to piecemeal New Labour reforms that point the British state in the direction of government procedures more compatible with EU processes.

However, while the range of domestic policies affected or indeed dictated by the EU is considerable, the machinery of the British state has responded to EU membership by adding to rather than radically reforming its structures and processes. The Westminster/Whitehall tandem, rather than notions of multilevel governance, remains an important political statement for political leaders dealing with a Eurosceptic public. This, together with the concern of successive governments to maintain "red lines" that indicate to the elector the preservation of national sovereignty (of which EMU, control of taxation and borders, and negativity to the idea of a European Constitution are examples), creates a notion of powerful, historically based veto points that preclude a "European takeover" of the British policy process.

When one factors in the numbing effects of global recession, the external constraints for policy makers are all too evident. But whether perceived by a British government as an ally in economic adversity or part of the problem for national recovery, the EU remains an integral structure within the British policy process. Subsequent chapters examine this assertion in relation to three policy arenas.

FURTHER READING

Peter Dorey, *Policy-Making in Britain: An Introduction* (2005a) gives an overview; Michael Hill (2004) presents a more theoretical perspective. Richard Pyper summarizes changes to the civil service in *Britain's Modernized Civil Service* (2007). For an examination of the bureaucracy's role in policy making see *Policy Bureaucracy: Government with a Cast of Thousands* (2005) by Edward Page and Bill Jenkins. Notions of the regulatory state and decentralization are included in Stephen Ludlam and Mike Smith (eds.) *Governing as New Labour: Policy and Politics under Blair* (2004). A close check is made on the quango state by Democratic Audit (see the book's website). Vernon Bogdanor (ed.) considers the viability of *Joined-up Government* (2005b). Simon Bulmer and Martin Burch explore the Europeanization of British government (2004) and in a forthcoming monograph (2009). Policy transfer is considered by David Dolowitz et al. *Policy Transfer and British Social Policy* (2000) and Simon Bulmer et al. *Policy Transfer in European Union Governance* (2007).

The Impact of devolution is observed in Michael O'Neill's edited volume *Devolution and British Politics* (2004) and also by Simon Bulmer and others in *British Devolution and European Policy Making* (2002). The Europeanization of specific policy arenas is considered in Ian Bache and Andrew Jordan (eds.) *The Europeanisation of British Politics* (2006) and in Philip Giddings and Gavin Drewry (eds.) *Britain in the European Union* (2004). Applying notions of cohesion and MLG to British policy, Ian Bache observes changes in British governance from 1989 to 2006 in *Europeanization and Multilevel Governance* (2008). Finally, Mark Bevir and Rod Rhodes apply the concepts utilized here in *Interpreting British Governance* (2003).

10

Economic Policy in Britain

Chapters 1 and 2 referred to the history, changes, and current characteristics of the British economy—a rich, developed, and trade-based entity. This chapter first outlines the key moments of post–World War II British economic policy and the perceived problems and solutions tried by governments of differing political persuasions. In its conclusions it also records the responses of the Brown government to the onset of recession since 2008. While contemporary circumstances demand short-term "fixes" to immediate problems, the scenario that surrounds government decision making has remained the same: how to best provide conditions for the British economy so as to obtain maximum domestic benefit from its international (global) connectivity while recognizing a growing and contentious reliance on a regional (EU) political economy. Once again, the triangle of globalization, Europeanization, and domestic pressures provides the framework for analysis of governmental policy.

A BACKGROUND

Until comparatively recently the British economy depended on its manufacturing and international financial sectors for its strength. As the "workshop of the world" in the mid-nineteenth century, the prosperity of the country depended on the export of British manufactured goods and the facilitation of trade through the use of British shipping services, the provision of international credit, and British foreign investment. This situation was to continue through to the 1950s, bolstered by a massive extension of government intervention in such industrial sectors as coal, steel, energy, and rail and road transportation—the nationalized industries of the postwar Labour government. Either indirectly, through infrastructural investment, or directly, through subsidy or regional grants, the manufacturing sector was cushioned from international competition by government aid within the "mixed economy" of the postwar period. As such, regional economies, particularly those of Wales, Northern Ireland, and Scotland, were able to sustain a workforce and local communities often based on single-industry employment. Sheffield steel; Scottish, Yorkshire, and Welsh coal; Belfast and Glasgow shipbuilding continued to be the basis of regional economic wealth into the 1960s.

Dealing with Industrial Decline

Economic historians trace the roots of Britain's decline from the late nineteenth century (Hobsbawm 1999; Barnett 1972). However, the impact of post–World War II international competition from recovering West European states such as Germany and Italy, later from the Far East, and inevitably the United States undermined still further Britain's long-term economic advantage in manufacturing and international trade. This period, from the mid-1950s through the 1970s, coincided with the loss of Empire/Commonwealth market dependability, and in the 1960s, Labour governments struggled to revitalize the domestic economy and find new ways of improving international competitiveness through the "white heat of technology," a Labour election catchphrase.

In chapter 1 we discussed attempts to "join Europe," that is to apply for European Economic Community (EEC) membership. Though eventually achieved under the Conservative Heath administration in 1973, this did little to ameliorate the impact of deindustrialization of the British economy. Economic problems included government expenditure that had risen to 50 percent of GDP by 1975, mostly on the welfare state; high government borrowing and levels of taxation; and a lack of new manufacturing investment and skills training (Jenkins 1989).

An inflexible and union-dominated labour force exacerbated these problems. Unionization, facilitated by nationalization of many industrial sectors in the 1940s and the corporate style of National Prices and Incomes policy in the 1960s, reached a peak in the 1970s, with 54 percent of the workforce being union members by 1979. The public sector workforce was particularly unionized. Miners strikes in 1972 brought a wage settlement of 27 percent, this set against an inflation rate of 9.2 percent in 1973 and over 1 million registered unemployed (a phenomenon known as "stagflation"). Union unrest and strikes led to a general election in 1974, when Edward Heath asked the question "who rules?" Heath was defeated, as was the Labour PM, Jim Callaghan, in 1979, after the strikes of 1978–1979 in what came to be known as the "Winter of Discontent."

From Keynesianism to Thatcherism

Events in the 1970s were to affect the direction of economic policy making with the same force as the postwar 1940s changed the direction of domestic policy in Britain. The shared assumptions of full employment and high levels of taxation to support welfare programs, subsidized nationalized industries, and public utilities were broken on the back of the sterling crisis of 1976. Since the breakdown of the Bretton Woods agreement (1972), the pound as an international currency had struggled to survive in a world of floating and unstable exchange rates. High-priced imports, especially of oil after the Yom Kippur War (1973), and declining exports of industrial goods in a situation of wage inflation were a recipe for economic disaster. A formal application to the IMF by the then Labour government for support amounting to $3.9 billion was the largest amount ever requested (Grant 2002: 33). Though granted, the strings attached wrecked Keynesian assumptions surrounding economic policy making that had supported one-nation Conservatism and the social welfarism of the Labour Party for thirty years. The cuts in public expenditure required by the IMF, and made by the Labour government, were no more than a prelude to the profound changes to economic policy that occurred following the election of Mrs Thatcher's Conservatives in 1979.

Useful parallels may be made here with US economic policy under Reagan. "Reaganomics" and "Thatcherism" were clearly associated with the neoliberalism of Milton Friedman and the Chicago School, geared to the supply side of the economy. The principles and instruments listed may overstate the coherence of each period of economic policy making, but they represent a starting point for their analysis. Thatcherism, as much as the use of demand-led Keynesian policy between 1945 and 1976, was skewed to win elections—and did so with considerable success for the Conservatives in the years 1979–1992. The changes involved stressing a supply-side economic strategy to beat inflation. This objective replaced commitment to full employment, which was seen as "an error made by previous governments" (Grant 2002: 35). A summary of the characteristics of Keynesianism and Thatcherism along with Labour's "Third Way," which followed Thatcherism, is available on the book's website.

NEOLIBERAL BRITAIN

To achieve this new objective, the political economy of Britain would be transformed, first by a major withdrawal of government from the economy, and second, by reducing the powers of trade unions to protect wage and employment levels. The former was to be achieved by "privatization"—of nationalized industries and public utilities, as well as, whenever politically possible, a reduction in public expenditure on welfare service provision. Trade unions were substantially weakened by legislation that reduced their power to strike and their opportunities for mutual support, and thus their membership and financial base. The battle to transform "welfare Britain" to "market Britain" was epitomized by the bitter national strike of miners in 1984–1985 that split the union movement and the public. The Thatcher government, better prepared than the Heath government of 1970–1974 and enjoying majority support in opinion polls, succeeded in breaking the strike, thus creating a political space for the achievement of an ambitious policy agenda.

Prior to the miners' strike, monetarist policies, including controlling the money supply, applying high levels of interest rates, reducing income taxes to "restore incentives," and increasing value added tax (indirect taxation), had already impacted on the economy. While inflation levels fell, unemployment increased massively, especially within the manufacturing sector. The rejection of Keynesian-style intervention as a palliative for a rapid increase in unemployment was evident in 1981, when, despite a cabinet revolt, the public sector borrowing requirement (PSBR), which is the amount the government must borrow to meet its budgetary needs, was cut as a test of resolute leadership (Kavanagh 1997: 123). A framework for a medium-term financial strategy (MTFS) set out a path of targeted reductions of the money supply and PSBR to tame inflation. Though inflation fell sharply in the mid-1980s, this was associated more with a fall in world commodity prices. Problems associated with the control of the money supply led, instead, to the use of the exchange rate to encourage economic growth within the cherished objective of price stability. In effect, monetary policy, that is the predominant use of control of the money supply to achieve policy ends, lasted for only four years (1980–1984), when interest and exchange-rate instruments took over as the primary tools of economic management.

A move from a mixed to a market-led economy also involved a repositioning of the state. This involved a restructuring of state services and wherever possible a withdrawal of state control and direct involvement in industry, that is, the privatization of state-owned assets and deregulation. Between 1981 and 1995 nationalized industries and public utilities were sold off in a series of well-publicized campaigns to induce a "democratization" of share ownership. British Telecom (1984), British Gas (1986), British Airways (1987), the Electricity Industry (1990–1991), and British Rail (1995) are examples. In most cases the sale of these assets proved popular, resulting in a short-term rise in share prices, of which many individuals took full advantage by immediately reselling—their first and often only venture into the stock market.

Of more lasting effect on people's lives was the opportunity for those in council housing (social housing) to buy their previously publicly tenanted homes, often at substantial discounts for long occupancy. In ten years (1985–1995) 1.3 million homes were sold; for many families living in sought-after locations this was to mean a firm foot on the property ladder. For others on "problem" public estates the advantages were not so clear. More recently, lack of affordable housing, especially in the southeast of England, has been attributed to this policy of "right to buy," particularly for those averagely paid workers in such public sector jobs as teaching, social work, and health care. This has resulted in a reprioritization of social housing, made all the more imperative by the onslaught of recession and the collapse of the housing and mortgage markets.

ECONOMIC GAIN, POLITICAL COSTS

"Selling the family silver," as the Conservative ex-prime minister Harold MacMillan famously described these privatization policies, produced both short- and long-term gains for some, introduced a spirit of consumerism and individualism that fitted the neoliberal aims of the Thatcher administration, and eventually enabled the Treasury to pay off a considerable proportion of the national debt. As table 10.1 indicates, the impact on the British economy of the eleven years of the Thatcher administration was considerable. The shift from a manufacturing to a service base was hastened, as was the shift from public sector to private ownership. Both productivity and investment levels improved as a result of this sectoral and employment "shakeout." There was a shift in taxes from income to indirect taxation, though the proportion of taxation to GDP remained roughly the same. Inflation had been beaten, albeit temporarily, during the mid-1980s, assisting house sales. This, together with the "right to buy" policy, produced a claim by the Conservative Party that Britain had become a "property-owning democracy."

The "Misery Index" in table 10.1 illustrates that the price of such a profound change to the structure and values of the British economy was considerable, especially in the very human cost of unemployment in most parts of Britain other than the southeast. Income inequality increased more rapidly than in any other EU member state and, as a consequence, the level of necessary social security payments undermined the major reduction in public expenditure aimed for. Moreover, world recessions at the beginning and end of the Thatcher administration underlined the continuing external vulnerability of the British economy. It was recognition of this vulnerability that led to significant steps by the Conservative government in the 1980s in the direction of a regional (EU) solution to the unstable external environment.

Table 10.1.   Economic Indicators (1979–2005):The Bad and Good Years

	I	2	3	4	5	6
	Inflation (RPI)	Unemployment Rate (Age 16 and Over)	Misery Index * (RPI + Unemployment)	GDP	Public Sector Expenditure	Days Lost in Strikes
	%	%	Index	£M	%GDP	Thousands
1979	13.4	5.4	18.8	620611	38.2	29474
1983	4.6	11.5	16.1	632065	42.3	3754
1987	4.2	10.5	14.7	729638	38.6	3546
1992	3.7	10.0	13.7	779563	40.3	528
1997	3.1	7.0	10.1	908655	37.1	235
2001	1.8	5.1	6.9	1027905	36.6	525
2005	2.8	4.8	7.6	1129235	38.5	122*

	7	8	9	10	11	12
	Inflation (RPI)	Unemployment Rate (Age 16 and Over)	Misery Index* (RPI + Unemployment)	GDP	Public Sector Expenditure	Days Lost in Strikes
	%	%	Index	£M	%GDP	Thousands
1979	13.4	5.4	18.8	620611	38.2	29474
1983	4.6	11.5	16.1	632065	42.3	3754
1987	4.2	10.5	14.7	729638	38.6	3546
1992	3.7	10.0	13.7	779563	40.3	528
1997	3.1	7.0	10.1	908655	37.1	235
2001	1.8	5.1	6.9	1027905	36.6	525
2005	2.8	4.8	7.6	1129235	38.5	122**

	Total Public Sector Employment	Manufacturing % of Total Employment	Public Sector Debt, % of GDP	Owner Occupied, Outright or with Mortgage	Rented from Local Authority/ Housing Associations	Number of Property Transactions
	Thousands	%	%	%	%	Thousands
1979	7449	28.0	47.1	52	34	1306
1983	6952	23.6	44.8	57	32	1669
1987	6359	21.3	41.0	63	26	1937
1992	5783	17.9	27.4	67	21	1136
1997	4954	17.2	42.7	67	18	1440
2001	5212	14.9	31.5	68	15	1458
2005	5650	11.9	37.5	70	18	1537

* The Misery Index (Inflation rate + unemployment) peaked in 1980 (24.8%) dropping to 6.9 percent (2001–2002) (see Grant 2002).
** January–November
Source: ONS (2008b).

Entry to the Market

Proposals to "complete" the EU as a Single Market were seized by the Conservative government as providing considerable trade advantages for Britain's rapidly modernizing economy. A relatively unrestricted market for goods, services, capital, and labor between twelve European countries made "free market" Britain an attractive investment location for Far Eastern and US capital seeking easy access to the EU market. The former Conservative minister Lord Cockcroft, then European commissioner for the internal market, drew up the White Paper (1985) that presented an optimistic view of the EU's economic future, providing it pursued many of the policies already in place under the Thatcher governments. At an intergovernmental conference in 1986 the British delegation reluctantly accepted the parallel institutional and process reforms that were deemed necessary as part of the package to achieve the integration of member-state markets. As discussed earlier, these nonmarket reforms were later to provide the "backdrop for Conservative Euro scepticism that so damaged the Party during the 1990s" (Geddes 2004: 82).

The second economic policy engagement with the EU was the Conservative government's decision to join the Exchange Rate Mechanism (ERM) in 1990. Since the mid-1980s, the search for effective tools of monetary policy included a debate over the need to establish exchange-rate stability for sterling. Stability would bring external credibility for the government's controversial anti-inflationary objectives. The strongest advocate for exchange rate control, Chancellor Lawson, saw such an advantage in Britain joining the ERM, which had existed since 1979. The ERM was the central aspect of an early attempt by the EU, especially by France and Germany, to coordinate monetary policy through a European monetary system. Within the ERM, the deutsche mark was the benchmark currency. Thus "the Bundesbank was fast becoming the surrogate central bank of the EC" (Gowland et al. 2006: 292).

The Conservative administration divided over whether Britain should join the ERM, with Mrs. Thatcher adamantly against such a European intrusion into the pound's "sovereignty." Chancellor Lawson was equally adamant about seeking the security of such a mechanism, and commenced a policy of shadowing the value of the deutsche mark starting in 1987. Despite her growing and strident Euroscepticism, Mrs. Thatcher was forced to concede ERM membership, but not before losing her Chancellor (Lawson) and Foreign Secretary Geoffrey Howe over her negative EU stance. She was to resign herself shortly afterward.

Britain joined the ERM in unfortunate economic circumstances. Domestically, the economy was in recession with an inflation rate of 10 percent, and the need to sustain the value of the pound within permitted

ERM band fluctuation of plus or minus 6 percent necessitated "setting domestic monetary policy so tightly that the recession was prolonged as output continued to fall and employment continued to rise" (Thain 2005: 38).
But within two years inflation had fallen to 4 percent. However, on 16 September 1992 (Black Wednesday) currencies within the ERM came under
considerable international pressure, and the pound and lira were unable
to sustain their parities against a strong deutsche mark. Britain suspended
ERM membership, but not before experiencing a considerable drain on currency reserves, an enforced devaluation of the pound, and a consequent
rise in interest rates to 15 percent. As mortgage payments rocketed, this
not only had an immediate effect on the Conservatives' property-owning
democracy but was also "as significant a blow to the prestige and confidence of Britain's economic policy makers as the devaluation of sterling
in 1967 and the recourse to an IMF loan in 1976" (Thain 2005: 38).

Britain's exchange rate vulnerability and enforced withdrawal from
the ERM was a consequence of domestic factors (the depth of Britain's recession especially) and global and regional market instabilities. This, together with the unwillingness of the economically stronger ERM members
to jeopardize the system as precursor to full monetary union, resulted in
little collegial support for the weaker ERM currencies, which included
Britain's.

The political consequences for the Conservative government were
massive, contributing to a considerable decline in public support and an
upsurge in Euroscepticism within the Conservative Party. It further undermined any serious chance for British involvement in the moves toward
Economic and Monetary Union (EMU) and also led, ironically, to a reconsideration of monetary and fiscal policies that were to pave the way
for a remarkable transformation of the British economy from the mid-
1990s into the new century.

BETWEEN THATCHERISM AND THE THIRD WAY

The period after Britain's resort to an IMF loan in 1976 presented a weakened Labour government with an uncomfortable and limited set of economic policy choices and contributed directly to the neoliberal experiment
of the Thatcher government beginning in 1979. Similarly, the Major government of 1992–1997 took policy steps that were subsequently maintained by the 1997 New Labour government in its "Third Way" strategy.

In an attempt to reconstitute a monetary-based approach, inflation
was targeted with an explicit 1–4 percent range. In a bid to underscore the
serious objective of the target, the Bank of England published, starting in
1993, regular reports of its advice to the chancellor on the movement of

interest rates. This, together with quarterly reports from a panel of independent advisors, introduced both a transparent and technical character to decision making. With regard to fiscal policy, the Major government continued the Thatcherite shift from direct to indirect taxation. This was the significant difference between the tax system for the first year of the Thatcher government (1979) and the last year of the Major government (1997), for the net overall share of direct taxes (income tax and national insurance) remained steady at 34 percent of total revenue in 1979 compared with 35 percent in 1997. But while there was no explicit commitment to reduce public expenditure, fiscal policy was constructed within a medium-term (roughly five-year) cycle, as was the aim to balance the public budget.

Thus, in 1997 the new Labour government inherited a set of monetary and fiscal policy tools within an established context of price stability as an overriding economic objective. It also inherited what an unpopular Conservative government called "the green shoots of recovery," the result of a strong dose of neoliberal economics and political coercion during the Thatcher years. As will be seen, this legacy was reflected in New Labour's Third Way to economic growth that continued until the recession of 2008–2009.

THE INSTRUMENTS OF ECONOMIC POLICY

Before assessing the nature and success and weaknesses of a Third Way economy it is necessary to explore the character of economic policy making in contemporary Britain.

Institutions: The Treasury

As one writer comments, "two institutions and one office manage Britain's economic policies: HM Treasury, the Bank of England and the Prime Minister of the day"; and certainly during the past decade the Treasury has "held sway" (Thain 2005: 28). While there currently may be particular factors that have enhanced the position of the Treasury in relation to the executive (see below) there is no doubt that the British Treasury is no mere Department of Finance. Its self-designated aim is to "raise the rate of sustainable growth and achieve rising prosperities and better quality of life with economic and employment opportunities for all." Thus it is to the Treasury that the governing party looks for delivery of the conditions for electoral victory (shades here of US president Clinton's maxim "it's the economy, stupid"); and within those conditions discrete policy objectives are managed. The Treasury has interests in setting long-term economic goals, and by way of managing demand and utilizing fiscal policy (and thus public expenditure), its interests also extend to public-sector pay and service delivery efficiency and the management of the nation's public account. These have medium- and short-term goals. Since the success of the British economy depends heavily on global and EU positioning, the Treasury also has a key role in interpreting the impact of external economic factors in relation to the health of the British domestic economy. In effect, the Treasury sits astride policy making as a prioritizing, enabling, shaping, and sometimes negating force. Its organizational structure reflects these broad-based political, economic, financial, and administrative roles.

The institutional significance of the Treasury to British politics is historically underscored by the constitutional, though seldom-used, titles given to the prime minister, who is "first lord of the Treasury," and the chancellor of the exchequer, who is "second lord." In the Commons, the governing party whips, whose task it is to provide majorities for their first and second "lords," are also "lords commissioners" of the Treasury. The salience of the executive to the exchequer and the need to seek Commons approval for expenditure is reflected in these titular anachronisms. The chancellor is assisted in his/her political leadership of economic policy by the chief secretary to the Treasury responsible for public expenditure and European issues; the paymaster general (taxation and welfare policy issues); the financial secretary (microeconomic policy); and the economic secretary (financial services and international matters including preparation for EMU).

Taking Politics Out of Economic Policy: The Bank of England

The British Treasury, like all finance departments, enjoys a position of structural power by virtue of its control of the public purse, and in chapter 8, we have described the close but often fractious relationship that has existed between prime minister and chancellor in controlling the direction of public expenditure.

The decision to create an independent central bank, the Bank of England, was announced by Chancellor Gordon Brown just a few days after the election landslide of 1997. The decision surprised both political and economic commentators at the time and ranks alongside Scottish and Welsh devolution, the Human Rights Act, and the banning of smoking in British pubs (!) as momentous in the long list of New Labour's domestic reforms. The bank, nationalized in 1946 and perceived as little more than an extended arm of the Treasury into the City of London, is charged with the considerable task of maintaining interest rates within a target set by the chancellor. In effect, it is the governor of the Bank of England, advised by an expert Monetary Policy Committee, who has the responsibility of maintaining price stability (see the book's website). However, in doing so the bank must also be sensitive to other government policy objectives with regard to employment and economic growth. But these are, or were until recession hit in 2008, secondary to the overriding goal of price stability. Its previous responsibilities for financial services regulation were transferred to a separate authority (FSA). In this way the potentially conflicting Treasury roles of "the government banker, responsible for managing borrowing and debt, the regulator of the financial system, responsible for the stability of the financial system, the agent of the Treasury in adjusting interest rates, and intervening in the foreign exchange markets" to a considerable extent is resolved (Thain 2005: 41). The FSA has, however, received considerable criticism for its "light touch" approach to regulation following the banking crises that began to emerge in the autumn of 2007 (see above).

In effect, monetary policy—through interest rate control to achieve price stability—was shifted from the political domain of chancellor/PM/cabinet and governing party, to a technical-professional domain, approximating the monetary regime emerging through EMU in the late 1990s. One of the Maastricht criteria for membership in the eurozone (those member states that have adopted the euro as currency) was the establishment of an independent central bank (the influence of EMU on British economic policy is discussed below). However, the decision may equally have been the result of meetings that future chancellor Gordon Brown attended with Alan Greenspan of the US Federal Reserve prior to the 1997 Labour victory (Routledge 1998; Bower 2005). In effect, the eventual model for an independent central bank followed more that of the Federal Reserve than the ECB, which is less open in its decision making and follows a more singular aim in pursuit of price stability in the eurozone (Pym and Kochan 1998).

New Labour: A New Policy Process?

In surrendering interest rate control to the Bank of England, the 1997 Labour government moved toward the monetarist-oriented economic agenda that was reflected in Conservative government economic perspectives of the 1980 and 1990s. For the first two years of office, New Labour policy kept to the spending limits of the previous Conservative administration. Public expenditure as a percentage of GDP in the first four years of Labour government kept below that of the previous Conservative administration (table 10.1). A Code for Fiscal Stability (1998) contained two key elements: "the golden rule," whereby the government over an economic cycle would only borrow for investment and not to support current expenditure; and borrowing would be held at 40 percent of GDP over an economic cycle. Notwithstanding the problems of distinguishing between investment and current expenditure (is education capital or a current cost?), the semblance of a rule-based fiscal policy underpinned the chancellor's search for stability to encourage growth. One further constraint was also accepted: that public expenditure should be consistent with the rules of the EU Stability and Growth Pact—rules that chimed well with the avowed "prudence" of New Labour policies (see textbox 10.1). The fiscal code also committed the Treasury to produce an Economic and Fiscal Strategy Report for Parliament as part of the debate over the annual budget cycle.

Biannual comprehensive spending reviews reintroduced medium-term planning for policy expenditure, involving departmental public service agreements between department and the Treasury, that were to be monitored by a cabinet committee. Targets for in-service delivery were also agreed (see chapter 9). In effect, the Treasury under New Labour, while surrendering its control of monetary policy, enjoys a greater array of fiscal levers that indicate "a significant shift in power from departmental discretion to central control" (Thain 2005: 43). This, together with the particular interest shown in contributing to issues of Third World debt and international finance reform, indicated the interests of the Treasury in international economic agendas. This is no more evident than in the influence of Treasury perspectives on EU economic and social policies and its massive interventions in dealing with the banking crisis and global recession of 2008–2009.

Textbox 10.1. The Stability and Growth Pact (1997)

The Stability and Growth Pact is an agreement by EU member states related to their conduct of fiscal policy, to facilitate and maintain EMU. It is based on Articles 99 and 104 of the TEC (as amended in 1993 and 1997) and related decisions. It consists of mutual surveillance of fiscal positions and an excessive deficit procedure defined in the treaty. The criteria that member states must respect are:

- An annual budget deficit no higher than 3 percent of GDP
- A public debt lower than 60 percent of GDP or approaching that value.

It has been applied inconsistently and was temporarily suspended in 2005, after the Council of Ministers failed to apply sanctions against France and Germany. The then Commission president described it as "stupid" but was still required by the treaty to seek to apply its provisions. The pact has proved to be unenforceable against big countries such as France and Germany, and it has proved difficult to apply as member states struggle to apply recession-busting policies that involve deficit spending and higher public debt.

New Labour—New Policy Directions?

The period 1997–2001 may be characterized as one of consolidation of the slow economic recovery evident at the end of the Conservative administration. This period saw a squeeze on public expenditure and a windfall tax on privatized utilities (1997), which formed the basis for sizable investments in public services at the beginning of the second Labour term (2001–2005). These investments were to provide a cushion against the impact of global recession in the early years of the century. Various supply-side measures such as the welfare to work program, the Working Families Tax Credit system, and others including educational and training programs reflected a consistent message: the prioritization of work opportunities for the poor and the least equipped sectors of the population—in effect to make work pay for marginalized families and persons (Elliott 2006). The tax and benefits system was utilized to make work pay by guaranteeing minimum income levels. This remained an objective of New Labour policy throughout its period in office.

In its second administration the major theme was investment in public services, made possible by the previous public expenditure squeeze and a gradual rise in the tax base, particularly in indirect taxation—a continuation of the trend commenced by previous Conservative administrations. The impact of public investment in improving welfare services has proved patchy and politically unrewarding (see the book's website). Of equal concern for New Labour subsequently (2005 onward) is that critics point to the seemingly endemic problem of low productivity and investment. Thus "a combination of economic stability, public investment, low interest rates and tax breaks have not produced the longed for step change in investment: instead the UK economy has the same problem that it has had for half a century—consuming too much and producing too little" (Elliott 2006: 9).

ECONOMIC POLICY IN A GLOBAL AND EU PERSPECTIVE

Problems of low investment and high consumption must also be set in the context of Britain's position as a trading nation. While the concept of economic globalization may be contested, the fact that it is part of the discourse of political economy is irrefutable (see the book's website). Since, however, the character and depth of globalization is debatable, the interpretation of the concept chosen by economic decision makers is a vital aspect of their decision making.

Here we follow the analysis of one set of commentators who present three variants of the concept: *hyperglobalism*; national *political economy*;

and *open regionalism* (Baker, Gamble, and Seawright 2002; Grant 2002). If the hyperglobalist view is taken, then all a national government can do is implement policies that will command respect in global financial markets—and presumably keep its fingers crossed. If, however, the national political economy is viewed as a significant and independent player, this stresses a path-dependent view of national economies and prioritizes difference as a strength. From this perspective, resistance to change is evident in the protective stance taken by French governments to agricultural supports, or the Swedish to their model of welfare in the face of external expectations for prudent public expenditure and open markets. Finally, the open-regionalist perspective takes the view that, in circumstances of potentially unstable global markets, especially those associated with international finance, national economic futures are best pursued collectively for reasons of both protection and opportunity (Grant 2002: 47).

It is in the context of these three perspectives that economic decision makers view Britain as part of a global market, as a powerful EU member state, and as a rich and independent nation-state. They face the same dilemma as their colleagues in the FCO: which of three circles of interest to prioritize and what mix of policies can produce optimal results for British national interests. Since these circles of interest overlap and interact, prioritization of any one shapes the relationship that policy has with the others. From 1997 to 2007 the Treasury, led by Chancellor Brown, stressed the need to accommodate the harsh realities of globalization. This, suggests one commentator, is evident from a "preoccupation with [macroeconomic] credibility"—as demonstrated by the establishment of greater Bank of England independence "and [microeconomic] competitiveness" that involves flexible labor markets, education, and training to assist this flexibility, alongside low levels of corporate and personal taxation (Hay 2006: 250). In adopting this formula, Britain's position within the EU's political economy could be explained.

Since 1997, British governments have argued for the deregulation of EU labor markets as a vital factor in the creation of a competitive knowledge-based EU economy—through the 2000 Lisbon Strategy (see textbox 10.2; Hopkin and Wincott 2006). Promotion of this "Anglo-Saxon model" has resulted after fractious arguments between supporters of this approach and those states—especially France, Italy, and Germany—whose labor markets have enjoyed a comparatively high level of legal protection (a European social model). This has spilled over to domestic politics, notably in France, where public demonstrations, such as those in 2006 against proposed reductions in young workers' rights, produced violent protests. Since 2008 the response to global recession has included Britain's willingness to coordinate fiscal and monetary responses through G20 summitry and at

---

Textbox 10.2. The Lisbon Strategy

At the Lisbon European Council, March 2000, the EU responded to concerns that member states were unable to compete in a global marketplace with a strategy to make the EU within ten years "the most competitive and dynamic knowledge-based economy in the world" (European Council 2000). The strategy aims to establish global competitive advantage through investment, research, and structural reforms.

Economic competitiveness is to be accomplished alongside measures to sustain social cohesion—in effect a political compromise between the advocates of the Anglo-Saxon model and "Social Europe." An ambitious list of aims included measures to achieve high levels of e-governance and commerce, widening Internet access, establishing a European area for research and innovation, and a European patent system. Measures to assist commerce include reducing the remaining SEM barriers, especially in the service sector and financial markets; reducing tax burdens on individuals and small business; and improving access to training for the young and unemployed. Social cohesion is to be enhanced by the reform of social protection, especially with regard to pensions, and encouraging the social inclusion of those on low incomes. These measures were to be achieved by what is called the open method of coordination (OMC). This "soft" approach was to be assisted by a stocktaking of member-state/Union progress at one of three European Councils each year.

It was soon apparent that of the 117 target indicators only a few were likely to be achieved by 2010. Reducing unemployment in several population groups and solving the pensions crisis were particularly intractable problems in several member states. Progress was more evident in post-2004 member states than in older members such as France, Italy, and Greece.

EU level—in effect an open-regionalist perspective on globally derived economic difficulties.

Britain has been at the forefront of extending EU membership to other states. This must be seen not only as a means to stall policy integration but also to prioritize an open-market perspective for EU futures. Thus Britain offered consistent support for Turkey's application for membership; formal application procedures commenced during the British presidency (in October 2005). Britain has also consistently promoted completion of the SEM through elimination of remaining internal barriers. The most recent example is in relation to the energy market that remains heavily protected in several member states. Concern for completion of the internal market must be seen in the context of a further British policy "to favour a more liberal approach by the EU to international trade questions" (Grant 2002: 49). British influence over the direction of EU external trade policy was facilitated by the appointment of Peter Mandelson in 2000–2008 as commissioner for external trade. He, like a previous British trade commissioner, Leon Brittan, took a strong free-trade stance in leading EU external-policy negotiations. His subsequent return to domestic politics in 2008 as secretary of state for business to help deal with Britain's recession continued the free-trade mantra. It is in the attitude toward EU macroeconomic policy and EMU, however, that British EU perspectives have been and remain unresolved; and to this we now turn.

Britain and EMU: A Recurring Dilemma

Apart from the period 1990–1992, when Britain was a member of the ERM, the precursor to EMU, British governments have been either openly hostile or sought to avoid integrating monetary policy with their EU partners. As alluded to earlier, the decision to join the ERM was contested within the then Conservative government, and the subsequent withdrawal was disastrous for the political fortunes of the Major administration. The fairly rapid recovery of Britain's economic fortunes, it has been argued, dates from ERM withdrawal (Hay 2006: 254). It is therefore not surprising that the parallel moves toward full monetary union were not considered appropriate for the British economy of the 1990s, especially given the negative public attitudes to the project at a time when both Conservative and Labour parties were struggling to establish credibility as parties of government. Prime Minister Major's "opt-out" from Stage Three of EMU, achieved as part of the Maastricht negotiations for the Treaty of European Union, reflected both the economic and political limits at the time. By 2001, when twelve of the then fifteen EU member states replaced their domestic currencies with the euro, those limits had not radically altered for the New Labour government.

The first Labour administration (1997–2001) was returned to office on the premise of its ability to run the economy with a competence that had previously eluded its predecessors. The policy goal, price stability, was underscored by the immediate establishment of operational independence of the Bank of England, one requirement for any EU state wishing to join Stage Three of EMU. Rejoining a more flexible ERM at the same time was also an option, with the next logical step being full membership in the eurozone. A number of factors combined to preclude this option. An immediate move toward eurozone membership would have meant accepting the European Central Bank (ECB) as replacement for the newly independent Bank of England in the control of interest rates, exchange rates, and inflation levels. The Bank of England, as we have seen, works independently, but within a formulation shaped by the government. Thus, the "institutional features of the eurozone are perceived to pose a threat to the conduct of representative and responsible government as constructed in British Politics" (Buller 2004: 25). Similar arguments could be made for the constraining force of the Stability and Growth Pact, where balancing the budget on an annual basis could be economically damaging (Buller 2004: 25). Early EMU entry was also precluded by the lack of synchronization of the business cycle of the British economy with its Continental neighbors. This, together with the economic weakness of several EU member states and the uncertainty of the medium-term success of the EMU project, drove a cautious chancellor and a sceptical Treasury toward what amounted to the position of the previous Conservative administration—wait and see.

The Politics of the Euro

Political considerations were to weigh heavily on Treasury and government views toward euro entry. The loss of not just economic but also political independence expressed in terms of "parliamentary sovereignty," and thus national integrity, remained a simple panic button for Eurosceptics to press. Figure 10.1 illustrates that the majority of public opinion ran two to one against the euro and, but for short periods during 1998, has remained at that level throughout the period of three Labour governments. This, together with an overwhelmingly hostile press, allowed little opportunity for selling eurozone membership electorally, despite a current House of Commons that contains a majority of MPs in favor of membership (Hix 2000).

The idea of a referendum on the Single Currency was born out of this political dilemma. By October 1994, Blair, then leader of Labour's opposition, deemed the case for EMU entry to be constitutional, and therefore

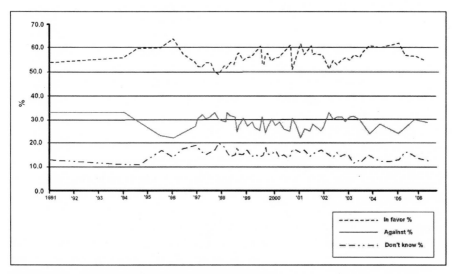

Figure 10.1.   Public Opinion on Joining the Euro

as requiring discussion by the British people. Thus, the promise of a referendum formed part of the 1997, 2001, and 2005 election manifestos. One of Blair's earliest problems after election in 1997 was when a euro referendum might be held. In response to media pressures, Chancellor Brown announced five "tests" through which membership would be decided—a "prepare and decide" strategy (Rawnsley 2001: 87).

The tests—sustainable convergence of the British and eurozone economies, flexibility to cope with economic change, impact on investment, the impact on the City of London, and whether it is good for employment—could be flexibly interpreted. However, various factors precluded the application of the tests prior to the 2001 election. A Treasury-organized "National Changeover Plan" was not to be completed within the Parliament's lifetime; resistance to an early decision also came from Treasury advisors and the then Bank of England governor, Eddie George, who, respectively, warned of the potential costs to public expenditure and the lack of British-Continental business cycle convergence. Public opinion in favor of joining rose only twice to a high point of 33 percent throughout the Parliament, with the opposition and Eurosceptical press relentless in pursuit of political advantage. Since Blair's overriding objective was success in a second "historic" term for his New Labour project, the issue of the Single Currency remained wrapped up in its tests. In June 2003 Gordon Brown presented a 1,700-page report to Parliament that formed the basis of his assessment of the "five tests." Only one "passed"—that related to the ability of the City of London to maintain its competitive advantage in global financial markets. The other four were deemed to have "failed."

A number of factors combined to push the Single Currency issue off the government's political agenda. The issue of a European Constitution replaced the Single Currency as a litmus test for British commitment to European integration. Politically trumped by the question of "what type of Europe in the twenty-first century," economic factors alone seem insufficiently convincing to sell euro membership to a still sceptical public (Hay 2006: 270). Until 2008, the headline successes of New Labour's economic policy—low inflation and interest rates, low unemployment, and modest economic growth—were consistently held by Gordon Brown as a mark of distinction from the experiences of other EU states within the eurozone. Much of this success was derived from consumption-led growth, in which the housing market has played a salient role. Since "households are more likely to engage in credit-based consumption in periods of low inflation . . . and . . . low interest rates," a calculation by householders that euro membership would be economically unfavorable could be profoundly destabilizing to what some observers believe to be a somewhat delicately balanced growth model (Hay 2006). This was coupled with the fact that both the pre-membership requirements (of the Stability and Growth Pact) and post-membership ECB control of monetary policy would reduce Treasury policy options to uncomfortable fiscal choices. "In effect should control of monetary policy pass from . . . the Bank of England to its equivalent in Frankfurt, the ability to soften any burden on mortgage holders . . . would be eliminated at a stroke (Hay 2006: 270). These circumstances, together with the stance of the Conservative opposition, ruled out British membership in the eurozone, suggesting that Britain's adoption of the Single Currency has been postponed indefinitely. The impact of recession on this probability is discussed below.

EUROPEANIZATION AND ECONOMIC POLICY

The homepage of the Treasury website (www.hm-treasury.gov.uk) places matters associated with the EU under "International Issues." Thus the euro and other EU-related economic issues are subsumed within a menu of other external Treasury interests such as international development, global economic challenges, the Commonwealth education fund, and action against terrorist financing. The then EU commissioner for trade, Peter Mandelson, saw the Treasury as "the most eurosceptic department in Whitehall since the end of the second world war. . . . It was Treasury thinking that kept us out of the European project in the first place and counselled against membership in successive generations. [But] scepticism doesn't equal hostility. It just means they are harder to persuade" (Watt 2006: 10). As one opponent of further EU integration, the Treasury was "the last remaining bastion of Euro scepticism in Whitehall" (Forster and Blair 2002: 57).

This opinion should not be surprising given the Treasury's traditional responsibility for control of state finances. Such responsibility is bound to be jealously guarded from profligacy—whether of domestic spending departments or costly procedures emanating from Brussels-based policy. Here we examine some of the dilemmas faced by chancellor and Treasury in influencing EU economic policy and their ability to shape, coordinate, and, if necessary, veto the implementation of EU policies as they affect Britain.

Shared or Contradictory Economic Values?

We have discussed above the particular stress New Labour has placed upon the impact of globalization since taking power in 1997. Their strategy involves a desire to gain maximum benefit from global economic opportunities. According to the Blair/Brown mantra, this entailed reducing EU protectionist tendencies, as exemplified by the CAP—a high-cost policy in terms both of expenditure inefficiency and international dispute. Notwithstanding the list of modernizing objectives included in the EU Lisbon

Agenda, the Blair/Brown mantra revolved around the establishment of a flexible labor market in which workers are sufficiently equipped with transferable skills to meet changes in labor supply/demand; and where wage levels are able to reflect change without restriction by regulation or overburdening trade union pressure. This "Anglo-Saxon model" is challenged by the "European Social Model" as its antithesis, the characteristics of which include high levels of labor protection; generous welfare supports; state investment in key industries; and, internationally, a protectionist expectation of state/EU. Politically, these views were publicly debated through periodic spats between Prime Minister Blair and President Chirac, who, however crudely, came to personify two markedly different views of European destiny. Prime Minister Brown and President Sarkozy currently hold closer views, but these are in the light of the more problematic and shared economic circumstances of recession during their administrations.

This "open versus closed Europe" discourse belies several commonalities between economic policies of member states. The Lisbon Agenda itself contains an undeniable social dimension. Britain with Sweden and Denmark have mostly operated their monetary policies within the structures of the Stability and Growth Pact; and monetary policy, variously applied, provided the assumed framework within which global economic credibility is sustained for all EU member states (Hay 2006: 250). Furthermore, the polarization of social versus economic arguments obscures the complexity of the issues involved.

However, there are more than two models of capitalism within the EU constellation. Moreover there is considerable evidence to suggest that EU state policies cannot be simply categorized within one view of capitalism but are generally hybrids that include specific economic and social policies that cut across different models of capitalism (Hopkin and Wincott 2006: 53). In several indexes that measure economic efficiency against social equity, Hopkin and Wincott find little correlation between, for instance, levels of competitiveness and income inequality. In fact, argue the authors, it is Scandinavian countries that have achieved the highest rates of competitiveness—alongside low rates of income inequality—with Britain not performing well on competitiveness and having a dismal record on social inequality (Hopkin and Wincott 2006: 60). But neither is Britain a particularly good model of a neoliberal economy, as it has engaged in "stealth redistribution" for some time—in effect an "Anglo-Social" rather than "Anglo-Saxon" model (Pearce and Paxton 2005). Whatever the veracity of this claim, those who argue for an economic *or* a social model are not consistent with most empirical observation regarding the European political economy—that European policy makers have sought hybrid solutions to the seeming clash between achievement of economic efficiency and reducing social inequality (see the book's website for a detailed discussion).

Britain's Partial European Economic Integration

As we point out above, Britain's decision to opt out of EMU and the subsequent "wait and see" policy with regard to membership was as much a commentary on politicians' fear of the political consequences of a common currency as it was a considered economic calculation. After 1997, the ceding of control over interest rates to the Bank of England depoliticized British monetary policy, as likewise the eurozone member states ceded control to the ECB. Similarly, the British government agreed to follow the guiding principles of EU fiscal rules included in the 1997 Stability and Growth Pact. However, joining the eurozone challenges notions of the role of representative, responsible, and accountable government in economic policy, and thus raises the emotive issue of parliamentary sovereignty. EMU was, until the debate over the EU Constitutional Treaty, the most powerful statement of progress toward European integration since the SEA, and it represented, for British, Danish, and Swedish Eurosceptical opinion, a bridge too far.

The consequence of nonparticipation has been the marginalization of the British government from European monetary policy deliberations. Meetings of Ecofin, the Economic Council of Ministers, have been overshadowed, since the creation of the eurozone, by a preliminary meeting that includes only eurozone ministers (the Euro Group). This meeting is also attended by the president of the ECB and the commissioner for economic affairs and is considered to be effective and decisive in its deliberations (*European Voice* 2006). By excluding non-eurozone members, including most post-2004 member states, a two-tier structure to European monetary policy deliberations is created. British contributions to any rethinking of the Stability and Growth Pact were also marginalized by eurozone outsider status.

One further difficulty for British political leadership in this arena is the niggling controversy surrounding the EU budgetary rebate negotiated by Mrs. Thatcher in 1982 and now considered to be redundant and inequitable by all member states but Britain. Political isolation was narrowly averted at the end of the British presidency (December 2005) when Prime Minister Blair offered to relinquish 20 percent of the €3.2 billion rebate as part of a final EU budget agreement. While the rebate remains, credible contributions to budgetary reform by British negotiators will be compromised (Geddes 2004).

As we have outlined above, British contributions to achievement of the Lisbon Agenda were vocal and often controversial. This was evident at the 2007 Brussels summit, when an attempt by France to de-emphasize competition as a Union objective in the Reform Treaty was resisted by then PM Tony Blair following vigorous protestations from Chancellor

Brown. The drive toward a competitive, open Europe has generally supported the European Commission, whose commentary is often amplified by Treasury and government statements (HM Treasury, 2005, 2006). For the most part, the Treasury position has been to argue for increased Commission powers to facilitate competition in EU labor, product, and capital markets. In other EU issue areas such as tax harmonization, the Treasury resisted Commission initiatives in support of the City of London's international competitiveness. Also, the Treasury has historically expressed concern over the financial implications of the domestic contribution to EU structural funding. This is in part an application of a Treasury view of receipts from the EU budget as *reimbursement* for British contributions rather than *additional* external funding. A system of financial control (EUROPES) locates such "income" and seeks out compensatory reductions in departmental spending. Though this has produced conflict with the Commission, "additionality" remains a contested concept for Treasury financial accounting.

A similar *non-communautaire* position has been associated with the Treasury attitude to the European budget (as well as Britain's net contribution). The Europeanization of British economic policy, when assessed in terms of support for economic integration, has been limited by a Treasury that views the EU suspiciously as a constraint on its policy options. EU norms have been internalized only when they fit an Anglo-Saxon perspective, which amounts to a "conditional and instrumental view of participation" (Dyson, as quoted in Geddes 2004: 173). The extent to which global recession has affected this detachment is discussed below.

Europeanization and Domestic Economic Policies

Our comments here are made in the context of two observations. The first is that the most significant policy-making institutions for economic policy, the Treasury and Bank of England, set frameworks within which public expenditure and the conditions for economic stability are to be achieved. As illustrated above, the decision to keep Britain outside EMU allowed for significant distance between current macroeconomic decisions of the eurozone policy makers and chancellor/Treasury decisions. Second, the growth in Treasury power over domestic policy since 1997 has been seen as unprecedented (Thain 2005: 40). Thus, "giving power resources to the Bank of England has freed the Treasury to focus on other policy arenas and here [Chancellor] Brown shaped the Treasury in his image to perform roles suited to his agenda for reform across the range of government policies" (Thain 2005: 40). This includes health service and education reform, child poverty relief, and international debt relief. These reflected the particular and, some would argue, unique, division of political responsibilities between the Blair/Brown "axis," and thus the personal agenda of a then powerful chancellor. Since then the Treasury has reinforced its control over the public purse and government policies as it leads the battle against recession.

Much of the pre-2007 New Labour agenda emanated from Chancellor Brown's US advisors and experiences (for example the welfare to work program). There are, however, two areas of regulatory policy that, to different degrees, may be perceived as Europeanized—in that the shape and implementation of policy "becomes part of the organisational logic of national . . . policy making" (Ladrech 1994: 70). The development of British competition policy since the 1998 Competition Act owes much to Confederation of British Industry (CBI) support for reform along the lines of EU Treaty Articles 81 and 82 (Suzuki 2000). Also, it must be noted that Britain was one of the first Western European countries to develop antitrust legislation and other policies regarding competition post-1945. There is, therefore, a complex relationship between national and EU sources of current British competition law that includes both uploading and downloading of policy preferences (Rosamond 2003).

Much the same arguments can be made when observing the development of British policy toward regulation of the financial sector. The Financial Services Authority (FSA), operating since 2000, took over responsibility for the regulation of financial institutions previously organized by several self-regulating industry bodies. The ineffective nature of some self-regulation, and a general desire to press on with perceived advantages in the EU financial services market, provided incentives to organize regulation within a single authority to facilitate a structured Single Market. EU directives, themselves the result of uploading from member state experience, formed the framework for comparability between member states' arrangements. Though it is difficult to establish clear lines of cause and effect, financial services regulations in Britain were "Europeanized" through both uploading and downloading of practice to minimize diversity between member states (Howell 2004). In the light of catastrophic banking failures however, the success of the FSA and other EU member state regulators has been called into question. It has also shaken EU economic policy assumptions to their core, and the likelihood of a more centralized EU-directed set of financial regulations is strong.

POLICY MAKING IN A CRISIS

British policy makers, like all their counterparts throughout the world, claim not to have had the opportunity to foresee the emerging "credit crunch" from 2007 onward. Neither did they recognize the depth of the financial crisis in time to forestall the economic recession that followed. Critics have argued that the lax regulation of British financial services and the ease of personal credit availability remain the government's responsibility in the final analysis. But perspectives would agree that the initial stimulus toward recession lay in a US-derived "credit crunch" (see the book's website).

The impact of the resulting financial crisis was devastating. Western leaders previously happy to advertise the lightness of their touch on the financial community were forced to invest trillions of dollars, euros, and pounds to prevent their domestic banking systems from total collapse. From the second half of 2007 and throughout 2008 the United States saw such established financial institutions as the Carlyle Group and Lehman Brothers fail. Others, such as Fanny Mae and Freddie Mac, Merrill Lynch, and AIG needed federal bailouts. Despite a $150 billion tax rebate in January, US consumers failed to show confidence in these measures. Rising unemployment and declining house prices continued throughout the year.

Britain's financial collapse paralleled that of the United States. Commencing with a housing mortgage lender, Northern Rock, that had indulged itself in domestic subprime lending and invested in US toxic debt in 2007 and continuing into 2008, other banks and mortgage lenders revealed massive debts. Bradford and Bingley, Royal Bank of Scotland, Halifax, and later HBOS and Alliance and Leicester, were rescued by direct Treasury intervention through government purchase of privately owned shares—in effect partial bank nationalization (apart from the fully nationalized Northern Rock). As in the United States, property prices went into freefall and unemployment began to rise, initially in the financial and construction industries, and then in other economic sectors. As the crisis continued, a range of measures were applied in the hope of avoiding recession turning to depression (see textbox 10.3).

By the spring of 2009 the British economy together with all other EU member states was in dire straits. British unemployment exceeded 2 million; the pound had reached parity with the euro and had lost twenty points against the dollar. Economic growth had shrunk in the last quarter of 2008 to officially establish the economy in recession. Retail sales in the electronics, white goods, and motor industry declined—car production dropped by 59 percent between February 2008 and February 2009. And as a result of a series of government interventions, tax cuts, and government borrowing, Britain's public sector borrowing requirement (2009–2010) would be highest amongst the G7 group, with estimates ranging from £110 billion to £200 billion. The per-capita loss of wealth for every adult in Britain between 2007 and 2009 as a result if the recession was estimated at £40,000 (*Independent* 19 March 2009).

**Textbox 10.3. The Government's Responses
to Recession (2008–2009)**

As unemployment increased to 2 million (March 2009), housing stock had lost 20 percent of its value since 2007. Several well-known shopping chains, most noticeably Woolworth's, had disappeared from the High Street. Interbank credit had dried up, and several commercial banks had requested and gained various government bailouts. The most optimistic forecast for even partial recovery was well into 2010. Like other EU member states, the British government's response was complex, deep intervention. By April 2009, these measures included:

- Interest rate cuts to .5 percent
- Bank and mortgage company bailouts to £400 billion, amounting to nationalization
- State backing to insure against exposure to "toxic debt"
- Public works initiative to £3 billion (brought forward to 2010)
- A cut in VAT (sales tax) from 17.5 to 15 percent
- Loans support for small business to £20 billion
- A home-energy efficiency program to £910 million
- Stamp duty tax on housing reduced and rescue packages for housing mortgage defaulters
- Increases in pensions and child benefits
- Increases in top-rate taxes and social security payments
- "Quantitive easing"—Treasury support to encourage interbank loans

---

British, EU, or Global Solutions?

Since the mid-1990s, Britain has emerged as a consumption-based market economy with relatively low levels of unemployment, inflation, direct taxation, and interest rates. This may be contrasted with the relatively high taxes, inflation, and public-sector domination of the 1970s or the high unemployment, social division, and strikes of the 1980s. The production base continued to move from manufacturing to the service/financial service sector; public sector ownership declined, to be replaced by provision of public utilities and energy by private companies. The revenue base shifted markedly in the direction of indirect rather than direct taxation, with the aim of providing incentives for higher productivity and investment commensurate with the competitive pressures of regional and global markets. The City of London still provided a considerable share of world financial services, and visible trade is mostly concentrated on the EU Single Market.

British responses to the credit crunch and recession have reversed or redirected many of the policy assumptions that have been sustained for the past fifteen years. The "golden rule" (government borrowing only for investment), a low level of PSBR, a 3 percent limit to the budget deficit, an "incentive-based" income tax philosophy, and light-touch regulation of financial services have all been found wanting in a crisis climate. A redistributive emergency budget in November 2008 with tax cuts and increases in capital expenditure, together with a cut in the indirect value added tax (VAT), injected £20 billion into the economy. Public sector borrowing rose to 8 percent of GDP. This, together with the effective nationalization of several banks, amounted to a return of Keynesian-style policies. The *new orthodoxy*, as one commentator put it, is that "it is better to spend, reflate and worry about the consequences for borrowing inflation and taxes later, than do nothing and allow the recessionary waves to engulf the economy" (*Independent*, 25 November 2008). Measures taken in the April 2009 budget reinforced partially this Keynesian strategy—while at the same time preparing for future massive cuts in public expenditure.

As noted earlier in chapter 8 Prime Minister Brown was quick to advertise these initiatives on the international stage. He encouraged the incoming Obama administration as well as his EU colleagues to a concerted reflationary action, at the same time preaching against the temptation to slip into trade protectionism, deemed in his March 2009 congressional address as "a race to the bottom." Neither this nor his call for a new international financial system was particularly well received by his US congressional audience. The prime minister's message received similar mixed reviews among EU colleagues, which reflected the lack of consensus regarding concerted EU action.

While all member states were adversely affected, each had its own particular difficulties and priorities. Thus British consumer and mortgage debt and the collapse of the financial sector as a wealth creator contrasts with the downturn in German manufacturing due to the loss of export markets, a problem also for France and Italy. Spain has particular problems with the decline in property markets and mortgage indebtedness. Central and Eastern European member states, as new market economies, are particularly vulnerable to a decline in foreign investment and the return of migrant workers. In effect the recession has produced considerable strains on the notion of a European Single Market, the viability of a common currency, and the effectiveness of an already strained Growth and Stability Pact.

A degree of concerted EU action was evident prior to the G20 meeting in March 2009. Thus a €50 billion rescue package for non-eurozone members was agreed, as was the establishment of an EU-wide regulatory system for financial markets, banks, hedge funds, and private equity groups (a European Systematic Risk Council). British policymakers were less enthused, arguing for a fiscal stimulus as a priority to get liquidity back into the financial system. Fear of a breakdown in the Single Market was evident in responses to President Sarkozy's decision to offer loans to the French auto industry, providing the resulting investment would lead to jobs for French workers and not for investment in other EU states. The Commission, in an attempt to sustain its role as guardian of the treaties, sought verification of the legality of the French initiative. It also threatened infringement proceedings against several states, including France and Spain and warned Britain for breaching the SGP. At the G20 conference held in London, April 2009, some semblance of agreement was reached between those who sought a reflationary approach and others who demanded tight internationally directed regulation for financial markets.

CONCLUSION

Britain's relative success as a global and regional economy in the past fifteen years was achieved via a mixture of Keynesian and monetarist policies nominated as the Anglo-Saxon—or more accurately the *Anglo-social*—model, a Third Way toward the holy grail of steady prices and noninflationary growth. Policies to achieve this were characterized by a rule-based technocratic approach to decision making in both monetary and fiscal policies that revolved around an operationally independent Bank of England and an independently regulated financial sector.

If economic policy has been "depoliticized," there nevertheless remain less clear and potentially controversial views of economic strategy: Where do the longer-term best interests of Britain lie? As a nation dependent on trading for its wealth and income, within what is generally accepted to be a globalized world, are Britain's interests stronger as a relatively independent global player or part of a powerful EU trading bloc? Its posture of standing aside from EMU and outside the eurozone and arguing for the benefits of the Anglo-Saxon model is indicative of a preference for a liberalized globalist future rather than one affected by the constrained choices of full EMU participation. The differences between an Anglo-Saxon and European social model, however, may prove more rhetorical than real, especially given the extent of common agreement around the evolving Lisbon Agenda and the acceptance of Keynesian intervention and financial regulation as a solution to the recession. In circumstances of persistent economic downturn, the regional market and economic union, including membership in the eurozone with all its social costs, may well prove to be a more convivial European home than current British policy makers have been prepared to admit to a sceptical British electorate.

FURTHER READING

For a comprehensive examination of British economic policy in the second half of the twentieth century see Wyn Grant (2002). For contrasting views of Britain's economic decline compare David Coates, *The Question of UK Decline* (1994) and Neal Crafts, *Britain's Relative Decline, 1870–1995* (1997). David Marquand examines the contrast between the economic postwar consensus and neoliberalism in *The Unprincipled Society* (1988), and Bernard Heffernan shows the connection between Thatcherite and New Labour policies in *New Labour and Thatcherism* (2000). *The Impact of the Euro: Debating Britain's Future* (Bainbridge et al. 2000) or the reader *From EMS to EMU: 1979 to 1999 and Beyond* (Cobham and Zis 1999) explain the nature of Britain's relationship with the eurozone. Robert Peston's *Brown's Britain* (2006) reviews Gordon Brown's long tenure as chancellor of the exchequer, and Vincent Cable's *The Storm* (2009) analyzes the effects of Brown's economic strategies in the context of recession. See also the book's website for a detailed discussion of Britain's welfare model and social expenditures.

⑪

British Environmental Policy
From Smog to Sustainability

It may come as a disappointment to foreign visitors that "a foggy day in London Town" is a phenomenon that no longer gets you down. The Clean Air Act (1956), together with slum clearance, helped to banish the fogs known as "pea soupers" that were part of Britain's urban and suburban winter scene. Subsequent clean-air legislation helped alleviate chronic lung diseases, especially among the elderly. The end of foggy nights and days left school children after the 1950s with no excuse for late arrival or the bonus of an afternoon off to walk rather than bus-ride in the general direction of home (as the author remembers). In addition to the positive health gains there were technological advances as well, because as legally stipulated smokeless coal–generated energy became more expensive, "clean" nuclear power generation was proffered as the future of energy production, and coal-fired trains turned to diesel, then electric, motive force. But while London's fog abated, gasoline-driven transportation emitted ever-increasing levels of carbon fuel pollution.

This early (and successful) example illustrates a number of features of British environmental policy up to the 1990s. The first is that it was *reactive*—fog killed over 4,000 people in 1952 and also disrupted the economy. The cure was *regulation* administered by local governments. Second, "solving" one problem created others: for much of the next twenty years nuclear energy was challenged as a possible replacement because of its potentially brutal impact on the environment and danger to human health. In the 1970s natural gas and oil from the North Sea came on line but proved over time to be expensive to produce and limited in supply. Imported oil was subject to world-market price fluctuations and source insecurity—and produced its own environmental problems. Third, smoke-free air cost both the public and private purse—in inspection administration and in investment for clean(er) technology or alternative energy sources. Local governments charged with administering Whitehall's clean-air regulations varied in their implementation of them, as economic pressures and conditions affected their enthusiasm. Once visibility had been improved, the political necessity of clean air—at both local and central level—was less evident. As Anthony Downs has pointed out, political concern for the environment has often been short lived, as public demand for action declines in the wake of political action and the recognition that continuing policy activity presents costs that may involve sacrifice in other policy areas (Downs 1973).

THE CHARACTERISTICS OF BRITISH ENVIRONMENTAL POLICY

As chapter 9 has illustrated, Britain's policy style might be generalized as consultative and negotiated consensus that tends toward incremental rather than radical change (Richardson and Jordan 1987). Until the considerable impact of an EU agenda, environmental policy was embraced within this consensus machine. More particularly, as a policy arena, it was further characterized by: a low political profile; variations in local implementation; reactive rather than proactive development; a reliance on voluntary, informal, and self-regulatory procedures; and a consequential reliance on local technical officials who, through close negotiation with affected interests, would seek practical solutions to particular environmental problems rather than legally derived national standards or targets (Lowe and Ward 1998). These characteristics describe the domestic policy process that was to mesh with EU environmental policy as it emerged during the last fifteen years of the twentieth century.

Historically, however, it must be pointed out that Britain could boast a solid list of European firsts in domestic environmental policy initiatives. As the first industrialized economy, Britain was first to experience consequent environmental problems; thus it could be claimed that Britain had the oldest pollution-control machinery in the world. Much of this, however, amounted to "end of pipe" solutions, where tall chimneys and sewage pipes moved pollution from one environment to another. More successful were attempts at nature conservation and, most significantly, town and country planning legislation (1947), especially after World War II (see table 11.1). It must also be pointed out that Britain played a significant role in early international environmentalism, especially with regard to fauna and flora preservation and marine pollution, "in keeping with its post-colonial outlook and the style and content reflected in its position as a major scientific and cultural power" (Lowe and Ward 1998: 10). The focus, however, was primarily domestic and with little concern for cross-frontier coopera-

Table 11.1.   The Development of British Environmental Legislation

Date	Legislation
1947	Town and Country Planning Act
1949	National Parks and to the Countryside Access Act
1954	Protection of Birds Act
1956	Clean Air Act
1969	Royal Commission on Environmental Pollution (permanent advisory body)
1973	Water Act
1974	Control of Pollution Act
	Health and Safety at Work Act
1976	Endangered Species Act
1980	Local Government Planning and Land Act
1981	Wildlife and Countryside Act
1982	Derelict Land Act
1985	Food and Environment Protection Act
1989	Water Act
	Air Quality Standards Act
	HM Inspectorate of Pollution (amalgamated from several inspectorates)
1990	Environment Protection Act
1991	Planning and Compensation Act
1994	Sustainable Development: The UK Strategy: White Paper
1995	Environment Act
1997	National Air Quality Strategy (periodic review)
1998	Scotland and Wales Acts (devolved environmental responsibilities)
2000	Transport Act and Ten-Year Plan
	Countryside and Rights of Way Act and Rural Affairs White Paper
2003	Waste and Emissions Trading Act
	Household Waste Recycling Act
2005	End-of-Life (vehicles) Regulation
	Clean Neighbourhood and Environmental Act
2007	Greenhouse Gas Trading Scheme Regulations

tion and regulation—Britain remains an offshore island with prevailing westerly winds and a circulation of currents that takes, fortuitously, domestic pollution abroad. So, through to the 1980s, British governments had little experience of or interest in international management of and solutions to environmental problems (Lowe and Ward 1998: 10).

The Greening of British Government

Since the 2005 general election, both Labour and Conservative Parties have promoted environmental issues to the upper reaches of crowded electoral agendas. Three government departments—the Department for Environment, Food and Rural Affairs (DEFRA); the Department for Communities and Local Government (DCLG); and the Department for International

Development (DFID)—in different ways, make "sustainability" a major aspect of their raison d'être (see textbox 11.1). Prime ministers Blair and Brown have associated themselves directly with support for and actions to implement the Kyoto Protocol and put issues of international climate change at the heart of Britain's environmental policy (DEFRA 2004). Similarly the leader of the Conservatives, David Cameron, has closely associated himself and his party with a range of green issues and images.

We may trace the emergence of green issues as mainstream politics over three periods. From the end of World War II to the early 1970s, concerns about environmental issues were reactive; piecemeal; domestically driven; and not disassociated from the drive for urban renewal, land use, and the preservation of a "green belt" from economic development and urban sprawl to mitigate the worst excesses of postwar industrialization. Rachel Carson's book *Silent Spring* (1962) challenged loosely managed environmentalism within economic growth and, indeed, the rosy future of industrial society. This was the first of an emerging critical literature that queried the sustainability of rapid economic growth. The Club of Rome Report (1972) projected a collapse of world ecology by 2000. A UN Conference on the Human Environment in 1972 led to the creation of the UN Environment Programme (UNEP). The establishment of international pressure groups such as Friends of the Earth (1969) and Greenpeace (1972) enhanced a growing British domestic environmental debate. The incoming Conservative government (1970) established the first Department of Environment (DOE) in part as a response to these pressures.

However the period 1970–1988 proved disappointing for a rapidly emerging environmentalist lobby in Britain. Despite the creation of a Green Party in 1973 and the adoption of environmental policy promises in the main parties' manifestos, the environment failed to make progress up the policy agenda. Labour's struggle to sustain Keynesian-driven economic growth in the 1970s, and the Conservatives neoliberal renewal in the 1980s, ensured that environmental policy was "nothing more than a token declaration, there to look good, but achieving little" (Robinson quoted in Fisher et al. 2003: 330). There were however, some notable successes, such as the campaign to switch from lead-based to lead-free gasoline. That campaign was instrumental in changing not just British government but also EC policy (Long 1998: 110). Earlier "firsts" that led to subsequent EC legislation included regulation of Health and Safety at Work, associated with harmful substances, and waste disposal in the Control of Pollution Act (both 1974). However, in these early years of EU membership, governments did little to promote in Brussels what was perceived in official government circles as Britain's advanced status in environmental affairs. Indeed, early Commission proposals for member states

Textbox 11.1. Environmental Governance: The Whitehall Actors

Title	Functions
Department of Environment, Food and Rural Affairs (DEFRA)	Includes animal health; farming, food, fisheries; rural affairs; sustainable development; wildlife and environmental protection.
Department for Communities and Local Government (DCLG)	Includes urban regeneration; housing; planning and local government.
Department of Transport (D of T)	Includes sustainable transport; environmental impact
Department for International Development (DFID)	Includes supports for combating climate change; sustainable agriculture/forestry; water and sanitation prospects
Department for Business, Enterprise and Regulatory Reform (BERR)	Includes sustainably energy; WEEE Directive
Foreign and Commonwealth Office (FCO)	Includes International negotiation on global warming (with DEFRA)

Policy-Coordinating Machinery

Cabinet subcommittees for Energy and the Environment and Housing, Planning, and Regeneration; also cabinet committees on Local Government and the Regions, Africa Trade, Families, and others have interests in the environment and sustainable development.

to consider statistical limits to pollutants were criticized as inferior and inappropriate to the British pragmatic approach to the subject (Lowe and Ward 1998: 18).

This insular and complacent perspective was exposed as the EU commenced its march toward a regional environmental perspective. The first Environmental Action Programme (EAP) (1973–1978) and its successors recognized the need for concerted action in an area that was politically invisible when the Treaties of Rome were signed in 1957. In an economically expanding market, the need to mitigate the pollutant element of production, trading, and consumption became necessary for both economic and political reasons: first to ensure that differing national standards did not form a non-tariff barrier to interstate trade and, second, to meet the public and specific lobby demands for improved "quality of life"—a factor loosely incorporated into Article 2 of the Treaty of Rome—"that the Community shall . . . promote throughout the Community, a harmonious development of economic activities, a continuous and balanced expansion [and] an accelerated raising of the standards of living." This somewhat loose legal justification for environmental policy was made solid by Articles 130R–130T of the Single European Act (1986), which were specifically devoted to the establishment of environmental standards as a vital aspect in the completion of the European Market. However, throughout most of the 1980s, Conservative administrations resisted what was perceived as the Commission's unwarranted and legally dubious encroachment into a set of fundamentally domestic policy issues.

Indeed, in the early years of the Thatcher period the concept was perceived as, at best, an irritant and, at worst, as a diametrically opposed factor in the perfection of a market-led growth economy. In a period of mass unemployment, environmental concern seemed a luxury. The tag of "the dirty man of Europe" seemed appropriate as the Commission and several Continental states criticized what were now perceived as limited and pernicious British attitudes to emergent common European environmental goals.

During the early and mid-1980s, as the EU developed community positions in a growing range of environmental areas, the British government found itself at loggerheads with Council and Commission over directives seeking to bring EU standards to sea bathing water, drinking water, and contamination from radioactive material in the Irish sea. At the same time, Britain was accused of being the source of deforestation in Scandinavia—the acid rain controversy. From 1987, the legal basis for EU environmental policy within the SEA, together with an emerging base of comparative statistical data, underscored EU-British divergences in policy and practice—all of which were not assisted by the Eurosceptical character of the Thatcher government. As we discussed in chapter 7, many

British-based environmental lobby groups shifted their attention away from Whitehall to Brussels, perceiving the Commission and European Parliament as allies. At the end of the decade, over one-third of complaints concerning noncompliance with directives were aimed at Britain, and the threat of legal action by the Commission "transformed what might have been comparatively minor wranglings . . . into matters of high politics" (Lowe and Ward 1998: 21).

THE ENVIRONMENT IN MAINSTREAM POLITICS?

The third period, beginning in the late 1980s, represents a sea change in British governmental attitudes toward environmental policy. A range of factors contributed to this. In 1986 the Chernobyl nuclear explosion illustrated to British island folk their vulnerability to international environmental disasters. Radioactive fallout on Welsh and Scottish highlands and the impact this had on farming communities was evidence enough. Some twenty years later, radiation levels in parts of North Wales still remain abnormally high. In 1984 the UN-instigated Bruntland Report introduced the notion and importance of sustainable development and the necessary political change to achieve it. The 1989 European Parliament elections resulted in a Green Party vote of 15 percent. Though no British Green EP seats were won under the then first-past-the-post (FPTP) system, this electoral "success" produced countervailing responses from the mainstream parties. The most startling conversion was that of Mrs. Thatcher, who, at the September 1988 Conservative Party conference, announced that "the core of Tory philosophy and the case for protecting the environment are the same. . . . And this government intends to meet the terms of [its environmental] lease in full." Institutional changes were to follow, and a broad examination of environmental policy was contained in a White Paper *This Common Inheritance* (DOE 1990). British negotiators adopted a more positive role in EU forums, accepting responsibility for acid rain and playing a positive role at the Earth Summit in Rio (1992). The post-Rio era has widened the environmental debate to "second generation" issues such as biodiversity and the current concerns over global warming and climate change. This global dimension to environmental policy has had consequences for British-EU environmental strategies as the scope for a concerted EU regional position in international forums has increased (see below).

The convergence of EU and British environmental policy emerged as a particular feature of the Major administration during the 1990s. There was, until the accession of the new "green" member states (Sweden, Finland, and Austria), a general easing of EU environmental legislation, as the issues of EMU and policy toward Central and East European Countries (CEECs) took center stage. The TEU, while extending QMV to environmental policy, also introduced the concept of subsidiarity to this policy area—a step strongly endorsed by the British EU presidency in 1992. This involved a step toward the softer EU policy instruments of national framework directives and voluntary codes—more acceptable to a Conservative government under considerable internal strain regarding EU-British relations in general. Thus, despite the trauma of the British beef BSE crisis in the mid-1990s, the general direction of British environmental policy has been toward convergence with the EU and a resultant pressure for higher standards in Britain (Lowe and Ward 1998: 28). The impact of this Europeanization on environmental policy outcomes is examined below. First, however, we will explore the political actors involved in the process of creating contemporary environmental policy in Britain.

GREEN ACTORS AND FACTORS

Central Government

The changes to the structure and competences of what was originally called the Department of the Environment (DOE) in 1970 indicate not just differing policy emphases over time but also, perhaps, doubts in the minds of political leaders as to what environmental policy should encompass. Thus transportation was moved out of the DOE in 1973; back in, in 1997; and then out again in 2001. In 1997 the title Department for Environment, Transport and Regions (DETR) reflected the incoming (New Labour) government's concern with devolved government and public transportation issues. By 2001 the emphasis had changed, as a series of rail accidents and a food and rural crisis led to the creation of the Department for Environment, Food and Rural Affairs (DEFRA), with transportation regaining its independent status. While each incarnation (DOE, DETR, DEFRA) represented both Conservative and Labour governments' concern to give the environment a public presence, the lack of agreement about what elements of public policy to join up in order to create environmental policy is evident and seems to reflect immediate political concerns rather than commitment to any environmental "ideal." In 2006, as part of a cabinet reshuffle to revive the creditability of a government beset by ministerial errors, Prime Minister Blair created, from the body of the Office of Deputy Prime Minister, the Department for Communities and Local Government (DCLG), with a responsibility to promote community cohesion, urban regeneration planning, and local government. The foreign secretary was, however, a key player in the 2006 British presidency, alongside the secretary of state for the environment, and has played a significant role in the post-Kyoto agenda.

The task of policy coordination is not easy, given the splits in functional responsibilities. Within DEFRA, a significant group of civil servants, the Environmental Protection Group (EPG), has the task of driving policy initiatives within a large department whose responsibilities extend to the farmer, the food and fishing industries, and the consumer. The EPG has increased its presence within and outside of its home department, but still works with fellow bureaucrats with their own interests to promote. Controversial arguments, for instance to cull the badger population to attack bovine tuberculosis, as many farmers suggest, present an obvious dilemma for DEFRA, which faces opposition to this idea from conservationists and support for it from farmers. The problems ensuing from not having responsibility for transportation or urban planning are similarly evident when dealing with such issues as aircraft pollution or road usage. Since 1997 the appointment of "green ministers" within every government department to champion the ecological consequences of their department's policies was a powerful political statement indicating the "mainstreaming" of green issues throughout Whitehall. The existence of a cabinet committee for energy and the environment and the stress on "sustainability" within all departments of state have underscored the salience of environmental policy recently. Yet both lobby groups and, as we shall see, the European Commission dispute departmental policy, and outcomes on environmental issues remain mixed. As an example, what to do about carbon emissions from aircraft, especially with the increase in "low-cost flights" throughout Europe, or agreement to build a third Heathrow runway, proved particularly problematic for the three departments involved (DEFRA, Transport, and BERR). It is further complicated by its EU-wide (and indeed) global dimensions.

Official Advisors and Central Implementation

The permanent Royal Commission on Environmental Pollution set up in 1969 had, for many years, argued the case for a coordinating body to manage diverse inspectorates involved in Britain's environmental protection. The Environment Agency (EA) was created in 1996 to unify and enhance the inspectoral role in water conservation and quality and waste disposal in England and Wales. A Scottish Environmental Protection Agency (SEPA) has similar responsibilities but also includes aspects of air pollution that in England and Wales remain the responsibility of local government. The EA enjoys a higher public profile than the previous inspectorates and has prosecuted, shamed, and educated polluters more rigorously and consistently. However, the separation of Scottish and English/Welsh inspectoral functions is indicative of traditional decentralized regulatory structures. This separation is also apparent in the division between urban/industrial environmental protection and rural conservation, which are each the responsibility of a separate agency (see textbox 11.2). Advice and, since 2006, watchdog responsibilities for sustainable development are undertaken by the Sustainable Development Commission (SDC). It is through the concept of "sustainability" that the coherence of environmental policy may be more effectively progressed and, importantly, is made more politically viable (see below).

Textbox II.2. Official Advice, Watchdogs, and Regulation

Agency	Responsibilities
Environment Agency (EA) and Scottish Environmental Protection Agency (SEPA)	licensing/controlling water use, conservation and quality; waste disposal disposal regulation; air quality (SEPA only)
Natural England	nature conservation; sustainable leisure; landscape protection; and rural development (separate agencies for Scotland/Wales)
Royal Commission on Environmental Pollution	independent advice to government.
Sustainable Development Commission (SDC)	advice, appraisal, and monitoring of government departments/policies
House of Commons Environment Committee	appraises work of DEFRA
House of Commons Environmental Audit Committee	monitors central government and other public bodies on environmental protection and sustainable development

Supra- and Subnational Actors

Of policy areas discussed in this book, the environment lends itself to the conceptual lens of multilevel governance fairly convincingly. Historically, environmental matters were dealt with at the local level on the one hand and, on the other, contemporary policy is intertwined with EU and international institutions, conventions, and treaties. Moreover, devolution of powers to Scotland, Wales, and Northern Ireland reinforced a further multilevel dimension to this complex agenda.

Britain in an EU Environment

As we have suggested, most British environmental legislation emanates from EU sources. In brief, the EU institutions involved are the Commission, in particular DG Environment (DGENV); the Environment Council of the Council of Ministers; the EP, whose Committee of the Environment, Public Health and Consumer Protection is a driving force; and, through European case law, the ECJ. The European Environment Agency provides an independent source of scientific knowledge from which EU actors may draw policy supports. Within the EU policy process "the Commission is present throughout the entire policy cycle" (Lenschow 2005: 312). As with DEFRA, the problem of bringing other bureaucratic sectors on board is problematic, and DGENV often finds it politic to sell environmental policy in terms of political and economic advantage and de-emphasizing regulatory burdens or costs to national budgets. In seeking to progress potential legislation, DGENV seeks out not just advice from EU-based interest groups, but also support from national officials on related committees within the EU's comitology (committee system) process. In this way, resistance to policy proposals within the Council of Ministers may be minimized.

The EP is the most enthusiastic of EU institutions for environmental policy, and through co-decision, is integrally involved in the shape of EU legislation. At this writing (2009) the Group of Green/European Free Alliance makes up only 7 percent, or ten MEPs, of whom two are British.

In general terms, the environmental politics of the Council may be crudely divided between richer northern states (Germany, Sweden, and Denmark) and laggard states of Southern and Eastern Europe (Portugal, Greece, and Slovakia), and Britain sits somewhere in the middle. The ECJ has, since enactment of the SEA (1987) and TEU (1992), played a significant role "in emancipating the environmental agenda from the single market agenda" (Lenschow 2005: 317). Infringement procedures, initiated mostly by the Commission against member states, led to the Court seeking compliance with the threat of financial sanctions. Thus, legal action was taken against the British government in 2004 on two occasions—over tardiness in introducing legislation to protect wild birds and failure to comply with EU legislation on environmental impact assessments (EIAs). The threat of a massive ECJ fine of several thousand euros per day, as in a case against Spain in 2003 for failing to reach EU bathing water standards, is enough to produce compliance.

The EU also plays a significant role, on behalf of its member states, as an international environmental actor. If 80 percent of British EU legislation has its origins in Brussels then, so one Commission official claimed, one-third of contemporary EU legislation emanates from international agreements (Lenschow 2005: 323). Despite problems associated with the legal position of the EU—for most international agreements are signed by sovereign states, the EC (which enjoys formal legal personality in international law within its areas of competence) is a signatory to many so called "mixed agreements" alongside its member states. These include the Vienna Convention on the Ozone Layer (1985), the subsequent Montreal Protocol (1987), and the Climate Change Convention (1994). Despite problems over who actually speaks for the EU (EU presidency or the Commission?), member states, including Britain, recognize the regional clout offered by Community leadership and communitarian positions. Most recently, the EU has given legs to a flagging Kyoto Protocol and, for some environmentalists, has established "a dimension of green regional actorness" (Bretherton and Vogler 2006: 110). The consequences of this international dimension for British environmental policy are dealt with below.

The International Context

The international dimension to environmentalism is not new to British policy makers. Governments played a major role in seeking international agreements over such issues as marine pollution and protecting endangered species throughout the last century. Britain and several other European states were signatories to such international agreements as the Man and Biosphere Programme (1970), the World Conservation Strategy (1980), and the Convention on Biological Diversity (1992). Since then, the recognition of "second-generation problems" that cluster around the issues of global warming and biodiversity has rewritten both the environmental agenda and the arena within which domestic policy makers operate. The two conventions signed at the Rio Earth Summit (1992)—on climate change and biodiversity conservation—and the Agenda 21 program on sustainable development created an international stage that former prime minister Blair strode across, from his early rebukes of US laggardness on climate change at the G7 Summit (June 1997) to the Gleneagles G8 Dialogue on Climate Change, Clean Energy and Sustainable Development

launched in 2005. The Blair administration also cooperated enthusiastically with the EU in promoting the Kyoto Protocol "for the sake of greater
effectiveness in pursuit of shared and common international goals" (Smith
2006: 169). His successor, Gordon Brown, advertised his commitment to
international action by joining forces with President Obama to push for a
low-carbon industrial revolution at the 2009 London G20 Summit. This
was to act as a precursor to a later climate change Summit in Copenhagen
(*Independent*, Sunday, 8 March 2009).

The complexity and urgency of global environmental politics have also
contributed to a new agenda of "sustainability" that, for both EU and
British policy makers, has meant changes to the scope, priorities, and organization of the policy process. As early as 1987, the UN Bruntland Report linked economic and social development and environmental
objectives in a "paradigm" that implied compromises, tradeoffs, and policy linkage necessitating a "joined-up" approach within multilevel governance. Kyoto targets in carbon emission levels, for instance, have
concentrated attention on transportation and energy policies that inevitably have global and EU as well as domestic facets. The 2001 Labour
Manifesto commitment to a 23 percent cut in greenhouse gas emissions
by 2020 is challenged some seven years later by problems of recession, oil
costs, and a dwindling supply of natural gas anticipated for energy generation. Reluctance to implement a major public shift from (private) road
transportation to bus/rail transportation, and to deal with the polluting
impact of cheap air travel, collides with international and EU constraints
and domestic electoral promises. However, a combination of internationally negotiated agreements, EU directives, and a growing public awareness
of global and domestic environmental issues has now placed the environment in a prominent position on the moral agenda for any aspirant to political power in Britain.

Subnational Environmental Governance

Historically, local government in Britain has played an integral role in "first
generation" environmental policy, pollution control, and public health.
Through the application of planning law, and in particular land-use planning, Britain's local authorities have contributed to conservation and
economic development in their areas. English local authorities remain responsible for air quality and waste collection and disposal, among other environmental functions. Local governments have a key role in achieving
recycling targets, now a significant aspect of EU pollution and sustainability control. More recently, second-generation issues of climate control and
sustainability have also found their way into local government through the
Rio Summit initiative, Agenda 21, as successive central governments have

recognized the potential for delivering sustainable development through locally derived Agenda 21 strategies (see the book's website). EU regulations/standards have presented local authorities with imposed standards and practices, often not necessarily from Brussels, but from overzealous Whitehall intervention. There are similar concerns about the decline of local discretion in planning regulation.

Scottish and Welsh devolution has, however, created new subregional environmental actors and, while the Scottish Parliament has broader legislative capacity, both it and the Welsh Assembly have unique responsibility for progressing sustainable development agendas, and they have taken this seriously. The Scottish Assembly has considerable powers in the field of transportation and, following the London government's decision, has mooted the idea of road charges for Scottish cities. Finally, the central government's regional offices in England have responsibility for ensuring implementation of a sustainability agenda both on behalf of central government and in vetting EU funding when it is sought for regional development (see chapter 9).

While the actors and character of the subnational agencies contributing to environmental policy may be changing, they remain, together with the functional central agencies, a vital aspect of both the multilevel governance of pollution control and the broader and new agenda of global warming, biodiversity, and sustainability.

Lobbying and Issue-Based Politics

According to the Charity Commission, in 2005 there were 1,841 registered charities with environmental improvement listed in their objectives. The growth of a green lobby and the impact that this has had on the main political parties and government is well documented (Garner 2000; Jordan 2002; Lowe and Ward 1998; McCormick 1991). Older, single-issue conservation and protection groups, such as the National Trust or the Royal Society for the Protection of Birds (RSPB), have been augmented since the 1970s by more broad-based ecological groups such as Greenpeace and Friends of the Earth. These and other groups highlight the connectivity, internationalism, and depth of contemporary green issues, and they provide often-controversial analyses and high-profile activities to publicize particular concerns.

Periodic campaigns, often on the back of national and international environmental crises, have shifted the emphasis of public concern as well as made environmental politics ubiquitous. The safety of nuclear energy generation, food scares, anti–road building campaigns, animal rights issues, land-use planning disputes, and water shortages and/or flooding are persistent concerns around which both established and anomic interests have formed. As an example, nuclear energy safety was a public issue for periods in the 1970s, 1980s, and 1990s and is currently back on the political agenda as the government struggles with an energy policy that seeks to square the circle of safe, cheap, secure, plentiful, and ecologically acceptable energy supplies for the next generation. Thus the issue of nuclear safety collides with the more general imperative of coping with climate change.

The complexity of environmentalism today is reflected in the character of the environmental lobby in Britain. Direct protest has taken the form of local, national, and international activity. Attempts to stop road building (Twyford Down in the 1980s and Newbury in the mid-1990s); the London Countryside Alliance demonstrations across a range of rural issues (2004); and the cross-national Greenpeace campaign against the disposal of an oil rig, Brent Spar (1995) illustrate the multilevel nature of environmental protest. Environmental umbrella groups, such as the Institute for European Environmental Policy (IEEP) and more recently the Green Alliance, indicate the interrelated nature of group interests in the field and a willingness to campaign on a broad environmental front. Membership in environmental groups and the associated funding is currently strong. Thus the National Trust has around 2.7 million members, and the RSPB over 1 million. Membership in the Labour Party was, in 2005, less than 200,000 (Maloney 2006).

Inevitably, powerful lobby groups provide opportunities for "informed" opinion, and government agencies have been open to their inclusion in policy formulation. Thus, the Green Alliance claimed "a central role in the UK environmental movement working closely with decision makers in government and business." Along with the IEEP, the Alliance was commissioned by DEFRA to identify the key priorities [for the EU environmental agenda] for the 2005 UK presidency. It also claimed "a coordination process of engagement with the ODPM to inject an environmental dimension in the strategic thinking of the department" (Green Alliance 2006). Involved in this process were the National Trust, RSPB, World Wildlife Fund, and other pressure groups.

The growth of the environmental lobby has played a significant role in the dissemination of knowledge regarding environmental issues for public and policy makers alike. This is particularly significant for the formulation of environmental policies and is reflected in the relative openness of the "policy communities" associated with green issues. However, lobbyists are conscious of the opportunities that pressure at EU level can exert on British decision makers, and alliances at EU and international level have, on occasion, been effectively exploited (see below).

The Greening of Political Parties

The role of political parties in the articulation and aggregation of British environmental policy is worth comparing with its German counterpart. The British Green Party, though predating the German Greens (Die Grunen), has failed to make any significant impact on local or national politics in terms of electoral success. In the 2005 general election the Greens won 1.1 percent of the total vote—up 0.4 percent on the 2001 result. They have never won a House of Commons seat, but have 7 seats in the Scottish Assembly and two seats in the London Assembly (2008). They have yet to gain a seat in the Welsh Assembly. At the local level in England and Wales they have relatively strong representation in some areas (Brighton, Lancaster, Lewisham, Oxford, and Stroud) but overall hold only 115 seats (2008). It is at European level that the Greens have performed best, and in 1989 the party won 15 percent of the vote but gained no EP seats under the then FPPS. The situation was unusually favorable, with the issue of Chernobyl still in the public mind and a divided Liberal/Social Democrat center. The 2009 EP elections, held under PR, resulted in an 8.6 percent Green vote and 2 Green MEPs. The lack of domestic electoral success is partly the result of the iniquity of the FPTP system but also the reluctance of the party to organize itself along conventional party lines, with the 2009 EP elections causing a party split between "realists and fundamentalists." The marginality of the British Greens may be contrasted with the pivotal position of Die Grunen, who, in 1998, joined a Social Democrat coalition and remained in power, with three cabinet ministers, until 2005. Their position was assisted by a more favorable PR electoral system and a willingness to make compromises at Länder and federal level in order to achieve national recognition.

If the Green Party has remained marginal to British electoral politics when compared with the major lobby groups, it has played its part in repositioning the more established parties in environmental politics. The Liberal Democrats, especially after the 1989 EP elections, have presented strong green credentials in their manifesto commitments. But the more significant changes are evident in the Labour Party and, most recently, the Conservatives under the leadership of David Cameron. A number of factors have combined, through a process of push-me, pull-you, to lift green policies to prominence in British politics.

The British media has consistently highlighted the overwhelming evidence of global warming. Catastrophic events such as Hurricane Katrina in 2006 and the more localized water shortage during the summer months in southeast England (2006) and widespread flooding (in the summers of 2007 and 2008) have reinforced these concerns. The relationship between global warming, carbon-based energy sources, the limits and insecurity of energy supply, and the search for "renewable" energy, have spotlighted the threat to the sustainability of living standards in a country that has enjoyed several years of economic prosperity. While some commentators have pointed to the difficulty of sustaining public interest in green issues, and others have suggested that the environment as a political issue only enjoys priority in economic good times, catastrophes, real or anticipated, are difficult to exclude from the political agenda for long (Downs 1973; Weale 1992).

Thus, New Labour's commitment to sustainability since 1997 has involved a strong international stance on Kyoto targets, with Britain to reduce greenhouse carbon emissions by 23 percent of the 1990 level and to adopt a recycling target for household waste (35% by 2015). This is not without controversy, because of the implied need for nuclear energy policy to achieve 10 percent of Britain's energy needs by 2010. The barriers to achieving these targets have proved both economic and political. Energy plans to phase down coal-fired production have hit at least medium-term problems, as North Sea natural gas supplies have run down faster than planned and as replacement imports have proved expensive. The intended switch from coal to gas generation to around 60 percent by 2005 still meant reliance on 80 percent of supplies coming from the Middle East, Africa, and Russia. By 2006, the arguments for nuclear provision to fill the "gap" while alternative clean technologies are developed were being put forcefully (Wintour and Adams 2006). More recently, the Brown government has called for a carbon-capture system for coal-fired power generation as a compulsory aspect of any public financial support for new commercial energy ventures.

Labour's early commitment to an integrated transportation policy, which included a reduction in car use, was seriously hampered by a series of rail accidents that emanated from a historic lack of investment in track and railway safety. Improvements have only recently begun to percolate through for rail users. Gasoline costs in 2000 produced fuel protests that led to the abandonment of "escalator" fuel taxes as an environmental charge. Other public pressures, such as resistance to the rapid development of genetically modified crops (2002), and a campaign to improve the sourcing and thus quality of children's school meals (2005), have changed government policies. Concern over food quality and public health have been reinforced, and produced policy changes after recent animal disease crises— most notably foot-and-mouth disease in cattle and sheep (2001). Rural tensions over fuel and transportation costs, rights of way for walkers, and the banning of fox hunting have sustained the environmental and urban/rural debate between the political parties throughout Labour's administration. It is in this context that David Cameron, elected as leader of the Conservative Party in 2005, commenced a review of Tory environmental policies that, if implemented, will place the issue (as Blair persistently argued) at the top of the public agenda as an electoral issue. However a sustained period of economic recession may produce a diminution in party political enthusiasm for costly environmental policies unless presented as part of Britain's economic renewal.

THE EUROPEANIZATION OF BRITISH ENVIRONMENTAL POLICY

"British environmental politics and policy have been profoundly affected by European integration" (Lowe and Ward 1998: 285). The authors cite the transnational nature of many environmental problems that make it both logical and easier to work within an EU arena; there is also a higher threshold of public support for environmental action than for a collective monetary or foreign policy and, finally, since the 2005 election there has been little conflict between the major political parties over either the worthiness of environmental policy or the need for collective action to solve problems. Politicians are thus much less likely to incur a sneering tabloid headline attacking an EU directive designed to recycle old auto components, which for most thinking (or even unthinking) Britons would be perceived as "a good thing."

But perhaps this fair wind for EU supranational action has held only because environmental policy has been of secondary importance when compared to the more contentious issues of EMU—foreign or immigration policy. What happens when, having placed environmental concerns high on their agendas, political parties are faced with incorporating EU directives that involve economic costs and potentially negative political reaction—involving energy policy, carbon taxes, and more expensive technologies to achieve CO_2 targets? How much has changed since the 1980 "dirty man of Europe" jibe goaded more positive action from a skeptical Thatcher administration? In responding to these questions, we commence with an evaluation of the congruence of British and EU environmental policy objectives: Do values now meet in the climate of climate change?

Common Regional Objectives

The EU is now within its sixth Environmental Action Plan (2002–2012). Since the first (1973–1976), these frameworks have developed in scope, to encompass such issues as climate change and biodiversity. As well as the explicit references to international perspectives and solutions, the objectives also involve the "greening of the market" and the need to establish an "educative dialogue" between citizens and other "stakeholders" to encourage a broad ownership of the actions involved (see textbox 11.3). A progression of policy principles may be observed that include the *preven-*

**Textbox 11.3. The Sixth Environmental
Action Program (2002–2012)**

The EAP identifies four environmental areas:

- climate change
- nature and biodiversity
- environment, health, and quality of life
- natural resources and waste

The Commission has prepared seven thematic strategies: air pollution; prevention and recycling of waste; protection/conservation of the marine environment; soil; sustainable use of pesticides; sustainable use of resources; urban environment.

The strategies are considered in long-term perspective and will identify the most appropriate means to achieve objectives; that is, the least burdensome and most cost-effective possible legislation is to be simplified and proportionate to the task in hand.

Implementation is through the following avenues:

- the achievement of common baselines for member states via effective legislative enforcement
- integration of environmental concerns and solutions
- blending different approaches—not just legislation
- promoting participation and partnership with businesses, other NGOs, and social partners—via open information and education

All of this is in the context of the Sustainable Development Strategy. This link is to be evident in the inclusion of environmental priorities when setting objectives for growth, competitiveness, and employment.

Source: Adapted from www.europa.eu/environment/new prg.

tative (precautionary) principle and the polluter-pays principle (from EAP 1977–1981); the need for *integration* of environmental policies, impact assessment, and the development of clean technologies (1982–1986); the establishment of *legally enforceable standards* and their effective implementation (1987–1992); and, significantly, the implementation of the concept of *sustainable development* in sectoral areas such as transportation, energy, agriculture, tourism, and industry (1993–2000).

Sustainable development has become a bridge between the often-conflicting perspectives of producers and environmentalists and, as such, has proven an important political formula for agreements and cooperation between member states. For the EU, sustainability allows the recognition of environmental perspectives in the Lisbon Agenda (for economic transformation); makes more palatable the considerable implications of the Kyoto Protocol; presents a conditionality for overseas aid that has some moral justification; and provides a linkage between business, environmental agencies, and government. Inevitably, DG Environment battles hard to sustain the Lisbon Agenda's environmental thrust against those pursuing its economic aims.

For British governments from the 1990s, sustainability has proved a similar comfort for politicians seeking "realistic" environmental solutions. "Sustainability" was adopted, promoted, and eventually institutionalized by successive governments, and it is evident in the organization of cabinet and ministerial offices and the work of the SDC. The notion of sustainability was embraced under the British presidency at the Cardiff Summit of 1998, from which member states committed to the development of an integrated approach and to share "best practices" for environmental policy making. Later, at the Gothenburg Summit in 2001, sustainability became an official objective in the EU's bilateral negotiations for international development. For some commentators, it now forms "part of the identity that the Union is constructing for itself" (Bretherton and Vogler 2006: 104)—and in the context of this construction Britain has played a leading role (see below). While sustainability has international roots in several treaties and conventions, the EU's demands on its member states, and thus Britain, to meet (for instance) CO_2 reduction targets, provide a pressing regional basis for policy action.

The EU has also forced on Britain "a more preventative, source based approach to policy making" (Jordan 2003: 12). While this judgment applies to some policies, for instance air, sea, and drinking-water quality, it is less appropriate in others, for instance land-use planning and biodiversity protection "where traditional British notions of environmental problem solving" (practical compromise solutions) still apply (Jordan 2003: 12). Fixed numerical environmental standards, and the publication of comparative EU statistics, have led to a begrudging acceptance of principles based on targets; maximum emission statements; and, importantly, precaution. This acceptance has also produced a more proactive contribution to the making of EU environmental policy in Brussels by British policy elites.

Britain, EU Environmental Policy, and Integration

Britain has passed through distinct periods of interaction with the EU. Before the formalization of EU environmental policy through the SEA (1987), with some exceptions, British (mainly junior) ministers and civil servants took either a benign interest in what was perceived as a relatively unimportant (and nonenforceable) policy dimension or, during the 1980s, a blocking role, vetoing Environmental Council proposals in such areas as ozone depletion and dumping at sea. Once the legal basis of EU environmental policy was established and EU policies emerged at pace, consider-able effort was made to "upload" British policy. This change reflected a rapid policy learning curve created by both domestic demands for gov-ernment action and a more willing acceptance of an EU policy agenda set by environmentally active member states such as Germany and the Netherlands. The Department of Environment, especially under the lead-ership of the Conservative minister John Gummer in the 1990s, com-menced not just an organizational restructuring to intercede at European level with purpose, but also a European professional program to educate civil servants and to provide links between member states and EU insti-tutions (Jordan 2000). The DOE moved from policy taker to policy shaper, monitoring areas of strength associated with environmental integration processes, frameworks for local action, and other agents of good environ-mental governance. DOE officials have learned to utilize communitarian tactics by establishing themselves within UKRep to shadow the work of the Environmental Council and work with the EP, given its co-decision powers in the area. One DOE official produced a handbook to assist col-leagues mapping their way through the Brussels maze (Humphries 1996).

While EU directives remain the most significant instrument of envi-ronmental governance (Jordan et al. 2003), "new instruments" such as vol-untary agreements and market-based instruments have developed both at EU and domestic levels. While slower to engage with new instruments than other EU states, for example the Netherlands or Denmark, a more environmentally positive Labour government has not only adopted some EU actions but also promoted and uploaded domestic initiatives to EU level. Thus, an EU emissions-trading scheme was considered "a constraint upon and not a spur to, domestic change," but during the discussions around carbon trading, British negotiators fought hard to convince the Commission to adopt a more broadly based and voluntaristic British scheme (Jordan et al. 2003: 196). A scheme for ecomanagement and audit evolved alongside an EU system, as did a scheme for eco-labelling. But even before the more positive EU/environmentalist positioning of New Labour, the Department of Environment had taken steps to engage with Brussels institutions to "get a firmer grip on EU policy or risk more and more policy misfits" (Jordan 2003: 21). Inevitably, in engaging positively with European environmental policy integration, EU and British policies have been adapted and, in some cases, transformed.

THE EUROPEANIZATION OF DOMESTIC POLICY

Below we evaluate the EU's contribution to the transformation of British environmental policy and its role as a regional regulatory body. This can be examined in four ways: its impact on policy scope and content, on policy process, on institutions, and on the bureaucratic culture of environmental policy.

Shades of Green

With regard to policy scope and content, we have demonstrated the almost exponential growth of an environmental perspective across almost all arenas of government policy. Discrete, limited, and pragmatic responses to environmental problems were challenged by a tide of regulatory controls and standards for air, water, noise, and chemicals policy. From the 1970s, when the EU began to regulate the emission of dangerous substances in water, to the 2001–2002 directives for disposal of automobiles and electrical appliances (see textbox 11.4), successive British governments have responded to external regulatory impetus. Some policies were accepted only after belligerent defense of a national position, such as control of hazardous chemicals. Others were reluctantly accepted and slowly transposed, as in the case of the safe disposal of refrigerators (2002). A few—for instance the emergence of an EU Rural Development policy as part of CAP

Textbox 11.4. Disposing Old Autos:
The End-of-Life Vehicle Directive (ELVD)

The aim of the ELVD (2000) was to reduce the amount of waste produced by autos and small commercial vehicles and increase the recovery and recycling of parts and materials. In Britain over 2 million vehicles are scrapped every year. The directive demanded transposition (implementation) in member states by 21 April 2002, setting a reuse and recovery target of 85 percent for all ELVs by 1 January 2006. Producers must limit the use of hazardous materials and increase their use of recycled material, designing vehicles for ease of recycling. Starting 1 January 2007, producers must pay all or a significant part of the take-back costs of ELVs and meet a 95 percent recycling target set for 2015. "Treatment facilities" must have licences to operate and work to high environmental standards.

There were a number of problems that the government had to face in transposing the directive. These included how to ensure that disposal systems met EU standards before the issue of a license, and thus adequate numbers of disposal points; how to encourage manufacturers to meet timetabled requirements for the use of recycled material; and who was to pay the full cost of disposal—producers, consumers, or some mixture of both parties. After 2007 and in compliance with the directive, vehicle producers will meet ELV costs for all vehicles produced after 2002. A subsequent vehicle scrappage scheme where consumers can obtain a £2,000 grant to scrap vehicles over ten years old when purchasing a new vehicle was introduced in 2009.

reform (1999) or the eventual government stance on genetically modified crops—helped formulate the EU's position. In second-generation issues, on CO_2 emission or biodiversity, we have noted the considerable influence of the broader international community and, especially under post-1997 Labour governments, the willingness to accept and indeed lead international initiatives. However, it has been the EU that has turned summitry rhetoric into "objectives of national policy more environmentally ambitious [by specifying] the instruments to be used to achieve them and the manner in which they should be applied" (Jordan 2003: 11).

A Greened Process?

With regard to environmental policy processes, the EU's (mainly) regulatory, standards-based approach has altered but not entirely transformed the traditional, locally negotiated pragmatism of British policy implementation. EU numerical standards and compliance deadlines have eroded the subregional technical discretion and negotiation capacity of locally based inspectorates. Thus the Brussels-negotiated Urban Wastewater Treatment Directive largely prescribes the standards of sewage treatment. As against this, the devolved responsibility for environmental policy to Scottish and Welsh assemblies has reinforced the multilevel characteristics of policy implementation. In this context, voluntary agreements or local tax-based initiatives, such as road pricing and differentiated charges for waste collection, have added variety to local policy options. This is reflected in the EU's Sixth EAP, which seeks to involve stakeholders in shared responsibility. New instruments reflect New Labour and New Conservative thinking for governance, rather than government, in public policy. Finally, environmental law is now mostly subject to the ECJ supremacy and direct effect that, particularly through the technical and regulatory role of the Environment Agency, shapes policy implementation (Jordan 2003: 18).

While policy processes may be adapting to an increase in EU regulatory demands, there is little to suggest that the institutional arrangements for environmental policy have followed an EU-derived formulation. The Department of Environment, in its various guises, has adapted its organization to meet its role in an EU arena, but its structure has been determined, as we suggested above, more by domestic political priorities. In its current formulation (DEFRA), it is shorn of responsibilities for local government and transportation and faces a Department of Energy tasked with providing policies that may well be dictated by supply security rather than environmental concern. Similarly the creation of regulators or functional agencies is a legacy of the Conservative Next Steps reform from 1988 (see chapter 9). However, the privatization of water and energy supplies, and the requirements to meet environmental standards and targets, created obligations for utility companies that are shaped by EU directives. New institutional arrangements—with parliamentary scrutiny committees in Whitehall departments and cabinet government, as well as in subgovernment, are evidence of the arrival of environmentalism as a policy arena in British politics. However, the EU has provided an impetus for adaptive change rather than new, radically "Europeanized" institutions (see textbox 11.5).

A Change of Style

Finally, to what extent may we observe the impact of Europeanization on policy style? We have already noted the significance of contemporary pressure-group politics, which plays an important part not only in the articulation, but also in the aggregation and implementation of policy. Importantly, pressure groups are now located in Brussels as well as Whitehall. These NGOs are likely to be umbrella organizations or the more established international groupings, including the European Environment Bureau, Friends of the Earth, Greenpeace, and the European Federation for Transport and Environment. These and other groups have enjoyed some Commission financial support and have provided information and personnel on temporary contracts to EU environmental offices. They also play a role in policy implementation and enforcement at domestic level (Lenschow 2005). Their contribution, both in Whitehall and Brussels, has been not only to sustain environmental issues within these decision-making arenas but also to contribute to an openness that has "perturbed the quasi-secretive world of pollution control, as has the advent of public registers of information and . . . the incorporation of the Human Rights Act into British Law" (Jordan 2003: 19). The same author also argues that the regulating authorities for water and electricity (Ofwat and Ofgen) have played their part in pressing private utilities and government to offer more publicly accessible information about financial calculations and policy performance in pursuit of environmental quality issues. This has also spread to the private sector where, for instance, larger UK supermarket companies such as Tesco's, Sainsbury's, and Waitrose have seen some advantage in advertising the nature of food production through content labelling or stating the environmentally and ethically friendly sources of supply.

But if EU regulation requirements have assisted in broadening environmental debate, and thus the range of actors involved, it has also contributed to the centralization of its implementation. In pursuit of effective compliance, DEFRA and its agencies are, like other British ministries, dutiful implementers of EU legislation. Compliance by Britain, a large mem-

Textbox 11.5. The EU Effect on Britain's Waste Management Processes

1989	Community Waste Strategy: The SEA and Fifth EAP; defines "waste"
1991	Hazardous Waste Directive
1991	Batteries and Accumulators Disposal Directive
1994	Invention of Hazardous Waste Directive
1994	Directive on Packaging and Packaging Waste
1996	Cross-media Prevention and Control Directive
1999	Landfill Directive
2000	End-of-Life Vehicles Directive
2000	Ozone Depleting Regulations
2001	Waste Electrical and Electronic Equipment Directive
2003	Directive on Emissions Tracking Scheme
2006	Waste Disposal Directive

This suite of directives and regulations has had a profound effect on waste disposal systems. Heavily reliant on landfill disposal, directives associated with control and standards of disposal of hazardous and nonhazardous waste have seen Britain struggle to meet timetables and to acquire the necessary technology to meet EU demands. New regulations concerning hazardous waste disposal meant a decline in legally operating landfill sites from 2002 to 2004, a problem not fully addressed some three years later in several parts of the country. Similar fears of "fridge mountains" and the countryside littered with abandoned cars were expressed in the same period. Tight controls of the export of waste from the EU plus the lack of technological expertise in other forms of waste disposal have not helped. Initial reluctance on behalf of government environmental agencies and businesses to respond to EU directives has recently been replaced by a more positive attitude, as commercial opportunities and public awareness of the issues have developed. For instance, private companies have imported German machinery that meets EU standards for refrigerator disposal in order to open legal and profitable recycling disposal sites. Supermarkets have experimented with the use of biodegradable packaging and advertised this as responsible capitalism. In 2006 DEFRA has called local authorities to increase waste incineration from 9 percent to 25 percent by 2020 (and has made available financial support to assist). Also, since 2003 the idea of tradable allowances for waste disposal between waste disposal authorities in England has provided the possibility of a "market" solution for waste pollution.

ber state with a laggard reputation, is relatively good, save in the case of "bad application" cases of water regulations (European Commission 2005). We have already noted the organizational responses to the EU, by the DOE, through the decision to "upload" rather than react to policy change and consequently the use of more *communautaire* language—"yes but" rather than a straight "no" to Commission proposals— although observers note still the tendency of British negotiators to view defense of a national position as the default stance in the Council (Jordan 2003: 21).

CONCLUSION

Labour government has been credited with taking a high-profile stance within international forums on climate change and sustainable development. While this has been criticized as not being well reflected in domestic policy, the issue of climate change and public awareness of its consequences has been heightened by the leadership and high profile offered by (former) PM Blair and his then chancellor, Gordon Brown, as well as the leader of the Conservative opposition, David Cameron. Each of the three major party leaders has stressed the importance of prioritizing environmental policies, despite the onset of a world economic recession in 2008. Indeed, in what was hailed as a groundbreaking 2009 budget, the chancellor announced a "green" stimulus of £375 million as part of a recovery strategy and recommitted Britain to a reduction in carbon omissions of 34 percent by 2020.

We have also noted the more positive role that British policy makers have played in contributing to EU legislation in particular policy areas. But EU directives have, like those on electrical appliance waste disposal, often shocked ministers by their cost. However, they have been implemented diligently, if slowly. British environmental policy, suggests Jordan, has been "Europeanized indirectly, stealthily and largely contrary to the expectations of the British government" (Jordan 2003: 24).

All postindustrial states have responded to international and domestic demands for policies that, for some, will lead to sustainable development and, for others, are necessary to save the planet, improve health, or preserve a rare species. British governments increasingly, since the 1980s, have responded to international and domestic pressures accordingly. The EU dimension to environmental policy has been of great importance, however. While we have suggested various examples where domestic pressures have resulted in policy advances or have hindered intended policy outcomes, EU directives and regulations have expanded the range of policies and to a considerable extent dictated the pace of change. Importantly, there has been a shift in regulatory culture, especially through acceptance of the precautionary principle.

While we might conclude that British environmental policies would have changed anyway, once directives are agreed at Council level their functional implementation by bureaucrats has impacted on the style, content, and strength of British environmental policy. One final point: one view of Europeanization is "a process of mutual learning and adjustment between co-evolving political systems" (Jordan 2003: 193). Recent EU environmental policy has been more pragmatic and voluntarist, and thus more akin to the traditional British policy style. Consequently, in this most Europeanized field of public policy, the process of "mutual learning and adjustment" is likely to continue.

FURTHER READING

The development of British environmental policy is traced in Neil Carter's *The Politics of the Environment* (2001) and Tim Gray (ed.) *UK Environmental Policy in the 1990s* (1995). An early examination of the impact of the EU on British environmental policy is in Philip Lowe and Stephen Ward (eds.) *British Environmental Policy and Europe* (1998). Andrew Jordan updates this in *The Europeanization of British Environmental Policy* (2002). Andrea Lenschow provides a picture of environmental policy making at EU level in Wallace, Wallace, and Pollack (2006). Pressure groups and the British-EU nexus are described by Andrew Jordan's essay in Bache and Jordan (eds.) (2006) and in comparison with other interest-group activity in Justin Greenwood's *Interest Representation in the European Union* (2007). Robert Garner's *Environmental Politics* (2000) examines the changing stances of political parties on environmental issues.

12

Britain's Foreign Policy and External Security

On face value, an examination of British foreign policy lends itself to an assessment of the effect of Europeanization in *each* of the perspectives identified in the introduction. Foreign policy is an external manifestation of the values, aims, and aspiration of any state. The Foreign Ministry of each member state of the EU plays a unique representational role for its national interests in the Council of Ministers and is a significant player in negotiating the shape of European integration and contributing to a European Common Foreign and Security Policy (CFSP). Finally, the role of the Foreign and Commonwealth Office (FCO) is vital in providing a focus for *all* British policy interests, as they are shaped by, and attempt to shape, EU policies. However, changes and adaptations to British foreign policy in recent years must also be interpreted as reactions to such broader factors as interdependence, the collision of domestic and international interests and, inevitably, globalization (Allen 2002: 251).

THE COORDINATES OF BRITAIN'S EXTERNAL INTERESTS

One description of its foreign policy especially favored by British diplomats is that Britain "punches above her weight." This view is encouraged by a number of historic and cultural factors, several of which were discussed in chapter 1. In summary, imperial hegemony during the nineteenth and early twentieth centuries, Britain's international trading and financial interests, and a long history of successful military adventurism for both defense and national profit have combined to sustain this perception of Britain as a world player. The spoils of World War II victory entitled Britain, together with another world middleweight, France, to permanent seats on the UN Security Council alongside the more evidently heavyweight forces of the United States and the Soviet Union (and China). This, together with the acquisition of an "independent" nuclear capability and the positioning of Britain's postwar interests close to those of the United States, ensured a place for Britain at top tables despite the rapid postwar decline of imperial status and the reality of international economic challenges, not least from the United States.

Britain's continuing role as a world player is conceptualized by Winston Churchill's "overlapping circles model" of British world presence, which neatly summarizes conventional interpretations of British foreign policy in the past sixty years. His view, expressed in 1946, was that Britain enjoyed the position of sitting within the intersection of three circles of interest—the Commonwealth, Europe, and the "English-speaking world." Britain was thus uniquely placed to influence each, and to encourage relationships between the actors within these "majestic" circles. They were not to be perceived, however, as having equal value. Foreign policy is essentially a reactive exercise and the salience of any particular sphere of interest is influenced by events and contemporary assessments of the future. Thus Churchill is, in the 1940s, purported to have observed to Charles de Gaulle that "whenever we have to choose between Europe and the open seas, we shall always choose the open sea" (Richard et al. 1971: 26). By 2003, in a speech to the US Congress, Prime Minister Blair saw Britain's European interests somewhat differently: "You know, people ask me after the past months when, let's say, things were a little strained in Europe, "why do you persist in wanting Britain at the center of Europe?" And I say maybe if the UK were a group of islands twenty miles off Manhattan, I might feel differently. But actually we are twenty miles off Calais and joined by a tunnel."

The ups and downs of the "special relationship" are discussed separately, but they have passed through the best and worst of times. The erosion of the Commonwealth as a priority sphere, however, is rather more clearly evident, as European rather than Commonwealth trade and defense issues become prominent in the listings of important external events of the period. Nevertheless, the sphere of Commonwealth interest, albeit diminished, continues into the twenty-first century and still provides a backdrop to more pressing issues of British external policy. During the second half of the twentieth century, periods of migration to and from Britain, shared cricket and rugby sporting interests, and royal visits did their part in sustaining the image of a "United Kingdom" to its inhabitants and the mother country to its diaspora. A table of the main events in Britain's "three circles" of influence is available on the book's website.

These residual domestic sentiments are perceived by politicians as being sufficiently powerful, still to be a factor affecting foreign policy. This is especially relevant for governments when addressing Britain's objectives within the European circle of interest, which, in relation to economic and security issues, is possibly more salient to national interest than Britain's transatlantic commitments. However, if only in a historic and symbolic sense, the Commonwealth circle remains one of the coordinates of foreign policy in the new millennium.

THE OBJECTIVES AND DILEMMAS OF BRITISH FOREIGN AND SECURITY POLICY

Textbox 12.1 presents an official and contemporary statement of British foreign policy priorities in the first decade of the twenty-first century. It differs little from principles that have existed for six decades. Save for the specific mention of current issues of security in the fields of immigration, crime, terrorism, and energy, these objectives are contained in most foreign policy analysts' listings of British objectives: that is, to play a *major* role in international relations; to promote economic interests, especially free trade; to maintain a strong conventional and nuclear military capability; to ensure a strong and prosperous European Union; but also to commit to close relations with the United States and to sustain ties and responsibilities with respect to the Commonwealth (Martin and Garnett 1997; Harris 2003).

Textbox 12.1. International Policy Priorities for Britain

1. A world safer from global terrorism and weapons of mass destruction
2. Protection of the UK from people smuggling, drug trafficking, and other international crime
3. An international system based on the rule of law that is better able to resolve disputes and prevent conflicts
4. An effective and globally competitive EU in a secure neighborhood
5. Promotion of UK economic interests in an open and expanded global economy and secure energy supply
6. Achieving climate security within a sustainable global economy
7. Security and good governance of the UK's overseas territories
8. Sustainable development and poverty reduction underpinned by respect for human rights and good governance
9. Managing migration and illegal immigration
10. Delivery of high-quality support for British nationals

Source: FCO (2007), Capability Review of the FCO.

In pursuit of these objectives, successive British governments, however differently they may have behaved while in opposition, have played an active role in the EU, NATO, and the UN; maintained a nuclear capability; and searched for influence within the United States through a perceived "special relationship." National, Commonwealth, and other security interests continue to lead to the deployment of British forces, usually as part of multinational interventions, and are most recently evident in Iraq and Afghanistan.

The main political parties, with some exceptions, have differed more in emphasis than over the principles that emerged during the Cold War. As will be seen below, differences have narrowed further during the 1990s, as national interest has become an often-difficult balancing act between what may not always be congruent objectives. Dilemmas of British foreign policy may be seen in the following questions:

- Is the national interest better served with a European or a transatlantic emphasis?
- Should there be a credible/flexible independent defense capability outside of NATO or EU security frameworks?
- Should ethical issues (human rights, armament exports, environmental sustainability, etc.) or national economic interest guide foreign policy?
- What are the boundaries between domestic and foreign policy when considering British–EU relations?
- How can growing global and regional economic interdependence be managed, especially in the context of economic downturn?

In the twenty-first century, in much diminished diplomatic and military circumstances, British strategy, still set at the intersection of three majestic circles, may be seen as a millstone rather than an opportunity for influencing world affairs. A brief examination of the development of British foreign policy since 1945 illustrates the overreach that this can bring to a small island off the coast of Continental Europe.

Developments in Foreign Policy since 1945

1945–1989

The distinguishing feature of this period is Britain's adjustment from a major power to middle-rank status in world affairs. Initially the postwar "big three" included Britain, whose historic and moral weight gave the new Labour government (1945–1951), under Prime Minister Attlee and Foreign Secretary Ernest Bevan, a potential mediating role between Stalin's USSR and the United States. Despite the end of imperial control of the subcontinent of India (1947), postwar Britain retained army battalions in forty countries (Coxall and Robins 1998). Also, Britain was an atomic power through its independent deterrent force of V-bombers. Still basking in a postwar sunset, British-Commonwealth interests remained significant: economically in trading and investment; politically as successive British governments encouraged independence among African and Asian colonies; and strategically, by policing and, if necessary, giving military support to emerging independent regimes.

The division of Europe between a communist east and capitalist west, and the breakdown of cooperation between the Soviet Union and the United States, France, and Britain thrust the European circle into prominence from 1946. Once again it was Churchill in his Fulton, Missouri, speech who set the scene. "From Stettin in the Baltic to Trieste in the Adriatic, an iron curtain has descended across the continent." The subsequent Truman Doctrine, which committed the United States to come to the aid of "free peoples" and the American dollars made available through the Marshall Plan for all *democratic* European states, provided a political and economic boost to vulnerable West European postwar governments.

For most West European states, including Britain, the continued presence of the United States within the "European theater" was a strategic necessity. In this context, Ernest Bevan played a vital role in establishing NATO (1949), which acted as a European security umbrella throughout the second half of the twentieth century. The organization institutionalized a West European-US defense interest that went some way toward resolving Britain's transatlantic-European dilemma; two of Churchill's spheres of influence interacted through a common security structure. US military power alongside European allies contributed to preserving the Cold War status quo in Europe during the entire post-1945 existence of the USSR and the Warsaw Treaty Organisation, NATO's military rival.

The European "theater" was perceived, nevertheless, by all British governments in the first fifteen years of the postwar period as of lesser significance in terms of national economic interest. The rejection of offers to join the European Coal and Steel Community (ECSC) in 1951 and talks to set up a European Economic Community (Messina in 1955) emanated from a continued assumption of a British world presence and an economic and moral commitment to the Commonwealth. Britain's global reach extended not just to a continued presence in a diminishing number of colonies and protectorates, but also as policeman and security guarantor to emergent states in such hotspots as Malaysia, Borneo, Aden, and Kenya. Britain also contributed to the UN-led defense of South Korea alongside the United States and other forces (1950–1952). However, the Anglo-French and Israeli invasion of Egypt (1956), an attempt to rein in the Arab socialist aspirations of General Nasser, turned to debacle as world, and especially US, opinion criticized the incursion. The Suez Crisis illustrated the problem of military overreach for both Britain and France, as well as the necessity for US approval for external interventions. But it was not until some twelve years after that a Labour government (1968) decided to cut back on Britain's military presence and withdraw from East of Suez.

Suez, together with the reluctant recognition of British dependence on the US for a nuclear delivery system, was an important factor in the shift of foreign policy toward a more limited multilateral approach that included attempts to join the European Community (EC). An initial move to form a counter to the EC through the European Free Trade Association (1959) proved a weak imitation of the real thing. Britain's applications, in 1961 and 1967, were rejected, the first because of a perceived lack of serious intent and the second because of a breakdown in negotiations over economic terms of entry and the continued negativity of the French president, Charles de Gaulle. The application was finally accepted in 1972 under the enthusiastic leadership of the Conservative prime minister, Edward Heath, and with the more supportive perspective of the new French president, Georges Pompidou. In joining the EC, British governments recognized not only the increasing significance of the European theater, but the diminishing significance of the Commonwealth for Britain's economic security. However, the recognition of a new EC partnership did not detract from the continuing significance of the United States as a guarantor of political and military security through NATO. This must be set within the Cold War perspective of Britain's security from the 1960s to the early 1990s.

Britain's security interests during this period fixed around defense of Western Europe's eastern borders from the Soviet Union's conventional forces, maintaining a capacity for deterrence against nuclear attack, and sustaining a military capability flexible and powerful enough to protect particular economic and postcolonial interests (of which the 1982 Falklands/Malvinas War is the main example). Such interests were dependent on multilateral and bilateral relationships, for which NATO and the United States played a pivotal role. There was, however, no doubt that the United States was by far the major player within NATO political and military structures, and on several occasions British governments, whether from necessity or political choice, positioned themselves closer to the United States than some European allies would have wanted. The British perception of the US/UK "special relationship" transcended even the political/organizational linkages that the NATO alliance provided.

This relationship was evident on several occasions: during the 1980s Margaret Thatcher's neoconservative nationalism, manifest in the Falklands/Malvinas dispute, revived a sense of Britain as a world player. UN and especially US support was essential to the success of that operation.

Similarly, the British government strongly supported the US decision to deploy Cruise and Perishing II missiles in Western Europe. Similar support was offered for President Reagan's "star wars" initiative and related and tough negotiations for Soviet-US nuclear weapons reduction in 1981–1982. Again, in December 1987, Margaret Thatcher was to claim a mediator's role in reviving US-Soviet negotiations on intermediate nuclear arms reductions. The Thatcher government also offered support for the US bombing of Libya in 1986. Despite a less fulsome relationship with President Bush, who saw Japan and West Germany as more powerful partners, Thatcher's and later John Major's support in the 1990–1991 Gulf War again reinforced US-UK relations.

By attaching British interests to those of the United States, Britain could continue to punch considerably above the country's military weight and so might enjoy a world-class diplomatic status despite second-class economic performance. Britain's armed forces, dwarfed in comparison with those of the United States, USSR, or China, were still the most powerful in Western Europe and, more significantly for the United States, were those that were most flexible to deploy. Defense expenditure reached a high point of 5.3 percent of GDP in 1984–1985, falling to 4 percent in 1992. This was higher than similar NATO partners (France 3.4%; Germany 2.2%; Italy 2%), reflecting the political will of successive British governments to fulfill international obligations. There was also the need to sustain an armaments industry, which depended on a subsidized, secure home market to recoup its research and development costs and so compete successfully in the export market. Britain is currently the second-largest world arms exporter after the United States.

Britain in the Post–Cold War Period (1989–2001)

The ending of the Cold War disturbed many of the foreign and defense policy assumptions that British governments had shared for over forty years. By 1990, Central and Eastern Europe had become a diverse collection of newly democratizing and potentially unstable neighboring states. Within two years, the USSR had ceased to exist and the former Yugoslavia had reverted to its unpleasant and (perhaps) historically inevitable path of ethnic and civil strife. World recession on the one hand, and the Maastricht negotiations for the Treaty on European Union on the other, were the backdrops to the end of Cold War certainty. The first precluded the United States from providing the extensive economic support to the Central and East European countries that was on offer to West European countries at the end of World War II. With no new Marshall Plan, the EU, at the behest of the G24 group of donor countries, played the leading role in the economic development of its new neighbors (Mannin 1999). This reinforced long-term US demands that European countries should shoulder more of the financial and military responsibilities for European defense and also coincided with the collapse of the Yugoslav Republic and the emergence of CFSP machinery in the Treaty of European Union. Added to these external pressures were Britain's own domestic economic difficulties and a public expectation of a "peace dividend" that had been encouraged by the findings of the 1990 defense review *Options for Change*—recommending a 20 percent cutback in army expenditure and heavy piecemeal cuts in the RAF and Royal Navy.

The old and relatively simple model of Cold War security was complicated by these challenges, which now contained economic, environmental, societal, and political dimensions. Insecure Eastern European boundaries, conflagration in the Balkans region, and the need to secure Central European democracy implied a multilateral and multidimensional response. Here the European Union, with its policies of close association and potential membership, implied, for the UK, closer linkage with EU rather than US interests. Nevertheless NATO remained the only military organization capable of responding to system breakdown, as events in Kosovo were to show. However, Tony Blair's willingness to commit British ground forces contrasted with US unwillingness to do so, and by late 1998 his frustration over the Kosovo operation strengthened a newfound enthusiasm for a European Security and Defense Policy (ESDP).

Nevertheless, the resilience of the three-circles model is evident in the response of the UK government to the US policy toward Iraq. Subsequent to the Conservative government's full support during the first Gulf War, Iraq's treatment of its Kurdish minority, and later its prevarication over the full implementation of UN resolution 1137 on armaments inspection, led to US-British air strikes and the imposition of "no-fly" zones. British support for the United States came, however, in the face of criticism from its European allies, which was to be repeated before and during the 2003 Iraq War.

The opportunity for a repositioning of British foreign and defense policies to prioritize the "European circle" of influence relied on attitudinal changes by the British government toward the role of the EU and its nascent ESDP, and US support for a more independent European presence—and thus new NATO arrangements to allow a separate European capacity to operate using NATO assets. The new arrangements, in turn, assumed a new entente between France and Britain concerning the role of NATO (since Britain and France were the more militarily powerful European NATO states). In this respect, the traditionally contradictory views of French and British governments over the role of NATO (the former seeking an independent European capacity, the latter maintaining an Atlanticist vision of European security) were still evident when New Labour assumed office in 1997. A year later, however, the British-French St. Malo Declaration indicated British willingness to accept an autonomous capacity for military involvement in peacekeeping (the Petersberg Tasks) by the EU (see textbox 12.2).

There was every hope that at last there existed a will in British government to ensure that there was "no contradiction between being a good European and being a good Atlanticist" (Smith and Tsatsas 2002: 42). There followed considerable efforts on the part of the Europeans to construct the European Security and Defence Policy (ESDP), including development of institutional structures within the EU and commitment of forces to a 60,000 strong Rapid Reaction Force (RRF), declared operational at the Laaken Summit in December 2001. Before these efforts reached fruition, however, the Twin Towers were destroyed.

A RENEWED SPECIAL RELATIONSHIP?

The British government and, in particular, Tony Blair's response to the tragedy of 9/11 and the subsequent Afghan war seemed unconditional. While Article 5 of the NATO Treaty was invoked for the first time on 12 September, so committing *all* NATO allies to the defense of the United States, in practice NATO was called upon to act only in a marginal capacity to assist aerial patrols of US air space in the aftermath of 9/11. Blair, however, pledged complete bilateral support for any US military action to be taken on the war against terrorism. In Afghanistan the British presence, at least from the perspective of the British government and press, was seen as the most significant and, in subsequent official statements of support, the case that Britain's interests were identical with those of the United States was openly broadcast. Thus the British defense secretary's pronouncement

---

Textbox 12.2. Petersberg, St. Malo, and Helsinki

The Petersberg Tasks (1992) included in the Treaty of Union at the Amsterdam Summit (1997) proposed a raison d'être for military action by EU-designated forces in support of humanitarian rescue and peacekeeping missions, including crisis management. The St. Malo Declaration between Britain and France (December 1998) supported the development of a Rapid Reaction Force for autonomous action that did not challenge the role of NATO. The Helsinki Summit and subsequent Headline Goal (2003) to create and sustain corps strength (around 60,000 troops with rapid reaction capability) facilitated the notion of an EU Security and Defence Policy. This has been further strengthened by development of cooperative EU battlegroups, the first eleven of which became operational at the end of 2007.

that he saw no divergence between US and British security interests "whether as part of a close bilateral alliance or as within wider defense alliances such as NATO" (*Guardian* 2002). This statement, made immediately prior to the November 2002 Prague NATO Summit, was illustrative of the British government's diplomatic commitment to its transatlantic ally, with all that it implied for continued military support for the United States. The Prague Summit resulted in an invitation to six more CEECs to join the alliance.

While remaining at the very junction of European and transatlantic circles of interest, the changing role of NATO and diminished US commitment to the transatlantic alliance has seen the further evolution of an EU-led security and defense framework. Nevertheless, following 9/11, the Blair administration's prioritization of diplomatic and military support for the United States and its "war on terrorism" produced tensions between Britain and its EU partners—as well as considerable domestic opposition in Britain, notably toward the 2003 military action in Iraq. Labour's relatively poor performance in the 2005 election and the decline in domestic popularity of PM Blair were attributed in no small part to the Iraq war. No other EU member state offered such unequivocal political and military support to the Bush administration in its uncompromising policy toward Iraq. Britain's diplomatic support for the US delegation at the UN and subsequent military contributions to President Bush's call for a "coalition of the willing" seemed unswerving, with Blair often playing a leading role in the presentation of the US-British stance. This was in direct contrast to the internationalist stance taken by Germany, Russia, and particularly France.

The rift between European states, encapsulated in Donald Rumsfeld's dichotomy of "new and old Europe," dealt a serious blow to the vision of the EU as a global actor. "Old Europe," characterized as protectionist and idealist, contrasted with a globalist/realist "New Europe" of which Britain seemed a leading member, alongside Spain (temporarily) and some of the Central and East European democracies, notably Poland (Kagan 2002).

Praised for his courage in much of the US press, Prime Minister Blair was pilloried in most sections of the British media for adopting such a dangerous path. Apologists for the British government's stance could point to the role played by Blair in prolonging the search for a UN diplomatic resolution to the crisis and in mitigating the ferocity of the early assaults on Iraqi cities. In these terms the British role was little more than that of the Atlantic bridge or broker between US and European perspectives. Others saw in these events a painfully dogmatic and intransigent stance by the British government leading to irreparable damage to both Britain and the EU (Young 2003; Woollacott 2003). But even at the height of these controversies, considerable progress was seen in the development of ESDP, with British involvement in the first three operations, which took place in Macedonia, Bosnia-Herzegovina, and the Congo during 2003.

In the aftermath of the hostilities, events seemed much less dramatic, ongoing EU matters receiving a business-as-usual reception. British postponement of adoption of the euro in June 2003 was received with genuine regret by EU elites and most commentators. Subsequently, however, commentary on the success or otherwise of Britain's presidency of the EU (June–December 2005) was mixed. The outcome, which included a last-minute compromise on the EU budget, was perceived more a victory for the negotiating skills of the new German chancellor, Angela Merkel, than the leadership of the Council president, Tony Blair, thus a further indication of waning British enthusiasm for aspirations to oversight in EU matters (Whitman and Thomas 2005; see also the book's website).

Under the leadership of Tony Blair the British government sought to retain its "special relationship" with the United States as well as encourage new directions in European integration post-enlargement. There is, however, no doubt that "the war on terror" complicated what, in 1998 at St. Malo, might have been a path toward British prioritization of its European circle of interests above the others.

Under the Brown administration there were initial indications that the notion of Britain as an "Atlantic bridge" had proven less successful than anticipated. But the election of President Obama opened up opportunities for fresh EU-US relationships, as the divisions between "old and new" Europe articulated during the Bush administration have diminished, a point emphasized in Prime Minister Brown's speech to Congress (March 2009). Brown's foreign secretary, David Miliband, expressed both a multilateral and European dimension to his philosophy, and Brown's speech to the EP in March 2009 indicated that Britain was to be "a country that does not see itself as an island adrift from Europe, but as a country at the centre of Europe, not in Europe's slipstream but firmly in its mainstream" (Prime Minister's Office 2009). In his speech to Congress Brown also sought to "renew our special relationship for our generation and our times." Being "at the point of junction" offers the British government opportunities to influence the US administration as its closest ally; on the other hand the potential for being seen as the stooge of US foreign policy still seems to sit uncomfortably with British aspirations to be at the heart of Europe.

ACTORS IN FOREIGN AND SECURITY POLICY

Institutionally, there are three main departments involved in the making and processing of foreign and security policy. These are the Foreign and Commonwealth Office (FCO), with origins dating back to 1782; the Ministry of

Defence (MOD); and the relatively new Department for International Development (DFID), created in 1997. Other departments with particular interests in external affairs include the Treasury, whose ministers play a vital role in British representation within international organizations such as the International Monetary Fund (IMF), the World Bank, the Group of Eight major economies (G8 and the new G20), and in EU economic councils; the Department of Trade and Industry; the Home Office, with its responsibilities for immigration and asylum matters; and the Ministry for Justice, with specific constitutional and legal responsibilities for Britain's remaining associated territories. As we will see below, EU institutions now take an increasing responsibility for what were originally Whitehall foreign interests. This is clearest in trade policy and negotiation, which is for the most part concluded and implemented by the European Commission on behalf of the member states, including Britain. We have already mentioned the emergence of a European CFSP and more recently ESDP, which have imposed (albeit limited) obligations and constraints on British policy makers.

In addition to the blurring of boundaries between Whitehall and EU jurisdictions, further complexity is provided by the input of an increasingly wide range of traditional and new nongovernmental actors who seek to influence British foreign and security policy. A twenty-four-hour news service, Internet accessibility, and freer access to official information have provided the potential for a new openness and accountability in foreign affairs as well as a public appreciation of the interdependence of domestic and external events (Kennedy Pipe and Vickers 2003).

The armaments industry has traditionally and successfully represented its commercial interests, sometimes to the detriment of intended government policy direction. Thus the 1997–2001 Labour government's intentions to move toward a closer European defense identity were thwarted by the objections of the giant defense company British Aerospace to merge with a German company. Instead they preferred to consolidate by taking over a British company, Marconi, and commenced moves toward further takeovers, but in the direction of the United States. Appreciation of a growing public interest in foreign policy, as well as the predilections of Labour politicians, particularly the late Robin Cook, led to attempts to establish an ethical perspective in the late 1990s (see the book's website). The limits of such attempts were quickly exposed, however, by human rights campaigners who relentlessly protested against the continued sale of arms to Indonesia—which would be capable of being used against rebels in East Timor and in direct contravention of the Labour administration's stated aim to adopt a regulated, ethical arms policy (Wheeler and Dunne 1998). Some contracts were subsequently cancelled.

We have already illustrated how interdependence, global information exchange, and a growing European agenda have impacted on the role of the prime minister as an international and domestic political actor (chapter 8). Both the Cabinet Office and Prime Minister's Office provide considerable support to the PM's representational and decision-making activities in external affairs. The role of foreign secretary, some argue, has consequently been downgraded to an assistant or delegatory status in the context of the emergence of a "presidential executive." Notwithstanding the veracity of this claim, the FCO remains at the heart of a process that needs considerable coordination in the light of a complex interdependence of domestic and international issues and policy.

THE ORGANIZATION AND ROLE OF THE FCO

It is the foreign secretary, with the considerable support services that the FCO offers, who is constitutionally responsible for Britain's foreign policy, in close association with the Ministry of Defence and, in recent years, the Department for International Development.

The foreign secretary is assisted in his/her work by three junior ministers. In 2008 their portfolios were: economic and "global issues," including the environment, human rights, the UN, the Commonwealth, Asia/Oceania, and Afghanistan; the Middle East, terrorism, North and South America, and international crime; and Europe (both EU and non-EU). The foreign secretary may also seek assistance from a minister appointed from the House of Lords who speaks on trade and investment. The permanent under-secretary (PUS) is one of the most senior civil service appointments, and he/she takes responsibility for the management of the whole diplomatic service.

The basis of the FCO remains the geographic "desk," which reflects Britain's global interests, despite some attempts to reorganize on functional lines. However, multilateral "commands" and functional necessity have cut into geographic divisions of responsibilities as the FCO's arrangements for representing Britain's European interests illustrate (see below). Given the significance of foreign policy for Britain's destiny, in both historical and contemporary terms, the conduct of policy has been subject to several pressures that have at once increased and limited the scope of the FCO.

THE FCO AS A MULTILATERAL ACTOR

Britain's splendid isolation, independence, and imperial hegemony of the nineteenth century contrast vividly with the role that British governments play in world affairs today. Partly through historic reputation, Britain still claims to punch beyond its weight, but it has since the end of World War II

promoted solutions to world problems through international organiza-
tion(s) and agreements. The FCO inevitably conducts much of its business
through its missions to international organizations and its advice and
proactivity within international bureaucracies. Britain's mission to the
UN is substantial (see table 12.1). Britain holds and makes full use of a
permanent seat on the UN Security Council. Similarly, British governments have been fully involved in Commonwealth conferences, accepting their decisions in relation to the conduct of, especially, African affairs.
Membership in NATO remained the hub of security for Britain throughout the Cold War period. More recently Britain has played a leading role
in the construction of ESDP and in seeking international solutions to
global environmental problems through supporting EU efforts to conclude
the Kyoto Agreements in 1997.

While the roles of its FCO and the diplomatic service remain, the international standing of the prime minister has been enhanced through
his/her undoubted ability as national leader to present a crucial political
weight and legitimacy when present in these international forums. In addition, attendances at more informal international meetings (G8/20 or
Davos are examples) and frequent bilateral meetings with other heads of

Table 12.1. The FCO: Distribution of Staff

Number of FCO Officials Working in International Organizations (2006)	
United Nations	
UN, New York	37
UN, Vienna	10
UN, Geneva	18
Other	15
Total	80
NATO	31
UK Delegation to the Western European Union (c/o UKRep)	10
Council of Europe	5
Organization for Economic Cooperation and Development (OECD)	7
UK Delegation to the Organization for Security and Cooperation in Europe (OSCE), Vienna	12
IMF and World Bank	9
Overall Total	152

Number of FCO Officials Working in the EU*	
EU 25 member states (excluding UK European Directorate)	653
UK Representation to the EU	79
European Directorate (250 in UK)	760
Total	1,492

* includes some locally engaged staff
Source: FCO (2006).

state, have given successive PMs a statesperson status that the foreign secretary can seldom emulate. Furthermore, the organization of the Prime Minister's Office and the Cabinet Office, together with the support of foreign policy advisors, gives the PM an alternative, if not necessarily competing, source of policy advice from that provided by the foreign secretary and FCO. While no British prime minister has attempted to create a Prime Minister's Office that would be a major challenge to the role of the FCO, the Blair administration moved two cabinet secretariats (for Overseas Aid and Defence, and for Europe) into Downing Street. PM Brown has retained a strong advisory component within his office with two units devoted to external affairs. Thus it can be argued that the FCO is no longer "the unchallenged determinant of overall British Foreign interest" (Allen and Oliver 2004: 12). Throughout 2008–2009, with the onset of global recession, PM Brown played a highly proactive external role in attempting to stimulate support, globally, for a collective response to the crisis.

THE FCO AND "EUROPE"

In the later stages of her administration, Margaret Thatcher mused over the idea of creating a Foreign Affairs Unit with a similar role to that of the US National Security Council (Allen and Oliver 2004: 6). Her fear was that the FCO was shaping British foreign policy too much in the direction of the EU. To what extent, almost twenty years later, were her fears justified?

As a repository of Britain's external interests, the organization of the FCO may be a significant pointer to the priorities of state with regard to the changing face of economic and physical security. In 1968, and coinciding with Britain's withdrawal of a strong military presence "east of Suez," the Foreign Office was combined to include Commonwealth interests and became the FCO. At the same time, and corresponding with Britain's second application for EU membership, the FCO increased its resources directed toward the European sphere. Britain's eventual accession to the EC in 1972 only reinforced an FCO adaptation already underway, which some observed as a diplomatic replacement for loss of Empire (Forster and Blair 2002: 57). While there was some brief flirtation with the idea of creating a Ministry for Europe in the early 1970s, the FCO was successful in maintaining its influence over this new arena of policy. Some thirty years later an examination of the structure of the FCO reveals the depth of its EU activities. But, as we shall argue, this has been accompanied by a complexity of relationship that has not necessarily maintained FCO control of EU policy.

A minister of state for Europe (junior minister) is one of the four ministers who assist the foreign secretary in his/her overall responsibilities for foreign policy. This political team is assisted by a diplomatic bureaucracy headed by the permanent under-secretary (PUS) and eight directors general. Of these, one has responsibilities for the EU. However, the director general (political) was created originally to assist in the task of facilitating Britain's role in the EU's early attempts at foreign policy (known as European Political Cooperation). The political director, though now not solely concerned with European policy, is the top advisory post to the foreign secretary, and it is he/she that "clocks up the air miles" with the foreign secretary or PM while the PUS "stays at home to look after the shop" (Allen and Oliver 2004: 10). Thus, the role of political director is a reflection of the considerable increase in scope of FCO responsibilities in the EU, associated in part with the deepening of integration provided by the Single European Market. This, together with the further deepening of the EU's policy portfolio as a result of the 1992 Treaty of Union, has produced a range of domestic policy activities and resources directed at maintaining a coordinating role for British European policy. But, while maintaining exclusive policy rights in the fields of CFSP and in advising and supporting the prime minister and other ministers in intergovernmental conferences, the FCO has ceded ground to specialist home ministers in many new European fields. Thus the expertise of the Home Office on immigration and asylum matters, DTI for export and investment, or Department of Health on public health issues, indeed almost all home government departments, is now an integral part of an FCO remit in these "intermestic" policy arenas.

THE PERMANENT HIGH REPRESENTATION TO THE EU (UKREP)

The centrality of the FCO in coordinating this plethora of EU/British policy interests, together with the need to share these responsibilities, is most clearly evident in the activities of UKRep (see textbox 12.3). The holder of the office of permanent representative (Britain's EU ambassador) is always an FCO appointment; however, most of his/her staff are seconded from other departments. As such, the permanent representation is akin to a mini-Whitehall in Brussels. While there are other embassies (Washington) or missions (the UN) that utilize the home civil service for specialist expertise, UKRep is exceptional for its range and depth of functions and its pivotal role for home departments and the executive in dealing with European policy. With Brussels only a short flight and slightly longer train ride away, there exists "an intensive and ever changing dialogue with London" and the permanent representative returns every Friday to brief and receive instruction on policy from the FCO and Cabinet Office (Allen and

**Textbox 12.3. Permanent Representation
to the European Union (UKRep)**

UKRep's remit is to represent the UK's interests in the EU. It is based in Brussels and staffed by civil servants drawn from British government departments. Devolved administrations (Scottish Executive, Welsh Assembly, and Northern Ireland Executive) have a degree of autonomy, with their own offices in Brussels. Its job is to monitor EU institutions, liaise with other member states, negotiate on behalf of the British government and interest groups, and relay information to Whitehall. It carries considerable domestic influence and is staffed by over 100 officials of exceptional caliber. UKRep is headed by the permanent representative, who has overall responsibility for its work, and sits in the UK seat in the Committee of Permanent Representatives (COREPER). This body works to the Council of Ministers in preparing and negotiating policy proposals. The permanent representative is, historically, an ambassador from the FCO. Three other key positions are the deputy permanent representative, a representative to the Political and Security Committee, and a military representative to the EU.

In 2008 UKRep was formally divided into seven sections:

- Political Affairs
- External Relations, Development and Trade Policy
- Institutions
- Agriculture and Fisheries
- Industry and the Internal Market
- Social, Environmental and Regional Affairs
- Economic Affairs, Finance and Tax

These portfolios are staffed by a range of first-, second-, and third-grade officials from relevant Whitehall departments. However, "in practice, officials work more or less directly to the permanent representative or the deputy" (Kassim 2001: 57).

Oliver 2004: 15). As the demand for expertise in EU matters, including CFSP, has increased, so the numbers of FCO staff whose work is wholly or partially associated with European policy has also increased.

Until 2008, when under the Brown administration it was suspended, there existed a dedicated recruitment process, the European Fast Stream. Supplanting the "Arabists" who dominated the service in the mid-twentieth century, its graduates supply both UKRep and the embassies to European states with skilled specialist diplomats. Developments in CFSP and ESDP have resulted in the need for increased Brussels-based activity, not only through the twice-weekly meetings of the Political and Security Committee of the Council, but also regular meetings bilaterally between British and other MS officials, especially in France and Germany.

DEVOLUTION AND FOREIGN POLICY

There is no doubt that the deepening of Britain's association with the EU has significantly affected the processes of British foreign policy and the direction and scope of the FCO as a central player in external relations. However, a further factor influencing the direction of contemporary British foreign policy is the potential impact of devolved government to Scotland, Wales, and Northern Ireland. While having no constitutional responsibilities for external affairs, these recently formed administrations do have considerable interest in EU matters. Each administration enjoys full diplomatic recognition in Brussels, unlike British regional or local government, and therefore gains access to EU processes in a similar fashion to the German Länder. Scotland, currently with more functional and legislative responsibilities, has beefed up its separate Brussels representation and during the 2005 EU presidency represented Britain in fisheries negotiations at the invitation of the British central government. Devolved government has moved responsibilities in such fields as agriculture, environment, and economic development away from Whitehall; yet ministers represent overall British interests in these and other areas in Brussels. While ad hoc and informal meetings between devolved, central government, and UKRep actors have so far worked reasonably satisfactorily, the ultimate responsibility of the British government for European policy fits uncomfortably with the principles of devolution, which could represent a potential challenge to the current position of the FCO and UKRep as controlling and coordinating bureaucracies with regard to the EU.

IS BRITISH FOREIGN POLICY EUROPEANIZED?

Commitment to support US-led military incursions in Iraq and Afghanistan, as well as diplomatic and security initiatives as part of the "war on terror," have led to the potential of overstretching Britain's external capabilities, as well as damaging Britain's credibility as a leading EU actor. As one commentator suggests, Britain's dual-track "Atlantic bridge" role seems dependent on tensions between the EU and United States not becoming "overly pronounced" (Marsh 2005: 91). It is, however, worth exploring how far Britain's continuing attempt to play a military and diplomatic world role is challenged by circumstances that are beyond the ambitions of Britain's foreign policy actors. How far has membership in the EU constrained Britain's traditional external pretensions as an independent world power? How much foreign policy has been ceded to EU external policy processes? How far have British foreign policy processes been "domesticated" by the necessary "low politics" of EU engagement? These and other factors are examined below, utilizing the three perspectives of Europeanization detailed in the introduction to this book.

EU and British Foreign Policy Interests and Values

In the sense of "shared values," is British foreign policy congruent with the aims and objectives of the CFSP? This question is not difficult to answer, since the CFSP proclaims support for values that are generally espoused by Western states, including all EU member states. Thus, the TEU, which established Pillar II of the EU's treaty structure, offered such broad objectives for CFSP as: safeguarding the integrity and security of the Union in conformity with the principles of the UN; preserving peace and international security and promoting international cooperation; and developing and promoting democracy, the rule of law, and human rights (TEU Title V). The Treaty of Amsterdam (1997) and the Treaty of Nice (2000), which developed the EU security dimension leading to ESDP, subsequently strengthened CFSP in its operational detail. We have already mentioned the British government's contribution to an EU security dimension emanating from the Franco-British St. Malo Agreement in 1998. The British government was also party to the creation of the 2003 EU Security Strategy. This seeks to address "key threats" to EU security and to promote international order through multilateralism (European Council 2003). Add to CFSP and ESDP the overriding free trade objectives of the Common Commercial (trade) Policy and one is able to observe little difference between EU external policy objectives and those stated as British foreign policy objectives in textbox 12.1.

Despite these shared objectives, CFSP is intergovernmental in its essence, and the machinery for its implementation, though increasing in scope, remains weak in political effectiveness when compared with that of states. This is not to say that, when applied to particular events, the EU, with Britain as a full participant, has not been effective. A major triumph for EU and British foreign policy was the consolidation of eight Central and Eastern European states as market democracies, leading to their incorporation as EU members in 2004. Expansion of the EU remains a major foreign policy objective for successive British governments. Though unsuccessful in dealing with the medium-term consequences of the breakup of Yugoslavia, there has emerged a more effective EU role in the Western Balkans through the Stabilization and Association process, which is linked to the future prospect of EU membership. This process, together with the EU military and policing missions in Bosnia-Herzegovina and Macedonia, has ensured that the EU (with full British participation) is now the most important player in the region. In addition, EU-based diplomatic initiatives in the Middle East, notably toward Palestine/Israel and over the nuclear capability of Iran, have been strongly supported by the British government. Much of Britain's diplomatic perspective toward such Eastern neighbors as Ukraine, Moldova, Belarus, and the South Caucasus is contained within the EU's (2003) European Neighbourhood Policy, and the British government has attempted also to manage relations with Russia in the context of the EU-Russia "strategic partnership." Here, however, MS differences, particularly since the 2004 enlargement, have prevented an effective common policy toward Russia. This reminder of the intergovernmental nature of CFSP has relevance, also, for areas where British and EU perspectives diverge.

While Britain has fully supported the "soft power" approach commensurate with the traditional view of the EU as an "island of peace" for its geographic hinterland (Tunander 1997) there remains a significant dilemma for British foreign policy. The Labour government's support for US military intervention in Afghanistan and Iraq reflects both historic and contemporary traditions of British foreign policy—a history of global interventionism and a powerful Anglo-American relationship since 1945.

Britain, EU Integration, and External Policy

Here we examine the extent to which British external policy is shaped by and shapes the external policies of the EU—that is, whether British foreign policy is becoming integrated with the machinery of EU external policies and outcomes.

As already mentioned, there are some areas of British external policy that are already ceded to the EU, and in particular the European Commission. As chapter 11 illustrates, the EU conducts much of the international dimension of Britain's environmental policy, and, though processes are complex, "EU member states have become increasingly willing to coordinate their positions and act collectively" (Lenschow 2005: 323).

While EU environmental policy is an arena that has emerged as a response to a changing international agenda, conduct of trade policy has been a treaty-based European Community competence from the outset. It is the European Commission, under the watchful eye of the Council of Ministers, that negotiates external trade agreements, which the Council can accept or reject by QMV—the classic "community method" of policy making. It must also be noted that the agenda of trade policy has broadened from matters of tariffs and quotas, to involve such related issues as labor, ethics, product safety, environmental factors, and other related areas. Britain's deep interests in international trade are evident from the appointment of successive trade commissioners—Peter Mandelson; his successor, Baroness Ashworth; and his predecessor, Leon Britton, were appointments made at the behest of the British government. Moreover, it is claimed, since Britain's accession, EU trade policy "has been shaped by a [UK] state that has deep liberal traditions" (Woolcock 2005: 390). The FCO, through its Economic Affairs Directorate and UKRep, are closely involved in the representation of British interests through COREPER II and contacts with the DG Trade. A specific cabinet subcommittee on European trade issues supplies political direction. British policy actors are thus firmly inserted into this arena of external policy; however, while opportunity for national lobbying is evident, "the key policy decisions are taken in Brussels" (Woolcock 2005: 398).

From its inception as European Political Cooperation (EPC) in the 1980s, successive British governments have attempted to shape the development of an EU foreign and security policy. Through close involvement, Britain has sought to preserve an image of leading status in matters diplomatic and to pursue its particular interests, not least to avoid undermining Britain's Atlanticist predisposition. Thus the pillar structure of the TEU, which clearly delineated CFSP in a separate (Pillar II) intergovernmental form and stressed the veto power of member states, was supported by Britain. As CFSP gained credence, it was a British proposal in 1999 to create a permanent committee of national diplomats to provide direction. The aim was to keep external policy in the orbit of the Council of Ministers; this led to the creation of the Political and Security Committee in 2000. Subsequently, the 2003 European Security Strategy echoed many British concerns, reflecting important input by British diplomats (Allen and Oliver 2004: 27). These and other examples represent successful uploading of British preferences to CFSP/ESDP and, as such, illustrate both effective bargaining and adaptive features of British foreign policy within this aspect of European integration.

In addition to its contribution to CFSP, the FCO provides considerable resources for British participation in the EU's intergovernmental conferences (IGCs)—sets of high-level meetings established to agree on major treaty amendments. Together with the European advisor in the Prime Minister's Office, a "position" on every aspect of an IGC agenda is established. The UK permanent representative in Brussels is appointed as a "personal representative" of the British government whose pre-decision bargaining skills are vital to a positive political outcome (Forster and Blair 2002: 104; Wall 2008). The issues involved are often highly technical and legalistic, and British negotiators have gained a reputation for their detailed examination of these matters that has, for some, confirmed an inherent negativity to any significant steps toward European integration. Since the political outcomes of an IGC produce considerable domestic commentary in Britain, such a cautious style would seem inevitable. Politicians must return home to face a generally Eurosceptic audience and must present the negotiations as a victory for Britain. Nevertheless, there has never been a situation where British "awkwardness" has, in itself, vetoed an eventual outcome (Forster and Blair 2002: 107).

As a major player within the EU, British foreign policy has adapted through its European dimension to share the objectives of CFSP and has influenced its direction through organizational changes so as to assert maximum influence on the EU's external dimension. To the extent that considerable foreign policy resources have been utilized in achieving an effective European policy outcome, British foreign policy has been integrated within CFSP. This bureaucratic adaptation is underscored by the attention given to European policy by the British executive and especially the prime minister, who, through the Prime Minister's Office, the Cabinet Secretariat, and "special advisors," attempts to provide political direction across controversial and complex issues.

But while British foreign policy and its processes have played a significant role and have integrated with the EU external dimension, it must be stressed that this integration is limited both by defense of Britain's Atlanticist perspective and by the limited scope of CFSP/ESDP itself. This is evident in Britain's insistence on a European defense capability that respects the presence of NATO, and thus the United States, and in the concern of successive British governments (in common with most other MS governments) to preserve the intergovernmental and thus limited CFSP processes originating in the TEU. In this way, aspects of British foreign policy have become integrated with an EU external face, but within a perspective that successfully sustains British aspirations to an Atlanticist, independent external presence. Symbolically, the FCO rejects the concept of sharing external diplomatic missions with other member states despite the obvious resource savings this would bring.

Europeanization and Intermestic Policies

A clearer perspective on the Europeanization of British foreign policy may be evident when considering the salience of the FCO in coordinating EU and UK (domestic) policy formulation. Since the SEA, the EU has deepened its policy competence considerably. As we have noted in chapter 9, British domestic policy processes are to a greater or lesser extent shaped by EU competences in this "intermestic" scenario. The FCO, and in particular the UKRep, seek to provide policy coordination by facilitating horizontal (uploading/downloading) and vertical (MS/MS) policy networks. The FCO may thus claim a "gatekeeper role" in the overall management of Britain's European policy.

In this context, UKRep is akin to a mini-Whitehall and is the Brussels home of civil servants from most domestic ministries. These officials provide representation and linkage with their London offices, link with relevant Commission DGs, and provide contact points for interest and issue groups. More recently, since the European Parliament has acquired an enhanced legislative role, British officials have spent time lobbying British MEPs and parliamentary groups to facilitate acceptable policy outcomes (Forster and Blair 2002: 80).

The expansion of the role of UKRep has produced a mixed outcome for the integrity of the FCO. On the one hand, a formal network of European policy coordination has emerged between senior officials of UKRep, the FCO, and the Cabinet Secretariat/PM's Office, within which UKRep plays a pivotal role. On the other hand, the FCO has conceded much of its formal gatekeeping role, as domestic ministries seek bilateral contact with their MS counterparts and EU institutions in the search for clear-cut policy information and outcomes (Forster and Blair 2002: 66). Thus it is tempting to conclude that the FCO has neither won nor lost in its new intermestic role within British European policy, but has adapted its processes to facilitate and coordinate policy outcomes across domestic and international boundaries.

Foreign and Security Policy in the Twenty-First Century

Our picture of the FCO at the hub of British foreign policy reflects several of the dilemmas for policy noted above. The expanded tasks of the FCO to cope with global economic interdependence require bi- and multilateral intervention of considerable complexity. In particular, the economic and political significance of the EU mixes traditional intergovernmental and bilateral contacts with the less traditional demands of "low politics" and intermestic issues that need effective Brussels representation and Whitehall coordination. The moves toward devolved government also present dilemmas for any single British external representative face.

As we suggest, foreign policy must be effective within clear coordinates. As an exploratory device, Churchill's three circles of interest may still be clung to, but with several caveats: the Commonwealth remains significant only insofar as it helps sustain an image of global reach for British diplomacy; the European circle has increased massively in terms of its salience to Britain's national interests, yet it fits uneasily with British pretensions to being a world player; while the emergence of the United States as the only global superpower in the post–Cold War period underscores Britain's need to sustain close transatlantic ties. To place Britain firmly at the intersection of European and US circles of interest and to gain the reputation of the "transatlantic bridge" was a key objective for successive governments throughout the 1990s. To a considerable extent it remains so today.

With the advent of the Bush administration and the US response to 9/11, standing firmly at the intersection of EU/US interests became more complex. Preventive actions to gain advantage in the "war on terror" and a reluctance to follow UN processes by the United States created a split in US-EU relations that was particularly evident in relation to the invasion of Iraq. The Blair government's steadfast support for President Bush revealed a division of EU opinion between "Atlanticists" and "Europeanists" that disrupted Britain's bridge-building capabilities. To balance this aspect of a dominant special relationship, Britain followed a consistent EU line, and thus opposed the US position on the Kyoto Protocol, the comprehensive Nuclear Test Ban Treaty, the International Criminal Court, and the Ottawa Convention (on land mines). Significantly, Britain has no choice but to support EU positions within the WTO and has therefore been party to several EU-US disputes, notably on US steel tariffs (2002) and the continuing arguments associated with agricultural subsidies and genetically modified crops. The EU's external (trade) policy remit also has had important impacts on Britain's relations with China and India, whose rapid economic growth in the past decade is of major global significance. Also EU-Russian relations are of significance, not least with regard to supplies of oil and gas to Europe—and thus Britain.

In common with the foreign policy of all states, Britain will take pragmatic initiatives to solve emerging problems within coordinates set by historic political and economic pathways. The war on terror produced strengthened support for the United States as a longtime ally. But as for all major players in international politics, the impact of global recession in 2008–2009 and the incoming Obama presidency have disturbed some of the more recent assumptions around which British foreign policy has been pursued. The new US president's willingness to adopt a more multilateral approach to US foreign policy and a willingness to open dialogues with previously shunned states has aligned the United States and the EU more closely. The necessity for Britain to make a choice between US or EU predispositions toward Iran; nuclear arms reduction; or, more generally, on the issue of climate change has eased. And as the March 2009 G20 conference in London illustrated, countries in the midst of a global recession have shown a willingness to adopt cooperative solutions to their economic difficulties. Despite a reported division in opinion between an Obama-Brown fiscal stimulus and a regulatory approach favored by France and Germany, the outcome of the conference was perceived as a diplomatic success. While these unusual circumstances remain, the pressure to choose between an Atlanticist- or EU-oriented foreign policy is reduced. It could be that Britain's long-term economic interests and, indeed, resolutions to security problems associated with terrorism, energy, and the environment may lie in closer regional ties within CFSP/ESDP. If this is the case, the events of 9/11, Afghanistan and the Iraq War, and the 2008–2009 global recession may be seen as only between parentheses in the reprioritization of Churchill's foreign policy interests toward a European destiny.

FURTHER READING

The FCO website (www.fco.gov.uk) is accessible and lucid. Brian Hocking and David Spence provide a comparative review of foreign ministries in the EU with a chapter on Britain by David Allen (2002). A historical review of Britain's foreign policy is contained in David Saunders's *Losing an Empire—Finding a Role* (1990). A concise account of postwar Britain's relations with Europe is in Alex May's *Britain and Europe since 1945* (1999). A longer and comprehensive review is in Hugo Young's excellent *This Blessed Plot: Britain and Europe from Churchill to Blair* (1998). The special relationship is a carefully observed in John Dumbrell's book *A Special Relationship: Anglo American Relations since 1960* (2000). Britain's EU foreign policy is explored in Anthony Forster and Alasdair Blair's *The Making of Britain's European Foreign Policy* (2002). On the Labour period 1997–2005, see Anthony Seldon and Dennis Kavanagh (eds.), *The Blair Effect* (2005); and for the Iraq war read *Blair's Wars* by John Kampfner (2003), or Con Coughlin, *American Ally: Tony Blair and the War on Terror* (2006).

A Conclusion—and Postscript

Spring 2009 was a less-than-ordinary three months in British politics. The prime minister hosted the G20 group of nations, receiving international and domestic praise for "brokering a $1.1 trillion injection of financial aid into the global economy" (*Guardian* 4 April 2009: 12). For this success a beleaguered Labour government received a short-lived "Brown bounce" in domestic opinion polls. There was hope that an economic recovery based on the encouragement of new and green technologies, along with planned public investments brought forward and a continued aspiration to meet targets in carbon reduction and international aid might lead to a fourth election victory.

Later in April a budget laid the financial ground for such a strategy. It also produced a desperately gloomy picture for Britain's medium-term economic future. Huge levels of national debt and deficit budgets that could only be dealt with by higher taxation and public service cuts were predicted as inevitable. Though not immediate in negative effect, the 2009 budget was deemed by one newspaper as "the budget from hell"! (*Observer* 19 April 2009). Nor were the government's woes purely financial. A close aide to Gordon Brown, Damien McBride, resigned after his proposals for a dirty-tricks Internet campaign against the Conservative opposition were exposed. An ill-advised appearance on YouTube by the prime minister revealed the limits of his public persona. And a well-organized campaign led by the popular actress Joanna Lumley brought government defeat in the House of Commons over the rights of ex-Gurkha soldiers who had served in the British army to settle in Britain. The withdrawal of British troops from Basra on 30 April, a promise that the Brown government had kept, was overshadowed by these domestic circumstances.

Faced with economic and financial problems and domestic faux pas, dealing with the outbreak of the Mexican swine flu pandemic might have been perceived as welcome political relief! This, however, was overshadowed in May–June by a further storm, as the issue of MPs' use of their allowances was brought to the fore by a newspaper, the *Daily Telegraph* (see chapter 4). The drip feed of details of how members had maximized their various allowance claims was to affect all parties; the *Telegraph*, a Conservative supporting daily, concentrated its initial blast on the government and Labour backbenchers. By the second week in May an opinion poll gave the Labour party its lowest standing in the polls (23%) since 1943 and public trust in their Westminster representatives had collapsed. Inevitably the results of the June European Parliament and local elections were devastating for the government.

Away from these headlines there is another less exciting account of British politics during spring 2009. In its fourteenth report for the 2008–2009 parliamentary session, the Commons European Scrutiny Committee invited debate over the posting of the Workers Directive in the Commons. DEFRA announced an implementation timetable for the Water Framework Directive. The ECJ delivered a judgment that denied the Dutch company TNT exemptions from value added tax similar to that for the Royal Mail. The Commission expressed concern with regard to Britain's deficit budget breach of the Stability and Growth Pact. The European Investment Bank, as part of a pledge to support Europe's car industry, was in negotiation with the British government for a supporting investment loan for the Jaguar-Landrover company. British ministers agreed to the creation of a European Systematic Risk Council that would have "macro prudential policy making powers" over all financial centers, including the City of London (*Guardian* 21 March 2009). And EU rules for controlling hedge funds were posted for negotiation by national ministries and the EP. In these two months the exceptional and complex nature of the British political system was illustrated in political Technicolor—and the House of Commons European Select Committee, DEFRA, the ECJ, and Commission continued with EU-British business as usual.

Other months have been and will be equally useful as examples of the complex realities of the British political system, but this short period is particularly apposite. The Westminster model seemed in one respect in rude health. The defeat of the government over Gurkhas' rights of settlement illustrated the strength of public opinion and the necessity of governments to take backbench opinion into consideration. The prime minister's albeit brief ascendency as an international leader illustrates the opportunities that come to a potential presidential persona. But without a supporting media, realizing leadership popularity is tough. The Westminster model also needs fair press winds. Scandals over MPs' allowances drained the remaining public legitimacy of the mother of Parliaments to the extent that one commentator offered it the title, "The Damned Parliament" (*Observer* 5 October 2009).

In the midst of headline calamities for government and Commons, "routine politics" continued, including in relation to the flow of interdependent British-EU governmental processes. "Direct effect" regulations, adjustments to EU directives, ECJ decisions, and the Commission's critical appraisal of the British government's economic decision making were all part of that two months in British politics. Policies that were designed to help the EU economy and British companies out of recession as well as regulations that would entail a new financial era were also applied to Britain and other member states. The "intermestic" nature of British public policy and its multilevel character were manifest even in this most unusual sixty-one days.

Each of these perspectives has its place in interpreting what goes on in British politics; indeed, they would seem symbiotic in their use, for it would be difficult to interpret what happens without reference to each. Exceptionalism and interdependence cannot be explained simplistically. However, as we have seen throughout this text, the notion of Europeanization as "the new kid on the conceptual block" must also be drawn into the analysis.

In this book's introduction it is argued that the sui generis nature of the EU reaches, through the treaty obligations of membership, into the domestic affairs of its member states. Thus the Europeanization of British politics and governance is as much part of "how things are" today as the iconic institutions of Westminster government or an evaluation of the undoubted powers of a British prime minister. Whether viewed as a set of shared values or as a phenomenon associated with the structures and processes of EU integration or as part of the examination of many British public policies, it cannot be ignored.

As is argued in chapters 9–12, evidence for the impact of Europeanization is clear in many arenas of British public policy. In some, such as CAP and external trade, Britain is one cog in a supranational process; in others, such as the environment and equal opportunities, objectives are set and the British policy and legal process implement them in a manner that reflects the spirit of EU legislation; other policy arenas—education, personal health, taxation, and trade union regulation—are kept at a political distance from supranational or shared decision making. But even in the areas of foreign affairs or monetary policy there are obligations that may curtail autonomous decision making. Thus a commitment to an EU Rapid Reaction Force has resource implications, while infringement of budget deficit limits set by the Stability and Growth Pact would produce a public embarrassment that the British Treasury could do without.

In so many respects, British public policy has become Europeanized. And in either implementation (downloading) or attempting to shape policies (uploading), policy actors have adapted to the multilevel nature of EU governance. This adaptation, as we discussed in several chapters, involves new pathways for pressure groups and opportunities for subgovernments to act institutionally in influencing the outcomes of British-EU negotiations and agreements. It involves the (horizontal) search for allies across national boundaries as well as (vertical) networking.

We have also noted the synonymous use of the terms *Europeanization* and *integration*, which implies not just the harmonization or approximation of policies in several arenas by different member states, but also the establishment of transformed MS institutions and processes within a supranational EU political system. This involves a full engagement within EU institutions by political actors of all member states as well as a necessary adjustment to supranational and intergovernmental processes by domestic institutions and players. Since 1973, political, technical, and bureaucratic resources have been directed to enhance Britain's membership. Ministers and prime ministers must devote an extensive part of their time and political capital in making the EU "work" for Britain. The civil service and devolved institutions, indeed all subgovernments, have also adapted their organizations and priorities to deal with an EU "dimension." Some of these adaptations might be considered transformational. The creation of the Brussels-based UKRep and its central coordinating role in EU external and domestic policy has produced a refocus of resources and personnel within Whitehall. A European "stream" of bureaucrats was one result; another was the creation of regional government offices as part of a coordinating strategy to enhance the links between British and EU regional policies.

But for the most part, most institutional adaptation to EU integration has been more incorporative than transformational. There is no Ministry for Europe, only a (junior) minister. Parliament has created two select committees to oversee the flow of EU policies, both of which would seem poorly resourced for the tasks they undertake. While MEPs are now elected by proportional representation, public interest in their activities is minimal; and within the "core executive" the attention to advice and the institutional position of European affairs within the PM's Office/Cabinet Office and in the cabinet is within the remit and predilections of the PM of the day.

If there is only limited evidence of the direct transformational impact of European integration on British government, there is room for conjecture over the impact that devolved powers to the Celtic nations may have on London's ability to control and coordinate EU-British affairs. The potential for disagreement between politically vocal devolved governments is only one unknown on a path that may lead to the fundamental re-assessment of Britain's unitary system and thus the relationship of its na-tions with the EU.

Finally, since European integration is not only about organizational and institutional change of member states, but also about the direction of the "European Project," concluding comments must deal with the issue of Europeanization as shared (European) values. The Irish "no" in June 2008, sub-sequently reversed in a second referendum (October 2009), however imperfect a proxy it may be for British attitudes to the Reform Treaty, high-lighted some common difficulties that both states have in coming to terms with an EU of the twenty-first century. While there may have been special factors that explain the negative response by the Irish electorate (abortion, neutrality, CAP, etc.) a major contributing factor was, it was claimed by "no" voters, a lack of knowledge about the treaty and the EU in general.

The EU was created by elites in historic circumstances, the aftermath of a world war, that encouraged expectations of a de facto popular legiti-mation of their idealism, for the EU was presented as a peace project. As discussed in chapter 1, British elites and popular opinion did not share this idealism. A different history and different wartime experience shaped a belief in the exceptional character of Britain as a world-class nation-state. Joining the EU in 1973 was therefore a pragmatic economic step—not a step into a European dream. A historic antipathy to Continental rivals, memories of nineteenth-century hegemonic status, and the links with the Commonwealth and the United States were, and remain, countervailing factors to a shared European destiny.

Substantial sectors of Britain's populace have strong reactions to Eu-rope, manifest in a pervasive Whig-imperial view of the past and enshrined in a myth of parliamentary sovereignty. These views are reinforced by a famously hostile national press, and thus parties and their leaders have a politically understandable tendency to avoid disturbing the EU elephant in the room. The British electorate, perhaps even more than their Irish counterparts, have little opportunity to overcome a considerable ignorance of matters EU. For most, therefore, Europeanization today is as it was in the 1970s—a matter of economic necessity rather than an ideal. At worst it is no ideal at all but rather the antithesis of an independent nation-state.

There is, however, another perspective to this scenario. Since 1997 a considerable majority of MPs have adopted pro-EU credentials; the House of Lords has, since its partial reform, also produced a more positive EU outlook. Governments since 1973, save for short periods, have played an initially reluctant but mostly constructive role in decision making and, once agreement has been reached, have implemented EU policies effec-tively. The Lisbon Agenda and enlargement to twenty-seven members largely met the strategic objectives of both Conservative and Labour perspectives of a wider open market–driven EU. Demographic and social changes in Britain, demonstrated in chapter 2, have brought, in the guise of labor mobility, travel, and consumerism, a new awareness of Continental neighbors and their lives and some notion of the advantages of social and economic interdependence within a European Community. Finally, the recession and the need to find international solutions to its impact may yet produce a willingness on behalf of British elites to view the EU as part of the solution rather than the problem. It is in the light of these factors that the politics of Britain in Europe and Europe in Britain should be observed.

The European Union
An Official Interpretation

The following is taken directly from the Foreign and Commonwealth Office website *Britain and the EU*. As such, it is an official public iteration of the role of Britain's position within the EU in 2008. Additional comments by the author are in italics.

WHAT IS THE EU?

The European Union (EU) is a unique partnership in which countries work closely together for the benefit of all their citizens.

The twenty-seven current **member states** of the EU have agreed to work together on issues of common interest, where collective and coordinated initiatives can be more effective than individual state action.

Born out of the devastation of the Second World War, this unprecedented cooperation has developed over the last fifty years to consolidate the peace and prosperity of Europe and create a powerful collective voice on the world stage.

The EU represents the latest development of the European Economic Community, which was established in 1958 by just six nations: France, West Germany, Belgium, the Netherlands, Italy, and Luxembourg.

The EU extended the scope of the European Economic Community and was formally created on 1 November 1993 when the **Maastricht treaty** entered into force.

The EU is governed by a series of treaties, negotiated at intergovernmental conferences (IGCs) and ratified by each member state. Its work is carried out by a number of different institutions, from the European

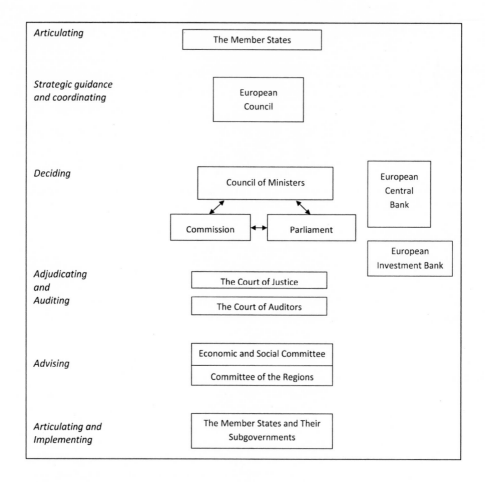

Council and Council of Ministers through to the European Commission, European Parliament, and European Court of Justice.

WHY DO THE EU TREATIES MATTER?

The EU has developed through a series of treaties that define its rules. They also define the institutions that carry out the work of the EU.

These treaties must be agreed by each member country, and when ratified according to its own national processes establish the basic rules and institutions that the union need to function, and which members are expected to follow.

The key treaties in the development of the EU (including the dates they were signed) are set out below.

The Treaty of Rome (signed 1957, entered into force 1958)

This Treaty established the European Economic Community (EEC), the forerunner of the EU with six original members.

The Single European Act (signed 1986, entered into force 1987)

This treaty was designed to give the power to the EEC to make laws in areas that supported the goal of free flow of goods and services across Europe.

The Maastricht Treaty (signed 1992, entered into force 1993)

The Maastricht Treaty established the European Union, which encompasses the European Community and co-operation in **common foreign and security policy** and **justice and home affairs**. The Treaty also established the groundwork for a single European currency.

There have been other treaties, such as Amsterdam (signed 1977, entered into force 1999) and Nice (signed 2001, entered into force 2003), which address particular issues and amend previous treaties.

The Proposed Constitutional Treaty (signed 2004)

At the end of 2004 the governments of member states agreed a new treaty, known as the Constitutional Treaty, designed to rationalize and streamline the operation of the union. The Constitutional Treaty would have replaced all existing EU treaties and re-founded the EU, *but it was rejected by French and Dutch referenda (2005).*

The Lisbon Treaty (signed 2007)

The Lisbon Treaty will make the changes needed for an EU of twenty-seven to work more effectively. It will allow the EU to move on from debating institutional changes and focus on issues which matter to citizens: energy security, organized crime and terrorism, globalisation, further enlargement and making Europe's voice more effective internationally.

The mandate for a new Treaty was agreed by the leaders of all twenty-seven EU member states at the European Council in June 2007. The Lisbon Treaty is not a freestanding document, like the Constitutional Treaty, but instead like the Single European Act and the Treaties of Maastricht, Nice and Amsterdam, will only amend existing EU Treaties.

The Lisbon Treaty will have to be ratified by all member states according to their own constitutional procedures. As with all treaties, the UK Parliament must be satisfied that it is in the national interest before it can be implemented in national law. *In a referendum in June 2008, the Irish people rejected the ratification by the Irish government. This decision was reversed in a second referendum in October 2009. As of this date only the Czech Republic has not ratified the treaty.*

THE INSTITUTIONS

What Does the Council of Ministers Do?

The Council of Ministers is the EU's most important decision-making body. Its main task is to approve European laws. Though a single institution, the Council meets in a variety of configurations: for instance the general Affairs and External Relations Council (GAERC) and the Economic and Financial Affairs Council (Ecofin). These councils are formed by ministers from each member state, usually with a national responsibility for the subject under discussion. For example, if the proposed legislation concerned agriculture, the UK would send its Minister for Agriculture.

The member state holding the presidency is responsible for organizing the business of the Council, assisted by a permanent secretariat based in Brussels.

What Does the European Council Do?

The European Council meets quarterly to set the EU's agenda and priorities. It provides the EU with strategic direction and impetus. European Council conclusions signal the future course of action for the EU.

The European Council is formed by the presidents or prime ministers of each member state, also bringing together their foreign ministers and the president of the European Commission.

The meetings (usually called European "summits") are chaired by whichever country holds the European presidency, which rotates every six months from one member state to the next. *If the Lisbon Treaty is ratified, the chair of the council, its presidency, will be elected by its members with a 2½-year period of office. Candidates need not be from the existing Council.*

What Does the European Commission Do?

The European Commission implements the agenda set by the European Council. It does this by:

- Developing and drafting legislation or other non-legislative measures and
- Monitoring implementation

The Commission is the executive organ of the European Community (the equivalent of our civil service). It is based in Brussels and organized in twenty-four directorates, each led by a European commissioner.

Every member country currently nominates one commissioner, who has a particular area of responsibility for five-year term, such as agriculture or trade. The commissioners' work is overseen by the president of the Commission.

The Commission acts as the guardian of the **treaties**, ensuring that member states respect the treaties and community law, and that they implement adopted legislation. The Commission's role is less developed in the "intergovernmental" activities of the **Common Foreign and Security Policy** and **Justice and Home Affairs.** *Under the Lisbon Treaty, after 2014 only two-thirds of the member states will provide a commissioner at anytime, with every country taking equal turns.*

What Does the European Parliament Do?

The members of the European Parliament (MEPs) are elected directly for a five-year term by the populations of the member states. The elections use a system of proportional representation. The next elections for the European Parliament take place in 2014. There are currently 732 MEPs (the UK has 78). The elected MEPs sit in seven political groups and not as national delegations.

Like national parliaments, much of the work is done in smaller committees of MEPs, which prepare reports for consideration by the full Parliament. These full or "plenary" sessions are held in either Strasbourg or Brussels. In these sessions MEPs review proposals in the light of these committee reports and move to an agreed position on each proposal.

MEPs must:

- Consider most of the laws proposed by the Commission before submission to the Council of Ministers
- Monitor the actions of other EU bodies
- Approve the EU's budget.

They can also hold the Commission to account.

There are three main formal decision-making processes through which the Parliament is involved in the enactment of the EU's legal instruments: consultation, assent, and co-decision.

With consultation, the Parliament must be consulted, but its view will not be binding on the Council, which has the final decision-making power. Key areas for consultation include agriculture, competition, discrimination, tax, and legal migration.

In the assent procedure, Parliament legislates jointly with the Council of Ministers. They may meet in "conciliation committees" to resolve differences and agree a joint text.

The co-decision procedure applies to most areas of legislation, notably the internal market, citizenship rights, and free movement of labor, employment, and social policy, environmental and consumer protection, development cooperation, visa and asylum policy, and illegal immigration. *Under the Lisbon Treaty co-decision is the "default" procedure for EU legislative process.*

What Do the European Courts Do?

Each member country sends a judge to the Luxembourg-based European Court of Justice (EC).The 27 judges are assisted by nine advocates general. The court exists to ensure that laws passed at a European level are applied and interpreted correctly. Some areas (notably the common foreign and security policy—CFSP) are outside its jurisdiction. In certain circumstances, individuals can also bring proceedings against EU institutions before the ECJ.

The Court of Auditors, based in Luxembourg, also has one member nominated from each member state for a renewable six-year term. It is a different kind of court altogether. Its job is to review the accounts of the European Union. The court must verify that the funds available to the EU are used legally, economically, efficiently, and effectively, and for the intended purpose. It audits the accounts of the EU's revenue and expenditure to promote maximum value for the citizens of the EU. The court submits an annual report on the use made by the EU of public funds.

How Do EU Laws Get Made?

The **European Commission** monitors the functioning of the EU. Where problems (for instance inequalities in trading) arise it may draft a new law or suggest other measures to tackle them, provided the necessary powers have been given to the EU in the treaties.

The European Parliament and Council will review, and may amend, the Commission's proposals. In many cases, especially Single Market measures, the European Parliament and the Council of Ministers are "co-legislators"—sharing decision-making power. For the sensitive areas (tax, foreign policy, and defence), every member nation has a veto: if just one country opposes the law, then it won't be passed. In most other areas, decisions are taken in the Council of Ministers through "**qualified majority voting**" (QMV).

For a law to be approved under QMV, at least half the member nations must vote for it. What's more, these votes should represent at least 62 percent of the total population of the EU. And, finally, a minimum of 232 votes out of a total of 321 weighted votes (allocated to each country according to population) must also be in favor.

Under the Lisbon Treaty, a new double-majority voting system will be introduced with a minimum of 55 percent of EU members representing 65 percent of the population before legislation is progressed.

In practice this system has proved highly effective in pulling down trade barriers, ensuring that all member countries have equal access to each other's markets.

Once a law has been agreed at European level, member states are obliged to ensure their national laws are consistent with it. They must do so even if they opposed the law in the Council of Ministers but were outvoted by the majority. Any nation joining the EU must agree that laws passed at a European level take precedence over national law. Without this principle—called the Primacy of European Law—the EU would not function. Members could pick and choose which laws they obeyed, making those laws meaningless. For instance when France tried to ban certain beef imports from the UK, the court ruled that the ban was illegal and forced France to abandon it.

EU Policies

Fundamental to the EU is the idea that many areas of policy can be more effective if established at a supranational rather than a national level. Policy areas include removing trade barriers to boost growth and jobs; improving our environment; and fighting international crime and illegal immigration. In many cases these policies must then be turned into law, binding across borders. The EU has created a framework of processes and institutions to do this. The framework has evolved through a series of intergovernmental conferences (IGCs) and **treaties** that must be ratified by each member state.

Above all, European laws underpin **the single European Market**, designated to create uniform trading conditions and the free movement of goods, persons, services, and capital between all EU member states. Overall, the EU has proved remarkably successful in balancing the individual interests of member states against the benefits of pan-European collaboration.

How Is EU Policy Developed?

There are essentially three levels of policy making within the EU.

Treaty changes can only happen with the agreement of all governments of the member states. The **treaties** must be ratified by national Parliaments. Everything the EU does must be consistent with the treaties. The broad direction of European policies, within that framework, is set by the European Council every three months.

The European Commission then works within the policy direction set by the European Councils to identify requirements for detailed policy development. It will engage directly with the relevant departments of member governments to formulate policy proposals that can be taken forward for legislation.

In the UK for instance, an EU policy on agriculture would be considered by the Department for Environment, Food and Rural Affairs, but the treaty would also have a view on budgetary implications. Any disagreement between departments would be resolved at ministerial level, with meetings chaired by the foreign secretary.

The EU has four different types of legal instrument:

- Regulations, which are binding and directly applicable in all member states
- Directives, which define a required result but leave member states to decide the best means to achieve it
- Decisions, which are binding on the bodies to which they are addressed
- Opinions and recommendations, which have no binding force

There are three main decision-making processes to enact these instruments: consultation, assent, and co-decision.

Does the EU Really Matter?

As the fifth-largest economy in the world, the UK is important to the prosperity of the EU, but the EU is equally important to the UK economy. Some simple facts speak volumes.

Over half our trade in goods and service is with other EU countries. Eight of our top trading partners are EU member states. One-seventh of all UK income and production is linked to trade with other EU members. Over 3 million jobs in the UK are linked to exports to the EU.

The EU forms the largest single market in the world and accounted for 40 percent of global trade in 2004. There are over 450 million people in this market for **EU businesses**. 100,000 Britons work in other EU countries, and another 350,000 live in those countries.

Single-market competition has halved the price of air travel within Europe. The price of international phone calls has fallen within the EU by 80 percent since 1984.

The Cost to Britain

Britain's contribution to the EU amounts to approximately £175 per head of its population per year. This money is funded from general taxation. But that's only half the story. We put this money in, but we also get a lot back through:

- Funding for projects
- Funding specifically targeted at the country's economically deprived areas
- Support for agriculture, etc.

This funding means the real direct cost is about £50 per head per year, or about £1 per person per week.

But it's also estimated that membership is worth about £300 per head per year to the UK economy as a whole, through increased trade, lower cross-border costs, and so on. In other words, membership is certainly a good financial investment for the UK. That estimate looks only at quantifiable benefits. Membership also brings less tangible benefits like better environment and better security. Many of the benefits of EU membership are also not directly financial.

Better cross-border cooperation can create real benefits in areas like **security** or policies on **climate change**. But if the financial equations did not add up, then the other areas of cooperation would have been much harder to achieve.

The EU is a complex entity, and so are its finance. But there's no real doubt that our membership brings economic as well as tangible benefits. The challenge is to ensure that those benefits are maximized in the changing conditions of the world.

UK-EU FACTS

The 2007 Spring Council underlined EU global leadership on **climate change** and set Europe on a fast track to becoming the world's first competitive, energy secure, low-carbon economy. The Council reached a historic agreement to an independent commitment to cut greenhouse gas emissions by at least 20 percent from 1990 levels to 2020.

The Commission estimates that business and consumers could save up to £19 billion a year from the **cost of cross-border transactions** once the Payments Service Directive is implemented.

Three million jobs in the UK are linked, directly and indirectly, to the export of goods and services to the EU. The estimated **employment gains** from the single market amount to 1.4 percent of total employment in the EU in 2006—equivalent to 2.7 million jobs.

Approximately 70 percent of UK employment is in services. Economic analysts estimate that the recently agreed **Services Directive** could be worth approximately £5 billion annually to the UK economy, and could deliver around 600,000 new jobs.

British nationals made 53 million **visits to the rest of Europe** in 2006—a 50 percent rise since 1998. Five percent of British nationals—that's 2.2 million—now own property overseas. Four percent are elsewhere in Europe.

More than half the money spent to help poor countries comes from the European Union and its member states, making the EU **the world's biggest aid donor.** In May 2005, EU ministers agreed to a new collective target of 0.56 percent of the GNP of the member states for 2010, which would result in an additional €20 billion of aid by that time. They also set 2015 as the date for reaching 0.7 percent.

Each year, well over 1 million EU citizens of all ages benefit from EU-funded **educational, vocational, and citizenship-building programs.** The EU funds initiatives in the member states for educational establishments and for students via a Lifelong Learning Programme. More than €7 billion has been allocated to this initiative for 2007–2013.

Consumers across the European Union will benefit from tougher holiday protection when they buy and resell **timeshare holidays;** timeshare-like holidays on cruise boats, canal boats, or caravans; and popular "discount holiday clubs" under new rules proposed by the European Commission.

Fifty-seven percent of total **British trade** is with the EU; British companies exported approximately £150 billion worth of goods to the EU27 in 2006—that is, 62 percent of total exports, and a rise of 24 percent compared to 2005.

Full liberalization of the "network" industries in the EU (e.g., telecommunications, air travel) could increase prosperity by a further 1.3–1.7 percent of GDP—up to €95 billion—and increase employment by between 140,000 and 360,000 jobs.

Abolition of customs duties already saves British businesses an estimated £135 million a year.

Enlargement is one of the EU's most successful policies, strongly backed by the UK, establishing peace and prosperity in an ever-widening

Union. During the UK presidency in 2005 Turkey and Croatia opened their accession negotiations. UK support was instrumental in opening accession negotiations with Romania, Bulgaria, the Slovak Republic, Latvia, Lithuania, and Malta in 1999. EU accession negotiations with Hungary, Poland, Estonia, the Czech Republic, Slovenia, and Cyprus began under the UK's presidency of the EU in 1998.

The European Defence and Security Policy has enabled the EU to make a real difference in the Balkans, the Middle East, Africa, and post-tsunami Indonesia, with 16 missions to date, deploying over 11,000 military personnel and around 600 civilians.

On the **Middle East peace process**, the EU contributes to the international community's efforts. There are currently two EU missions in the region, one supporting the Palestinian Civil Police and the other the Rafah border mission—for which the EU was the only monitoring party acceptable to both Israelis and Palestinians. The EU gave a total of €680 million to the Palestinians in 2006, more than in any previous year.

Britain's Institutional Representation (2009)

The European Council	PM as UK representative
The Council of Ministers	Ministers as required (1 per functional Council)
Commission	1 commissioner (out of 27)
European Parliament	72 MEPs (out of 736)
Court of Justice	1 judge
Court of Auditors	1 member
European Central Bank	Bank of England Chairman on General Council only (Britain outside eurozone)
European Investment Bank	designated minister on Board of Governors. 1 nominee on Board of Directors
Economic and Social Committee	24 members (appointed)
Committee of Regions	24 local and regional politicians
UK Permanent Representation (UKRep) (diplomatic/bureaucratic support)	FCO and Whitehall representation in Brussels as "embassy" to the EU
UK National Parliament Office	small office
Scottish, Welsh, Irish, and several English Regional Offices	separate Brussels-based offices
EU Council and Commission bureaucracy	British advisory and bureaucratic presence in the complex of technical profession committees, supporting Council of Ministers and Commission DGs (comitology)
Functional Agencies	Britain also has professional/technical staff working in functional agencies such as the European Environment Agency, Europol, Food Safety Authority, etc.

References

Allen, David. 1992. "European Union, the SEA and 1992." In Dennis Swann (ed.), *The Single Market and Beyond*, pp. 26–52. London: Routledge.

———. 2002. "The United Kingdom: Adapting to the European Union within a Transformed World." In Brian Hocking and David Spence (eds.), *Foreign Ministries in the European Union*, pp. 250–72. Basingstoke: Macmillan.

Allen, David, and Tim Oliver. 2004. "The Europeanisation of the Foreign and Commonwealth Office." ESRC/UACES Europeanisation of British Politics Conference, Sheffield University, March.

Almond, Gabriel. 1958. "A Comparative Study of Interest Groups and the Political Process." *American Political Science Review* 52 (March): 270–82.

Anderson, Benedict. 1991. *Imagined Communities: Reflections on the Origin and Spread of Nationalism*. London: Verso.

Anderson, Peter. 2004. "A Flag of Convenience? Discourse and Motivations of the London-based Eurosceptic Press." *European Studies* 20: 161–71.

Anderson, Peter, and Anthony Weymouth. 1999. *Insulting the Public? The British Press and the European Union*. London: Longmans.

Ashley, Jacky. 2006. "Brace Yourselves: Labour Is Getting a Big Issue Right." *Guardian*, Monday, May 22, p. 33.

Aughey, Arthur. 2005. *The Politics of Northern Ireland: Beyond the Belfast Agreement*. London: Routledge.

Bache, Ian. 2008. *Europeanization and Multilevel Governance*. Lanham, MD: Rowman & Littlefield.

Bache, Ian, and Matthew Flinders (eds.). 2004. *Multi-level Governance*. Oxford: Oxford University Press.

Bache, Ian, and Andrew Jordan (eds.). 2006. *The Europeanisation of British Politics*. Basingstoke: Palgrave, Macmillan.

Bache, Ian, and Alex Marshall. 2004. "Europeanisation and Domestic Change: A Governance Approach to Institutional Adaptation in Britain." Queens Papers on Europeanization. Belfast: Queens University.

Bagehot, Walter. 1963. *The English Constitution*. London: Fontana.

Baggott, Rob. 1995. *Pressure Groups Today*. Manchester: Manchester University Press.

Bainbridge, M., B. Burkitt, and P. Whyman. 2000. *The Impact of the Euro: Debating Britain's Future*. Basingstoke: Macmillan.

Baker, David. 2003. *The Shotgun Marriage: Managing Eurosceptical Opinion in British Political Parties, 1972–2002*. EUSA Eighth Biennial International Conference, Nashville, TN, March 27.

———. 2005. "Islands of the Mind: New Labour's Defensive Engagement with the European Union." *Political Quarterly* 76 (1).

Baker, David, Alex Gamble, and David Seawright. 2002. "Sovereign Nations and Global Markets." *British Journal of Politics and International Relations* 4 (3): 399–428.

Baker, David, and David Seawright (eds.). 1998. *Britain for and against Europe: British Politics and the Question of European Integration*. Oxford: Clarendon Press.

Bale, Tim. 2005. *European Politics*. Basingstoke: Palgrave.

Barnett, Correlli. 1972. *The Collapse of British Power*. London: Alan Sutton.

Bartle, John, and Samantha Laycocks. 2006. "Elections and Voting." In Patrick Dunleavy et al. (eds.), *Developments in British Politics 8*, pp. 77–97. Basingstoke: Palgrave Macmillan.

Beloff, Lord. 1998. "Amery on the Constitution: Britain and the European Union." *Government and Opposition* 33 (2): 167–82.

Bevir, Mark, and Rod Rhodes. 2003. *Interpreting British Governance*. London: Routledge.

Blair, John. 2000. *The Anglo-Saxon Age*. Oxford: Oxford University Press.

Blair, Tony. 2000. "Superpower: Not Superstate?" *European Essay* no. 12.

Bogdanor, Vernon. 1999. *Devolution in the UK*. Oxford: Oxford University Press.

———. 2001. "Gladstone's Hour." *Prospect* (February), 22–25.

Bogdanor, Vernon (ed.). 2005a. *The British Constitution in the 20th Century*. Oxford: Clarendon.

———. 2005b. *Joined-up Government*. London: The British Academy.

Bort, Eberhard. 2005. "The New Institutions: An Interim Assessment." In Michael O'Neill (ed.), *Devolution and British Politics*, pp. 295–307. Harlow, UK: Longman.

Borzel, Tanja. 2003. "Shaping and Taking EU Policies: Member States' Responses to Europeanization." Queens Papers on Europeanization, no. 2-2003. Belfast: Queens University.

Bower, Tom. 2003. *Gordon Brown*. London: Harper Collins.

———. 2005. *Gordon Brown*. Rev. ed. London: Harper Perennial.

Brazier, Alex (ed.) 2004. *Parliament, Politics and Law Making*. London: Hansard Society.

Bretherton, Charlotte, and Liz Sperling. 1996. "Women's Networks and the EU." *Journal of Common Market Studies* 34: 477–508.

Bretherton, Charlotte A., and John Vogler. 2006. *The European Union as a Global Actor*. London: Routledge.

Brewer, Mike, et al. 2005. *Poverty and Inequality in Britain: 2005*. London: Institute of Fiscal Studies.

British Election Study. 2005. 2005 Elections, University of Essex. Available at: http://www.essex.ac.uk?bes/2005.

Broad, Roger, and Virginia Preston. 2001. *Moored to the Continent? Britain and European Integration*. London: Institute of Historical Research, University of London.

Bromley, Catherine, John Curtice, and Ben Sneyd. 2004. *Is Britain Facing a Crisis of Democracy?* London: Constitution Unit.

Brussels European Council. 2007. *Presidency Conclusions*. Brussels: Council of the European Union. CONCL 2, 21–22 June.

Buller, James. 2004. "The Disadvantage of Tying One's Hands: Towards an Understanding of the Controversial Nature of Europeanization in the Area of British Monetary Policy." *Britain in Europe—Europe in Britain: The Europeanization of British Politics*. ESRC/UACES Conference. University of Sheffield, 16 July.

Buller, James, and Alex Gamble. 2004. "Conceptualising Europeanisation." *ESRC/UACES Study Group on the Europeanisation of British Politics and Policy-Making*. Research Paper. University of Sheffield.

Bulmer, Simon, et al. 2007. *Policy Transfer in European Union Governance*. London: Routledge.

Bulmer, Simon, and Martin Burch. 1998. "Organising for Europe: Whitehall, The British State and the European Union." *Public Administration* 76 (4): 601–28.

———. 2004. "The Europeanization of UK Government: From Quiet Revolution to Explicit Step Change?" *Britain in Europe—Europe in Britain: The Europeanization of British Politics*. ESRC/UACES Conference. Sheffield Town Hall, 16 July.

———. 2009. *The Europeanization of Whitehall: UK Central Government and the European Union*. Manchester: Manchester University Press.

Bulmer, Simon, and C. M. Radaelli. 2004. "The Europeanization of National Policy?" Queens Papers on Europeanization, no 1-2004. Belfast: Queens University.

Bulmer, Simon, et al. 2002. *British Devolution and European Policy Making: Transforming Britain into Multi-Governance*. Basingstoke: Palgrave Macmillan.

Bulpitt, James. 1967. *Party Politics in English Local Government*. London: Longman.

———. 1983. *Territory and Power in the United Kingdom*. Manchester: Manchester University Press.

Burch, Martin, and Simon Bulmer. 2001. "The Europeanisation of Central Government: The UK and Germany." In G. Schneider and M. Aspinall (eds.), *The Rules of Integration: Institutional Approaches to the Study of Europe*. Manchester: Manchester University Press.

Burch, Martin, and Ricardo Gomez. 2006. "The English Regions 82–97." In Ian Bache and Andrew Jordan (eds.), *The Europeanization of British Politics*. Basingstoke: Palgrave Macmillan.

Butler, David, and Gareth Butler. 2006. *British Political Facts since 1979*. Basingstoke: Palgrave MacMillan.

Butler, David, and Uwe Kitzinger. 1976. *The 1975 Referendum*. London: Macmillan.

Cabinet Office. 1999. *Modernising Government* (Cm 4310). London TSO.

Cable, Vincent. 2009. *The Storm: World Economic Crisis and What It Means*. London: Atlantic Books.

Cannadine, David. 1998. *History in Our Time*. New Haven, CT: Yale University Press.

Carey, Sean, and Jonathan Burton. 2004. "Research Note: The Influence of the Press in Shaping Public Opinion towards the European Union." *Political Studies* 52: 623–40.

Carson, Rachel. 1962. *Silent Spring*. Boston: Houghton Mifflin.

Carter, Elizabeth, and Robert Ladrech. 2007. "Government Change, Organizational Continuity: The Limited Europeanization of British Political Parties." In Thomas Poguntke et al. (eds.), *The Europeanization of National Political Parties*. London: Routledge.

Carter, Neil. 2001. *The Politics of the Environment: Ideas, a Division, Policy*. Cambridge: Cambridge University Press.

Chapman, Rachel. 2006. "The Third Sector." In Ian Bache and Andrew Jordan (eds.), *The Europeanization of British Politics*, pp. 168–73,. Basingstoke: Palgrave, Macmillan.

Childs, David. 1992. *Britain since 1945: A Political History*. 3rd ed. London: Routledge.

Childs, Sarah. 2006. "Political Parties and Political Systems." In Patrick Dunleavy et al. (eds.), *Developments in British Politics 8*, pp. 56–76. Basingstoke: Palgrave.

Chitty, C. 2005. "Education Policy." In P. Dorey (ed.), *Developments in British Public Policy*, pp. 46–66. London: Sage.

Chryssochoou, D. 2007. "Democracy and the European Polity." In M. Cini (ed.), *European Union Politics*, pp. 359–74. Oxford: Oxford University Press.

Clarke, Harold, David Sanders, Marianne Stewart, and Paul Whiteley. 2004. *Political Choice in Britain*. Oxford: Oxford University Press.

CIA. 2008. *World Factbook*. Available at: www.cia.gov/cia/publications/factbook/index.html (accessed 20 July 2004).

Club of Rome. 1972. *Limits to Growth*. New York: Universe Books.

CM7170 [Ministry of Justice]. 2007. *The Governance of Britain* (Green Paper). London: HMSO.

Coates, David. 1994. *The Question of UK Decline*. Hemel Hempstead, UK: Harvester Wheatsheaf.

Cobham, D., and G. Zis (eds.). 1999. *From EMS to EMU: 1979 to 1999 and Beyond*. Basingstoke: Macmillan.

Cohen, Nick. 2000. *Cruel Britannia: Reports on the Sinister and the Preposterous*. London and New York: Verso.

Coleman, James. 1973. *The Mathematics of Collective Action*. London: Heinermann.

Copus, C. 2004. *Party Politics and Local Government*. Manchester: Manchester University Press.

Corbett, Richard, Frances Jacobs, and Mike Shackleton. 2003. "The European Parliament at Fifty: One View from the Inside." *Journal of Common Market Studies* 41 (2): 353–73.

———. 2007. *The European Parliament*. 7th ed. London: John Harper.

Cornford, James (ed.). 1975. *The Failure of the State: On the Distribution of Political and Economical Power in Europe*. London: Rowman and Littlefield.

Coughlin, Con. 2006. *American Ally: Tony Blair and the War on Terror*. New York: HarperCollins.

Coxall, Bill, and Lynton Robins. 1998. *British Politics since the War.* New York: St. Martin's Press.

Cowley, Philip. 2006. "Making Parliament Matter?" In Patrick Dunleavy et al. (eds.), *Developments in British Politics 8*, pp. 36–55. Basingstoke: Palgrave Macmillan.

Cowley, Philip, and Jane Green. 2005. "New Leaders—Same Problems: The Conservatives." In Andrew Geddes and Jon Tonge (eds.), *Britain Decides: The UK General Election, 2005*, pp. 46–69. Basingstoke: Palgrave.

Crafts, Neill. 1997. *Britain's Relative Decline, 1870–1995.* London: Social Market Foundation.

Craig, David, and Richard Brooks. 2006. *Plundering the Public Sector.* London: Constable.

Crewe, Ivor. 2002. "A New Political Hegemony?" In Anthony King (ed.), *Britain at the Polls, 2001*, pp. 207–32. New York: Chatham House.

Crowson, Neill. 2006. *The Conservative Party and European Integration since 1945.* London: Routledge.

Curran, James, and Jean Seaton. 2003. *Power without Responsibility: The Press and Broadcasting in Britain.* London: Routledge.

Curry, D. 2002. *Farming and Food: A Sustainable Future.* London: Cabinet Office.

Curtice, J. S. Fisher, and M. Steel. 2005. "The Results Analyzed." In Dennis Kavanagh and David Butler (eds.), *The British General Election of 2005*, pp. 235–59. Basingstoke: Palgrave.

Daddow, Oliver. 2006. "Euroscepticism and the Culture of the Discipline of History." *Review of International Studies* 32: 1–20.

Davies, Norman. 1996. *Europe: A History.* Oxford: Oxford University Press.

———. 1999. *The Isles: A History.* Basingstoke, Macmillan.

Davis, Aeron. 2002. *Public Relations Democracy: Public Relations, Politics and the Mass Media in Britain.* Manchester and New York: Manchester University Press.

DEFRA (Department for Environment, Food and Rural Affairs). 2004. "Defra Celebrates Its Third Anniversary." Available at: http://www.defra.gov.uk/news/latest/2004/anniversary.

Democratic Audit. 1994. *Ego Trip: Extra-Governmental Organizations in the UK and Their Accountability.* Essex: Essex Human Rights Centre: University of Essex.

Denham, A. 2003. "Public Services." In Patrick Dunleavy et al. (eds.), *Developments in British Politics 7*, pp. 202–301. Basingstoke: Palgrave Macmillan.

Denver, David. 2005. "'Valence Politics': How Britain Votes Now." *British Journal of Politics and International Relations* 7: 292–99.

———. 2007. *Elections and Voters in Britain.* 2nd ed. Basingstoke: Palgrave Macmillan.

DCLG (Department of Communities and Local Government). 2005. *Citizenship Survey: Active Communities Topic Report.* London: HMSO.

Department of Health. 2006. *Our Health, Our Care, Our Say: A New Direction for Community Services*, Cm 6499. London: HMSO.

Department of Work and Pensions. 2006. *Security in Retirement: Towards a New Pensions Scheme*, Cm 6841. London: HMSO.

Dicey, Albert V. 1959. *An Introduction to the Study of the Law of the Constitution*, 10th ed. London and Basingstoke: Macmillan.

DOE (Department of the Environment). 1990. *This Common Inheritance: Britain's Environmental Strategy* (White Paper on the Environment, Cm L200). London: HMSO.

Dolowitz, David, Rob Hulme, and Mike Nellis (eds.). 2000. *Policy Transfer and British Social Policy.* Buckingham: Open University Press.

Dorey, Peter. 2005a. *Policy-Making in Britain: An Introduction.* London: Sage Publications.

Dorey, Peter (ed.). 2005b. *Developments in British Public Policy.* London: Sage Publications.

Dorling, D. 2005. "Why Trevor Is Wrong about Race Ghettos." *Observer.* 24 September, 14–15.

Downs, Anthony. 1957. *An Economic Theory of Democracy.* New York: Harper.

———. 1973. "Up and Down with Ecology." In J. Bains (ed.), *Environmental Decoy.* Boston: Little, Brown.

Drewry, Gavin. 2004. "Immigration and Asylum: Law and Policy in Action." In Philip Giddings and Gavin Drewry (eds.), *British in the European Union: Law Policy and Parliament*, pp. 199–218. London: Palgrave.

DTLR (Department of Transport, Localities and Regions). 2001. *Strong Local Leadership: Quality Public Services.* London: HMSO.

———. 2002. *Your Region, Your Choice: Revitalizing the English Regions.* London: HMSO.

Dumbrell, John. 1997. *American Foreign Policy, Carter to Clinton.* Basingstoke: Macmillan.

———. 2000. *A Special Relationship: Anglo American Relations since 1960.* Basingstoke: Macmillan.

Duncan, Ben. 2002. "Health Policy in the European Union: How It's Made and How to Influence it." *British Medical Journal* 324 (April 27): 1027–30.

Dunleavy, Patrick. 2006. "The Westminster Model and the Distinctiveness of British Politics." In Patrick Dunleavy et al. (eds.), *Developments in British Politics 8*, pp. 315–41. Basingstoke: Palgrave Macmillan.

Dunleavy, Patrick, et al. (eds.). 2000. *Developments in British Politics 6.* New York: St. Martin's Press.

———. 2003. *Developments in British Politics 7.* New York: Palgrave Macmillan.

———. 2006. *Developments in British Politics 8.* Basingstoke: Palgrave Macmillan.

Duverger, Maurice. 1954. *Political Parties.* London: Methuen.

Dyson, Kenneth. 2000. "Europeanization, Whitehall Culture and the Treasury as an Institutional Veto Player: A Constructivist Approach to Economic and Monetary Union." *Public Administration* 78 (4): 897–914.

Eckstein, Harry. 1960. *Pressure Group Politics: The Case of the British Medical Association.* Stanford: Stanford University Press.

Egeberg, Marten. 2007. "The European Commission." In Michelle Cini (ed.), *European Union Politics.* 2nd ed., pp. 140–53. Oxford: Oxford University Press.

Eising, Raynor. 2007. "Interest Groups and the European Union." In Michelle Cini (ed.), *European Union Politics*, pp. 202–21. Oxford: Oxford University Press.

Elazar, David. 1987. *Exploring Federalism.* Tuscaloosa: University of Alabama Press.

Electoral Commission. 2007. *An Audit of Political Engagement 4.* London: Electoral Commission and the Hansard Society.

————. 2009. UK General Election 2005. Available at: www.electoralcommission .org.uk/elections/results/general_elections.

Elliot, Larry. 2006. "The Secret of Longevity in the Chancellor's Job Is to Become Indispensable." *Guardian*, 23 March, 8–9.

Esping-Anderson, Gosta. 1990. *The Three Worlds of Welfare Capitalism*. Princeton, NJ: Princeton University Press.

Eurobarometer. 2005. *Standard Barometer 63*. Brussels: European Commission.

————. 2006a. *EU Communication and the General Public*. Flash Barometer Series #189a. Brussels: The Gallup Organization (Hungary) for the Directorate-General Communication.

————. 2006b. *National Report: United Kingdom*. Standard Eurobarometer 66, Autumn. Brussels: European Commission.

Europa. 2007. "Boosting the Diversity of European TV." Available at: http:// europa.eu/rapid/pressReleasesAction.do?reference=IP/07/311&format=HTML&a ged=1&language=EN&guiLanguage=en.

European Commission. 2005. "Sixth Annual Survey of the Implementation and Enforcement of Community Environmental Law 2004." Staff Working Paper; SEC (2005) 1055, DGENV August. Brussels: European Commission (DGENV).

————. 2006. *General Report on the Activities of the European Union*. Luxembourg: European Commission.

European Council. 2000. *Presidency Conclusions*. Lisbon European Council, 23–24 March.

————. 2003. *A Secure Europe in a Better World*. European Security Strategy, 12 December.

European Voice. 2006. "Ministers Bid to Spice Up Rigid Ecofin Meetings." *European Voice*, 16–22 March, 1.

Fairbrass, Jenny. 2003. "The Europeanization of Interest Representation: A Strategic Decision-Making Analysis of UK Business and Environmental Interests." *ESRC/UACES Study Group on the Europeanization of British Politics*, 13 January.

————. 2004. "The Europeanization of Interest Representation: UK Business and Environmental Interests Compared." *Britain in Europe—Europe in Britain: The Europeanization of British Politics*. ESRC/UACES Conference. Sheffield Town Hall, 16 July.

————. 2006. "Organized Interests." In Ian Bache and Andrew Jordan (eds.), *The Europeanization of British Politics*. Basingstoke: Palgrave Macmillan.

Farrell, David, and Richard Scully. 2005. "Electing the European Parliament." *Journal of Common Market Studies* 43 (4): 969–84.

————. 2007. *Representing Europe's Citizens?: Electoral Institutions and the Failure of Parliamentary Institutions*. Oxford: Oxford University Press.

FCO (Foreign and Commonwealth Office). 2006. *HM Diplomatic Service Overseas Reference List*. London: HMSO.

————. 2007. *Britain in the EU*. Available at: www.fco.gov.uk/servlet.

Featherstone, Ken, and Claudio Radaelli (eds.). 2003. *The Politics of Europeanization*. Oxford: Oxford University Press.

Feeney, Brian. 2004. *The Troubles*. Dublin: O'Brien Press.

Fieldhouse, Edward, and David Cutts. 2005. "The Liberal Democrats: Steady Progress or Failure to Seize the Moment?" In Andrew Geddes and Jon Tonge (eds.), *Britain Decides: The UK General Election 2005*, pp. 70–88. Basingstoke: Palgrave Macmillan.

Fielding, Steven. 2005. "Labour's Campaign—Neither Forward nor Back." In Andrew Geddes and Jon Tonge (eds.), *Britain Decides: The UK General Election 2005*, pp. 27–45. Basingstoke: Palgrave Macmillan.

Finer, Sam. 1969. *Anonymous Empire*. London: Pall Mall.

Fisher, Justin, et al. 2003. *Central Debates in British Politics*. Harlow, UK: Pearson Education.

Flinders, Matthew. 2006. "The Half-Hearted Constitutional Revolution." In Patrick Dunleavy et al. (eds.), *Developments in British Politics: 8*, pp. 117–37. Basingstoke: Palgrave Macmillan.

Foley, Michael. 1999. *The Politics of the British Constitution*. Manchester: Manchester University Press.

———. 2000. *The British Presidency: Tony Blair and the Politics of Public Leadership*. Manchester and New York: Manchester University Press.

Forster, Anthony, and Alasdair Blair. 2002. *The Making of Britain's European Foreign Policy*. Harlow, UK: Pearson Education.

Fox, Kate. 2004. *Watching the English: The Hidden Rules of English Behavior*. London: Hodder Headline.

Franklin, M. 2004. *Voter Turnout and the Dynamics of Electoral Competitions in Established Democracies since 1945*. New York: Cambridge University Press.

Freedland, Jonathan. 1999. *Bring Home the Revolution: The Case for a British Republic*. London: Fourth Estate.

Gamble, Andrew. 1990. "Theories of British Politics." *Political Studies* 30: 404–20.

———. 2003a. *Between Europe and America: The Future of British Politics*. New York: Palgrave Macmillan.

———. 2003b. "Remaking the Constitution." In Patrick Dunleavy et al. (eds.), *Developments in British Politics 7*, pp. 18–38. Basingstoke: Palgrave Macmillan.

———. 2006. "British Politics after Blair." In Patrick Dunleavy et al. (eds.), *Developments in British Politics 8*, pp. 295–312. Basingstoke: Palgrave.

Garner, R. 2000. *Environmental Politics*. Basingstoke: Macmillan.

Geddes, Andrew. 2004. *The European Union and British Politics*. Basingstoke: Palgrave Macmillan.

———. 2005. "Nationalism: Immigration and European Integration at the 2005 General Election." In Andrew Geddes and Jon Tonge (eds.), *Britain Decides: The UK General Election 2005*, pp. 279–93. Basingstoke: Palgrave.

———. 2006. "Political Parties and Party Politics." In Ian Bache and Andrew Jordan (eds.), *The Europeanization of British Politics*, pp. 119–34. Basingstoke: Palgrave Studies in European Politics.

Geddes, Andrew, and Jon Tonge (eds.). 2005. *Britain Decides: The UK General Election 2005*. Basingstoke: Palgrave.

George, Stephen. 1990. *An Awkward Partner: Britain in the European Community*. Oxford: Oxford University Press.

Gibson, Owen. 2007. "BBC Chairman Will Oversee Reforms to Win Back Public Trust." *Guardian*, 9 August, 4.

Giddings, Philip, and Gavin Drewry, eds. 2004. *Britain in the European Union: Law, Policy and Parliament*. New York: Palgrave Macmillan.

Giddins, Anthony. 1998. *The Third Way: Renewal of Social Democracy*. Cambridge: Polity Press.

Glendinning, C. 2003. "Health Policies." In N. Ellison, and C. Pierson (eds.), *Developments in British Social Policy 2*, pp. 194–210. Basingstoke: Palgrave Macmillan.

Government Equalities Office. 2008. "Women's Representation in the UK: Fact Sheet." Available at: www.equalities.gov.uk/PDF/womens_Rep_in_uk_sept08.

Gowland, David, Richard Dunphy, and Charlotte Lythe. 2006. *The European Mosaic*. 3rd ed. Harlow, UK: Financial Times–Prentice Hall.

Gowland, David, and Arthur Turner. 2000. *Reluctant Europeans: Britain and European Integration, 1945–1998*. Harlow, UK: Pearson Education.

Grant, Wyn. 1997. *The Common Agricultural Policy*. London: Macmillan.

———. 1999. *Pressure Groups and British Politics*. London: Palgrave Macmillan.

———. 2002. *Economic Policy in Britain*. New York: Palgrave.

———. 2004. "Pressure Politics: The Changing World of Pressure Groups." *Parliamentary Affairs* 57 (2): 408–19.

Gray, Tim (ed.). 1995. *UK Environmental Policies in the 1990s*. Basingstoke: Macmillan.

Graziano, Paulo, and Maarten Vink (ed.). 2006. *Europeanization: New Research Agendas*. Basingstoke: Palgrave Macmillan.

Green Alliance. 2006. "Green Alliance: Thinking, Talking, Acting." Available at: http://www.green-alliance.org.uk (accessed 1 February 2006).

Greenwood, Justin. 2007. *Interest Representation in the European Union*. Basingstoke: Palgrave Macmillan.

Guardian. 2002. "The US Will Be Legislator, Judge and Executioner." *Guardian*, 18 November, 22.

Guild, E. 2006. "International Terrorism and EU Immigration, Asylum and Border Policy: The Unexpected Victims of 11 September 2001." In F. Carr and A. Massey (eds.), *Public Policy and the New European Agendas*, pp. 233–48. Cheltenham, UK: Edward Elgar.

Hague, Robert, and Martin Harrop. 2007. *Comparative Government and Politics*. Basingstoke: Macmillan Palgrave.

Hailsham, Lord. 1976. "Elective Dictatorship." *Listener* (October), 496–500.

———. 1978. *The Dilemma of Democracy: Diagnosis and Prescription*. London: Collins.

Halsey, A. H. 2000. "A Hundred Years of Social Change." *Social Trends* 30: 15–24.

Hansard Society. 2006. *Scrutiny of European Union*. Hansard Society Briefing Paper No. 8: Issues in Law Making. London: Hansard Society.

Harris, Kenneth. 1988. *Thatcher*. London: Weidenfeld and Nicholson.

Harris, Paul. 2003. "Foreign and Defence Policy." In Justin Fisher, David Denver, and John Benyon (eds.), *Central Debates in British Politics*, pp. 311–28. Harlow, UK: Pearson Education.

Harris, Richard. 1990. *Good and Faithful Servant*. London: Faber and Faber.

Harrison, Brian. 1996. *The Transformation of British Politics, 1869–1995*. Oxford, New York: Oxford University Press.

Hay, Colin. 2006. Managing Economic Interdependence. In Patrick Dunleavy et al. (eds.), *Developments in British Politics*. Basingstoke: Palgrave MacMillan.

Hazell, Robert (ed.). 2006. *The English Question*. Manchester: Manchester University Press.

Heath, A., and C. Payne. 2000. "Social Mobility." In A. H. Halsey and J. Webb (eds.), *Twentieth Century Social Trends*, pp. 254–80. London: Macmillan.

Heath, Anthony, et al. 2001. *The Rise of New Labour Party Policies and Voter Choices*. New York: Oxford University Press.

Heffernan, Bernard. 2000. *New Labour and Thatcherism*. Basingstoke: Macmillan.

Held, David, and Anthony McGrew. 2002. *Globalization and Anti-Globalization*. Cambridge: Polity.

Henis, M. 2001. "Europeanisation and Globalisation." *Journal of Common Market Studies* 39 (5).

Hennessy, Peter. 1995. *The Hidden Wiring: Unearthing the British Constitution*. London: Trafalgar Square.

———. 2001. *The Prime Minister: The Office and Its Holders since 1945*. New York: Palgrave.

Heppell, T. 2002. "The Ideological Composition of the Parliamentary Conservative Party 1992–97." *British Journal of Politics and International Relations* 4 (2): 299–324.

Hettne, Bjorn. 1995. *Development Theory and the Three Worlds*. London: Longman.

Heywood, Andrew. 2002. *Politics*. 2nd ed. New York: Palgrave.

Hill, Michael. 2004. *The Public Policy Process*. London: Longman.

Hix, Simon. 2000. "Britain, the EU and the Euro." In Patrick Dunleavy et al. (eds.), *Developments in British Politics*, 6, pp. 47–68. Basingstoke: Palgrave.

Hix, Simon, Amie Kreppel, and Abdul Noury. 2003. "The Party System in the European Parliament: Collusion or Competitive?" *Journal of Common Market Studies* 41 (2): 289–308.

H M Treasury. 2002. *Reforming Britain's Economic and Financial Policy: Towards Greater Economic Stability*. Basingstoke: Palgrave.

———. 2005. *Growth and Opportunity: Prioritizing Economic Reform in Europe*. Norwich: HMSO.

———. 2006. *The Case for Open Markets: How Increased Competition Can Equip Europe for Global Change*. Report to ECOFIN (April), London: HMSO.

Hobsbawm, Eric. 1999. *Industry and Empire*. London: Penguin.

Home Office. 2004. *Home Office Citizenship Survey*. London: Home Office.

Hood, C. 1995. "Contemporary Public Management: A New Global Paradigm?" *Public Policy and Administration* 10 (2): 104–17.

Hopkin, J., and D. Wincott. 2006. "New Labour Economic Reform and the European Social Model." *The British Journal of Politics and International Relations* 8 (1): 50–68.

House of Commons. 2003. *Government by Appointment: Opening Up the Patronage State*. Public Administration Select Committee Report HC165. London: House of Commons.

———. 2005. *UK Parliament and European Business*. House of Commons Library Research Paper 05/85, 2 December. London: House of Commons.

House of Lords. 2007. *The Work of the House of Lords (2005–06)*. London: House of Lords Information Service.

Howell, K. E. 2004. "Uploading, Downloading or European Integration? The Europeanization of Financial Services Regulation." *Politics* 24 (1): 20–35.

Humphries, J. A. 1996. *Way through the Woods*. London: Department of the Environment, HMSO.

Hutton, Will. 1995. *The State We Are In*. London: Jonathan Cope.

ICM. 2001. *Most Significant Issues in Voting*. Available at: http://www.icmresearch.co.uk/issuesinvoting.

———. 2005. *Most Significant Issues in Voting*. Available at: http://www.icmresearch.co.uk/issuesinvoting.

IMF (International Monetary Fund). 2008. World Outlook Database: United Kingdom. Available http://at www.imf.org/external/np/sec/pr/2008.

IPPR (Institute of Public Policy Research). 2005. "Britain's Immigrants: An Economic Profile." London: Institute of Public Policy Research.

Ipsos MORI. 2005. *EMU Entry and European Constitution*. London: MORI for Citigroup.

———. 2006. *Public Perspectives: The Future of Party Funding in the UK: Final Report*. London: HMSO Electoral Commission.

ITU. 2009. "ICT Development Index 2009." Available at: www.itu.int/publications.

Jacoby, M., and M. Finkin. 2004. *Labor Mobility in a Federal System: The United States*. Social Science Research Network. Available at: www.ssrn.com.

Jardine, Lisa. 2008. *Going Dutch: How England Plundered Holland's Glory*. London: Harper Press.

Jeffrey, C. 2007. "The Unfinished Business of Devolution." *Public Policy and Administration* 22 (1): 92–142.

Jenkins, Peter. 1989. *Mrs. Thatcher's Revolution: The Ending of the Socialist Era*. London: Pan Books.

Johnson, Nevil. 2004. *Reshaping the British Constitution: Essays in Political Interpretation*. Basingstoke: Palgrave Macmillan.

Jones, Digby. 2005. *UK Parliamentary Scrutiny of EU Legislation*. London: The Foreign Policy Centre, 2005.

Jordan, Andrew. 2000. "The UK Department of the Environment: Manager or Cypher of the Europeanization of Environmental Policy?" Working Paper GEC 2000-05. London/East Anglia: Centre for Social and Economic Research on the Global Environment; University of East Anglia; and University College, London.

———. 2002. *The Europeanization of British Environmental Policy*. London: Palgrave.

———. 2003. "The Europeanization of British Environmental Policy: From Policy 'Taking' to Policy Shaping." ESRC/UACES Conference, Department of Politics, University of Sheffield, 2 May.

Jordan, Andrew, et al. 2003. "Policy Innovation or Muddling Through? New Environmental Policy Instruments in the United Kingdom." *Environmental Politics* 12 (1): 179–98.

Jordan, G., and Jeremy Richardson. 1982. "The British Policy Style or the Logic of Negotiation." In Jeremy Richardson (ed.), *Policy Styles in Western Europe*. London: Allen and Unwin.

———. 1987. *Governing under Pressure*. London: Martin Richardson.

Joseph Rowntree Foundation. 2007. *Poverty and Wealth across Britain, 1968–2005*. York, UK: Joseph Rowntree Foundation.

Joshua, J. M. 2002. "A Sherman Act Bridgehead in Europe or a Ghost-Ship in Mid-Atlantic? A Close Look at the United Kingdom's Proposals to Criminalize Hard-core Cartel Conduct." *European Competition Law Review* 23 (5): 231–45.

Jowell, J., and David Oliver. 2004. *The Changing Constitution.* 2nd ed. Oxford: Oxford University Press.

Judge, David. 2005. *Political Institutions in the United Kingdom.* Oxford: Oxford University Press.

Kagan, Richard. 2002. "Power and Weakness." *Policy Review* (June–July): 3–28.

Kampfner, John. 2003. *Blair's Wars.* London: Free Press.

Kassim, Hussein. 2001. "Asymmetric Devolution and European Politics in the UK." In Kassim, B. Hussein, Guy Peters, and Vincent Wright (eds.), *The National Coordination of EU Policy: The European Level,* pp. 47–74. Oxford: Oxford University Press.

Katz, R., and P. Mair. 1995. "The Ascending of the Party in Public Office: Party Organizational Change in Twentieth-Century Democracies." In R. Gunter et al. (eds.), *Political Parties: Old Concepts and New Challenges.* Oxford: Oxford University Press.

———. 1995. "Changing Models of Party Organization and Party Democracy: The Emergence of the Cartel Party." *Party Politics* 1 (1): 5–28.

Kavanagh, Dennis. 1997. *The Reordering of British Politics: Politics after Thatcher.* New York: Oxford University Press.

Kavanagh, Dennis, and David Butler. 2006. *The British General Election of 2005.* Basingstoke: Palgrave Macmillan.

Kearney, Hugh. 2006. *The British Isles: A History of Four Nations.* Cambridge: Cambridge University Press.

Kellas, J. 1989. *The Scottish Political System.* 4th ed. Cambridge: Cambridge University Press.

Kennedy Pipe, C., and R. Vickers. 2003. "Britain in the International Arena." In Patrick Dunleavy et al. (eds.), *Developments in British Politics 7,* pp. 321–37. Basingstoke: Palgrave Macmillan.

King, Anthony. 2001. *Does the United Kingdom Have a Constitution?* London: Sweet and Maxwell.

King, Anthony (ed.). 1985. *The British Prime Minister.* Basingstoke: Macmillan.

———. 2002. *Britain at the Polls, 2001.* London: Chatham House.

Knill, Christoph. 2001. *The Europeanization of National Administration: Patterns of Institutional Change and Persistence.* Cambridge: Cambridge University Press.

Krieger, Joel. 1999. *British Politics in the Global Age: Can Social Democracy Survive?* Oxford: Oxford University Press.

Kuhn, Raymond. 2007. *Politics and the Media in Britain.* Basingstoke: Palgrave Macmillan.

Kyambi, S. 2005. *Beyond Black and White: Mapping New Immigrant Communities.* London: Institute of Public Policy Research.

Labour Party. 2006. *300+ Gains from Our Labour Government 2006.* London: Labour Party/USDAW.

Ladrech, Robert. 1994. "Europeanization of Domestic Politics and Institutions: The Case of France." *Journal of Common Market Studies* 32 (1): 67–87.

Laffan, Brigid, Rory O'Donnell, and Michael Smith. 1999. *Europe's Experimental Union*. London: Routledge.

La Palombara, Joseph. 1961. "The Comparative Role of Groups in Political Systems." *SSRC Items* 15 (June): 18–21.

Lavenex, Sandra, and William Wallace. 2005. "Justice and Home Affairs: Towards 'a European public order.'" In Helen Wallace, William Wallace, and Mark Pollock (eds.), *Policy-Making in the European Union*, pp. 457–80. Oxford: Oxford University Press.

Leach, Robert. 2002. *British Political Ideologies*. Basingstoke: Palgrave Macmillan.

Lecky, William. 1908. *Democracy and Liberty*. Vol. 1. London: Longmans, Green and Co.

Leibfreid, Stephen. 2006. "Social Policy: Left to the Judges and the Market?" In Helen Wallace, William Wallace, and Mark Pollock (eds.), *Policy-Making in the European Union*. 5th ed., pp. 244–77. Oxford: Oxford University Press.

Leigh, David, and Edward Vulliamy (eds.). 1997. *Sleaze: The Corruption of Parliament*. London: Fourth Estate.

Lenschow, A. 2005. "Environmental Policy: Contending Dynamics of Policy Change." In Helen Wallace, William Wallace, and Mark Pollock (eds.), *Policy-Making in the European Union*, pp. 303–27. Oxford: Oxford University Press.

Lewis, J. 2007. "The Council of the European Union." In M. Cini (ed.), *European Union Politics*, pp. 154–73. Oxford: Oxford University Press.

Lightfoot, Simon. 2005. *Europeanizing Social Democracy*. London: Routledge.

Lipset, S. M., and Stein Rokkan. 1967. *Party Systems and Voter Alignments: Cross-National Perspectives*. New York: Free Press.

Local Government Association. 2009. *National Census of Local Authority Councillors*. London: Local Government Association.

Long, A. 1998. "The Environmental Lobby." In P. Lowe and S. Ward (eds.), *British Environmental Policy and Europe: Politics and Policy in Transition*. London: Routledge.

Lowe, P., and S. Ward (eds.). 1998. *British Environmental Policy and Europe: Politics and Policy in Transition*. London: Routledge.

Ludford, Sarah. 2007. "Blair 'EU Leading Role' Undermined by Ministerial Absences." Available at: www.sarahludfordmep.org.uk/news/00832.

Ludlam, Stephen, and Mike Smith (eds.). 2004. *Governing as New Labour: Policy and Politics under Blair*. Basingstoke: Palgrave Macmillan.

Lynch, Phillip. 1999. *The Politics of Nationhood Sovereignty: Britishness and Conservative Politics*. New York: Macmillan Press.

Macaulay, James. 1848. *The History of England from the Accession of James II*. London: Everyman.

Mackintosh, John. 1962. *The British Cabinet*. London: Stevens.

Madgewick, P., and D. Woodhouse. 1995. *The Law and Politics of the Constitution of the United Kingdom*. Hemel Hempstead, UK: Harvester, Wheatsheaf.

Maloney, William. 2006. "Political Participation beyond the Electoral Arena." In Patrick Dunleavy et al. (eds.), *Developments in British Politics 8*, pp. 98–116. Basingstoke: Palgrave Macmillan.

Mandelson, Peter. 2007. "Where We Have Failed." *Guardian*, 17 January, 31.

Manin, B. 1997. *The Principles of Representative Government*. Cambridge: Cambridge University Press.

Mannin, Michael L. 1999. "Democratic Governance in CEE: The Conditions for Change." In Michael Mannin (ed.), *Pushing Back the Boundaries: The European Union and Central and Eastern Europe*, pp. 98–131. Manchester: Manchester University Press.

———. 2004. "Britain in Europe." In R. Tiersky (ed.), *Europe Today*, pp. 297–344. Lanham, MD: Rowman & Littlefield.

———. 2006a. "Acting Global—Thinking Local: Balancing Historic Marginality and Political Change in a Small Island 'State.'" *Policy and Politics* 33 (3): 387–405.

———. 2006b. "Regional Policy in the EU." In Fergus Carr and Andrew Massie (eds.), *Policy Making in the New Europe*. 2nd ed., pp. 297–330. Sussex: Elgar.

Marquand, David. 1988. *The Unprincipled Society*. London: Jonathan Cape.

———. 2008. *Britain since 1918*. London: Weidenfield and Nicholson.

———. 2009. "How Free Are We? Liberty in Britain." *History Today* 59 (3): 6-8.

Marsh, D., and R. A. W. Rhodes (eds.). 1992. *Policy Networks in British Government*. Oxford: Oxford University Press.

Marsh, S. 2005. "Foreign Policy." In Patrick Dunleavy et al. (eds.), *Developments in British Policy 7*, pp. 67–91. Basingstoke: Palgrave.

Marshall, Adam. 2006. "Local Government." In Ian Bache and Andrew Jordan (eds.), *The Europeanization of British Politics*, pp. 98–115. Houndsmills, UK: Palgrave Macmillan.

Martin, L., and J. Garnett. 1997. *British Foreign Policy*. London: Royal Institute of International Affairs.

Massey, Andrew. 2004. "Modernisation as Europeanisation: The Impact of the European Union on Public Administration." *Policy Studies* 25 (1): 19–33.

Mather, Janet. 2004. "The Impact of European Integration." In Michael O'Neill (ed.), *Devolution and British Politics*, pp. 269–94. Harlow, UK: Longman.

May, Alex. 1999. *Britain and Europe since 1945*. Seminar Studies in History. Harlow, UK: Addison Wesley Longman.

McCormick, J. 1991. *British Politics and the Environment*. London: Earth Scan.

———. 2008. *Understanding the European Union: A Concise Introduction*. Basingstoke: Palgrave Macmillan.

McMillan, J., and Andrew Massey. 2004. "Central Government and Devolution." In Michael O'Neill (ed.), *Devolution and British Politics*, pp. 231–50. Harlow, UK: Longman.

Monbiot, George. 2000. *Captive State: The Corporate Takeover of Britain*. London, Basingstoke: Macmillan.

Moran, Michael. 1985. *Politics and Society in Britain: An Introduction*. New York: St. Martin's Press.

———. 2005. *Politics and Governance in the UK*. Basingstoke: Palgrave Macmillan.

Morgan, Kenneth (ed.). 1998. *The Oxford Popular History of Britain*. Oxford: Paragon Book Service and Magpie Books.

Mori Opinion. 2005. *Long-Term Monarchy Trends*. Available at: Ipsos-Mori.com/feed.xml.

Murkens, Jo, et al. 2002. *Scottish Independence: A Practical Guide*. Edinburgh: Edinburgh University.

Murray, C. 1990. *The Emerging British Underclass*. London: Institute for Economic Affairs (IEA Health and Welfare Unit).

Nairn, Tom. 2000. *After Britain*. London: Granta.

———. 2003. *The Breakup of Britain*. 2nd ed. London: Verso.

Naughtie, James. 2004. *The Accidental American: Tony Blair and the Presidency*. New York: Public Affairs.

Newman, J. 2001. *Modernizing Governance: New Labour, Policy and Society*. London: Sage.

Norton, Philip. 2001. *The Conservative Party: Is There Anybody Out There?* In Anthony King, *Britain at the Polls*, pp. 68–94. London, Chatham House.

———. 2003. "Governing Alone." *Parliamentary Affairs* 56 (4): 543–59.

———. 2004. "The Crown." In B. Jones et al. (eds.), *Politics UK*. 5th ed., pp. 339–61. Harlow, UK: Pearson Education.

———. 2005. *Parliament in British Politics*. Basingstoke: Palgrave.

———. 2007. "The House of Commons." In B. Jones et al. (eds.), *Politics, UK*. 6th ed., pp. 407–52. Harlow, UK: Pearson Education.

Nugent, Neill. 2006. *The Government and Politics of the European Union*. Basingstoke: Palgrave Macmillan.

Nugent, Neill, and Janet Mather. 2006. "The United Kingdom: Critical Friend and Awkward Partner?" In Eleanor Zeff and Ellen Pirro (eds.), *The European Union and the Member States*. 2nd ed., pp. 129–50. Boulder, CO: Lynne Reinner.

O'Hara, Kieron. 2007. *After Blair: David Cameron and the Conservative Tradition*. London: Icon Books.

O'Neill, Michael (ed.). 2004. *Devolution and British Politics*. Harlow, UK: Pearson Education.

ONS (Office of National Statistics). 2003. "Socio-Economic Classifications." London Office of National Statistics. Available at: www.ons.gov.uk/aboutstatistics/classifications.

———. 2007. "Regional Indications." London Office of National Statistics. Available at: www.statistics.gov.uk.

———. 2008a. "UK Snapshot: Gender Pay Gap." London: Office of National Statistics. Available at: www.statistics.gov.uk/cci/nugget.asp?id=167.

———. 2008b. "UK Snapshot: Economic Trends." London Office of National Statistics. Available at: www.statistics.gov.uk.

———. 2009a. "UK Snapshot: Population of Britain." London Office of National Statistics. Available at: www.statistics.gov.uk.

———. 2009b. "A Distribution of Wealth." London Office of National Statistics. Available at: www.statistics.gov.uk.

Osborne, D., and T. Gaebler. 1992. *Reinventing Government*. Reading, MA: Addison Wesley.

PAC (Public Account Committee). 2001. *Mapping the Quango State*. Fifth Report of the Public Account Committee. London: HMSO.

Page, Alan. 2003. "Balancing Supremacy in EU Membership and the Constitution." In Philip Giddings and Gavin Drewry (eds.), *Britain in the European Union: Law, Policy and Parliament*, pp. 37–59. Basingstoke: Palgrave Macmillan.

Page, Edward, and Bill Jenkins. 2005. *Public Bureaucracy: Government with a Cast of Thousands*. Oxford: Oxford University Press.

Parker, Simon, Phil Spiers, Faizal Farook, and Melissa Mean. 2008. *State of Trust: How to Build Better Relationships between Councils and the Public*. London: Demos.

Pattie, Charles, Patrick Seyd, and Paul Whitely. 2003. "Civic Attitudes and Engagement in Modern Britain." *Parliamentary Affairs* 56: 616–33.

———. 2004. *Citizenship in Britain: Values, Participation and Democracy*. Cambridge: Cambridge University Press.

Paxman, Jeremy. 1999. *The English: A Portrait of a People*. London: Penguin Books.

Paxton, Will, and M. Dixon. 2004. "State of the Nation 2004: An Audit of Injustice in the UK." Available at: www.ipps.org.uk?research/files/term41rp.

Pearce, Nick, and Will Paxton (eds.). 2005. *Social Justice in a Challenging World: The Emerging Anglo-Saxon Model*. London: Politics.

Peston, Robert. 2006. *Brown's Britain*. London: Short Books.

Peterson, John, and Mark A. Pollack. 2003. *Europe, America, Bush: Transatlantic Relations in the Twenty-First Century*. London: Routledge.

Philips, H. 2007. *Strengthening Democracy: Fair and Sustainable Funding for Political Parties*. London: HMSO.

Pierson, P. (ed.). 2001. *The New Politics of the Welfare State*. Oxford: Oxford University Press.

Pocock, J. G. A. 2006. *The Discovery of Islands*. Cambridge: Cambridge University Press.

Poguntke, Thomas, Nicholas Aylott, Elizabeth Carter, Robert Ladreach, and Kurt Luther (eds.). 2007. *The Europeanization of National Political Parties*. London: Routledge.

Porter, H. 2007. "Less a Servant of the People, More a Hammer of Parliament." *Observer*, 25 February, 31.

Prime Minister's Office. 2009. PM's Speech to the European Parliament. Available at: www.number10.gov.uk/page18718.

Putnam, Robert. 2000. *Bowling Alone: Collapse and Renewal of American Community*. New York: Simon and Schuster.

Putnam, Robert (ed.). 2002. *Democracies in Flux: The Evolution of Social Capital in Contemporary Society*. Oxford: Oxford University Press.

Pym, Hugh, and Nick Kochan. 1998. *Gordon Brown: The First Year in Power*. London: Bloomsbury.

Pyper, Richard. 2007. *Britain's Modernized Civil Service*. Basingstoke: Palgrave Macmillan.

Quinn, Thomas. 2004. *Modernizing the Labour Party: Organizational Change since 1983*. Basingstoke: Palgrave Macmillan.

Radaelli, Claudio. 2000. "Whither Europeanization? Concept Stretching and Substantive Change." European Integration Online Papers No 4. Available at: http://www.eiop.or.at/eiop/texte/2000-008.htm.

Rawlings, Richard. 2003. *Delineating Wales: Constitutional, Legal and Administrative Aspects of National Devolution*. Cardiff: University of Wales Press.

Rawnsley, Andrew. 2001. *Servants of the People*. London: Penguin Books.

Rentoul, John. 2001. *Tony Blair: Prime Minister*. Rev. ed. London: Warner Books.

Rhodes, Rod. 1988. *Beyond Westminster and Whitehall*. London: Allen and Unwin.
———. 1994. "The Hollowing out of the State: The Changing Nature of Public Service in Britain." *Political Quarterly* 15: 138–51.
———. 1997. *Understanding Governance: Policy Networks, Governance, Reflexivity, and Accountability*. Buckingham, UK: Open University Press.
Richard, I., et al. 1971. *Europe or the Open Sea*. London: Charles Knight.
Richards, D., and M. J. Smith. 2001. "New Labour, the Constitution and Reforming the State." In S. Ludnam and M. J. Smith (eds.), *New Labour in Government*. Basingstoke: Palgrave Macmillan.
Richards, S. 2007. "Forget George Bush and America—the Big Foreign Policy Challenge for Britain Is Europe." *Independent*, 31 July, 29.
Richards Commission. 2004. *Report of the Richards Commission*. London: TSO.
Richardson, Jeremy (ed.). 1993. *Pressure Groups*. Oxford: Oxford University Press.
Richardson, Jeremy, and Andrew Jordan. 1987. *British Politics and the Policy Process*. London: Unwin Hyman.
Rieger, E. 2005. Agricultural Policy: Constrained Demands." In Helen Wallace, William Wallace, and Mark Pollock (eds.), *Policy-Making in the European Union*, pp. 161–90. Oxford: Oxford University Press.
Rieu, Alain-Marc, et al. 1995. *European Democratic Culture: What Is Europe?* Rev. ed. London: The Open University and Routledge.
Riker, W. H. 1962. *The Theory of Political Coalitions*. New Haven, CT: Yale University Press.
Robertson, David. 1984. *Class and the British Electorate*. Oxford: Basil Blackwell.
Robbins, Keith. 2005. *Britain and Europe, 1789–2005*. London: Hodder Arnold.
Robins, Lynton, and Bill Jones. 2000. *Politics Today: Debates in British Politics Today*. Manchester: Manchester University Press.
Robinson, M. 1992. *The Greening of British Party Politics*. Manchester: Manchester University Press.
Rogers, Robert, and Rhodri Walters. 2006. *How Parliament Works*. 6th ed. Harlow, UK: Pearson-Longman.
Rogers, Simon (ed.). 2004. *The Hutton Inquiry and Its Impact*. London: Polito's Guardian Books.
Rosamond, Ben. 1993. "National Labour Organisations and European Integration: British Trade Unions and 1992." *Political Studies* 41: 412–34.
———. 2003. "The Europeanization of British Politics." In Patrick Dunleavy, et al. (eds.), *Developments in British Politics 7*, pp. 39–59. Basingstoke: Palgrave.
Rose, Richard. 1980. *Politics in England: An Interpretation of the 1980s*. 3rd ed. Boston: Little, Brown.
———. 1982. "Is the United Kingdom a State? Northern Ireland as a Test Case." In P. Madgewick and Richard Rose (eds.), *The Territorial Dimension in the United Kingdom Politics*, pp. 100–136. London: Longman.
———. 2001. *The Prime Minister in a Shrinking World*. Cambridge: The Polity Press.
Routledge, Paul. 1998. *Gordon Brown: The Biography*. New York: Simon and Schuster.
Rush, Michael. 2001. *The Role of the Member of Parliament since 1868*. Oxford: Oxford University Press.

Russell, Andrew. 2005. *Neither Left nor Right: The Liberal Democrats and the Electorate.* Manchester: Manchester University Press.

Sabato, L. J. 1991. *Feeding Frenzy: How Attack Journalism Has Transformed American Politics.* New York: Free Press.

Sakwa, Richard, and Anne Stevens. 2006. *Contemporary Europe.* London: Palgrave.

Sampson, Anthony. 2004. *Who Runs This Place? The Anatomy of Britain in the 21st Century.* London: John Murray Publishers.

Sartori, Giovanni. 1976. *Parties and Party Systems: A Framework for Analysis.* Cambridge: Cambridge University Press.

Saunders, David. 1990. *Losing an Empire—Finding a Role: Britain's Foreign Policy since 1945.* Basingstoke: Macmillan.

Schumpeter, Joseph. 1962. *Capitalisim, Socialism and Democracy.* 3rd ed. New York: Harper and Row.

Scottish Parliament. 2001. *Scotland and Europe.* European Seminar.

Scully, R., and D. Farrell. 2003. "MEPs as Representatives: Individual and Institutional Roles." *Journal of Common Market Studies* 41: 269–88.

Seidentop, Larry. 2000. *Democracy in Europe.* London: Penguin Books.

Seldon, Anthony. 2001. *The Blair Effect: The Blair Government, 1997–2000.* London: Little, Brown.

———. 2004. *Blair.* London: Free Press.

Seldon, Anthony (ed.). 2007. *Blair's Britain, 1997–2007.* Cambridge: Cambridge University Press.

Seldon, Anthony, and Dennis Kavanagh. (eds.). 2005. *The Blair Effect 2001–5,* Cambridge: Cambridge University Press.

Seldon, Anthony, and Peter Snowden. 2004. *The Conservative Party.* London: The History Press.

Seyd, P., and Paul Whiteley. 2002. *New Labour's Grass Roots: The Transformation of the Labour Party Membership.* Basingstoke: Palgrave Macmillan.

Seymour-Ure, Colin. 2002. New Labour and the Media. In Anthony King (ed.), *Britain at the Polls, 2001,* pp. 117–42. New York: Chatham House.

Shore, Peter. 1973. *Europe—The Way Back.* Fabian Tract 425. London: Fabian Society.

Smith, Julie, and Mariana Tsatsas. 2002. *The New Bilateralism: The UK's Relations within the EU.* London: Royal Institute of International Affairs.

Smith, Martin J. 1999. *The Core Executive in Britain.* Basingstoke: Palgrave.

———. 2003. "The Core Executive and the Modernization of Central Government." In Patrick Dunleavy et al. (eds.), *Developments in British Politics 7,* pp. 60–81. Basingstoke: Macmillan.

Smith, Mike. 2006. "Britain, Europe and the World." In Patrick Dunleavy et al. (eds.), *Developments in British Politics 8,* pp. 159–73. Basingstoke: Palgrave Macmillan.

Social Trends. 2004. *Focus on Religion.* Available at: http://www.statistics.gov.uk/cc1 (11 October).

Sombart, W. 1976. *Why There Is No Socialism in the United States.* London: Macmillan.

Starkey, David. 2006. *Monarchy: From the Middle Ages to Modernity.* London: Harper Collins.

Statham, P., and E. Gray. 2005. "The Public Sphere and Debates about Europe in Britain." *Innovation* 18 (1): 61–81.

Stephens, Phillip. 2004. *Tony Blair: The Making of a World Leader*. London: Viking.

Stevens, A. 2002. "Europeanization and Administration of the EU." Queens Papers on Europeanization, no 4-2002. Belfast: Queens University.

Stevens, Christopher. 2004. "English Regional Government." In Michael O'Neill (ed.), *Devolution in British Politics*, pp. 251–64. Harlow, UK: Longman.

Stoker, J. 2000. *The New Politics of British Local Governance*. Basingstoke: Palgrave Macmillan.

Sutton Trust. 2005. *The Educational Background of Members of the House of Commons and House of Lords*. London: Sutton Trust.

Suzuki, K. 2000. "Reforms of British Competition Policy: Is European Integration the Only Factor?" Working Paper No. 94. European Institute of Japanese Studies. Stockholm: Stockholm School of Economics.

Thain, Colin. 2005. "Economic Policy." In Peter Dorey (ed.), *Developments in British Public Policy*, pp. 24–25. London: Sage.

Thatcher, Margaret. 1988. The Bruges Speech (speech to the College of Europe). Available at: www.margaretthatcher.org/speeches/displaydocument.

———. 1993. *The Downing Street Years*. New York: HarperCollins.

Tiersky, Ronald. 1994. *France in the New Europe: Changing Yet Steadfast*. Belmont, CA: Wadsworth.

Tiersky, Ronald (ed.). 2004. *Europe Today: National Politics, European Integration and European Security*. 2nd ed. Lanham, MD: Rowman & Littlefield.

Tompkins, A. 2005. *Our Republican Constitution*. London: Hart.

Tonge, Jon. 2002. *Northern Ireland: Conflict and Change*. London: Pearson.

———. 2005a. *The New Northern Ireland Politics*. Basingstoke: Palgrave Macmillan.

———. 2005b. "Meltdown of the Moderates, or the Redistribution of Moderation." In Andrew Geddes and Jonathan Tonge (eds.), *Britain Decides: The UK General Election, 2005*, pp. 129–48. Basingstoke: Palgrave.

Townsend, Ian. 2004. *Income Wealth and Inequality*. House of Commons Library Research Paper 04/70. House of Commons, 15 September.

Trench, A. (ed.). 2004. *Has Devolution Made a Difference? The State of the Nations 2004*. Exeter: Imperial Academic.

Tunander, O. 1997. "Post-Cold War Europe: Synthesis of a Bipolar Friend-Foe Structure and a Hierarchic Cosmos-Chaos Structure." In P. O. Tunander, P. Baev, and V. I. Einagan (eds.), *Geopolitics in Post-Wall Europe: Security, Territory and Identity*, pp. 17–44. London: Sage.

Van der Maas, Erin. 2004. "British Labour and the European Union: The Europeanization of Trade Unions?" ESRC/UACES Seminar on Europeanization, Dept. of Politics, University of Sheffield, 16 January.

———. 2006. "Trade Unions." In Ian Bache and Andrew Jordan (eds.), *The Europeanization of British Politics*, pp. 152–67. Basingstoke: Palgrave Macmillan.

Wall, Stephen. 2008. *A Stranger in Europe: Britain and the EU from Thatcher to Blair*. Oxford: Oxford University Press.

Wallace, Helen. 2000. "Europeanisation and Globalisation: Complementary or Contradictory Trends?" *New Political Economy* 5 (3): 369–82.

Wallace, William, Helen Wallace, and Mark Pollock (eds.). 2006. *Policy-Making in the European Union*. Oxford: Oxford University Press.

Watt, N. 2006. "What Peter Did Next." *Guardian*, 17 March, 8–13.

Watts, R. L. 1999. *Comparing Federal Systems*. 2nd ed. Kingston, ON: Institute of Intergovernmental Relations.

Weale, Albert. 1992. *The New Politics of Pollution*. Manchester: Manchester University Press.

Webb, P. 2000. *The Modern British Party System*. London: Sage.

Weiler, Joseph. 1999. *The Constitution of Europe*. Cambridge: Cambridge University Press.

Westlake, M. 1999. *The Council of the European Union*. London: Catermiller.

Wheeler, N., and T. Dunne. 1998. "Good International Citizenship: A Third Way for British Foreign Policy." *International Affairs* 64 (4): 847–70.

Whitman, Richard, and G. Thomas. 2005. "Two Cheers for the UK's EU Presidency." Briefing paper EPBP 05/05. London: European Research Chatham House.

Wickham, J. 2001. "The End of the European Social Model: Before It Began?" Irish Congress of Trade Unions Essay Services.

Wilkinson, R., and K. Pickett. 2009. *The Sprit Level: Why More Equal Societies Always Do Better*. London: Penguin Books.

Wilson, David, and Chris Game. 2006. *Local Government in the United Kingdom*. 4th ed. Basingstoke: Macmillan.

Wintour, P., and D. Adams. 2006. "Blair Presses the Nuclear Button." *Guardian*, 17 May, 1–2.

Women and Equality Unit. 2008. *Women in Public Life*. Available at: www .equalities.gov.uk/pdf/publiclife.

Woolcock, S. 2005. "Trade Policy." In H. Wallace, W. Wallace, and M. A. Pollack (eds.), *Policy-Making in the European Union*, pp. 377–99. Oxford: Oxford University Press.

Woollacott, Martin. 2003. "Never Mind Iraq, the Battle for Europe Is Much Bigger." *Guardian*, 6 June, 12.

Wright, Alex. 2001. "Scotland in Europe: Independence or Federalism." European Essay, no. 18. London: The Federal Trust

Young, Hugo. 1991. *One of Us: A Life of Margaret Thatcher*. London: Macmillan.

———. 1998. *This Blessed Plot: Britain and Europe from Churchill to Blair*. London: Macmillan.

———. 2003. "WMD or Not, Blair Had Already Made His Mind Up." *Guardian*, 6 June, 2.

Young, John W. 2000. *Britain and European Unity, 1945–1999*. New York: St. Martin's Press.

Index

agricultural policy. *See* Common Agricultural Policy
American Revolution, 15
Amsterdam Treaty (1997), 79
"Anglo-Saxon" versus "Continental" cultures, 8

Bagehot, Walter, 82
Bank of England, independence of, 264–65, 270
Beloff, Lord, 85
Beveridge Report (1942), 20
Bill of Rights (1689), 15
Blair, Tony, 25–26, 143–45, 193, 218, 220–24; Brown, Gordon, and, 211–12; cabinet government and, 208–10; European Union and, 25–26, 232–33, 312; international affairs and, 216, 312; Labour Party and, 143–45; quasi-presidentialism and, 220–24; United States and, 218–19, 319–20, 334
Britain: as a state, 1–2, 11–13; characteristics, 26–27, 54–58; citizenship, 77–78; Civil Service, 226–27; constitution, 59–64, chap. 3 *passim*; constitutional reform, 18, 80–85; democracy, 133–36; democratic-collectivist interpretation, 13; demographic change, 43–45; devolution,

15–16, 29–30, 56, 68–69, 109, 113–20, 236–38; economy, 20–22, 39–41, 219–20, chap. 10 *passim*; elections, 71, 93; electoral issues, 158–59; electoral systems, 80, 93, 138–42; empire of, 17–19; environment policy, chap. 11 *passim*; ethnicity, 46–48; European Commission and, 127–29; European elections and, 80, 129–32; European integration and, 6, 85; Europeanization and, 7–8, 134, 339–42; European Parliament and, 79–80, 106–7, 129–32; the executive, chap. 8 *passim*; executive sovereignty, 64, 70–71, 76–77; Financial Services Authority, 277; foreign policy, chap. 12 *passim*, 76–77, 343–353; gender, 45–47; government departments, restructuring of, 209–10; incomes, 41–43; interests, organized, 171–85; judiciary, 71–73, 75–76; local government, 67, 109–13; Lords, House of, 98, 100–103, 105; media, 185–97; Members of European Parliament, 129–32; Members of Parliament, 89, 92–95, 144; Monarchy, 13–15, 17, 48, 53, 63–67, 70, 203, 214–15; Parliament, 90–107; parliamentary sovereignty, 7, 28–29, 70,

About the Author

Michael L. Mannin is the Jean Monnet Chair of European Studies at Liverpool John Moores University. He has researched and published widely in the fields of European Union Studies, European Politics, and British government. He has taught and researched in the United States as a Fulbright Fellow at New York University and as Loewenstein Fellow in Political Science at Amherst. He is also a visiting professor at the University of Lyon Lumière II and associate lecturer at the University of Portsmouth.

Breinigsville, PA USA
10 January 2010
230443BV00002B/2/P